EARLY MODERN ENGLISH

Charles Barber

EDINBURGH UNIVERSITY PRESS

© 1976, 1997 by Charles Barber

Edinburgh University Press
22 George Square, Edinburgh

First published in 1976 by André Deutsch Limited

Typeset in Times
by Nene Phototypesetters, Northampton, and
printed and bound in Great Britain

A CIP record for this book is available
from the British Library

ISBN 0 7486 0835 4

CONTENTS

PREFACE

In the original (1976) version of this book, I expressed my warm gratitude to a number of friends and colleagues to whom I was indebted. Sadly, two of them, Frank Behre and Simeon Potter, are no longer with us. To the other three, I repeat my expression of gratitude: Alvar Ellegård of the University of Gothenburg, Peter Meredith of the University of Leeds, and Robin Alston, also formerly of the University of Leeds. In preparing this new version I have been grateful for advice once again from Peter Meredith, and also from Jonathan Hope, formerly of the University of Leeds and now of the University of Middlesex. Finally, my thanks to a newer friend, Manfred Görlach of the University of Cologne, from whose wisdom I have profited in recent years.

The book contains a large number of quotations from English works of the sixteenth and seventeenth centuries, the majority of which have been taken directly from the earliest editions. Most of these are not accessible to the ordinary present-day reader, and there seems little point, in a book designed for the non-specialist, in giving page or line references for them. In the quotations, abbreviations have been silently expanded, and obvious errors (like turned letters) have been silently corrected in cases where the emendation does not affect the point being illustrated. Normally, the use of capital letters and of italics is kept as in the original. In Chapters Four and Five, however, there are many short quotations illustrating points of grammar, and in these I use italics to indicate the form being commented on: in such cases, I remove any italicisation found in the original text, to avoid confusion. Occasionally it has proved necessary to use modern editions for the quotations: in such cases there may sometimes be silent modernisations, especially of punctuation.

On first mention, books are usually given their short title in old spelling. In subsequent references, the title is modernised, unless (as with *The Faerie*

Queene) it is common present-day practice to use the old-spelling title. In the case of Shakespeare's plays, however, the usual present-day title is used even for the first reference. In Chapters Four and Five, where there are numerous brief quotations, I often use abbreviated titles, which I hope will be sufficiently clear. The text of Shakespeare's plays is taken from the First Folio of 1623 unless the contrary is stated.

Leeds, 1996   Charles Barber

PHONETIC SYMBOLS

VOWELS

as in

[ɪ]	RP *sit*		[i:]	German *sie*
[y]	French *cru*, German *Hütte*		[y:]	French *sûr*, German *führen*
[e]	French *été*		[e:]	German *zehn*
[ɛ]	French *même*		[ɛ:]	French *faire*, German *fährt*
[æ]	RP *hat*		[æ:]	London English *bad* (long [æ])
[a]	French *la*, German *Mann*		[a:]	Australian English *park*
[ɑ]	American English *hot*		[ɑ:]	RP *park*
[ɒ]	RP *hot*		[ɒ:]	lengthened [ɒ]
[ɔ]	French *donne*, German *von*		[ɔ:]	RP *law*
[o]	French *dos*		[o:]	French *chose*, German *wo*
[ʊ]	RP *put*		[u:]	German *Uhr*
[ʌ]	RP *cup*		[ɜ:]	RP *bird*
[ə]	RP fath*er*, *a*dmit		[ə:]	lengthened [ə]

CONSONANTS

as in

[f]	RP *far*		[v]	RP *voice*
[θ]	RP *thin*		[ð]	RP *this*
[s]	RP *sit*		[z]	RP *zoo*
[ʃ]	RP *shoe*		[ʒ]	RP *measure*
[p]	RP *peel*		[b]	RP *bee*
[t]	RP *took*		[d]	RP *deed*
[k]	RP *coy*		[g]	RP *go*

[tʃ]	RP *church*		[dʒ]	RP *judge*
[m]	RP *may*		[l]	RP *lee*
[n]	RP *no*		[j]	RP *yes*
[ŋ]	RP *sing*		[w]	RP *woe*
[h]	RP *hat*		[r]	RP *red*
[ç]	German *ich*		[x]	German *ach*

Diphthongs are represented by two symbols, the first showing the vowel-position at which the diphthong starts, and the second showing the position towards which it glides. So the diphthongs in the words *here* and *boy* in PresE (RP) are represented as [ɪə] and [ɔɪ]. The symbol ['] is used to mark stress, and is placed *before* the stressed syllable. The symbol [ˌ] is similarly used to mark secondary stress. Phonemic transcriptions are enclosed within slopes, while phonetic or allophonic transcriptions are enclosed in square brackets. In transcriptions of Present-day English (RP) I use the phoneme system of Gimson (1989), the standard work on the subject.

LIST OF FIGURES

ABBREVIATIONS

---

adj.   adjective
adv.   adverb
aux.   auxiliary
EME   Early Middle English (1100–1300)
eModE   Early Modern English (1500–1700)
LME   Late Middle English (1300–1500)
LModE   Later Modern English (since 1700)
ME   Middle English (1100–1500)
ModE   Modern English (since 1500)
n.   noun
OE   Old English (before 1100)
OED   The Oxford English Dictionary
PresE   Present-day English
p.p.   past participle
pres.p.   present particle
p.t.   past tense
RP   Received Pronunciation
S-V-O   Subject-Verb-Object (or Complement)
StE   Standard English
v.   verb
{ }   used to enclose morphemes

Chapter One

VARIETIES OF
EARLY MODERN ENGLISH

The concern of this book is factual, not theoretical. Its aim is not to illuminate or extend linguistic theory, but to present some of the known facts about Early Modern English (eModE) – about its vocabulary, its grammar, its phonology, the attitudes of its speakers towards it. In particular, I shall try to bring out the main ways in which it differed from Present-day English (PresE). The book is therefore intended for people who are interested in the history of English, and for people who read works written in eModE – plays, poems, historical documents, philosophy, or whatever.

This does not mean that theory is rejected: linguistic matters can only be discussed adequately within a theoretical framework. But the framework used in this work is a fairly traditional and simple one, influenced somewhat by the structural linguists of the 1940s and 1950s, and I hope that it will not be found difficult by non-specialist readers.

I am taking eModE to be the English language between 1500 and 1700. All such divisions are arbitrary, for linguistic change is continuous; but there are a number of features in the language of that period which mark it off fairly clearly from Middle English (ME) and Later Modern English (LModE). Some scholars, on the other hand, take the eModE period to end in 1660, and there are indeed marked differences in the language after the Restoration. Nevertheless, many of the grammatical and phonological changes of eModE are completed around the year 1700, so that it is convenient to include the Restoration period in our study.

Early Modern English was not monolithic, but consisted of a large number of sub-languages. There were different varieties of English according to region, social group, field of discourse, and context of situation (e.g. the social relationship between speaker and hearer, the degree of formality of the

1

situation). Although we have less direct evidence of this, there were also differences according to the medium used: ordinary spoken language differed in many ways from written language; and language written in order to be read aloud (like some sermons) was probably different again. In this chapter we shall look at a number of passages which illustrate some of the varieties of the language in the Early Modern period.

VARIATION WITH TIME

Two hundred years is a substantial length of time in linguistic history, and the language changed considerably between 1500 and 1700. So we shall begin by looking at four prose passages from different dates, and at the same time we can notice some of the obvious features of the language in the period.

The first passage is from *The boke named the Gouernour* (1531), by Sir Thomas Elyot. This is the first book in English on the new-style humanist education, and, like so many of the courtesy books that followed, it prescribes an education in Arms and Arts which will enable a gentleman to serve his sovereign. The passage is from the section on the physical exercises suitable for a gentleman:

> But the moste honorable exercise in myne opinion / and that besemeth the astate of euery noble persone / is to ryde suerly and clene / on great horse and a roughe / whiche vndoubtedly nat onely importeth a maiestie and drede to inferiour persones / beholding him aboue the common course of other men / dauntyng a fierce and cruell beaste / but also is no litle socour / as well in pursuete of enemies and confoundyng them / as in escapyng imminent daunger / whan wisedome therto exhorteth. Also a stronge and hardy horse dothe some tyme more domage vnder his maister / than he with al his waipon: and also setteth forwarde the stroke / and causethe it to lighte with more violence.
>
> Bucephal / the horse of great kynge Alexander / who suffred none on his backe saulfe ['save'] onely his maister / at the bataile of Thebes beinge sore wounded / wolde nat suffre the kinge to departe from hym to a nother horse / but persistyng in his furiouse courage / wonderfully continued out the bataile / with his fete and tethe betyng downe and destroyenge many enemies. And many semblable maruailes of his strength he shewed. wherefore Alexander / after the horse was slayne / made in remembrance of hym a citie in the countray of India / and called it Bucephal / in perpetual memorie of so worthy a horse: which in his lyfe had so well serued hym.
>
> What wonderfull enterprises dyd Iulius Cesar achieue by the helpe of his horse? whiche nat onely dyd excell all other horsis in fiercenesse and swyfte rennynge / but also was in some parte discrepant in figure from

2

other horsis / hauing his fore hoeues ['hooves'] like to the feete of a man. And in that figure Plinius writeth / that he sawe hym kerued ['carved'] before the temple of Venus. Other remembrance there is of diuers horsis / by whose monstruous power / men dyd exploite ['achieve'] incredible affaires: but by cause the reporte of them contayneth thinges impossible / and is nat writen by any approued autour: I will nat in this place reherce them.

Perhaps the things that strike the modern reader first are punctuation and spelling. The punctuation marks used are the full stop, the colon, the question mark, and the virgule (oblique stroke). The virgule is common in early English printed books. In the sixteenth century it is gradually replaced by the comma, which was introduced from the continent in the 1520s.

There is one feature of eModE that I have not reproduced, namely the use of 'long s'. In printed books throughout the period there are two forms of the letter s: an ordinary *s* like the present-day one, and 'long s', which is like an 'f' without its cross, thus: ſ. When *s* occurs as the last letter in a word, 'short s' is invariably used. In other positions 'long s' is normal, though 'short s' appears occasionally, especially before *b*, *k*, and *f*. So in the Elyot passage the word *persons* appears as *perſones*. I have also silently expanded abbreviations: the original text often has & for *and*, and frequently uses a tilde for *m* or *n*, printing *daunting* as *daũtyng*, and *from* as *frõ*.

One striking feature of the spelling is the distribution of the letters *u* and *v*. The letter *u* can be used to represent a vowel (*but*) or a consonant (*euery*). The letter *v*, too, can represent either a vowel (*vnder*) or a consonant (*violence*). At first sight it looks as though the printer has used *u* and *v* indiscriminately. This is not so, however: for the first letter of a word, the printer invariably uses *v*, and in other positions he invariably selects *u*. This distribution is a normal printer's convention in the sixteenth and early seventeenth centuries, though it is not always observed in manuscripts. Originally, *u* and *v* were merely variant ways of writing the same letter, and could be used interchangeably. In late ME, however, it became common to use *v* initially and *u* elsewhere, and this practice was continued by the printers. In the sixteenth century, printers observe the convention pretty strictly, and one rarely finds exceptions to it. The present-day convention, whereby *u* is used as a vowel symbol and *v* as a consonant symbol, came in round about 1630, under continental influence.

The letter *j* does not occur in the passage: where today we write *j*, it uses *i*, as in *maiestie* 'majesty'. Originally, *j* was merely a variant form of *i*, and in the sixteenth century it was only used as a capital letter, and also in the combination *ij*. This is found, for example, in Latin-style numbers, like *iij* 'three'. The present-day convention, whereby we use *i* as a vowel symbol and *j* as a consonant symbol, also came in round about 1630.

3

When once we have got used to these conventions, the spellings of the passage present no serious difficulty. We are not troubled by the *y* in *ryde* and *tyme*, since we ourselves use spellings like *rhyme* and *scythe*, and similarly with the final *-ll* of *cruell*, the *ay* of *slayne*, the *-ie* of *citie*, and the final 'mute e' in words like *moste* and *backe*. Most of the conventions are ones we are familiar with, but they are applied in different ways, and with greater freedom. Elyot has *memorie* and *citie*, but *hardy* and *worthy*, whereas we have standardised the *-y* spelling. We use *ai* in medial position, and *ay* in final position; Elyot has *ay* in medial position, in *slayne*, but he could equally well have written *slaine*. In eModE there was no single set of universally accepted spellings. There were many widely accepted spelling conventions, but within those conventions considerable variation was possible. Moreover, one person (or one printer) could use variant spellings inside a single work: in the second paragraph of the Elyot passage, we see the spellings *kynge* and *kinge*, both in the same sentence. It was not until the late seventeenth century that spelling was more or less standardised. Even then, such spellings were confined to printed books: in their private writings people continued to spell idiosyncratically.

What is not immediately apparent is the pronunciation represented by any of Elyot's spellings. The spelling system of a language can tell us things about its phonological system, for there is bound to be some kind of correspondence between them. But the spellings, by themselves, cannot tell us how the words were pronounced. To get any idea of that, we have to turn to other kinds of evidence. There are indeed spellings in the passage which suggest pronunciations different from those of PresE, such as *autour* 'author', *daunger* 'danger', *domage* 'damage', *kerued* 'carved', and *nat* 'not'. What we are noticing here, however, is the relationship of these particular words to other words in the system: we notice that *autour* has medial *t* like *citie*, not *th* like *other*; that *daunger* has the same *au* spelling as *causethe*; that *kerued* has *er* like *persone*, not *ar* like *hardy*; and so on. But how all these words were pronounced by Elyot in 1531 is another question. In a later chapter we shall consider the phonology of eModE. In the meantime, it is worth making one small point about it: in eModE spellings, the final *-e* in words like *moste* and *persone* does not represent any vowel-sound. Word-final unstressed *-e* had ceased to be pronounced in the fourteenth century, so in eModE this final *-e* was silent, and the word *moste* was monosyllabic, as today. Just occasionally, however, especially in the early sixteenth century, final *-e* was written where we have *-y*, and it is then to be pronounced, as in *cite* 'city'. Where such forms occur, I shall add an accent on the *-e*, as in *cité*.

In vocabulary, there is nothing in the passage that is absolutely unfamiliar, though there are some words which now sound old-fashioned, like *daunt*, *succour* and *semblable*. This last word is certainly obsolete in the sense of 'similar', and there are other words used with unfamiliar meanings, such as

4

importeth 'betokens', *confounding* 'destroying', *suffered* 'permitted', and *other remembrance* 'other records'.

In grammar, there are several differences from PresE. Among the verb-forms, the passage contains many examples of the third-person singular of the present tense, and without exception the {-eth} morpheme is used for the inflection, not {-es}, as in *besemeth, importeth, dothe*. In the phrase *with al his waipon*, the noun *waipon* is an uninflected plural, 'weapons'. In *myne opinion*, the pronoun-determiner *mine* is selected, not *my*, because the following word begins with a vowel. There are adverbs which are identical in form with adjectives, i.e. lacking the suffix *-ly*, as in 'ryde suerly and *clene*', '*sore* wounded'. In *who suffred none on his backe*, the pronoun *none* means 'nobody', and the relative pronoun *who* is used to refer to a horse (though in two later references to horses the relative pronoun *which* is used). In the expression *like to the feete of a man* we see the compound preposition *like to*, which is common in eModE. Auxiliary *do* is inserted in positions where we should not use it, as in *men dyd exploite incredible affaires* 'men achieved incredible things'. The noun phrase *a great horse and a roughe* has a structure which we could hardly use today, and there are sentences where the order of the elements would not come naturally to a present-day writer of prose, like *Other remembrance there is of diuers horsis*.

My second extract is taken from *The Principall Nauigations, Voiages, Traffiques and Discoueries of the English Nation*, the monumental work by Richard Hakluyt, which was published in 1589, and then again, enlarged in three volumes, in 1598–1600. The extract comes from the account by 'M. Edward Haies gentleman' of the loss at sea of Sir Humphrey Gilbert, returning from Newfoundland in 1583. Gilbert was in a small frigate, the Squirrel, and Hayes was in the other ship, the larger Golden Hind. The Squirrel was known to be unsafe, and the weather was bad, but Gilbert resisted persuasions to transfer to the larger ship, saying that he would not desert the company with which he had passed through so many storms and perils. No doubt he felt that, as commander-in-chief of the expedition (or 'General', as they called him), he could hardly ask his ship's company to run risks that he was unwilling to take himself, especially as he was sensitive (as Hayes remarks) about 'hard reports giuen of him, that he was afraid of the sea'. The narratives in Hakluyt have a tendency to directness and matter-of-factness, and we see in this extract how the everyday matter-of-fact tone gets carried over from such things as the routine accounts of course and wind-direction to the more moving and momentous incidents of the voyages.

By that time we had brought the Islands of *Açores* South of vs, yet wee then keeping much to the North, vntil we had got into the height and eleuation of *England*: we met with very foule weather, and terrible seas, breaking short and high Pyramid wise. The reason whereof seemed to proceede either of hilly grounds high and low within the sea, (as we see hilles and dales vpon the land) vpon which the seas doe mount and fall: or else the cause proceedeth of diuersitie of winds, shifting often in sundry points: al which hauing power to moue the great Ocean, which againe is not presently setled, so many seas do encounter together, as there had bene diuersitie of windes. Howsoeuer it commeth to passe, men which all their life time had occupied the Sea, neuer saw more outragious Seas. We had also vpon our maine yarde, an apparition of a little fire by night, which seamen doe call *Castor* and *Pollux*. But we had onely one, which they take an euill signe of more tempest: the same is vsuall in stormes.

Munday the ninth of September, in the afternoone, the Frigat was neere cast away, oppressed by waues, yet at that time recouered: and giuing foorth signes of ioy, the Generall sitting abaft with a booke in his hand, cried out vnto vs in the *Hind*, (so oft as we did approch within hearing) *We are as neere to heauen by sea as by land*. Reiterating the same speech, well beseeming a souldier, resolute in Iesus Christ, as I can testifie he was.

The same Monday night, about twelue of the clocke, or not long after, the Frigat being ahead of vs in the *Golden Hinde*, suddenly her lights were out, whereof as it were in a moment, we lost the sight, and withall our watch cryed, the Generall was cast away, which was too true. For in that moment, the Frigat was deuoured and swallowed vp of the Sea. Yet still we looked out all that night, and euer after, vntill wee arriued vpon the coast of *England*: Omitting no small saile at sea, vnto which we gaue not the tokens betweene vs, agreed vpon, to haue perfect knowledge of each other, if we should at any time be separated.

In punctuation, the virgule has now disappeared and been replaced by the comma. By this date, the semicolon was also in use, having come in during the 1570s, but there are no examples in the passage. The piece of direct speech, *We are as neere to heauen by sea as by land*, is not placed within inverted commas, which were not generally used for this function until the eighteenth century: in eModE, direct speech was sometimes italicised, as here, and sometimes not marked in any way at all.

The spelling conventions for *u/v* and *i/j* are the same as in Elyot. The spellings, however, are slightly more modern: *nat*, for example, has been replaced by *not*, and there are no spellings that look as strange to us as Elyot's *astate*, *saulfe*, and *hoeues*.

The vocabulary of the passage is familiar enough, but there are some expressions used in unfamiliar meanings, like *height and eleuation* 'latitude', *occupied the Sea* 'followed the occupation of sailor', and *Omitting* 'disregarding'. As in Elyot, there is an adverb with no {-ly} suffix (*neere cast away*), and there is one with the suffix {-wise} (*Pyramid wise*).

In grammar, there are many features like those in Elyot. The third-person singular inflection is still invariably {-eth}, as in *proceedeth*, *commeth*. The preposition *of* is used where we should use *by* ('swallowed vp *of* the Sea') or *from* ('proceedeth *of* diuersitie'). In Elyot, there was an example of the relative pronoun *who* used with a non-personal antecedent: in this passage there is an occurrence of relative *which* with a personal antecedent ('men *which* ... occupied the Sea'). There are affirmative declarative sentences with auxiliary *do* inserted, indeed more than in the Elyot passage ('the seas *doe* mount', 'seas *do* encounter', 'seamen *doe* call', 'we *did* approch'). There is also a sentence which is negated without the use of *do* or any other auxiliary ('we gaue not the tokens').

My third passage is taken from Milton's *Areopagitica*, which was a pamphlet addressed to Parliament in 1644 arguing in favour of unlicensed printing.

> I deny not, but that it is of greatest concernment in the Church and Commonwealth, to have a vigilant eye how Bookes demeane themselves, as well as men; and thereafter to confine, imprison, and do sharpest justice on them as malefactors: For Books are not absolutely dead things, but doe contain a potencie of life in them to be as active as that soule was whose progeny they are; nay they do preserve as in a violl the purest efficacie and extraction of that living intellect that bred them. I know they are as lively, and as vigorously productive, as those fabulous Dragons teeth; and being sown up and down, may chance to spring up armed men. And yet on the other hand unlesse warinesse be us'd, as good almost kill a Man as kill a good Book; who kills a Man kills a reasonable creature, Gods Image; but hee who destroyes a good Booke, kills reason it selfe, kills the Image of God, as it were in the eye. Many a man lives a burden to the Earth; but a good Booke is the pretious lifeblood of a master spirit, imbalm'd and treasur'd up on purpose to a life beyond life. 'Tis true, no age can restore a life, whereof perhaps there is no great losse; and revolutions of ages doe not oft recover the losse of a rejected truth, for the want of which whole Nations fare the worse. We should be wary therefore what persecution we raise against the living labours of publick men, how we spill that season'd life of man preserv'd and stor'd up in Books; since we see a kinde of homicide may be thus committed, sometimes a martyrdome, and if it extend to the whole impression, a kinde of massacre, whereof the execution ends not in the slaying of an elementall life, but strikes at that ethereall and fift essence,

the breath of reason it selfe, slaies an immortality rather then a life. But lest I should be condemn'd of introducing licence, while I oppose Licencing, I refuse not the paines to be so much Historicall, as will serve to shew what hath been done by ancient and famous Commonwealths, against this disorder, till the very time that this project of licencing crept out of the *Inquisition*, was cacht up by our Prelates, and hath caught some of our Presbyters.

The letters *u* and *v* are now used for vowel and consonant respectively, and *j* is used as a consonant symbol. The spellings are nearer to PresE usage than those of the sixteenth-century passages. For example, with one exception (*slaies*), *ai* and *ay* are distributed as they are today, and final *-y* occurs more frequently than final *-ie*. Some words, however, still occur in more than one spelling: *Booke* and *Book*. A usage typical of the later part of the period is the spelling *-'d*, as in *us'd, imbalm'd*; it is especially common in poetry, where it shows that the {-ed} morpheme is not to be pronounced as a syllable. Milton's spelling *armed* in this passage perhaps indicates a disyllabic pronunciation. On the other hand, the absence of an apostrophe in the possessive ending of nouns (*Dragons teeth*, *Gods Image*) is normal until the late seventeenth century. The spelling *then* 'than' is also quite common, at least until the Restoration, and perhaps represents the unstressed form [ðən]. The form *fift* 'fifth' is the historical one (OE *fifta*); the form *fifth* is analogical, influenced by *fourth*, and is first found in the fourteenth century.

In vocabulary the passage is strikingly modern, and word meanings are also ones common today. In grammar there are some differences from the two earlier passages. For the third-person inflection of verbs the {-es} morpheme is normal, as in *kills, destroyes, lives*; there are only two occurrences of the {-eth} morpheme, both in the form *hath*. There are examples of the subjunctive, which by chance did not occur in the two earlier passages, as in *if it extend*. In contrast to the earlier passages, the relative pronouns *who* and *which* are distributed as they are today, *who* being used with personal antecedents (*hee who destroyes*) and *which* with non-personal ones (*a rejected truth, for the want of which*). But the use of *who* as an indefinite pronoun (*who kills a Man kills a reasonable creature*) is found throughout the period.

As in the earlier passages, auxiliary *do* sometimes occurs in affirmative declarative sentences: *Books ... doe contain, they do preserve*. There are negative sentences formed without *do* or any other auxiliary: *I deny not, the execution ends not, I refuse not*. But beside these there is a negative with *do*, as today: *ages doe not oft recover*. In Milton, forms with and without auxiliary *do* are in free variation, and in fact this is also the case with Elyot and Hakluyt, though forms with auxiliary *do* are rarer in the early sixteenth century than in the central part of the period. In grammar, as in spelling, there was greater freedom of choice than in PresE, and this is also illustrated by the final sentence of the passage, which contains two different past-tense forms of the verb *to catch*, namely *cacht* and *caught*.

My fourth passage is taken from the preface to John Dryden's *Fables Ancient and Modern*, a collection of translations published in 1700, the last year of our period. It was also the last year of Dryden's life, when he was nearly seventy, and can be taken as an example of conservative educated usage in the final years of the Early Modern period. Dryden is discussing Chaucer, some of whose poems he had translated.

> He must have been a Man of a most wonderful comprehensive Nature, because, as it has been truly observ'd of him, he has taken into the Compass of his *Canterbury Tales* the various Manners and Humours (as we now call them) of the whole *English* Nation, in his Age. Not a single Character has escap'd him. All his Pilgrims are severally distinguish'd from each other; and not only in their Inclinations, but in their very Phisiognomies and Persons. *Baptista Porta* could not have describ'd their Natures better, than by the Marks which the Poet gives them. The Matter and Manner of their Tales, and of their Telling, are so suited to their different Educations, Humours, and Callings, that each of them would be improper in any other Mouth. Even the grave and serious Characters are distinguish'd by their several sorts of Gravity: Their Discourses are such as belong to their Age, their Calling, and their Breeding; such as are becoming of them, and of them only. Some of his Persons are Vicious, and some Vertuous; some are unlearn'd, or (as *Chaucer* calls them) Lewd, and some are Learn'd. Even the Ribaldry of the Low Characters is different: The *Reeve*, the *Miller*, and the *Cook*, are several Men, and distinguish'd from each other, as much as the mincing Lady Prioress, and the broad-speaking gap-tooth'd Wife of *Bathe*. But enough of this: There is such a Variety of Game springing up before me, that I am distracted in my Choice, and know not which to follow. 'Tis sufficient to say according to the Proverb, that here is God's Plenty. We have our Fore-fathers and Great Grand-dames all before us, as they were in *Chaucer's* Days; their general Characters are still remaining in Mankind, and even in *England*, though they are call'd by other Names than those of *Moncks*, and *Fryars*, and *Chanons*, and *Lady Abbesses*, and *Nuns*: For Mankind is ever the same, and nothing lost out of Nature, though every thing is alter'd.

Like Milton, Dryden makes regular use of the spelling -*'d* for the {-ed} morpheme, except in *distracted*, where the ending constitutes a syllable. Like Hakluyt and Milton, he makes more use of initial capital letters than we do; but in the Dryden passage their use is less sporadic, for all nouns are capi-

9

talised, and so is the first word after a colon. Apart from these two points, the spelling is almost exactly as in PresE, the only words that differ being *Phisiognomies*, *Vertuous*, *Bathe*, *Moncks*, *Fryars*, *Chanons*, and *every thing* 'everything'. The possessive singular of nouns is given an apostrophe: *God's Plenty*, *Chaucer's Days*.

In the vocabulary there is nothing which is now archaic. There is one word used in an obsolete meaning: when Dryden says that the reeve, the miller, and the cook are 'several Men', he means that they are various, distinct, distinguished from each other.

The grammar is almost as in PresE. The third-person singular inflection is invariably {-es}, as in *gives* and *calls*, never {-eth}: Milton used *hath*, but Dryden uses *has*. There are no examples of auxiliary *do* being used in an affirmative declarative sentence, but there is just one example of a negative sentence being formed without do or any other auxiliary: *I ... know not which to follow*. There are two examples of verbs being used in a progressive form: *is ... springing up, are remaining*. In the three earlier passages there is not a single example of a progressive tense; such tenses were indeed in use, but were rarer than today.

REGIONAL VARIATION

There was undoubtedly a good deal of regional variation in the language spoken in England in the Early Modern period. This does not appear very clearly in the written records, however, because there was something approaching a standard literary language in England by this time, and it was only in the spoken language that much regional variation occurred. It may seem to us that there was a great deal of freedom of usage in the written language, especially in the sixteenth century, but the extent to which there was an accepted literary language becomes clear if we compare the situation with that in Middle English. Even in the fourteenth century, texts from different regions display great differences, not only in spelling, but also in vocabulary and grammar. *Sir Gawain and the Green Knight* in the north-west Midlands, *Piers Plowman* in the south-west Midlands, the devotional writings of Richard Rolle in Yorkshire, the poems of Chaucer in London – these are all written in very different regional varieties of English. It was during the late fourteenth century and the fifteenth century, when French was finally disappearing from England as a normal language of administration, education, and culture, that a standard literary form of English gradually became accepted. This new literary standard was based on the ME dialect of the East Midlands, which by now had become the form of English used in the court and the capital. Its dissemination was encouraged by the introduction of printing with movable type, first brought to England by William Caxton in 1476, and by the early sixteenth century it was fairly widely used.

In the printed texts of the Early Modern period, therefore, we find very little reflection of regional variation inside England. Occasionally, poets or dramatists or writers of prose fiction attempt to reproduce regional speech in their dialogue. Such attempts, however, cannot be relied on to give an accurate reproduction of a regional dialect: they tend to reflect stereotyped metropolitan beliefs about rural speech, and often jumble together forms from different regions. One motive for such attempts is the creation of a 'rustic' atmosphere, especially in works within the pastoral tradition. This can be seen, for example, in some of the eclogues in Edmund Spenser's *Shepheardes Calender* (1579), a set of pastoral verse dialogues, one for each month of the year. The eclogue for April opens as follows, with Thenot addressing Hobbinoll:

> Tell me good Hobbinoll, what garres thee greete?
> What? hath some Wolfe thy tender Lambes ytorne?
> Or is thy Bagpype broke, that soundes so sweete?
> Or art thou of thy loued lasse forlorne?

The phrase *garres thee greete* is genuine Northern English dialect: it means 'causes you to weep', and the ME examples of the two verbs are almost exclusively Northern English or Scots. Spenser expected his readers to be unfamiliar with the phrase, because in the notes at the end of the eclogue he glosses it as 'causeth thee weepe and complain'. This gloss calls attention to another feature: *garres* has the {-es} morpheme for the third-person singular, while *causeth* has the {-eth} morpheme. The {-es} form was originally northern, and, although it had spread to the south by Spenser's time, it had not yet supplanted {-eth}, at any rate in the written language. Spenser knew a good deal about Northern English dialect, but not all of his 'rustic' expressions are northern. The past participle *ytorne* has the prefix *y-*, descended from OE ȝe-, and this is certainly not northern, for it had disappeared in the north by about 1200, and in the rest of the country by the middle of the fifteenth century. In the sixteenth century, therefore, it is an archaism, and the combination of archaisms and dialect forms is found in much of Spenser's poetry. The word *lasse* 'girl, sweetheart' was also northern by origin; by Spenser's time it was well-known in the south, but was used especially in pastoral or rustic contexts, as here.

Sometimes, however, attempts are made to depict regional dialects in non-pastoral contexts, especially in the drama. In Shakespeare's *King Lear* there is a scene where the disguised Edgar, defending his father from the steward Oswald, adopts a rustic style of speech:

Stew. Let go his arme.
Edg. Chill not let go Zir,
    Without vurther 'casion.

11

Stew.   Let go Slaue, or thou dy'st.

Edg.   Good Gentleman goe your gate, and let poore volke passe: and
'chud ha' bin zwaggerd out of my life, 'twould not ha' bin zo
long as 'tis, by a vortnight. Nay, come not neere th'old man:
keepe out che vor'ye, or ice try whither your Costard, or my
Ballow be the harder; chill be plaine with you.

Edgar's speech there shows many non-standard characteristics. Since the
scene is set in Kent, these are presumably meant to represent Kentish dialect
forms, but in fact they are a mixed bag. Some forms could indeed be Kentish:
spellings like *Zir* and *vurther* clearly indicate pronunciations with voiced
initial fricatives: in Middle English such forms occurred everywhere south of
the Thames and the Severn, and this may still have been true in Shakespeare's
day. Edgar uses *che* or proclitic *ch-* for the personal pronoun *I*, as in *chill* 'I
will' and *chud* 'I would', where *ch* is from an earlier strong form *ich*. Such
forms are often used in Shakespeare's time to indicate rustic speech, but are
not specifically Kentish. And the expressions *goe your gate* 'go your way, go
away' and *ice* 'I shall' are if anything northern rather than south-eastern, while
the word *ballow* 'cudgel' is unrecorded by the OED except in this passage.
Shakespeare is probably just drawing on stock theatrical ideas about the way
rustics talked.

In addition, writers of the period sometimes comment on the existence of
regional dialects, and occasionally give examples of dialect forms. The following comes from *A Restitution of Decayed Intelligence* (1605), by Richard
Verstegan:

we see that in some seueral partes of *England* it self, both the names of
things, and pronountiations of woords are somwhat different ... and of
this different pronountiation one example in steed of many shal suffise,
as this: for pronouncing according as one would say at *London*, *I would
eat more cheese yf I had it* / the northern man saith, *Ay sud eat mare
cheese gin ay hadet* / and the westerne man saith: *Chud eat more cheese
an chad it*. Lo heer three different pronountiations in our owne countrey
in one thing and heerof many the lyke examples might be alleaged.

Verstegan says that these examples illustrate differences of pronunciation, but
in fact they also illustrate grammatical differences, as in the variation between
I and *ch-*, and that between *yf*, *gin* and *an*. Like Shakespeare, he represents
regional pronunciations by using spellings not normally found in his time, like
ay 'I' and *hadet* 'had it'. In other words, variations in pronunciation are normally concealed in written works by the existence of a standard literary language. In the surviving texts, then, we shall on the whole be dealing with a
standard literary language, with little regional variation, whereas there can be

little doubt that in speech there was considerable regional variation, especially in pronunciation. It was perhaps common for members of the gentry to speak with a local accent, and for some of them also to use regional lexical and grammatical forms. As late as the eighteenth century, some country gentlemen in works of fiction are depicted as using such regional forms. Such, for example, are Sir Wilful Witwoud (a sympathetic character) in William Congreve's play *The Way of the World* (1700), and Squire Western (an unsympathetic one) in Henry Fielding's novel *Tom Jones* (1749). The language of the court, however, and the court accent, had great prestige. George Puttenham, in *The Arte of English Poesie* (1589), advises the writer on the kind of speech he should base his poetical language on. The purest language in a country, he says, is usually that spoken in the king's court, or in good inland towns, not in seaports or in border regions or uplandish villages. The poet must use the language of the educated classes, not of artisans. And he must use the present-day language, not that of Chaucer and other older poets. He continues:

> neither shall he take the termes of Northern-men, such as they vse in dayly talke, whether they be noble men or gentlemen, or of their best clarkes all is a matter: nor in effect any speach vsed beyond the riuer of Trent, though no man can deny but that theirs is the purer English Saxon at this day, yet it is not so Courtly nor so currant as our Southerne English is, no more is the far Westerne mans speach: ye shall therfore take the vsuall speach of the Court, and that of London and the shires lying about London within lx. myles, and not much aboue. I say not this but that in euery shyre of England there be gentlemen and others that speake but specially write as good Southerne as we of Middlesex or Surrey do, but not the common people of euery shire, to whom the gentlemen, and also their learned clarkes do for the most part condescend.

This testifies to the prestige of the language of the Court, and of south-eastern England generally (within a radius of sixty miles!), but at the same time gives evidence for the continuation of regional speech even among the upper classes. The poet is not to imitate the everyday language of northern England, even of noblemen, gentlemen, or scholars, nor the language of the far west. Puttenham hastens to add that he knows that in every county of England there are gentlemen and others that can speak *but specially write* good southern English: this suggests that it was common in all parts of England for educated people to write the standard literary language, but less common for them to speak with a south-eastern accent. At the end of the passage, the word *condescend* perhaps implies that the gentry used the local dialect when they talked with 'the common people', but among themselves used StE.

EARLY MODERN ENGLISH

One very distinctive regional variety of English was the form of the language used in Scotland. English was not the only language spoken there, for Scottish Gaelic was still the mother tongue of the north and the west, while the language of Orkney and Shetland was Norn, a form of Scandinavian. But English had been spoken in south-eastern Scotland since OE times, and by the sixteenth century was probably the normal language throughout the Scottish lowlands.

Scottish English had many features in common with the speech of Northern England, together with a number of distinctive features of its own, and was sufficiently different from southern English to be the subject for comment, jest and parody. There is an example in *Merie Tales of the mad men of Gotam*, one of those jest books that the sixteenth century was so fond of. It was written by 'A.B. of Phisike Doctour' (possibly Andrew Boorde) round about 1540. The eighteenth tale in the collection is about a Scot who took a house near London, which he wanted to make into an inn. For his inn sign, he wanted to have a boar's head.

> And he wente to London to haue a Bores head made. He dyd come to a Caruer (or a Joyner) saying in his mother tonge, I saye spek, kens thou meke me a Bare heade? Ye said the Caruer. Than sayd the skotyshman, mek me a bare head anenst Yowle, and thowse bus haue xx pence for thy hyre. I wyll doe it sayde the Caruer. On S. Andrewes daye before Chrystmas (the which is named Yowle in Scotland, and in England in the north) the skottish man did com to London for his Bores heade to set at a dore for a signe. I say speke said the skotish man, haste thou made me a Bare head? Yea said the Caruer. Then thowse a gewd fellow.The Caruer went and did bryng a mans head of wod that was bare and sayd, syr here is youre bare head. I say sayde the skotyshman, the mokyl deuill, is this a bare head? Ye said the caruer. I say sayd the Skotishman, I will haue a bare head, syk an head as doth follow a Sew that hath Gryces. Syr said the caruer, I can not tel what is a Sew, nor what is a Gryce. Whet horson, kenst thou not a sew that wil greet and grone, and her gryces wil run after her and cry a weke a weke. O said the Caruer, it is a pigge. Yea said the skotish man, let me haue his fathers head made in timber, and mek me a bird and set it on his skalps, and cause her to sing whip whir, whip whir. The caruer sayde, I can not cause her to singe whip whir. Whe horson sayde the skotish man gar her as she woulde singe whip whir.
>
> Here a man maye see that euerye man doth delight in his own sences, or doth reioyce in his fantasie.

The thing that the whole anecdote turns on, the pronunciation by the Scot of *boar* as *bare*, was a genuine mark of northern speech. The word *boar* is descended from OE *bár*, and one of the phonological differences between northern and southern dialects is the treatment of the OE long vowel *á*. South of the Humber it must have been a back vowel, and in Middle English it became closer, developing into [ɔ:]. North of the Humber it must have been a front vowel, and it too became closer, developing into [ɛ:]. OE *hám*, *bán*, and *hláford* have developed into present-day southern English *home*, *bone*, and *lord*, but into Scots *haim*, *bain*, and *laird*. So the Scot in the anecdote, wanting a boar's head, asked for a bare head. The carver interpreted *bare* as 'hatless' (a normal eModE meaning), and carved him the head of a man without a hat. There are also other genuine northern forms in the anecdote, such as *gar* 'cause', *greet* 'to cry', *gryce* 'piglet', *mokyl* 'great, powerful', and *syk* 'such'. This last word is also found in pastoral poems in the south, but then usually in the form *sike*. The word *mokyl* (*muckle*) and its variants like *mickle* are frequently found in northern texts with the word *devil*, as here. The author also attempts to represent Scots pronunciation, by spellings such as *mek* 'make', *gewd* 'good', and *whe* 'why'. On the other hand, there are forms in the Scot's speech which are alien to Scots, such as *doth*, *hath*, *kenst* and *she*: typical Scots forms would have been *dois*, *hes*, *kens*, and *scho*. So even though there are genuine Scots forms in the dialogue, the author is probably drawing to a considerable extent on southern stereotypes.

Since the author has to explain the meaning of *Yowle*, and since the carver does not understand the Scotsman's *sew* or *gryce*, it might be thought that the story is evidence against the existence of a standard form of the language in the Early Modern period. In fact, however, there were *two* standard languages, English and Scots. The standard literary language that I talked about earlier was the one that arose in England, but alongside it there was a rather different one in Scotland. Throughout the Middle Ages there was an independent Scottish kingdom. Its power centres were in the English-speaking lowlands, where the primary language of culture and administration was English, not Gaelic. Naturally enough, Scotland developed her own form of standard literary English, different from that which developed around London. The earliest substantial records of this Scots literary language are not found until the second half of the fourteenth century, with John Barbour's long narrative poem, the *Bruce* (about 1375). Thereafter, however, there is a well documented literary tradition, and a fine literature, which reaches its peak in the poetry of Robert Henryson and William Dunbar in the late fifteenth and early sixteenth centuries. Nowadays we usually refer to this early form of the Scots literary language as 'Middle Scots', but the Scots themselves called it *Inglis*. The first person to refer to it as *Scottis* seems to have been the poet Gavin Douglas, who translated Virgil's *Æneid* into Scots in the early sixteenth century.

So far, we have only seen a parody of Scots speech in an English jest book.

For a genuine example of the Scots literary language at the beginning of our period, let us look at an extract from the *Morall Fabillis* of Robert Henryson, probably written shortly before 1500. The extract comes from the tale of the cock ('Schir Chantecleir') and the fox (or *tod*, also called 'Lowrence'), a story which had earlier been handled by Chaucer in the *Canterbury Tales*.

> Ane vedow ['widow'] dwelt in till ane drop ['village'] thay dayis
> Quhilk wan hir fude off spinning on hir rok ['distaff'],
> And na mair had, forsuth, as the fabill sayis,
> Except off hennis scho had ane lyttil flok,
> And thame to keip ['protect'] scho had ane iolie cok,   5
> Richt curageous, that to this wedow ay
> Deuydit ['divided up'] nicht and crew befoir the day.
>
> Ane lyttil fra this foirsaid vedowis hows,
> Ane thornie schaw ['copse'] thair wes off grit defence ['security'],
> Quhairin ane foxe, craftie and cautelous ['cunning'],   10
> Maid his repair and daylie residence,
> Quhilk to this wedow did grit violence
> In pyking ['stealing'] off pultrie baith day and nicht,
> And na way be reuengit on him scho micht.
>
> This wylie tod, quhen that the lark couth sing,   15
> Full sair hungrie vnto the toun ['village'] him drest,
> Quhair Chantecleir, in to the gray dawing,
> Werie for ['because of'] nicht, wes flowen fra his nest.
> Lowrence this saw, and in his mynd he kest ['pondered']
> The ieperdies ['tricks'], the wayis, and the wyle,   20
> Be quhat menis he micht this cok begyle.
>
> Dissimuland in to countenance and cheir,
> On kneis fell, and simuland thus he said,
> 'Gude morne, my maister, gentill Chantecleir!'
> With that the cok start backwart in ane braid ['jerk'].   25
> 'Schir, be my saull, ȝe [ye] neid not be effraid,
> Nor ȝit ['yet'] for me to start nor fle abak;
> I come bot heir seruice to ȝow ['you'] to mak.'

As in the south, spelling was variable, but there were a number of distinctive Scots spelling conventions. Henryson writes *quhilk* 'which' (2) and *quhen* 'when' (15), where the southern language uses initial *wh-*. He writes *richt* (6) and *nicht* (7), corresponding to southern *right* and *night*. In words like *keip* 'keep, guard' (5), *befoir* 'before' (7), and *sair* 'sore' (16) the *i* in the spelling indicates a long vowel, not a diphthong. The word *sair* also illustrates a feature which we have already noticed, namely the different development of the OE long vowel *á* north and south of the Humber: in Henryson's time it was probably realised in Scots as [ɛ:] (a vowel similar to that of modern German *fährt*). The spelling *fude* 'food' also reflects a distinctive northern development: the OE long vowel *ó* became ME [o:] in the south, but in Scots it was rounded and fronted, and eventually became [y:] (similar to the vowel of modern German *führen*), represented in spelling by *u* or *ui*.

There are also distinctive grammatical forms. Plural and possessive forms of nouns have the ending *-is*, as in *dayis* 'days' (1) and *wedowis* 'widow's' (8). The third-person present singular of verbs also has the ending *-is*, as in *sayis* 'says' (3). The same ending could be used for the present plural of verbs, though there are no examples in the passage. The past tense of weak verbs has the ending *-it*, as in *Deuydit* 'divided, marked the end of' (7). The same ending is used in the past participle, as in *reuengit* 'revenged' (14). The present participle has the Scandinavian ending *-and*, as in *simuland* 'feigning, dissimulating' (23). The expression *couth sing* (15) means 'did sing, sang': it was possible to use the auxiliary *couth*, literally 'could', to form a past tense, rather like later *did*. The word *scho* is the normal northern form, corresponding to southern *she*.

In vocabulary, one striking feature of the passage is the complete absence of loans from Gaelic. There are some Gaelic loans in Scots, especially topographical words like *bog*, *cairn*, *crag*, *glen*, and *loch*, but the total number is not large. By contrast, there are a number of Scandinavian loans in the passage: *thay* 'those' (1), *thame* 'them' (5), *fra* 'from' (8), *baith* 'both' (13), *kest* 'cast'(19). These five words are not confined to Scots, however, for corresponding forms are found in the southern language. The word *fra* is from Old Norse *frá*, the corresponding OE form being *fram*. The Scandinavian word survives today in the phrase *to and fro*. In Scots there are in fact Scandinavian loans which are not found in the southern language, but if anything there are fewer Scandinavian loans in Middle Scots than in the ME dialects of northern England.

The medieval Scottish kingdom had close links with France, and there are many French loans in Middle Scots, especially in works written in a high style. In the passage there are about twenty French loans, such as *fabill* (3), *iolie* (5), and *curageous* (6). There are also two Latin words, *Except* (4) and *Deuydit* (7). There were some French and Latin loans which were distinctively Scots, but in fact all those in the passage are also found in the south. The only lexical item in the passage which is not found in southern England is *tod* 'fox', the etymology of which is doubtful.

That example of the Scots literary language comes from the very beginning of our period, and is in verse. We can usefully supplement it with another Scots passage from later in the period, and in prose. The following extract is

17

from Alexander Hume's *Orthographie and Congruitie of the Britan Tongue*, written round about 1617, but not published in his time. It is a work on the spelling and grammar of English, and was intended for use in Scottish schools. Hume, however, was interested in southern usage as well as in Scots, and hoped to influence southern spelling. In the passage quoted, he is arguing for the Scots spelling *quh-* instead of the southern *wh-*, and tells a story about an argument he had on the point with English colleagues:

> To clere this point, and alsoe to reform an errour bred in the south, and now usurped be ['by'] our ignorant printeres, I wil tel quhat befel myself quhen I was in the south with a special gud frende of myne. Ther rease ['rose'], upon sum accident, quhither ['whether'] quho, quhen, quhat, *etc.*, sould be symbolized with q or w, a hoat disputation betuene him and me. After manie conflictes (for we oft encountered), we met be chance, in the city of baeth, with a doctour of divinitie of both our acquentance. He invited us to denner. At table my antagonist, to bring the question on foot amangs his awn condisciples, began that I was becum an heretik, and the doctour spering ['asking'] how, ansuered that I denyed quho to be spelled with a w, but with qu. Be quhat reason? quod ['said'] the Doctour. Here, I beginning to lay my grundes of labial, dental, and guttural soundes and symboles, he snapped me on this hand and he on that, that the doctour had mikle a doe ['much ado'] to win me room for a syllogisme. Then (said I) a labial letter can not symboliz a guttural syllab ['syllable']. But w is a labial letter, quho a guttural sound. And therfoer w can not symboliz quho, nor noe syllab of that nature. Here the doctour staying them again (for al barked at ones), the proposition, said he, I understand; the assumption is Scottish, and the conclusion false. Quherat al laughed, as if I had bene dryven from al replye, and I fretted to see a frivolouse jest goe for a solid ansuer.

The doctor's rebuttal of the argument was perhaps not as frivolous as Hume suggests, for his syllogism does indeed rest on a 'Scottish assumption' about pronunciation. In Scots, words like *what* probably began with [xw-], the first consonant being a velar ('guttural') fricative (like that in German *ach*), whereas in the south such words began with [hw-] or [w-].

The passage contains some distinctively Scots forms, like *amangs*, *awn*, *gud*, *mikle*, *sould* 'should' and *sper-* 'ask'. But what is striking is the large number of southern forms. The word *gud* 'good' illustrates the normal Scots development of OE *ó* to [y:], and *gud* is the usual form in Hume. This, however, is exceptional: in the vast majority of cases, words with OE *ó* appear in his work with southern spellings, an example in the passage being *foot*. Similarly, words with OE *á* sometimes appear in Scots form, as with *awn* and *rease*, but more often in southern form, as in *both*, *hoat* 'hot', *noe*, and *ones* 'once'.

18

The spelling *quh-* is of course used, not southern *wh-*, but *laughed* has the southern *gh*, not Scots *ch*. Among grammatical features, we notice the verb inflection *-ed*, (*usurped*, *laughed*), not Scots *-it*, and the present participle ending *-ing* (*staying*), not Scots *-and*.

It might be thought that the context of the anecdote explains the large number of southern forms: when Hume reports the speech of an Englishman it is perhaps unsurprising that he writes *quho* rather than *quha*. But in fact the high proportion of southern forms is found throughout the work, not merely when Hume discusses the southern language. Sometimes the northern and southern forms of a word occur inside a single sentence, as when Hume says that adjectives are compared with *mare* and *mast*, and immediately gives the examples *more sueet*, *most sueet*. Some Scots usages occur pretty consistently: he usually writes *ald* 'old', and similarly *cald*, *hald*; words with OE *áw* appear with *aw*, like *awn* 'own', *knaw* 'know'; and he normally uses the forms *mikle* 'much', *quhilk* 'which', *sal* 'shall', *sik* 'such', and *sould* 'should'. But the indefinite article is usually *a* or *an*, only occasionally Scots *ane*; and words with OE *á* and *ó* appear more frequently in English spelling than in Scots. For the second and third person singular of verbs, Hume uses northern forms like *thou wrytes*, *it cumes*, not the southern *thou writest*, *it cometh*, but even so he uses the English spelling *-es* for the inflection, not the Scots *-is*; and occasionally he uses the southern forms *hath* and *doth*. Sometimes the *-es* inflection is used for the plural in the northern way, as when he writes *men confoundes*, but most often he uses the base form of the verb for the plural.

Hume had spent a number of years in England in the late sixteenth century, and knew the southern language well. He is not, however, just an isolated case of a Scot being influenced by southern forms: his writing is typical of what was happening to Scots in the seventeenth century. In 1500, there were two forms of standard literary English, one centred on London and the other on lowland Scotland. But in the course of the Early Modern period the Scots literary language fell into decay, and by the late seventeenth century there was in effect only one standard literary form of English, that centred on London. During the sixteenth and seventeenth centuries, the Scots literary language was increasingly penetrated by southern forms, and at the same time it became commoner for Scots to write in the southern language.

One reason for this influence was that the southern speech community was larger and richer than the English-speaking community in Scotland. It also had an impressive literary tradition, the works of Chaucer, Lydgate, and Gower being especially influential. The influence extended to the language, and as early as the fifteenth century there are occasional southern forms to be found in Scots writing. The number of such southern forms increased in the sixteenth century, and one important factor was the Reformation. The sixteenth-century Scottish reformers were influenced by the English reformers, whose works consequently were read in Scotland. But perhaps the Scottish Protestants were influenced even more by southern English translations of the Bible. The sixteenth century was a period of intense biblical translation in England, beginning with William Tyndale's New Testament of 1534. The various English protestant translations were not all completely new versions: rather, each translator began from the previous translations, and tried to improve and refine them, the whole process culminating in the great King James Bible of 1611. But the fact remains that there were numerous translations of the Bible available in English, all in the southern language. There was nothing comparable in Scotland. There was indeed a translation of the New Testament into Scots, probably made by Murdoch Nisbett round about 1520, but this was not published. It is notable, too, that it was not translated from the Greek or Latin, but was a Scotticisation of the fourteenth-century Wycliffite version. So Scottish protestants read English versions of the Bible, and especially, from the time of its publication in 1560, the Geneva Bible, with its calvinistic marginal comments. John Knox himself was in Geneva while the translation was being made, and may even have contributed to it, but the Geneva Bible was in southern English, and was a potent source of linguistic influence in Scotland. The influence of southern forms first becomes marked in Scottish writing in the second half of the sixteenth century.

In the seventeenth century, southern influence was further encouraged by the union of the crowns in 1603, when James VI of Scotland became James I of England. It was indeed only a union of the crowns: in all other respects, England and Scotland remained separate, each with its own administrative, judicial, and ecclesiastical system. But the union of the crowns meant that the king's court was in London, so that London became the centre from which patronage radiated, for English and Scots alike. This inevitably increased English cultural influence on Scotland.

In the seventeenth century, therefore, the Scots literary language became extremely mixed, with strong influence from the southern language. Moreover, it became increasingly common for Scots to write in southern English, and for books in southern English to be printed in Scotland, a practice that began in the late sixteenth century: in the passage quoted above, Hume complains about the 'ignorant printeres' of Scotland, who are adopting southern spellings. By the end of the seventeenth century, the Scots literary language had practically ceased to exist. In the eighteenth century, there were many distinguished Scots thinkers and writers, like David Hume, Adam Smith, and the historian William Robertson: those three were all born and educated in Scotland, but all three wrote in the southern literary language.

The fact that the southern literary language became standard in Scotland does not mean that the Scots changed the way they spoke. They went on talking in the same way, but in writing they adopted the conventions of the south.

But, since the southern literary language is based on an East Midland dialect of Middle English, extremely different from the dialects of the north, many Scots have been conscious of a certain discrepancy between their spoken and their written language. This, combined with Scots national feeling, has led to the production of a dialect literature in which writers have attempted to produce a written language which would mirror more closely the way in which Scots actually speak. This involves the use of spelling conventions different from those of the standard language, to represent the phonological characteristics of Scots, and the reproduction of Scots grammatical and lexical features. The father of the Scots dialect movement was Allan Ramsay (1686–1758), and its most renowned figure has been Robert Burns (1759–96). But having a dialect literature of this kind is not the same thing as having a standard Scots literary language. When Middle Scots was the standard literary language of Scotland, all written transactions (if not in Latin) were carried out in this language – official documents, private letters, contracts, sermons, pamphlets, works of scholarship. But since the eighteenth century, when Scotland has had a dialect literature, this has not been so: there have been plays and poems in Scots, but the contracts and the history books and the chemistry textbooks have been written in the southern literary language.

SOCIAL VARIATION

Social variation certainly existed in eModE, though, as with regional variation, its existence is to some extent concealed by the fact that there was a standard literary language. Earlier, we saw a passage in Puttenham in which he advises the poet to use the language of the court and of the London area. But he also warns the poet against modelling himself on speakers of the 'wrong' social class:

> neither shall he follow the speach of a craftes man or carter, or other of the inferiour sort, though he be inhabitant or bred in the best towne and Citie in this Realme, for such persons doe abuse good speaches by strange accents or ill shapen soundes, and false ortographie. But he shall follow generally the better brought vp sort, such as the Greekes call *charientes* men ciuill and graciously behauoured and bred.

Puttenham is referring to social dialects, not regional ones. The poet is not to imitate the language of craftsmen or carters, even if they live in the right region, but the language of 'the better brought vp sort'. The Greek word *charientes* means something like 'elegant men, accomplished men'; Puttenham probably assumes that these will be members of the gentry. When he condemns 'strange accents', he is probably not using the word *accent* in the sense 'mode of utterance peculiar to an individual or locality', for this meaning is not recorded in the OED until 1600. More probably he is referring to stress and intonation, for elsewhere in the work he discusses the 'accents' of classical Greek in such terms; but he does condemn lower-class pronunciation for its 'ill shapen soundes'. He is however concerned with the written language, for he condemns 'false ortographie', which means 'incorrect spelling'. He says nothing specific about vocabulary or grammar, but these are presumably things he objects to in the language of plebeians.

As with regional speech, we might hope to find some representation of lower-class speech in the drama, for the plays quite often depict artisans, apprentices, shopkeeping citizens, common soldiers, and similar characters from below the level of the gentry. It is not always possible, however, to take such representations at their face value, especially when the character is presented as an object of mirth, for the dramatist is likely to exaggerate and parody. The frequent use of malapropisms, and of long, rambling, inconsequential sentences (seen in characters like Shakespeare's Mistress Quickly and Juliet's Nurse), was not necessarily typical of the speech of uneducated women. All the same, the evidence of the plays probably has some value. The citizen classes, and especially London citizens, are frequently depicted on the stage, and the dramatists must have had some first-hand knowledge of their speech. The following is a specimen of London citizen speech from the Induction to Francis Beaumont's comedy *The Knight of the Burning Pestle* (1613). The speaker is a member of the Grocer's Company, and is suggesting to the Prologue that his apprentice, Rafe, should take a part in the play:

> Well remembred wife, come vp *Rafe*: Il'e tell you Gentlemen, let them but lend him a suit of reparrell, and necessaries, and by Gad, if any of them all blow winde in the taile on him, I'le be hang'd.

The pronunciation indicated by the spelling *Gad* became a fashionable affectation later in the century, but at this date it was a vulgarism, and here probably represents a city pronunciation. The word *reparrell* 'apparel' is not a malapropism, for it is a historically genuine form. This example, however, is the last recorded in the OED, and it was probably non-standard by this date. The Citizen's Wife also uses the word, but when the Prologue (i.e. a boy actor) replies, he uses the word *apparrell*. It is possible that the expression *blow winde in the taile on him* (? 'outdo him') was also a vulgarism. Similar representations of citizens' speech can be found in other plays: particularly common is the use of spellings to represent non-standard pronunciations. Such spellings occur in Thomas Middleton's city comedies, where we find forms like *chashock* 'cassock', *guesse* 'guests', *kiffe* 'kith', *kursen* 'christen', *misters* 'mistress', *Queen-hive* 'Queenhithe', and *shuter* 'suitor'.

In the plays, too, we sometimes find comments on the usages of different classes. In Shakespeare's *Henry IV Part 1* occurs the following piece of dialogue between Hotspur (son of an earl) and Lady Percy, his wife:

Hotsp. Come, Ile haue your Song too.
Lady. Not mine, in good sooth.
Hotsp. Not yours, in good sooth?
You sweare like a Comfit-makers Wife:
Not you, in good sooth; and, as true as I liue;
And, as God shall mend me; and, as sure as day:
And giuest such Sarcenet suretie for thy Oathes,
As if thou neuer walk'st further then Finsbury.
Sweare me, *Kate*, like a Lady, as thou art,
A good mouth-filling Oath: and leaue in sooth,
And such protest of Pepper Ginger-bread,
To Veluet-Guards, and Sunday-Citizens.

Hotspur is rebuking his wife for using the expression *in good sooth*, which he obviously regards as mealy-mouthed. It is the kind of oath, he says, which is used by London citizens, not by members of the nobility. A comfit-maker was a maker of sweets or crystallised fruits, a rather humble member of the citizenry. Finsbury Fields, just outside the city walls to the north-east, were a favourite Sunday walking-place for London citizens and their wives. The *Veluet-Guards* are citizens' wives dressed up in their Sunday best, wearing *guards* (ornamental bands or borders on the clothes) made of velvet. Hotspur throws in a few other phrases for similar condemnation – *as true as I live, as God shall mend me, as sure as day*. The implication is that these are citizen usages, whereas Lady Percy is a member of the nobility, and ought to use forthright oaths suitable to her class.

The cultivation of mild asseverations like 'in good sooth' may be a sign of puritan influence, for the puritans deplored swearing, and puritan influence was particularly strong among the citizenry. The puritans, however, cannot be considered to form a social class in sixteenth- and seventeenth-century England, for puritan ideas were found over a wide spectrum of society. They did however form a large and influential group within society, especially in the seventeenth century, and the puritan movement developed some language usages of its own. The distinctively puritan features were on the whole lexical rather than grammatical or phonological. Hostile commentators do indeed refer at times to the nasal mode of voice production considered typical of puritans. For example, in Ben Jonson's play *The Case is Altered* (1609), Count Ferneze's daughter Aurelia says:

beleeue me, if I had not some hope of your abiding with vs, I should neuer desire to go out of black whilst I liued: but learne to speake i'the nose, and turne puritan presently.

This alleged puritan nasality was perhaps a feature of citizen speech in East Anglia.

It was however the puritan vocabulary that attracted most attention. In many cases, the favourite puritan words existed in the general vocabulary of the language, but the puritans used them much more frequently than other people, or used them in different contexts. Such general words are *brethren* and *sisters* (used by puritan groups to refer to their own members), *abomination, antichristian, carnal, the discipline, edify, the holy cause, idol, profane, the saints* (i.e. the puritans), *spirit, tribulation,* and *zeal.* There were also words which were coined in puritan circles and hardly used at all by other speakers. For example, puritan hostility to the Mass (in their view a popish abomination) led to the rejection of the word *Christmas*: a puritan would talk instead of Christ's Nativity (as Milton did in the title of a famous poem), or could use the word *Christ-tide* (as Ananias does in Jonson's play *The Alchemist*). The puritans' habit of searching their consciences also led to the coining of numerous compounds in *self-*, like *self-conceitedness, self-condemned, self-deceit, self-denial, self-examination,* and *self-sufficiency.*

Today, many of us probably have our views of seventeenth-century puritanism coloured by the portraits of puritans in the drama. These are often very amusing, but we have to remember that they are caricatures: the seventeenth-century dramatists were nearly all hostile to the puritans, and depicted the more disreputable aspects of the movement, picking especially on the behaviour of the lunatic fringe. One of the most famous of these caricatures is Zeal-of-the-Land Busy, the ex-baker from Banbury, in Jonson's *Bartholomew Fair*, first performed in 1614. Busy is depicted as a casuistical hypocrite, justifying self-indulgences which he condemns in others. He uses the kind of puritan vocabulary already described, and moreover illustrates another alleged puritan habit, namely the use in everyday discourse of biblical and near-biblical words and phrases, especially ones from the Old Testament. In Busy's speech there are numerous such expressions as *Baal, a beam in the eye, the chariot wheels of Satan, fall down … and worship, Dagon, gnashing of teeth,* and *the heathen of the land.* Perhaps the word *verily*, which was also much used by puritans, is also due to this biblical influence. Busy's speech is also marked by a great deal of repetition of words and phrases, and this was possibly a feature of some types of puritan public speaking.

For puritan written usage, however, we need not rely on parody and caricature: the sixteenth- and seventeenth-century puritans themselves wrote an enormous amount, and a movement which included Milton and Bunyan in its ranks was hardly either mute or inglorious. The movement produced large numbers of sermons and works of edification, but also a fair amount of autobiography and a considerable amount of polemic. As a specimen of puritan writing, let us look at an extract from one of the Marprelate tracts, which fall into the polemical category. These were a series of pamphlets published by a secret press in 1588–9 under the pseudonym of Martin Marprelate, attacking episcopacy in general and the English bishops in particular. The pseudonymity was essential, for it was perilous to attack the established order: one of the probable authors, John Penry, was executed for his seditious views, and another, John Udall, died in prison. The Marprelate pamphlets are lively, uninhibited, sometimes witty, and often scurrilous, with juicy stories about the private lives of particular bishops and other church dignitaries. They were frowned on for their levity by many people of puritan sympathies, but they got under the skin of the authorities, who went to the length of employing professional writers like Thomas Nash and John Lyly to write replies to them in their own style.

Our extract comes from the pamphlet headed *O read ouer D. Iohn Bridges*, published in 1588. The abbreviations *ye* and *yt* denote *the* and *that*: in late Medieval times, *y* was often used to represent the runic symbol *þ* (correponding to our *th*), and this usage persisted to some extent in Early Modern English. Twice the writer breaks off to answer imaginary interruptions by bystanders. The second of these interruptions is in fact printed in the margin in the original, and says 'M. Marprelate you put more then the question in the conclusion of your syllogisme'. The passage is attacking episcopacy on the grounds that the Bible (which for puritans was the sole authority on church organisation and discipline) prescribes that nobody shall have pastoral authority over ministers of the church.

> They are pettie popes / and pettie Antichrists / whosoeuer vsurpe the authority of pastors ouer them / who by the ordinance of God / are to bee vnder no pastors. For none but Antichristian popes and popelings euer claimed this authoritie vnto themselues / especiallie when it was gainsaid / and accounted Antichristian / generally by the most Churches in the world. But our Lord bishops vsurpe authoritie ouer those who by the ordinance of God / are to be vnder no pastors / and that in such an age / as wherein this authoritie is gainsaid / and accounted Antichristian / generally by all the Churches in the world for ye most part. Therefore our Lord Bishops (what sayest thou man?) our Lord bishopps / (I say) as Iohn of Canterburie / Thomas of Winchester (I will spare Iohn of London for this time / for it may be he is at boules / and it is pitie to trouble my good brother / lest he should sweare too bad) my reuerend prelate of Litchfielde / with the rest of that swinishe rable / are pettie Antichrists / pettie popes / proud prelates / intollerable withstanders of reformation / enemies of the gospell / and most couetous wretched priests. This is a pretie matter / yt standers by / must be so busie in other mens games: why sawceboxes must you be pratling? you are as mannerly as bishops / in medling with that you haue nothing to doe / as they do in taking vpon them ciuill offices.

25

The jeer at the Bishop of London for his addiction to playing bowls and to swearing is one that occurs frequently in the pamphlets. One of the striking things about the passage is the absence of obviously puritan linguistic features. There are some typically puritan lexical items: *pope* (used in the sense 'one who assumes an unjustified position of authority') and its diminutive *popeling*, and *Antichrist* and *Antichristian*, but hardly anything else. And there is nothing in the grammar or the style which would identify it as a piece of puritan writing. Moreover it would be possible to quote from the Marprelate tracts many passages of this length which have no obviously puritan linguistic features at all. This suggests that the usages ridiculed by the dramatists were those of extreme or eccentric sects.

THE LANGUAGE OF ROGUES AND VAGABONDS

In looking at the language of puritans, we have moved from class dialects to the language of other kinds of group within society. There must have been many such sub-languages: the languages of sports and pastimes (hawking, hunting, bowls, archery, gambling), the languages of occupational groups (sailors, weavers, joiners, military engineers), and no doubt also such things as schoolboy and university slang. Words from such specialised groups sometimes drifted into the general vocabulary. Let us look at just one such sub-language, a rather strange one: the arcane language of rogues and vagabonds.

As a result of the social disorders of the fifteenth century, and the enclosures and evictions of the sixteenth, there was in our period a small army of 'sturdy vagabonds' roaming the English countryside. The authorities were alarmed by them, and passed severe punitive legislation, but this did not get rid of the problem. Many of the vagabonds were rogues and cheaters of various kinds, and formed a sub-community on the fringes of official society. This rogues' community had a language of its own, partly no doubt for reasons of security. The secrecy, however, was not so great as to prevent accounts of this language from appearing in print.

One brief account appears in a small book (hardly more than a pamphlet) called *The Fraternitye of Vacabondes*, by John Awdeley. The earliest surviving edition is dated 1575, but there had probably been an edition some ten or fifteen years earlier. Awdeley gives the cant names for various kinds of vagabond, with a brief definition of each. Some of these will sound a familiar note for readers of Shakespeare. An Abraham Man might be a character in *King Lear*:

> An Abraham man is he that walketh bare armed, and bare legged, and fayneth hym selfe mad, and caryeth a packe of wool, or a stycke with baken on it, or such lyke toy, and nameth himselfe poore Tom.

An Irish Toyle, 'that carieth his ware in hys wallet, as laces, pins, poyntes, and

26

such like', reminds us of Autolycus in *The Winter's Tale*. Autolycus, moreover, sings 'With heigh the Doxy ouer the dale', and Awdeley tells us that female vagabonds are called *Doxies*. But perhaps Awdeley's nicest definition is that of 'A Patriarke Co'. To appreciate this, you have to know that in eModE the verb *to depart* commonly meant 'to separate', and moreover that it was used in this sense in the marriage service in *The booke of the common praier* of 1549. In that ceremony, the bride and the groom promise *to haue and to holde* each other *tyl death vs departe* 'until death separates us' (departe being a subjunctive form). The vagabonds provide a parody of this, with a pun on the other common meaning of *depart*:

> A Patriarke Co doth make mariages, and that is vntill death depart the maried folke, which is after this sort: When they come to a dead Horse or any dead Catell, then they shake hands and so depart euery one of them a seuerall way.

A much more substantial book than Awdeley's is *A Caueat or Warening, for Common Cursetors* (meaning 'A Warning against Vagabonds') (1567), by Thomas Harman. Harman was a gentleman, a small landowner at Crayford in Kent. He was much interested in the trickeries of the vagabond community, and went to a good deal of trouble to inform himself about them. He begins, like Awdeley, with an account of the different kinds of rogue, each called by its cant name. But, whereas Awdeley has just a sentence or two on each type, Harman has longer accounts, sometimes running to pages, with detailed descriptions of the methods used for each type of trick, and sometimes anecdotes about specific occasions on which they were used. There are more species of rogue, too, than in Awdeley, and some of them have splendid names, like *A Prygger of Prauncers* (a horse thief), *A counterfet Cranke* (one pretending to suffer from epilepsy), *A Demaunder for glymmar* (a woman who pretends to have lost her goods in a fire), and *A bawdy basket* (a female pedlar/prostitute). Harman then names the main rascals operating in England at the time, and finally gives a section on their speech, 'the leud lousey language of these lewtering Luskes, and lasy Lorrels'. First he gives a glossary of about a hundred of their words, with his own translations, and then an invented dialogue between two vagabonds, again with translation. Some of the words in the glossary will be familiar to modern readers, for example *bowse* 'drink', *to cante* 'to speak', *drawers* 'hosen', and *to fylche* 'to rob'. Indeed, *drawers* is more immediately comprehensible to the modern reader than Harman's gloss, 'hosen'. A word that occurs several times in the glossary is *cofe*, meaning 'man', as in *a gentry cofe* 'a noble or gentleman'; this is perhaps the ancestor of the modern slang word *cove* 'fellow, chap'. Similarly, the words *booze*, *cant*, *drawers*, and *filch* may have come into the general vocabulary from rogues' slang.

Most of the words in the glossary, however, are opaque to the modern reader, as can be seen from the following examples:

autem, a church	*bynge a waste*, go you hence
cassan, cheese	*Crashing chetes*, teeth
dewse a vyle, the country	*fambles*, hands
gan, a mouth	*a gybe*, a writinge
the hygh pad, the hygh waye	*the lightmans*, the daye
a margery prater, a hen	*Nab*, a head
pannam, bread	*a pratling chete*, a tounge
quaromes, a body	*Rome bouse*, wyne
Rome mort, the Quene	*ruff pek*, baken
a skew, a cuppe	*stampers*, shooes
to towre, to see	*yaram*, mylke

The dialogue that follows the glossary suggests that this language was deviant only in vocabulary: the sentence structures are normal English, and it is merely the lexical items that are unfamiliar. This can be seen in the following extract from the dialogue between 'the vpright man' and 'the Roge':

Man. Why hast thou any lowre in thy bonge to bouse,
Why hast thou any money in thy purse to drinke.
Roge. But a flagge, a wyn, and a make.
But a grot, a penny, and a halfe penny.
Man. Why where is the kene that hath the bene bouse.
where is the house that hath the good drinke
Roge. A bene mort hereby at the signe of the prauncer.
A good wyfe here by at the signe of the hors.
Man. I cutt it is a quyer buose I bousd a flagge the laste darkmans.
I say it is small and naughtye drynke, I dranke a groate there the last night.
Roge. But bouse there a bord and thou shalt haue beneship.
But drinke there a shyllinge, and thou shalt haue very good.

Harman's translations have exactly the same structure as the original sentences: it is simply that different nouns, verbs, and adjectives are slotted into them.

Harman's book is a classic of its kind, and was extensively plagiarised by later writers, especially round the turn of the century, when coney-catching pamphlets and rogue literature generally had a boom. It is a first-class source of information on Elizabethan vagabonds and their language, and is also extremely entertaining.

VARIETIES OF EARLY MODERN ENGLISH

WRITTEN AND SPOKEN LANGUAGE

We can be certain that in eModE times there were differences between the written and the spoken language, just as there are today. Unfortunately, we have no records of eModE speech, since the gramophone and the tape recorder are relatively recent inventions. The best we can hope for is a written transcription of speech which reveals some of the characteristics of the spoken language. It is difficult to find things purporting to be transcriptions of everyday informal speech: there are indeed such things as legal documents that contain the depositions of witnesses, but the danger here is that the scribe may well have tidied up the language, and made it nearer to the written form. There are however court cases in which the precise words alleged to have been used by the parties are important, and in such cases the court clerk can hardly have changed them. Some work has been done on records of this type, and it is to be hoped that more will follow.

On the other hand, there is a good deal of material with verbatim reporting of formal occasions, especially in the seventeenth century. There are such things as parliamentary debates, and the remarkable records found in the Clarke Papers – councils of war, the Saffron Walden negotiations between the army and the parliamentary commissioners, the famous Putney debates. After the trial and execution of King Charles I in 1649, authorised accounts of the trial were published, containing what claim to be verbatim records of the proceedings. Some of the passages consist of long speeches, obviously prepared in advance, but there are also what look like more spontaneous exchanges, such as the following, which took place on 22 January 1649. The king is challenging the authority of the court to try him:

The King.	I will answer the same so soone as I know by what authority you do this.
Lord President.	If this be all that you will say, then Gentlemen you that brought the Prisoner hither, take charge of him back againe.
The King.	I doe require that I may give in my Reasons why I do not answer, and give me time for that.
Lord President.	Sir, 'Tis not for Prisoners to require.
The King.	Prisoners? Sir, I am not an ordinary Prisoner.
Lord President.	The Court hath considered of their jurisdiction, and they have already affirm'd their jurisdiction; if you will not answer, we shall give order to record your default.
The King.	You never heard my Reason yet.
Lord President.	Sir, Your Reasons are not to bee heard against the highest Jurisdiction.

The King.	Shew me that Jurisdiction where Reason is not to be heard.
Lord President.	Sir, We shew it you here, the Commons of England; and the next time you are brought you will know more of the pleasure of the Court; and, it may be, their finall determination.
The King.	Shew me where ever the House of Commons was a Court of Judicature of that kind.
Lord President.	Sergeant, Take away the Prisoner.
The King.	Well Sir, Remember that the King is not suffer'd to give in his Reasons for the Liberty and Freedome of all his Subjects.
Lord President.	Sir, You are not to have liberty to use this language; How great a friend you have been to the Lawes and Liberties of the People, let all England and the world judge.
The King.	Sir, under favour it was the Liberty, Freedome, and Lawes of the subject that ever I took – defended myselfe with Armes, I never took up Armes against the People, but for the Lawes.
Lord President.	The Command of the Court must be obeyed; no answer will be given to the Charge.
The King.	Well Sir.

The king is speaking without notes, and the transcript gives the impression of spontaneous speech, though the kind of speech appropriate to a highly formal situation. We cannot know, of course, how much the scribe tidied up the language while writing it down, but our faith in the transcription is increased by the king's penultimate speech in that extract, with its hiatus and change of grammatical construction. He is probably being jostled by his guards, for the president has already ordered him to be removed from the court. There is an even more remarkable passage at the end of the trial, when sentence of death has been passed on the king, and he tries in vain to make a speech to the court after the sentence:

King.	Will you heare me a word Sir?
Lord President.	Sir you are not to be heard after the sentence.
King.	No Sir?
Lord President.	No Sir, by your favour Sir. Guard, withdraw your Prisoner.
King.	I may speake after the sentence. – By your favour Sir, I may speake after the sentence ever.

> By your favour (hold) the sentence Sir. –
> I say Sir I do –
> I am not suffered for to speak, expect what Justice
> other people will have.

Stage directions are hardly necessary: through the king's final speech we can see the court rising in disregard of him, and he himself, still protesting, being removed by his guard.

We have to interpret all such transcriptions with caution, but there is another source of information about the spoken language, namely the drama, which puts characters on the stage and makes some kind of pretence that they are real people talking. Not, indeed, that anybody believes that the speeches of Marlowe's Tamburlaine or Shakespeare's Richard III bear any close resemblance to everyday speech in the 1580s or 1590s: they too obviously proclaim themselves as rhetorical structures. But there are scenes in sixteenth- and seventeenth-century drama which are in a more naturalistic style: such are the low-life scenes in some of Shakespeare's comedies, the citizen comedies of Middleton and Dekker, and (later) the comedy of manners developed by Shirley, Davenant, and Congreve. But here too we have to treat the evidence with caution. Drama is not a slice of life, and the straightforward reproduction of everyday speech, with its formlessness and incoherence, would probably have bored the audience stiff. The dramatists must surely have selected, compressed, parodied. Still, they presumably do attempt to reproduce some of the features of everyday speech in their time, and moreover they often depict speech in everyday situations, and it is not easy to find other sources for this. Let us look at a passage of drama which seems to be trying to give the illusion of everyday speech. The following is the opening part of a scene from Shakespeare's *Henry IV Part 1* (Q1 text):

> *Enter a Carrier with a lanterne in his hand.*
> 1. *Car.* Heigh ho. An it be not foure by the day ile
> be hangd, Charles waine is ouer the new
> Chimney, and yet our horse not packt. What
> Ostler.
> *Ost.* Anon, anon. 5
> 1. *Car.* I preethe Tom beat Cuts saddle, put a few
> flockes in the point, poore iade is wroong
> in the withers, out of all cesse.
> *Enter another Carier.*
> 2. *Car.* Pease and beanes are as danke here as a dog,
> and that is the next way to giue poore iades 10
> the bots: this house is turned vpside downe
> since Robin Ostler died.

31

1. Car. Poore fellow neuer ioied since the prise of
Oates rose, it was the death of him.

2. Car. I thinke this be the most villainous house   15
in al London road for fleas, I am stung like a
Tench.

1. Car. Like a Tench, by the Masse there is nere a
King christen could be better bit then I
haue bin since the first cocke.   20

2. Car. Why they will allowe vs nere a Iordane, and
then we leake in your chimney, and your
chamber-lie breedes fleas like a loach.

1.Car. What Ostler, come away and be hangd, come
away.   25

2. Car. I haue a gammon of bacon, and two razes of
Ginger, to be deliuered as far as Charing
crosse.

1. Car. Gods bodie, the Turkies in my Panier are
quite starued: what Ostler? a plague on thee,   30
hast thou neuer an eie in thy head? canst
not heare, and twere not as good deede as
drinke to break the pate on thee, I am a
very villaine, come and be hangd, hast no
faith in thee?   35

Enter Gadshill.

Gads. Good morrow Cariers, whats a clocke?

Car. I thinke it be two a clocke.

Gads. I prethe lend me thy lanterne, to see my
gelding in the stable.

1. Car. Nay by God soft, I knowe a tricke worth two   40
of that I faith.

Gads. I pray thee lend me thine.

2. Car. I when canst tell? lend me thy lanterne
(quoth he) marry ile see thee hangd first.

Gads. Sirrha Carrier, what time doe you meane to   45
come to London?

2. Car. Time enough to go to bed with a candle, I
warrant thee, come neighbour Mugs, weele
call vp the Gentlemen, they will along with
company, for they haue great charge. *Exeunt.*   50

Enter Chamberlaine.

Gads. What ho: Chamberlaine.

Cham. At hand quoth pickepurse.

Gads.   Thats euen as faire as at hand quoth the
          Chamberlaine: for thou variest no more from
          picking of purses, then giuing direction   55
          doth from labouring: thou laiest the plot
          how.
Cham.   Good morrow maister Gadshill.

The rest of the scene consists of a dialogue between Gadshill and the Chamberlain, in which plans are made for a highway robbery.

The passage gives the illusion of spontaneous informal speech, and it is not difficult to see some of the characteristics that create this illusion. The sentence structures are relatively simple, with successive co-ordinated clauses rather than subordinate clauses. Sometimes, as in the First Carrier's speech in lines 6–8, the successive clauses are simply juxtaposed, without even a co-ordinating conjunction. When subordinate clauses do occur, they are usually simple conditional or temporal clauses, introduced by *an* (meaning 'if') or *since*. There are no examples of sub-dependent clauses.

The speakers use many lexical items (both single words and whole phrases) from the informal end of the stylistic range. In eModE, just as in PresE, there is a stylistic spectrum, ranging from the most formal usages, through neutral ones, to the least formal, with slang at the bottom of the range. Most items are neutral. Indeed, both the highly formal and the highly informal usages depend for their effect on the contrast with ordinary neutral usage. Everyday speech tends to select items from the informal end of the spectrum, and there are certainly examples in the passage, such as *leake* 'urinate' (22), *as good deede as drinke* 'a good thing to do' (32–3), and *I when canst tell* 'not likely!' (literally 'Yes, when, can you tell?') (43). The use of such colloquialisms makes the scene more obscure to the modern reader, but some of the difficulty of the passage arises from the use of trade technicalities. The carriers, naturally enough, talk about the work they are doing as they bustle around preparing for their journey, and we get phrases like *put a few flockes in the point* 'put some flocks of wool under the pommel of the saddle' (6–7).

One of the colloquialisms is also a proverbial expression: *as good deede as drinke*.The use of proverbs and proverb-like phrases is a characteristic of informal speech, and there are other examples in the passage: *as danke ... as a dog* (9), *stung like a Tench* (16–17), *breedes fleas like a loach* (23), *a tricke worth two of that* (40–1), *Time enough to go to bed with a candle* (47), and *At hand quoth pickepurse* (52). These are not indeed all recorded as traditional proverbs (though the last one certainly is), but they all have a proverb-like quality, for example the balance, alliteration, and simile structure in *as danke ... as a dog*.

A proverb is a ready-made expression, a formula, and there are other kinds of formula which are common in speech. There are formulas for greeting people, and for replying to the greeting: in the passage we have *Good morrow*, used by Gadshill (36) and by the Chamberlain (58).There are also summoning formulas: the First Carrier calls *What Ostler* (3–4), using a formula normal for summoning inferiors. The Ostler (obviously off-stage) replies with the formula *Anon, anon* 'coming' (literally 'at once') (5). Gadshill's summoning formula *What ho* (51) is perhaps a trifle less peremptory than the Carrier's *What* (3) and *come away* 'come here' (24). In contrast to these peremptory summonses is his use, when addressing his fellow carrier, of *I preethe* 'I pray you' (6), which is used in courteous requests. It is also used by Gadshill, in the forms *I prethe* (38) and *I pray thee* (42).

Terms of address are also typical of speech. The first Carrier addresses the Ostler as *Ostler* (4, 24, 30), but calls his fellow carrier *Tom* (6), while the Second Carrier later addresses the first as *neighbour Mugs* (48). Gadshill greets the two carriers with *Good morrow Cariers* (36), and later addresses one of them as *Sirrha Carrier* (45), which is perhaps patronising. He addresses the Chamberlain as *Chamberlaine* (51) (and later in the scene as *Sirrha*), while in reply the Chamberlain uses the respectful *maister Gadshill* (58), which suggests that Gadshill has pretensions to some kind of social standing. The use of occupational names as terms of address (like *Ostler*, *Cariers*) is common in the period. Notice too the formulas for asking and telling the time (36, 37).

Another speech-like feature of the scene is the use of exclamations, oaths, and asseverations. The oaths and asseverations are *by the Masse* (18), *Gods bodie* (29), *by God* (40), *I faith* (41), and *marry* 'by (the Virgin) Mary' (44). The opening phrase of the scene, *Heigh ho*, is an exclamation, perhaps expressing a resigned weariness. Later, Gadshill uses the exclamation *tut*, expressing impatient or contemptuous dismissal of objections. Exclamations at the beginning of a sentence shade off into utterance initiators, the words or noises which we insert at the beginning of an utterance while we gather our thoughts. Such are *Why* (21) and *Nay* (40).

The passage also contains many weak forms characteristic of lively speech. The weak form of a word is the form it has in unstressed position, whereas the strong form is the one it has when stressed. Shakespeare has to leave a good deal to his actors in the matter of weak forms, but he often suggests some common ones by his spellings. The weak form of *will* occurs in *ile* (1, 44) and in *weele* (48); of *never* in *nere* (18, 21); of *been* in *bin* (20); of *it* in *twere* (32); of *in* in *I faith* (41); and of *is* in *whats* (36) and *Thats* (53).

Another characteristic of speech is ellipsis: items are omitted which would be considered essential in the written language. In *canst not heare* 'can you not hear' (31–2) the subject pronoun *thou* is omitted, and the same is true of *hast no faith in thee?* (34–5) and *canst tell?* (43). In *poore iade* (7), the definite article *the* has been omitted. There is one ambiguous case: *Poore fellow neuer ioied* (13). This could be an example of the omission of either the definite article ('The poor chap was never happy') or the subject pronoun *he* ('Poor chap, he was never happy').

The language of the passage, then, has many characteristics which suggest real informal speech: simple sentence patterns; lexical items from the informal end of the stylistic continuum; proverbs and proverb-like phrases; formulas of greeting, summoning, and so on; terms of address; exclamations, oaths, asseverations, and utterance initiators; spellings to suggest weak forms; and ellipsis. Many of these things take forms different from those we use today: we do not address people as *neighbour Mugs* or *Sirrha*; we do not greet people by saying *Good morrow*; *Gods bodie* and *marry* are not exclamations that rise naturally to our lips.

Despite all these speech-like qualities, the language of the passage probably lacks many of the characteristics of real informal speech. Our judgement in this matter is inevitably based on the characteristics of informal speech in our own time. We cannot be certain that these characteristics were also found in informal speech in Shakespeare's time, but it would be rather surprising if they were not. One such feature is repetition: in spontaneous informal speech, there are frequent repetitions of single words and short phrases, especially when the speaker is groping for words. Another is the use of pause fillers, the words or noises which we insert in our speech to occupy gaps while we think or hesitate: common pause fillers in PresE are *I mean*, *like*, *sort of*, *well*, and the noises usually represented in writing as *er* and *um*. Another common feature is change of construction in mid-sentence: a speaker begins with one grammatical construction, but breaks off and goes back to begin again; or there may be a switch of construction without any going back, so that what is produced would not be recognised as a grammatical sentence at all in the written language.

These features of real speech – frequent repetition, pause fillers, switch of construction – do not occur in the passage above, and it is not difficult to see why: any extensive use of such features is likely to produce dialogue which is slow-moving, lacking in point and clarity, and (except for occasional comic uses) somewhat tedious. Their absence from Shakespeare's dialogue is not really evidence for their absence from the speech of his time.

Moreover, Shakespeare's dialogue in scenes of this kind often uses more complex sentence structures than those that occur in the passage above. Later in the same scene, a speech by Gadshill contains the following sentence:

> tut, there are other Troians that thou dreamst not of, the which for sport sake are content to do the profession some grace, that would (if matters should be lookt into) for their owne credit sake make all whole.

There we have a main clause (*there are other Troians*) with a restrictive relative clause attached (*that thou dreamst not of*); then two non-restrictive relative clauses, introduced by *the which* and *that*; and inside the second of these a sub-dependent conditional clause introduced by *if*. This would not be at all complex in literary prose, but is rather complex for informal speech, in which non-restrictive relative clauses are rare, and ones containing a sub-dependent conditional clause even rarer. It could be argued, admittedly, that this was not so in Shakespeare's time. The educated classes were trained in rhetoric and in public speaking, and it is possible that their speech, even in informal contexts, was more deliberate and more highly structured than ours is. But it is also likely that the dramatists used complex sentences, even in informal dialogue, because structured writing of this kind is more satisfying to an audience, and easier to listen to, than the incoherences of real informal speech.

LANGUAGE WRITTEN FOR ORAL DELIVERY

We have few transcriptions of natural speech from our period, but we have large quantities of material in a somewhat different mode, written material designed to be read aloud. Volumes of sermons constitute a considerable part of the output of the press in Early Modern times, and a printed sermon is usually intended primarily for oral delivery. Attendance at church on Sunday was legally obligatory, and a sermon was a normal part of the service. The puritans attached especially high value to sermons, but the sermon was also cultivated by non-puritan Anglicans. Moreover, listening to sermons was not merely a tedious duty, at any rate not for everybody: some famous preachers drew large crowds of listeners. Because of the cult of the sermon, people were probably better trained as listeners than we are, and were more accustomed to following a long and sometimes complex argument in spoken form. This has to be borne in mind when we try to assess the characteristics of the audience in the Elizabethan and Jacobean theatre.

Let us first look at an extract from a sermon by a non-puritan Anglican, John Donne (1572–1631), one of the famous preachers of the Jacobean age. It was delivered in 1624, though not printed until 1640.

> But when the Church was newly conceived, and then lay like the egge of a Dove, and a Gyants foot over it, like a worm, like an ant, and hill upon hill whelmed upon it, nay, like a grain of corn between the upper and lower Mill-stone, ground to dust between Tyrans and Heretiques, when as she bled in her Cradle, in those children whom *Herod* slew, so she bled upon her crutches, in those decrepit men whom former persecutions and tortures had creepled before, when East and West joyned hands to crush her, and hands, and brains, joyned execution to consultation to annihilate her; in this wane of the Moon, God gave her an

36

instant fulnesse; in this exinanation, instant glory; in this grave, an instant Resurrection.

It is immediately striking how different that is from the extract from *Henry IV Part 1*, and how conspicuously it lacks all the speech-like features of that extract. It is an obviously rhetorical structure, and makes considerable use of rhetorical figures, as in the repetitions of *like* near the beginning, and in the three balanced phrases at the end. The clause structure is complex: the passage constitutes one single intricate sentence, with its main clause (*God gave her ...*) held back until the end. This kind of structure is alien to spontaneous speech. Nevertheless, a listener has no great difficulty in following it, which suggests that complex structures are avoided in speech because they are difficult for the speaker, not because they are difficult for the hearer. On the other hand, there is clearly a limit to the length of a complex sentence that a hearer can follow with comfort, especially if the main verb is held back, and this sentence of Donne's is probably near this limit. If we go outside the sermon, and look at seventeenth-century expository prose not intended for oral delivery, it is possible to find extremely long complex sentences, sometimes going on for pages (for example in the writings of Milton, Browne, Burton). Writers of sermons normally use shorter and simpler structures than these.

The Donne extract sounds literary, remote from spontaneous speech. By way of contrast, let us look at an extract from a sermon from an earlier generation than Donne's, a sermon which suggests much more strongly the voice of the improvising preacher. It is by Hugh Latimer (?1492–1555), who was one of the zealous reformers of the early Tudor period, and who was one of the protestant martyrs of the reign of Queen Mary. The sermon was delivered in January 1549, and printed a few weeks later. It is usually known as 'The Sermon of the Plough' or 'Sermon on the Ploughers'.

Moyses was a meruelous man, a good man. Moyses was a wonderful felowe, and dyd his dutie being a maried man. We lacke suche as Moyses was. Well, I woulde al men woulde loke to their dutie, as God hath called them, and then we shoulde haue a florishyng christian commune weale. And nowe I would ask a straung question. Who is the most diligent bishoppe and prelate in al England, that passeth al the reste in doinge his office? I can tel, for I knowe him, who it is; I knowe hym well. But nowe I thynke I se you lysting and hearkening, that I shoulde name him. There is one that passeth al the other, and is the most diligent prelate and precher in al England. And wl ye knowe who it is? I wyl tel you. It is the Deuyl. He is the most dyligent preacher of al other, he is neuer out of his dioces, he is neuer from his cure, ye shal neuer fynde hym vnoccupyed, he is euer in his parishe, he keepeth residence at al tymes, ye shal neuer fynde hym out of the waye, cal for him when you wyl, he is euer at home, the diligenteste preacher in all the Realme, he is euer at his ploughe, no lordynge nor loytringe can hynder hym; he is euer appliynge his busynes, ye shal neuer fynde hym idle, I warraunte you.

Latimer too uses rhetorical devices: paired words (*lysting and hearkening*), alliteration (*prelate and precher*), rhetorical question, suspense (the tantalising holding back of *It is the Deuyl*), and accumulation (the series of sentences at the end of the passage). But these, we feel, are the devices of popular oratory, not of learned rhetoric. The sentence structures are relatively uncomplicated, many sentences being simple one-clause affairs. Many lexical items come from the informal end of the stylistic scale (*Moyses was a wonderful felowe*) or at any rate from the neutral central part (*he is euer at home*). The audience are addressed directly by the *ye/you* pronoun. Use is made of speech-like utterance initiators (*Well, But nowe*). And the total effect is simple, direct, and colloquial. In fact it reads like an unscripted performance by a skilled and experienced preacher, reconstructed afterwards from the performer's notes and the transcripts of shorthand writers. This indeed may well be what it is, though we are not in a position to assert positively that this is the case. But there can be little doubt that it bears the mark of popular speech, as of popular purposes.

ARTLESS WRITTEN LANGUAGE

There are documents in the period which are not transcriptions of speech, but which reveal an absence of literary training, and have some characteristics that remind us of the spoken language, especially in their simplicity of clause structure. Diaries are sometimes of this type, but not always: some diaries show a high degree of literary sophistication, and some were obviously written with publication in mind (even if only posthumously, as in the case of Samuel Pepys). Some, however, especially ones written by non-standard speakers, are relatively artless. These sometimes throw light on non-standard vocabulary and grammar, and even, through their spellings, on non-standard pronunciations. A writer who was by no means uneducated, but whose writing is artless and is patently not influenced by a rhetorical training, is Celia Fiennes, who kept a remarkable record of the series of journeys she made around England between about 1685 and 1703. The following is her account of Leeds, which she visited in 1698:

Leeds is a large town, severall large streetes cleane and well pitch'd and good houses all built of stone, some have good gardens and steps up to their houses and walls before them; this is esteemed the wealthyest town of its bigness in the Country, its manufacture is the woollen cloth the Yorkshire Cloth in which they are all employ'd and are esteemed very rich and very proud; they have provision soe plentifull that they may live with very little expense and yet much variety; here if one calls for a tankard of ale which is allwayes a groate – its the only dear thing all over Yorkshire, their ale is very strong – but for paying this groat for your ale you may have a slice of meate either hott or cold according to the tyme of day you call, or else butter and cheese gratis into the bargaine, this was a generall custom in most parts of Yorkshire but now they have almost changed it, and tho' they still retaine the great price for the ale yet make Strangers pay for their meate, and at some places at great rates, notwithstanding how cheape they have all their provision; there is still this custome on a Market day at Leeds the sign of the Bush just by the bridge, any body that will goe and call for one tanckard of ale and a pinte of wine and pay for these only, shall be set to a table to eate with 2 or 3 dishes of good meate and a dish of sweetmeates after; had I known this and the day which was their Market, I would have come then but I happened to come a day after the Market, however I did only pay for 3 tankards of ale and what I eate and my servants was gratis; this town is full of Discenters there are 2 large Meeting places, here is also a good schoole for young Gentlewomen; the streetes are very broad the Market large.

The artlessness of that appears especially in the way the sentences are strung along one after the other, often without conjunctions and sometimes without even punctuation. The rambling and ill-coordinated sentences give the writing affinities with speech. But there is nothing to suggest non-standard speech, and Celia Fiennes indeed came from a prominent and well-connected non-conformist family. Her spelling, however, is slightly erratic, as with *Discenters*, a word which appears in several different spellings in her writing. This reminds us that in private documents there was still less standardisation than in printed books.

OTHER VARIETIES

There were many other varieties of English from specialised fields of discourse: the language of Acts of Parliament, of the law courts, of wills, of contracts, of mathematical text books, of medicine, of handbooks of alchemy and astrology, and so on. Moreover there is a whole range of language usages of a different kind. The examples we have looked at, whether verse or prose, have all been what might be called continuous discourse. But there were also such things as inventories, invoices, receipts, public notices, programmes, playbills, books of accounts, and advertisements, which have rather different characteristics. Some of these can be seen in the diary of Philip Henslowe, the business man and theatrical impresario, dating from the late sixteenth century and the early years of the seventeenth. Henslowe used the book to record a wide variety of transactions, both personal and commercial. These include lists of payments to building workers, records of Henslowe's takings as his share of theatrical performances, records of money lent to dramatists as advances, signed receipts, and records of Henslowe's pawnbroking business. There tend to be standard patterns for each type of entry, and standard abbreviations such as *pd* 'paid' and *Rd* 'received'. The diary as a whole has many spellings which are not common in printed books of the time, some of which suggest non-standard pronunciations.

In what follows, I shall not consider writings of the type found in Henslowe's diary, but shall confine myself to continuous discourse, both verse and prose. For the pure linguist, one type of language is as good as another as material for study, but I shall assume that readers of this book are most interested in certain types, and especially in those that involve continuous discourse – the language of Locke's philosophy, Elyot's writings on education, Bacon's essays, Donne's sermons, Milton's pamphlets, Marvell's lyrics, Shakespeare's plays. One aim of the book will be to improve people's reading of such works.

As far as medium is concerned, we have little choice: the material available is in the form of written texts, and these must be central to our study. This, however, does not prevent us from trying to reconstruct features of the speech of the period, nor does it preclude the study of eModE pronunciation, for which there are many sources of evidence.

I shall not give any further consideration to the Scots literary language, which was dying out in the Early Modern period, but shall confine myself to the southern form of English. Within this, I shall concentrate on the standard form of the language – the standard literary language, and the prestigious pronunciation of courtly circles in the south-east. Otherwise I shall try to be non-exclusive, handling both formal and informal styles, both prose and verse, and material from late and early in the period as well as from the central years.

FURTHER READING

A substantial account of Early Modern English is provided by Görlach (1991). On the history of Modern English, Wyld (1936) is still useful, as is Robertson (1954), a shorter and more popular work. A standard one-volume history of the English language is provided by Baugh (1993); a more advanced work, suitable for the student, is Strang (1970); a more introductory work is Barber (1993). The monumental *Cambridge History of the English Language* is in progress: the Early Modern period will be covered in Volume 3, edited by Roger Lass, which is expected to appear in 1997. Crystal (1995) is a beautifully illustrated book on English more generally, for the non-specialist reader. On the history of English spelling see Vallins (1965) and Carney (1994). On the habits of early printers, see Appendices 3 and 4 to McKerrow (1927). Books on the language of individual authors include Brook (1976, Shakespeare), Dahl (1951, Deloney), Emma (1964, Milton), Hope (1994, Shakespeare), Lake (1975, Middleton), Partridge (1953a, 1953b, Jonson), and Sugden (1936, Spenser).

On varieties of English, useful material will be found in Quirk (1962), which is a good book for the general reader, and in Crystal & Davy (1969). On English dialects, see Skeat (1911), which is very brief, Brook (1965), and the monumental Orton & Dieth (1962–71). On the language of puritanism see van Beek (1969), which gives an account of about 700 puritan words in the period 1566 to 1644. The characteristics of spoken English in the low-life scenes of Shakespeare are examined by Salmon (1967), while Hope (1993) examines transcripts of statements made in court cases.

The Early Modern texts from which excerpts have been taken are listed in Part I of the Select Bibliography at the end of the book.

Chapter Two

ATTITUDES TO ENGLISH

During the Early Modern period, educated English people were somewhat self-conscious about the English language. They were concerned about its prestige compared with other languages, its suitability for works of literature and scholarship, the adequacy of its vocabulary for various purposes, the merits of different methods of expanding the vocabulary, the necessity for spelling reform, and the desirability of 'regulating' the language (for example by producing dictionaries and grammars). On such topics there was vigorous debate throughout the period, but there was some shift of emphasis in the course of it: arguments about the suitability of English for works of literature and scholarship are typical of the early part of the period, while discussion of regulation is more typical of the seventeenth century, and continued in the eighteenth.

THE INFERIORITY OF ENGLISH

When the period opened, the English language had low prestige compared with some other languages known to educated English people. French still had high prestige as a literary language. The first book to be printed in English, William Caxton's *Recuyell of the Historyes of Troye* (c. 1475), was a translation from the French, as were many of Caxton's later publications, and Blake (1969) has shown that Caxton was attempting to cater for courtly taste by translating works that were fashionable at the Burgundian court. In his preface to the *Recuyell*, Caxton is apologetic about the 'symple and rude englissh' of his translation compared with 'the fayr langage of frenshe'. In part this may be purely conventional author's self-deprecation, but in the following hundred years there are many other such utterances comparing English unfavourably with French. Moreover, as the vernacular literatures of Italy and Spain became

42

better known in England, the Italian and Spanish languages are often added to the comparison. Thus Andrew Boorde, in *The fyrst boke of the Introduction of knowledge* (c. 1550), says:

> The speche of Englande is a base speche to other noble speches, as Italion Castylion and Frenche, howbeit the speche of Englande of late dayes is amended.

This occurs, moreover, at the end of a highly eulogistic account of England and things English: the only thing about England that is criticised is its language. In 1581 George Pettie published *The ciuile conuersation*, translated from the Italian of Guazzo. In his preface, he complains that many readers will undervalue his work because it is written in English:

> There are some others yet who wyll set lyght by my labours, because I write in Englysh: and those are some nice Trauaylours, who returne home with such quæsie stomackes, that nothyng wyll downe with them but *Frenche*, *Italian*, or *Spanishe*, and though a woorke be but meanely written in one of those tongues, and finely translated into our Language, yet they wyll not sticke farre to preferre the Originall before the Translation.

Clearly, however, Pettie does not share this opinion.

THE SUPERIORITY OF LATIN

English, however, had a more serious rival than the modern European languages, namely Latin, which was still the international language of scholarship in Western Europe, and continued to be so throughout the Early Modern period. It was not only the traditional subjects, like theology, grammar and logic, that continued to be handled in Latin: many of the seminal works of the New Philosophy (what we call science) were also published in Latin – for example works by Nicolaus Copernicus, Andreas Vesalius, Galileo Galilei, Renatus Cartesius, and, in England, William Gilbert, William Harvey, Isaac Newton. The most famous English propagandist for the New Philosophy, Francis Bacon, also published in Latin. His *Advancement of Learning* (1605) was indeed in English, but the work that he intended as his major contribution to scientific method, the *Novum Organum* (1620), was in Latin.

Education also continued to be dominated by Latin throughout the eModE period. In the grammar schools, the Latin classics were central. The pupils learnt to read and to write Latin. They read Latin literature, and were taught to explicate it in terms of the classical rhetorical tradition. And they read classical works of history, philosophy, geography, and natural science. The pagan classics, the humanist educators believed, could provide the basis for a complete education. Moreover, the pupils learnt to speak Latin. In *The Governor*,

Elyot insists that a nobleman's son must be taught to speak pure and elegant Latin (meaning classical, Ciceronian Latin, as opposed to Medieval Latin), and suggests methods of teaching spoken Latin to children before they reach the age of seven. A later Tudor educationalist, Roger Ascham, mentions the speaking of Latin on the title page of *The Scholemaster* (1570), which claims to give a 'plaine and perfite way of teachyng children, to vnderstand, write, and speake, the Latin tong'. In the later seventeenth century, there was a move towards a more modern type of education, seen for example in the Dissenting Academies, but even so the prestige of Latin remained high. In *Some Thoughts concerning Education* (1693), John Locke considers Latin 'absolutely necessary for a gentleman', though he deemed it absurd to teach it to children who were destined for trade and commerce. But by this time, it seems, spoken Latin was no longer taught in the schools, for Locke attacks the grammar-and-translation methods used in the grammar schools, and advocates oral methods of teaching Latin as a desirable reform.

If Latin was entrenched in the grammar schools, it was even more dominant in the universities. The texts studied were in Latin, and an essential part of the educational process was the disputation, carried on in spoken Latin. A parody of the method can be found in Thomas Middleton's comedy *A Chaste Maid in Cheapside* (1630), in which a foolish Cambridge student and his equally foolish tutor dispute endlessly in Latin about utterly trivial matters.

People brought up in this tradition of Latin scholarship had a vested interest in its continuance. It is not surprising that many of them resisted attempts to popularise knowledge, and so they put forward arguments to show that the English language was unsuitable for works of scholarship. The hostility to de-Latinisation was fiercest in groups whose professional status rested on their learning, like physicians. In the 1530s, Elyot published a book in English on the maintenance of health, called *The Castel of Helth*. The earliest edition has not survived. The second edition appeared in 1539, and thereafter it was reprinted frequently up to the end of the century, and was obviously a popular work. Elyot was careful to advise his readers to have recourse to a physician for diagnosis of illness, but this apparently was not enough to protect him from attack by the medical profession, for in the 1541 edition of the work he introduced a new preface answering such attacks. He defends himself from the charge that, as a layman, he is incompetent to write on the subject, but then has to answer another criticism, and defend the very fact of producing a medical work in the English language:

> But if physicions be angry, that I haue written physicke in englishe, let them remember that the grekes wrate in greke, the Romains in latin, Auicenna, and the other in Arabike, which were their own proper and maternall tongues.

And he goes on to suggest, with some asperity, that this medical obscurantism is un-Christian, and is motivated by envy and covetousness.

The use of Latin as a language of scholarship persisted all through the Early Modern period, and in 1699 Richard Bentley, the great Cambridge classical scholar, referred quite casually to Latin as 'the Universal Language of Learning'. We must distinguish, however, between scholarship and literature: the use of Latin was common in the former, but not in the latter. A certain amount of literature, it is true, was written in Latin: such things as More's *Utopia*, Latin plays for performance at Tudor grammar schools or universities, and Latin poems by Spenser, Milton, Marvell. But these were the exceptions, not the rule. Normally, an English person who wanted to write poetry or plays or prose fiction would write them in English. The books most likely to be written in Latin were the serious works of science and scholarship, especially those aimed at an international audience.

FORCES IN FAVOUR OF ENGLISH

In the course of our period, Latin, despite its continuing prestige, gradually declined in importance in England, and the prestige of the vernacular rose. Among the forces working in favour of the English language were national feeling, the expansion of the reading public, and the effects of the Reformation.

Nationalism was a powerful force in England as early as the fifteenth century, and was very strong during the Early Modern period. National feeling finds frequent expression in literature, as in the history plays of the 1590s, like Shakespeare's *King John* and *Henry V*. To us the attitudes often seem arrogant, as when Milton, in *Areopagitica* (1644), suggests that the English have a special relationship with God himself:

> Now once again by all concurrence of signs, and by the generall instinct of holy and devout men, as they daily and solemnly expresse their thoughts, God is decreeing to begin some new and great period in his Church, ev'n to the reforming of Reformation it self: what does he then but reveal Himself to his servants, and as his manner is, first to his English-men.

National feeling led to a pride in the national language, and to attempts to create a vernacular literature to vie with that of Greece and Rome.

The expansion of the reading public may have been encouraged by the introduction of printing, but it was already taking place in the middle of the fifteenth century, long before Caxton established his press at Westminster in 1476. The new public arose as a result of the expansion and secularisation of education. The grammar schools expanded in the fifteenth century, and alongside them were many new 'petty schools', which taught the reading and writing of English. When the Early Modern period opened, a substantial part of the population could read. In 1533, Sir Thomas More asserted that over half the population could read (Bennett 1973). Even if this was an overestimate, it is clear that there was a large potential reading public.

A considerable part of this reading public must have been unable to read Latin. Many of them, however, had a great desire for learning, and the citizen classes in particular had a thirst for self-improvement. Wright (1935) argues that, during the period 1550 to 1650, the citizenry had an uncritical faith in the grammar schools, and wished to obtain for their children at least a modicum of conventional school learning. Some of these children attended only the petty school, and so learnt to read English but not Latin. Even among those with a grammar school education, there must have been many whose Latin was not very fluent, and who preferred books in English. Such readers may nevertheless have obtained a taste for classical literature, and would want to read the classics in translation. Shakespeare is an example. As the son of a prominent Stratford citizen, he almost certainly went to Stratford grammar school, and there is evidence that he had been taught Latin. But there is also evidence that some of his favourite works were English translations, such as Golding's translation of Ovid, and North's translation of Plutarch.

In this situation, there was a great demand for translations from Greek and Latin, especially for poetry and history, and there are numerous such translations throughout the period. But even if a reader wanted to remain within the confines of the humanist syllabus, it was necessary to study rhetoric and logic as well as literature. Here again the basic texts were classical ones: Quintilian, Cicero, the *Ad Herennium*, Aristotle. From the middle of the sixteenth century, similar handbooks of rhetoric and logic begin to appear in English. Two of the early ones are by Thomas Wilson, the *Logique* (1552) and *The Arte of Rhetorique* (1553). Many others followed.

But a considerable number of readers wanted material from quite other fields. There were many practical men who wanted books on subjects like navigational instruments, geometry, warfare. If there were suitable texts in Greek or Latin, they could be translated, as was Euclid's *Elements of Geometry* (by H. Billingsley, 1570). In other cases, like the use of artillery or the magnetic compass, technical developments had made classical texts out of date, and new ones had to be written. And ordinary people wanted these to be written in plain English. Often, the first stage was the translation of classical texts, to be followed later by the production of independent works in English. This can be seen in books on the techniques of warfare. Despite the changes brought about by gunpowder, classical precepts and theories remained influential. Webb (1965) shows that the military literature of sixteenth-century England had its origins in classical works on history and strategy, especially those by Frontinus, Onosander, Julius Caesar, and Vegetius. Works by all four were translated into English between 1539 and 1572. Also influential were certain continental works, notably Machiavelli's *Dell' arte della guerra*, translated in 1560. The translations were followed by original works in English, like those of Barnaby Rich, Thomas Digges, Sir Roger Williams, and Humphrey Barwick. Between them, these four published ten such works in the period 1574 to 1618.

The English writers varied in the importance they attached to classical precept. When Digges wrote his *Stratioticos* (1579) he had no practical military experience, and the work is heavily dependent on the classics. At the other extreme is Barwick, the old soldier who scorns the theoreticians and takes an anti-classical line. In between are Rich and Williams, who are respectful towards the classics, but willing to modify classical theory in the light of their own practical experience. The opposition between military theoretician and old soldier is reflected in Shakespeare's *Othello*. There Iago sneers at Cassio, who has been promoted over him, as a 'great Arithmatician' who is solely versed in 'Bookish Theoricke'.

In addition to specialist interests of this kind, there was a voracious appetite, not least among the citizenry, for knowledge of all kinds. This was fed by a great variety of publications: English versions of encyclopedias of traditional scientific knowledge, like Stephen Batman's *Batman vppon Bartholome* (1582); works on geography and the Discoveries; herbals and popular medical works; works on psychology, like Robert Burton's *Anatomy of Melancholy* (1621); and many more.

The Reformation encouraged the use of English in two ways. First, the controversies were usually carried on in English, since the disputants wanted a wide national audience. The first large-scale controversy of the English Reformation was between Simon Fish and William Tyndale on the one hand, and Sir Thomas More on the other. When More wrote for the learned people of Europe, he wrote in Latin, as in his *Utopia* and his Latin poems. But when he undertook to answer the Reformers, which he did in seven works between 1528 and 1533, he wrote in English.

Secondly, the protestant insistence on biblical translation, and the existence and widespread use of English bibles, raised the prestige of the vernacular. Inevitably, too, the protestant party were led to argue that English was not an inferior language, but was suitable for the Scriptures. In *The obedience of a Christen man* (1528), Tyndale has a long section putting forward the protestant arguments in favour of an English Bible. In the course of it, he answers opponents who think that the English language is intrinsically unsuitable:

> They will saye it can not be translated in to oure tonge it is so rude. It is not so rude as they are false lyers.

And he goes on to argue that both Greek and Hebrew translate more naturally into English than into Latin. In general, because of the Catholic use of the Vulgate, and insistence on Latin as the liturgical language, there was a tendency to associate Latin with Catholicism, which worked to the disadvantage of Latin in strongly Protestant circles.

DISPUTES ABOUT THE USE OF ENGLISH

In the sixteenth century, then, there were forces favouring the use of English for purposes formerly reserved for Latin, but there was also opposition to the use of English for such purposes. Various arguments were advanced against the use of English instead of Latin. Learning would decay, because there would be no incentive to learn the classical tongues. It was dangerous to let learning get into the hands of the common people. English was unsuitable for scholarly works, because it lacked the necessary technical vocabulary. It was 'rude' or 'barbarous', lacking in expressiveness. It was unstable and changing, unlike classical Latin and Greek, which were 'fixed'. It was not commonly understood outside England, whereas Latin was an international language, and facilitated intellectual intercourse between scholars of different European nations.

The supporters of English advanced various arguments in reply. It was useful to have works of scholarship in English, so that time and effort did not have to be wasted in learning other languages. Those who wished to keep learning from ordinary people had sinister motives. Classical Greek and Latin had themselves once been mother tongues, and the Romans had written their science and philosophy in Latin, not in Greek. Deficiencies in the English vocabulary could be remedied by coining or borrowing new words. Producing important works in English would enrich the language, and it would cease to be rude or barbarous.

The arguments in favour of English are often found in authors' prefaces, especially in prefaces to translations. Their frequency, especially in the sixteenth century, suggests that opposition continued to be considerable right up to the middle of our period, and perhaps longer. As an example of one of these defensive prefaces, let us look at the translator's 'Epistle to the Reader' which is prefixed to the first English version of Petrus Ramus's *Dialecticae Partitiones*, published as *The Logike of the moste excellent Philosopher P. Ramus Martyr* (1574). This was published in London, but the translator was a Scot, and he sometimes refers to his language as 'English' and sometimes as 'Scottish'. He writes, however, in the southern form of the language. He begins by emphasising the public utility of his undertaking:

> Seing it is the dewtye of all Christians (beloued Reader) to labour by all
> meanes, that they maye profytte and ayde their bretherne, and to hyde or
> kepe secrete nothing, whiche they knowe maye bring great vtilitie to

the common wealthe: I thought it my dewtie (hauing perceyued the greate commoditie whiche this booke bryngethe to the Reader of what state and qualitie soeuer he be) to make thee and all others to whose knowledge it shall come pertakers thereof.

The translator hopes to benefit readers of all social classes ('of what state and quality soever he be'). The leaving of a useful text untranslated is a kind of concealment. And making useful knowledge available to everybody is a religious duty.

He next spends several pages explaining why Ramus's system of logic is so useful. Then, at the end of the preface, he answers those critics who would object to such a work being translated into English:

Heare I will speake nothing of the enuious, that thinkethe it not decent to wryte any liberall arte in the vulgar tongue, but woulde haue all thinges kept close eyther in the Hebrewe, Greke, or Latyn tongues. I knowe what greate hurte hathe come to the Churche of God by the defence of this mischeuous opinion.

Here we have the imputation of sinister motives to the adversaries: they are motivated by envy, and it is also implied that they resemble Catholics in their desire to keep things secret ('close') from ordinary people. In the phrase *any liberall arte*, the translator is referring to the Seven Liberal Arts which formed the basis of traditional education, of which logic was one. He next puts forward one of the standard arguments for using English:

Whether wrote Moyses (the Hebrewe and deuyne) and after hym Esdras in the Hebrewe and vulgar tongue or in some other straunge tongue? Did Aristotle and Plato Greke Philosophers, Hipocrates and Galen Greke Phisitions, leaue the Greke tongue, because it was their natiue language, to seke some Hebrewe or Latin? Did Cicero who was a Latinist borne write his Philosophie and Rethoricke in the Greke tongue, or was he content with his mother tongue? and suerly as he testifiethe hym self he had the perfecte knowledge of the Greke tongue, yet he wrothe nothing therin wich we haue extant at this daye. Shall we then thinke the Scottyshe or Englishe tongue, is not fitt to wrote any arte into? no in dede.

The word *straunge* is here used in the common eModE sense of 'foreign': the Greeks and Hebrews and Romans did not write in a foreign language, but in their native languages, and we should do the same. This was a common protestant argument in favour of biblical translation, and had been used by Tyndale in *The Obedience of a Christian Man*.

The translator next deals with the argument that English lacks the technical terms necessary for works of scholarship:

But peraduenture thou wylt saye that there is not Scottyshe wordes for to declare and expresse all thinges contayned into liberall artes, truthe it is: neither was there Latin wordes to expresse all thinges writen in the Hebrewe and Greke tongues: But did Cicero for this cause write no philosophie in Latin? thou will not saye so, lest I take the with a manifest lye. What then did Cicero? he laborethe in the Latin tongue, as Aristotle before hym did in the Greke, and thou enuious felowe ought to do in thy mother tongue what so euer it be, to witte he amplified his natiue tongue, thinking no shame to borrowe from the Hebrucians and Grecians suche wordes as his mother tongue was indigent of. What, shall we thinke shame to borrowe eyther of the Latin or Greke, more then the learned Cicero did? or finde some fitt wordes in our owne tongue able to expresse our meaning as Aristotle did? shall we I saye be more vnkynde to our natiue tongue and countrey then was thiese men to theirs?

Here the translator admits the deficiency in vocabulary, but replies that we should remedy it, as the Greeks and Romans had done, by borrowing words from other languages or by giving new meanings to existing words. He implies that this process would improve the language (Cicero *amplified* his native tongue), and that we should be unnatural (*vnkynde*) if we did not thus improve ours.

The translator next answers the accusation that English is a barbarous language:

But thou wilt saye, our tongue is barbarous, and theirs is eloquent? I aunswere thee as Anacharsis did to the Athenienses, who called his Scithian tongue barbarous, yea sayethe he, Anacharsis is barbarous amongest the Athenienses, and so are the Athenienses amongest the Scythyans, by the which aunswere he signified that euery mans tongue is eloquent ynoughe for hym self, and that others in respecte of it is had as barbarous.

As the contrast with *eloquent* shows, *barbarous* is here used (as often) in the sense 'unexpressive, lacking in eloquence'. At first sight, the answer to the accusation sounds sophistical, since it involves taking *barbarous* in its etymological sense of 'foreign' (Greek *bárbaros*). But what the translator is doing is to call attention to the double meaning of the word ('foreign' and 'barbarous'), which is a sign of Athenian bigotry. His comment on the story shows that he believes that English is indeed eloquent, because all languages are eloquent for their native speakers.

He ends his preface by once again suggesting the sinister motives of those who oppose translations like his:

> Thou seest (good Reader) what a grounde they haue to defende their opinion, and howe they labour only to roote out all good knowledge and vertue, and plante mere ignoraunce amongest the common people. Now for to conclude, it shalbe thy dutie to receiue this my litle paynes in a good parte, and to call vpon God that the vse therof, maye tende to the glorie of his holy name, and profitte of our bretherne.

This is a typically Protestant ending, with its emphasis on reading matter for 'the common people', and its insinuation that the Latinists wish to keep them ignorant and so to root out 'all good knowledge and virtue'. The choice of the text translated accords well with the writer's Protestant bias. Petrus Ramus (Pierre de la Ramée) was hostile to traditional scholastic philosophy, and was also a protestant martyr, dying in the St Bartholomew massacre of 1572. For both these reasons he became much admired in England, especially in educated puritan circles.

THE ELOQUENCE OF ENGLISH

Much of the case for the use of English rested on the fact that it was useful to have books in English. In the early part of our period, however, it was widely felt that, though English might be useful, it was not eloquent. Even writers who argue for the use of English often admit that it is 'rude' or 'barbarous'. There were exceptions: as we have seen, Tyndale denied that English was rude, and on this point his opponent More agreed with him. For the most part, however, the attitude to the language in the early Tudor period was apologetic, and many people shared Boorde's view that English was 'a base speche'.

This, however, was one of the things that changed in the course of our period. By the end of the sixteenth century, uncomplimentary comparisons of English with other languages have largely disappeared. In the seventeenth century, writers are more likely to go to the other extreme, and boast of the superiority of English to other languages. William Lisle, in the preface to *A Saxon Treatise* (1623), claims that:

> our language is improued aboue all others now spoken by any nation, and became the fairest, the nimblest, the fullest; most apt to vary the phrase, most ready to receiue good composition, most adorned with sweet words and sentences, with witty quips and ouer-ruling Prouerbes: yea able to expresse any hard conceit whatsoeuer with great dexterity; waighty in weighty matters, merry in merry, braue in braue.

Lisle, clearly, has no doubts about the expressiveness of English. But the belief that English was eloquent antedated the seventeenth century. It is found, for example, in Richard Mulcaster, the eminent Elizabethan headmaster and educational theorist. In the Peroration to *The First Part of the Elementarie*

(1582) he not only defends himself for writing in English, and deplores the bondage of Latin, but also argues for the positive qualities of English, which in some points excels all other languages.

So English, formerly considered barbarous, was now considered eloquent. When did this change of attitude take place? Jones (1953) has examined a large amount of material, and concludes that the change took place quite suddenly between 1575 and 1580. Before 1575, most writers agree that English is barbarous. After 1580, there is a whole chorus of voices proclaiming that English is eloquent. Jones also discusses the criteria for eloquence, the factors that were considered to have made English into an eloquent language. He finds that four features in particular were thought to be important.

First, a language was made eloquent by having important works written in it. The translators and the writers of works of original scholarship were doing their language a service by making it the key to a considerable body of learning. The poets were doing it a service by making it the key to an important literature. In the late Elizabethan age and the Jacobean age, great emphasis is placed on literature: people often talk as though it is poetry that makes a language eloquent. Jones thinks that the works of Sidney and Lyly and Spenser played a large part in convincing people round about 1580 that English was now an eloquent language.

Secondly, English had become eloquent because its vocabulary had expanded. The words which were especially thought to contribute to eloquence were those borrowed from Latin or Greek. Not all of these were technical terms: the prestige of the classical languages, and the belief that words derived from them were particularly expressive, led to the borrowing of large numbers of such words, even when a native synonym already existed. In the seventeenth century, it is often said that this vocabulary expansion has enriched the language. When English is praised as an eloquent language, a quality frequently singled out for praise is *copie*, meaning copiousness, richness of vocabulary.

Thirdly, a language was made eloquent by being adorned with the devices of classical rhetoric. In particular, the figures of rhetoric were thought to confer eloquence, and were assiduously cultivated in English writing from the time of Spenser onwards. There was also an anti-rhetorical movement, inspired partly by Puritanism and partly by the new science. But the classical rhetorical tradition was strong right to the end of our period, and the cultivation of the figures in late Elizabethan literature contributed to the conviction that English was now an eloquent language.

A fourth quality thought to contribute to eloquence was the fact that a language was 'fixed' or 'ruled'. The instability of English, the fact that it was subject to change, was one of the reasons for calling it rude or barbarous. Classical Greek and Latin, by contrast, were fixed and unchanging. If a language was fixed or regulated, there could be no doubts about what was good usage and what was not. With English, on the contrary, there was uncertainty – about spelling, about acceptable vocabulary, about grammatical usage. These two things (the fact of change, and uncertainty about good usage) are in fact different. But the people who wished to regulate the language tended to think of them together: the production of dictionaries and grammars of English would legislate for good usage, and at the same time prevent this usage from changing. By 1580 very little had been done about regulating English. The first English dictionary and English grammar had yet to be produced, and, although there had been discussion of spelling reform, English orthography had not yet been standardised. English was therefore considered an eloquent language despite the fact that it was unregulated. The movement in favour of regulation grew in strength during the seventeenth century, and was very powerful from the Restoration onwards.

Of the four features thought to contribute to eloquence, the first calls for no comment here, but something more will be said about the other three – vocabulary expansion, classical rhetoric, and regulation.

DISPUTES ABOUT VOCABULARY EXPANSION

The great expansion of the lexicon which took place in our period (and which will be examined in detail in Chapter Six) was a highly conscious affair, and people argued about it a good deal. There were three main schools of thought. The first, which we can call the neologisers, was in favour of loan words, especially from Latin. The second, which we can call the purists, advocated the use of existing English words, either by giving them new meanings for technical purposes, or by using them to make new words by compounding or affixation. The third, which we can call the archaisers, argued that obsolete English words should be revived. Since words which had died out in the standard language sometimes survived in regional dialects, this school of thought often advocated the use of dialect words as well as archaisms. The three schools of thought are not mutually exclusive, since a purist could also be an archaiser, but the neologisers were often assailed by the others, who attacked learned loans as 'inkhorn terms'.

The Neologisers

An obvious way for a translator or populariser to produce a new technical term was the borrowing or adaptation of a word from the classical languages, especially Latin. The writer's own training in the subject had been conducted in Latin, and Latin technical terms seemed the natural and right ones. The writer on logic, wishing to translate terms like *affirmatio* and *negatio*, would easily produce words like *affirmation* and *negation*. The process would not have seemed so easy and natural, however, but for the fact that there were already many words in the language which resembled these in structure, and offered a pattern. In ME there had been a great influx of French loans, producing English words like *condition* and *extortion*, the ultimate Latin origin of which was obvious to the learned. With such patterns to hand, our writer on logic coined his *affirmation* and *negation*, for these are influenced by French precedent, being derived from Latin oblique forms such as *negationem*, not from the nominative *negatio*. There were many such patterns to hand, as a result of earlier borrowings from French: prefixes like *con-* and *ex-* and *pre-*, suffixes like *-ence* and *-ity* and *-ment*. Indeed, it is not always possible to know whether an eModE loan word has been taken direct from Latin or from French: *negation* could equally well come from Latin *negationem* or from French *négation*.

Learned loans of this kind, however, had a disadvantage: their meaning was not obvious to a reader who knew no Latin or French; and it was often for the relatively unlearned reader that the translator or populariser was writing. Not surprisingly, opponents of loan words attacked them on this ground. To meet this criticism, the coiners of such words often explain their meaning when they introduce them. This is done by Sir Thomas Elyot, who was responsible for many Latin and Greek borrowings, like *animate*, *education*, *encyclopedia*, *frugality*, *metamorphosis*, *modesty*, *obfuscate*, and *persist*. All these words occur in *The Governor*, and are not recorded in the OED at any earlier date. When he used such words, Elyot often paired them with an easier synonym or with an explanatory phrase: *animate or gyue courage to others*; *the beste fourme of education or bringing vp of noble children*; *persist and continue*. Sometimes a little more explanation is necessary:

> in an oratour is required to be a heape of all maner of lernyng: whiche of some is called the worlde of science: of other the circle of doctrine / whiche is in one worde of greeke *Encyclopedia*.

Just occasionally, Elyot launches into more elaborate explanations. Such is the passage where he discusses the word *maturity*. He has invented this word, he says, because there is an excellent virtue for which there is no name in English:

> wherfore I am constrained to vsurpe a latine worde callyng it *Maturitie*: whiche worde though it be strange and darke / yet by declaring the vertue in a fewe mo wordes / the name ones brought in custome / shall be as facile to vnderstande as other wordes late commen out of Italy and Fraunce / and made denizins amonge vs.
>
> Maturitie is a meane betwene two extremities / wherin nothing lacketh or excedeth: and is in suche astate / that it may neither encrease nor minisshe without losinge the denomination of Maturitie ... *Maturum* in latine maye be enterpreted ripe or redy: as frute / whan it is ripe / it is at

the very poynte to be gathered and eaten: and euery other thinge / whan it is redy / it is at the instante after to be occupied. Therfore that worde maturitie / is translated to the actis of man / that whan they be done with suche moderation / that nothing in the doinge may be sene superfluous or indigent / we may saye / that they be maturely done: reseruyng the wordes / ripe and redy / to frute and other thinges seperate from affaires / as we haue nowe in vsage. And this do I nowe remembre for the necessary augmentation of our langage.

Elyot says that he has taken his new word from Latin. The only Latin word he quotes is the adjective *maturum*, but he must have modelled his word on the Latin noun *maturitas*. But *maturity* bears a more obvious resemblance to French *maturité*, and it is typical of the age that Elyot should think of his word as a Latin loan, even though he has given it the English suffix *-ity*, which is derived from French. The word *maturity* had in fact been used in English before, though Elyot obviously did not know this: the OED records two earlier examples, one by Barbour (c. 1375) and one by Lydgate (1426). This is not surprising. If the conditions exist for the coinage of such a word, it is quite possible that it will be coined independently by more than one person.

In explaining the meaning of his new word, Elyot distinguishes between *mature* and *ripe*. The latter he uses literally, of fruit, but to *mature* he gives a figurative or transferred (*translated*) sense, referring to human acts. He obviously thought that the language needed the distinction, and that he was improving it by his coinage. This is clear from his phrase about 'the necessary augmentation of our langage'. Elyot was consciously trying to remedy the deficiencies of English, and he says this again in the preface to a later work, *Of the knowledg whiche maketh a wise man* (1533). Referring back to *The Governor*, he says that in that book he had 'intended to augment our Englyshe tongue', so that men would be able to express their ideas more fully, having words apt for the purpose, and also would be able to make adequate translations into English out of Greek or Latin or any other language. He also claims that he has explained clearly the meanings of all the new words which he has introduced from French or Latin.

Elyot, then, is a neologiser with utilitarian aims, though his new words are not necessarily technical terms. But many neologisers coined fine new words from Latin or Greek with a different motive. Their users were aiming at a high style, at magniloquence. Mulcaster refers to the large number of loans entering the language in his time, and also to the two different motives for making them. He speaks of:

the latest terms which it [the English language] boroweth daielie from foren tungs, either of pure necessitie in new matters, or of mere brauerie, to garnish it self withall.

55

The word *daielie* gives vividly a contemporary's awareness of the flood of neologisms. Some words are borrowed *of pure necessitie in new matters*: this is the utilitarian motive. But others are borrowed *of mere brauerie*, which means 'out of pure ostentation' or 'from sheer love of finery'. The suggestion of splendid embellishment is reinforced by the final phrase, *to garnish it self withall* 'to decorate itself with'.

The Inkhorn Controversy

This coining of words for fine effect, for the achieving of magniloquence, sometimes led to abuse and excess. The 'bravery' of new words could easily degenerate into obscurity, affectation, and pomposity. Hence the many attacks on 'inkhorn terms', and defences of them, which make up the great inkhorn controversy. The dispute raged most strongly in the second half of the six-teenth century and the early years of the seventeenth.

One of the well-known attacks on inkhorn terms is in Thomas Wilson's *Art of Rhetoric*. In the section on style, he recommends plainness as a quality for an orator to cultivate. The first thing to learn, he says, is to avoid all strange inkhorn terms, and to speak as is commonly received. Under the general heading of Inkhorn Terms, he goes on to attack a wide range of affectations: the travelled gentleman who uses French or Italian words, the lawyer and the auditor who use the technical terms of their trade, the fine courtier who cultivates archaisms from Chaucer, the pseudo-learned eccentric who uses Latinisms. When, however, Wilson goes on to give examples of inkhorn terms, they are not legal technical terms, or courtiers' archaisms, or even brand-new words from France or Italy: overwhelmingly, they are learned coinages from Latin. They occur in what Wilson calls 'An ynkehorne letter', which he claims is genuine. It is a letter written by a Lincolnshire man to a gentleman in the service of the Lord Chancellor, asking him to use his influ-ence with the Lord Chancellor to procure a vacant benefice for the writer. It runs as follows:

> Ponderyng expendyng ['weighing'], and reuolutyng ['revolving'] with my self your ingent ['enormous'] affabilitee, and ingenious capacitee, for mundane affaires: I cannot but celebrate and extolle your magnificall dexteritee, aboue all other. For how could you haue adepted ['acquired'] suche illustrate prerogatiue ['illustrious pre-eminence'], and dominicall ['lordly'] superioritee, if the fecunditee of your ingenie ['intellectual powers'] had not been so fertile, and wounderfull pregnaunt. Now ther-fore beeyng accersited ['summoned'], to suche splendent renoume, and dignitee splendidious: I doubt not but you will adiuuate ['help'] suche poore adnichilate ['destitute'] orphanes, as whilome ware condisciples ['schoolfellows'] with you, and of antique familiaritie in Lincolneshire.

Emong whom I beeyng a Scholasticall panion ['companion'], obtestate ['beseech'] your sublimitee to extoll ['raise'] myne infirmitee. There is a sacerdotall dignitee ['ecclesiastical office'] in my natiue countrey, contiguate ['adjoining'] to me, where I now contemplate: whiche your worshipfull benignitee, could sone impetrate ['obtain'] for me, if it would like you to extend your scedules ['write letters'], and collaude ['praise'] me in them to the right honorable lorde Chauncellor, or rather Archigrammacian ['principal classical scholar'] of Englande. You know my literature ['literary culture'], you knowe the pastorall promocion, I obtestate ['beseech'] your clemencie, to inuigilate ['take pains'] thus muche for me, accordyng to my confidence ['as I rely on you to do'], and as you know my condigne merites, for suche a compendious ['profitable'] liuyng. But now I relinquishe ['cease'] to fatigate ['tire'] your intelligence with any more friuolous verbositie, and therfore he that rules the climates be euermore your beautreux [?'buttress'], your fortresse, and your bulwarke. Amen.

It is probable that, despite his denial, Wilson himself invented this letter. But he did not invent most of the highflown words in it. Only two words in the letter cannot be found in the OED, namely *Archigrammacian* and *beautreux*. The former is perhaps a printing error for *Archigrammarian*, but that word is not in the OED either (though both *archi-* and *grammarian* are). And it is possible that *beautreux*, as suggested by Moore (1910), is merely a form of the word *buttress*. If we leave these two words out of account, we find that all the words in the passage are recorded in other texts. Some indeed are rare: *accersited* p.p. and *adepted* p.p. each has only one example given in the OED, while *revolute* v. has only two. This is not surprising. Nor is it surprising that some of the words are not recorded until later than Wilson's book of 1553: *adepted* p.p. (1595), *adjuvate* v. (1599), *celebrate* v. (1564), *condisciple* n. (1554), *contemplate* v. (1592), and *obtestate* v. (1613). For three words, the earliest example given by the OED comes from this Wilson passage: *invigilate* v., *panion* n., and *revolute* v. If the conditions existed for the formation of new words, it is to be expected that such words should be coined independently by more than one person. And if such a word is rare, even the superb records of the OED may fail to register its earliest appearance in print. In any case, all the remaining words are recorded in the OED before 1553, even unusual and extravagant-sounding ones. It seems probable, therefore, that we can accept Wilson's examples of inkhorn words as genuine, not simply as parodies invented by himself.

It is difficult for the modern reader, however, to tell which words in the passage are intended as inkhorn terms, and which not. Some words which now seem affected may have been quite normal in the sixteenth century, and vice versa. The verb *contemplate* is an ordinary word for us, but the first example in the OED is dated 1592, so that when Wilson used it in 1553 it probably sounded startlingly new. Moreover, Wilson relies on a cumulative technique for his comic effect. Many of the words may have been unexceptionable in themselves, but when long and learned words are piled up one after the other the effect becomes ludicrous.

We can be sure, however, that the inkhorn terms in the letter are non-Germanic words. The words of English or Scandinavian origin are nearly all grammatical words (auxiliaries, conjunctions, determiners, prepositions, pronouns), and they are all ordinary everyday ones, even *whilome* 'formerly', which is now an archaism, but which in 1553 was still in common use. The lexical words in the letter (adjectives, nouns, verbs) are almost all French or Latin loan words. Some of these were ordinary everyday words in Wilson's time, and can hardly be inkhorn terms. Such are *affair*, *country*, *doubt*, *merit*, *poor*, and *rule*. These had all been borrowed from French in the thirteenth or fourteenth century, and were thoroughly naturalised by the sixteenth. The words most likely to have been considered inkhorn terms were probably those which had been coined most recently. There are twenty-five words in the letter which are recorded in the OED as having entered the language after 1500: *accersited* p.p., *adepted* p.p., *adjuvate* v., *antique* adj., *celebrate* v., *clemency* n., *collaud* v., *condisciple* n., *contemplate* v., *dexterity* n., *dominical* adj., *extol* v., *fatigate* v., *frivolous* adj., *illustrate* p.p./adj., *impetrate* v., *invigilate* v., *magnifical* adj., *obtestate* v., *panion* n., *revolute* v., *scholastical* adj., *sublimity* n., *superiority* n., and *verbosity* n. These words are the most likely to have been called inkhorn terms, and overwhelmingly they are loans from Latin. The word *panion* n. is a shortening of *companion*, itself a thirteenth-century loan from French. The word *magnifical* adj. is from French. Three words, *antique* adj., *superiority* n., and *verbosity* n. could be from either French or Latin. The remaining twenty words are from Latin.

Some of the words from before 1500 may also of course be inkhorn terms, especially those from the fifteenth century. In that period some writers adopted an 'aureate' style, a highly ornamented literary style which used high-flown words. Some of the fifteenth-century words in the letter are loans from French, like *condign* adj., *promotion* n., and *relinquish* v., and these may well be inkhorn terms. But many of the fifteenth-century words are from Latin. Moreover a number of them are rather rare words, like *contiguate* p.p./adj., *ingent* adj., and *splendidious* adj., and so probably inkhorn terms. It seems, therefore, that for Wilson an inkhorn word was most often a loan from Latin. It is striking that the letter contains no loans from Italian or Spanish, despite Wilson's attack on the affectations of travelled gentlemen.

Wilson does not, however, condemn all learned loan words. He admits that there are many Greek and Latin words in English which are perfectly acceptable, and which have enriched the language. As examples he gives *patents* (in the expression 'letters patentes'), *communion* and *prerogative*. The reason such words are acceptable is that they are generally received, but, Wilson says, it is folly to use:

> suche wordes, as fewe men doo vse, or vse theim out of place, when another might serue muche better.

The problem that Wilson avoids is that of transition. How does a new word get into the language if it has to be generally accepted before we can use it?

There are other writers, however, who are much more enthusiastic about learned loans. One such is George Pettie. In *The ciuile conuersation* (1581) he has a preface in which he attacks people who call English barbarous, yet at the same time sneer at those who try to enrich the language by introducing words from Latin. Borrowing from Latin is highly desirable,

> for it is in deed the ready way to inrich our tongue, and make it copious, and it is the way which all tongues haue taken to inrich them selues.

The richness of French, Italian, and Spanish, he argues, is due to the Latin words in those languages, and the richness of Latin is due to its borrowings from Greek.

> Wherefore I marueile how our english tongue hath crackt it ['its'] credite, that it may not borrow of the Latine as well as other tongues: and if it haue broken, it is but of late, for it is not vnknowen to all men how many woordes we haue fetcht from thence within these fewe yeeres, which if they should be all counted inkepot termes, I know not how we should speake any thing without blacking our mouthes with inke: for what woord can be more plaine then this word *plaine*, and yet what can come more neere to the Latine? What more manifest, then *manifest*? and yet in a manner Latine: What more commune then *rare*, or lesse rare then *commune*, and yet both of them comming of the Latine?

Like so many others, Pettie does not (and probably cannot) distinguish between French loans and Latin loans: *plain* and *common* are both ME loans from French. The language is already so full of Latin words, he is saying, that we cannot express ourselves without using them. He then answers people who, like Wilson, argue that we should not use a loan word until it is hallowed by use:

> But you wyll say, long vse hath made these woords curraunt: and why may not vse doo as much for these woords which we shall now deriue? Why should we not doo as much for the posteritie, as we haue receiued of the antiquitie? and yet if a thing be of it selfe ill, I see not how the

oldnesse of it can make it good, and if it be of it selfe good, I see not how the newness of it can make it naught ['bad']: Wherevpon I infer, that those woords which your selues confesse by vse to be made good, are good the first time they are vttered, and therfore not to be iested at, nor to be misliked.

Pettie here attempts to deal with the problem that Wilson had disregarded – the fact that all loan words now 'received' must at some time have been new.

There are, then, arguments about the general principles involved in creating new words. A great deal of the inkhorn controversy, however, is not about principles, but about particular practices. Writers who ridicule affected language, as Shakespeare and Jonson both do, are not attacking loan words, but the eccentricities of the lunatic fringe. And when writers attack others for their inkhornisms, they are often counter-attacked. There are a number of controversies in which literary men attack one another's usages, like the flyting between Thomas Nash and Gabriel Harvey in the pamphlet warfare of the 1590s, and that between Ben Jonson and John Marston in the war of the theatres round about 1600. In such controversies, both disputants use neologisms, but each thinks that his opponent's usages are ridiculous, while his own are acceptable. Harvey attacked Greene and Nash in his *Foure Letters* of 1592. In the same year, Nash replied with a pamphlet called *Strange News*, in which (among many other things) he attacked a number of Harvey's expressions as 'inkhornisme'. The words and phrases he takes exception to include (in modern spellings) *addicted to theory, the Aretinish mountain of huge exaggerations, artificiality, canicular tales, conscious mind, cordial liquor, deceitful perfidy, divine entelechy, effectuate, energetical persuasions, extensively employed, fantasticality, ingenuity, loud mentery, materiality, mechanician, negotiation, notoriety, perfunctory discourses, putative opinions, rascality*, and *valorous authors*. Harvey replied with *Pierces Supererogation* (1593), in which he defended the words attacked by Nash, asserting that every expression in *Four Letters* was 'autenticall English'. In turn, he attacked expressions used by Nash, calling them 'a mishapen rablement of absurde, and ridiculous wordes'. The expressions attacked include *a corregidor of incongruity, censorial moralisers, decrepit capacity, fictionate person, the horrisonant pipe of inveterate antiquity, inkhornism, a providitor of young scholars*, and *sacriligiously contaminated*. As often in such cases, some of the words ridiculed now sound perfectly normal, for example *artificiality, conscious, ingenuity, negotiation*.

Attacks and counter-attacks of this kind become rarer during the seventeenth century, but do not entirely cease. There is an example from the end of the period in the controversy between Richard Bentley and the Hon. Charles Boyle about the genuineness or otherwise of the *Epistles* attributed to Phalaris.

In his *Dissertations upon the Epistles of Phalaris* (1697), Bentley argued that the *Epistles* were a late forgery. Boyle (who had edited the *Epistles* in 1695) replied in 1698, and among other things accused Bentley of pedantry, because he had used Latin and Greek words when there were suitable English ones. The words attacked were *alien, commentitious, concede, idiom, negoce, putid, repudiate, timid,* and *vernacular.* Bentley replied in a second edition of his *Dissertations* in 1699, and neatly turned Boyle's argument by quoting him:

> A *second mark* [of a pedant] *is to use a* Greek *or* Latin *word, when there's an* English *one, that signifies the very same thing.* Now if this be one of his marks, Himself is a Pedant by his own confession: for in this very sentence of his, *Signifie* is a Latin word, and there's an English one, that *Means* the very same thing.

Bentley then defends the words that Boyle had attacked, arguing that they were in use in English long before his time; that words of this kind had been used by 'all the best Writers of our Nation'; and that they were all formed on correct etymological principles. Finally, he counter-attacks by criticising Boyle's use of the word *cotemporary*, which, he says, is a downright barbarism:

> For the Latins never use *Co* for *Con*, except before a Vowel, as *Coequal, Coeternal*; but before a Consonant they either retain the N, as *Contemporary, Constitution*; or melt it into another Letter, as *Collection, Comprehension*. So that the Examiner's [i.e. Boyle's] *Cotemporary* is a word of his own Coposition, for which the Learned World will cogratulate him.

On the whole, however, the inkhorn controversy died down in the seventeenth century. People went on coining new words from Greek and Latin morphemes, both for 'necessity' and for 'bravery'. There were many writers, like Sir Thomas Browne, who delighted in a highly Latinate vocabulary. But the process was now more generally accepted, and criticisms were rarer. English was now considered to be an eloquent language, one of its great virtues being copiousness, and it was a common seventeenth-century view that the flood of loan words had been necessary, and had enriched the language. Even William Lisle, an enthusiast for Old English, argues in his *Saxon Treatise* (1623) that it is no discredit to English that it has a vocabulary of mixed origins. This is true of all languages, and 'our language is improued aboue all others now spoken by any nation'. Even stronger statements of the enrichment view can be found in the prefaces to seventeenth-century dictionaries. In the preface to his *Glossographia* (1656), Thomas Blount asserts that:

> our best modern Authors ... have both infinitely enriched and enobled our Language, by admitting and naturalizing thousands of foreign

> Words, providently brought home from the *Greek, Roman, and French
> Oratories*; which though, in the untravel'd ears of our Fathers would
> have sounded harsh, yet a few late years have rendred them familiar
> even to vulgar capacities.

And Blount goes on to name some of the 'best modern Authors' who have
used such words.

A more critical note is sometimes heard in the Restoration period, when the
smart town set were self-conscious in matters of taste and etiquette, and critical of affectation. In plays of the period, characters are sometimes satirised for
their affected language. Often it is the affected use of French words which is
satirised, rather than of Latinisms. In Dryden's *Marriage à la Mode* (1673)
there is 'an Affected Lady' called Melantha who is 'one of those that run mad
in new *French* words'. She besprinkles her conversation with phrases like
bien tourné, charmant, honnete homme, mon cher, obligeant, ravissant and
voyag'd. But satire of this kind is not an attack on loan words in general.
Dryden himself defends them in the dedication prefixed to his translation of
Virgil's *Æneid* (1697). He compares imported words to coins: if they are good,
they will circulate. He himself trades both with the living and with the dead
(i.e. borrows both from the classical languages and from living languages), for
the enrichment of English. Our old Teuton monosyllables are all right for
'necessity', but if we want magnificence and splendour we must borrow words
from abroad. If he finds any elegant word in a classical author he uses it, and
if the public accepts it the word becomes naturalised. But not everybody is a
good judge of a loan, and the licence should be used sparingly. Here again we
have the distinction between 'necessity' and 'bravery' which Mulcaster had
made. Dryden, however, thinks that we need only borrow for 'magnificence',
since the language is perfectly adequate for utilitarian purposes.

The Purists

The purists opposed the introduction of loan words. They argued that the
vocabulary should be enlarged by the use of the existing resources of the
language – by compounding, affixation, giving new meanings to existing
words. One of the main arguments for this was that such words would be self-
evident in meaning, whereas loan words were opaque to the unlearned. Purists
also tended to invoke ideas of linguistic purity and naturalness, and to appeal
to patriotic feeling.

The outstanding purist of the early Tudor age was Sir John Cheke, the
Greek scholar. His opposition to loan words is expressed in a letter to Thomas
Hoby, dated 1557 and printed at the end of Hoby's translation of Castiglione's
Courtier (1561):

> I am of this opinion that our own tung shold be written cleane and pure,

vnmixt and vnmangeled with borowing of other tunges, wherein if we take not heed bi tijm, euer borrowing and neuer payeng, she shall be fain to keep her house as bankrupt.

The 'bankrupt' was obliged to stay indoors ('keep her house') to avoid arrest. It was perhaps to this passage that Pettie was referring when he denied that English had 'crackt it credit' (p. 59 above). Cheke's ideal is difficult to realise when one's language has been importing words for centuries. Indeed, the sentence quoted above contains no fewer than six non-Germanic words, one of which (*bankrupt*) is not recorded by the OED until 1533. Moreover, Cheke uses the Latinised form of this last word, which also existed in Italian and French forms, such as *banke rote* and *bankrout*. Cheke admits the difficulties, and allows that some loans may be unavoidable, but argues that they should only be admitted to the language if the need cannot be met from existing resources.

Cheke put his theories into practice in a translation of St Matthew's Gospel and the opening verses of St Mark's. He by no means avoids all loan words, but he does often use a traditional native form where (for example) the King James Bible has a more learned word. He has forms like *biwordes* 'parables', *hunderder* 'centurion', *onwriting* 'superscription', *tolbooth* 'receipt of custom', *tollers* 'publicans', and *vprising* 'resurrection'. In Chapter 3 of Matthew he uses the word *baptism*, but in Chapter 21 and in Mark Chapter 1 he changes over to *wasching*. All these forms are recorded before Cheke's time, but he uses *hunderder* and *biwordes* in quite new senses. He probably re-invented the word *onwriting*, for the only other example given by the OED is in a gospel translation of the tenth century.

There are other words in Cheke's translation which are unrecorded earlier, and which are presumably his own coinages. Such are *freschman* 'proselyte', *gainbirth* 'regeneration', *gainrising* 'resurrection', *groundwrought* 'founded', and *moond* 'lunatic'. Sometimes he has a learned word in the text of his translation, and explains it in a marginal note. Such words include *discipils*, *hypocrites*, *synagoogs*, and *propheets*. This last word he explains at length, and finally glosses with his own coinages, 'forschewers or forsaiers'.

Cheke's translation was not published until the nineteenth century, but he was a man of great eminence, and his ideas were probably well known in his own time. There were certainly other people in the sixteenth century with similar ideas. One of these was Ralph Lever, who in 1573 published a textbook on logic, entitled *The Arte of Reason, rightly termed, Witcraft*. To provide English technical terms for logic, Lever did not adapt the Latin terms he knew. Instead, he invented compound words, each formed from two existing English words. In the title of his book he invents the word *witcraft* 'logic'. To translate Latin *conclusio*, he coins the word *endsay*; and similarly *foresays* 'premissae', *ifsay* 'propositio conditionalis', *naysay* 'negatio', *saywhat* 'definitio', *shewsay* 'propositio', and *yeasay* 'affirmatio'. To us, the striking thing is that none of Lever's coinages has caught on, and that we use words formed from the Latin expressions that he was trying to replace (*conclusion*, *negation*, *premisses*, etc.).

In the *Forespeache* ('preface') to the work, Lever justifies his method of word formation. He argues that the art of reasoning can be taught in English. The English have powers of rational discrimination, like people of other nations, and they also have a language in which they can express anything which they conceive in their minds. Some people believe that our language has no technical terms in which the rules of logic can be expressed, and that this is an unalterable fact. But this is not true.

> For as time doth inuent a newe forme of building, a straunge fashion of apparell, and a newe kinde of artillerie, and munitions: so doe men by consent of speache, frame and deuise new names, fit to make knowen their strange deuises.

He does not, indeed, favour 'straunge and inckhorne termes', which are a misuse of language. But their existence does not prove any deficiency in the English language itself. There are, admittedly, more things than words, but this was true even of Greek, the most copious of all languages. And lack of vocabulary can be remedied in various ways: one word can be used to signify several different things; one language sometimes borrows from another; and people sometimes invent new names and compounded terms. If there is a new concept, the writer will find some means of expressing it; and the invention of new words is essential to the establishment of any art or science. The English language is especially well suited to the making of new compounds, because many English words consist of only one syllable, so that two or three of them can often be fitly joined together. He has himself, Lever says, formed many such new compound words. The main reason for using this method is comprehensibility.

> An arte is to be taughte in that toung, in whiche it was neuer written afore. Nowe the question lyeth, whether it were better to borrowe termes of some other toung, in whiche this sayde Arte hath bene written: and by a litle chaunge of pronouncing, to seeke to make them Englishe wordes, whiche are none in deede: or else of simple vsual wordes, to make compounded termes, whose seuerall partes considered alone, are familiar and knowne to all english men? For trial hereof, I wish you to aske of an english man, who vnderstandeth neither Greek nor Latin, what he conceiueth in his mind, when he heareth this word a backset, and what he doth conceiue when he heareth this terme a Predicate. And doubtlesse he must confesse, if he consider the matter aright or haue any sharpnesse

of wit at al, that by a backset, he conceiueth a thing that muste be set after, and by a predicate, that he doth vnderstande nothing at all.

This, Lever claims, will be found to be generally true when his own new technical terms 'compounded of true english words' are compared with 'the inkhorne termes deriued of straunge and forain languages'. The English compound will be self-evident in meaning. Or at the very least its meaning will be much easier to remember once it has been explained. If Lever's illustrative example is not very convincing to the modern reader, this is because the noun *predicate* is now a familiar one, whereas in the sixteenth century it was not: the earliest example in the OED is dated 1612.

In the phrase 'true english words', Lever is implicitly invoking the idea of linguistic purity, and at the same time appealing to patriotic sentiment. He goes on to do this more explicitly:

> We therfore, that deuise vnderstandable termes, compounded of true and auncient english woords, do rather maintain and continue the antiquitie of our mother tongue: then ['than'] they, that with inckhorne termes doe chaunge and corrupt the same, making a mingle mangle of their natiue speache, and not obseruing the propertie thereof.

He then returns to the subject of linguistic evolution. People who object to new words have not sufficiently considered the way in which 'speache groweth', or the reason why humankind devised it. Names are not given to things before the things themselves are invented, and old names will not serve for 'newe deuises'. Lever concedes, however, that it is folly to invent a new word when there is already an adequate one in use. He also recognises that the individual alone cannot change the language:

> For no man is of power to change or to make a language when he will: but when fit names are deuised and spoken, they force the hearers to like of them and to vse them: and so do they by consent of manye, growe to a speache.

For its age, this is an acute observation of the way linguistic innovations spread when they meet the needs of the speech community, until by the 'consent of manye' they become accepted usage. To aid the acceptance of his own coinages, Lever refers the reader to a glossary at the end of the book, where they are all gathered together and explained. The glossary, however, makes a final concession to the learned reader:

> There shalbe added also (for some mens better contentation) the Latine termes.

As we have seen, it is from these Latin terms that the PresE technical words are derived. For all Lever's eloquent advocacy of his compounds, they were stillborn.

65

The purist movement continued in the seventeenth century, and was especially likely to influence antiquarians (like John Selden) and people who cultivated Anglo-Saxon studies (like Richard Verstegan). A good deal of steam had been taken out of the movement, however, because of the successful way in which the English vocabulary had been expanded by loans, especially from Latin. After the Restoration, when everything French was the rage in smart society, the movement receded even more.

Nevertheless, purism continued to be a vocal force throughout the century, and it had some influence in scientific circles. In 1674 a Baconian scientist, a Doctor of Medicine with strong purist views, wrote a philosophical-scientific work in 'pure English', and the result was rather odd. The book is by Nathaniel Fairfax, and is called *A Treatise of the Bulk and Selvedge of the World*, meaning 'a treatise about the volume and the boundary of the universe'. It is about the puzzles raised by the very large and the very small – the infiniteness or finiteness of the universe, the infinite divisibility or otherwise of matter, infinite time – and is really rather sharp. It is also amusingly eccentric in its language, replacing most loan words by new native coinages or periphrases. Fairfax has a long preface in which he justifies his purist usages. As becomes a scientist of that period, he eschews eloquence:

> I could never open my mouth Charmwise, nor breath out Spells to bind down men.

He is very Baconian, talking about the Book of God's Word and the Book of God's Works, and emphasising practicality and usefulness. Indeed, the new twist that he gives to purist ideas is to argue that we have reached an age in which the important things are practical and physical, concerned with the mechanical arts. Philosophy has become 'workful', and a suitable language for our age must be drawn from the practical people, the yeomanry and the craftsmen, not from the Latin of bookish people in closets.

Fairfax is surprisingly successful in writing English prose devoid of obvious learned loan words. Occasionally his prose sounds natural. More often it sounds slightly odd, but is clear and comprehensible. And periodically he hits the reader with phrases like 'the great *Speech-break* at *Babel*'. Here are a couple of brief specimens of his writing.

> In that narrow Chat that I have had with Outlanders, it has been hugely to my liking, that hard upon the first greeting, I have been plyed with so many good words for our *Royal Society* in the whole, and Mr. *Boyle* alone.

We have no difficulty with *narrow Chat* 'limited conversation', or *Outlanders* 'foreigners'. But *in the whole* and *alone* are perhaps rather misleading for 'in general' and 'in particular'. The loan words in *Royal Society* were unavoidable, since it is a proper name. The two other non-Germanic words in the passage, *huge(ly)* and *(ap)ply*, are ME loans from French. They were thoroughly naturalised by Fairfax's time, and he was presumably unable to recognise them as loans.

The second passage comes from Fairfax's discussion of the very small:

> Wherefore we are about to say, that our atome *punctum* or leasting, is made only of body. And although it may be metesom by Mathematical measures of the minds making, yet it is not made up thereof, any more than the greater parts are, or the whole is.

There are a few non-Germanic words in that extract. Presumably Fairfax inserted 'atome *punctum*' as a gloss for his own coinage *leasting*. But this explanation does not apply to *Mathematical* and *measures*, which were perhaps helped into the text by alliteration. The word *metesom* means 'measurable, able to be given dimensions'. It is technical words of this kind which call for most ingenuity on Fairfax's part. Here are some further specimens: *biggen* (v.) 'increase'; *brain-breaks* 'enigmas, paradoxes'; *bulksomness* 'volume' (or 'mass'?); *cleavesomness* 'divisibility'; *flitting* 'transient'; *meteings* 'dimensions'; *roomthiness* 'extension in space'; *talecraft* 'arithmetic'; *unboundedness* 'infinity'; and *unthroughfaresom* 'impenetrable'.

The Archaisers

The archaisers were hostile to inkhorn terms, and advocated the revival of obsolete words and the use of words from regional dialects. They therefore overlap with the purists, many of whom (though not all) were also archaisers. Most often, the archaisms and dialect words are only recommended for use in literature, but occasionally a more general use is envisaged.

The most celebrated practitioner of the movement was Edmund Spenser, and a defence of archaisms can be found in the preface to his set of pastoral poems, *The Shepheardes Calender* (1579). The preface was not written by Spenser himself, but by a friend who signs himself 'E.K.' (perhaps Edward Kirke). E.K. begins by looking back to Chaucer as the great English poet of the past, comparing him favourably with Virgil. In the seventeenth century, purists were often hostile to Chaucer, regarding him as a corrupter of the language who had introduced a flood of foreign loan words. This, however, was not the usual sixteenth-century view. Next, E.K. discusses Spenser's use of archaisms. He admits that many things in *The Shepherd's Calendar* will seem strange, and the vocabulary will seem strangest, 'the words them selues being so auncient'.

> And firste of the wordes to speake, I graunt they be something hard, and of most men vnused, yet both English, and also vsed of most excellent

67

Authors and most famous Poetes. In whom whenas this our Poet hath bene much traueiled and throughly redd, how could it be, (as that worthy Oratour sayde) but that walking in the sonne although for other cause he walked, yet needes he mought be sunburnt; and hauing the sound of those auncient Poetes still ringing in his eares, he mought needes in singing hit out some of theyr tunes. But whether he vseth them by such casualtye and custome, or of set purpose and choyse, as thinking them fittest for such rusticall rudenesse of shepheards, eyther for that theyr rough sounde would make his rymes more ragged and rustical, or els because such olde and obsolete wordes are most vsed of country folke, sure I think, and think I think not amisse, that they bring great grace and, as one would say, auctoritie to the verse.

The words are justified because they are genuine English words, and have been used by excellent authors. Moreover, they are appropriate to the rustic characters of pastoral: and here E.K. explicitly equates archaisms with dialect words. He goes on to support his view that 'auncient solemne wordes' are a 'great ornament' by citing the examples of Livy and Sallust, and the precepts of Cicero, who says that 'ofttimes an auncient worde maketh the style seeme graue, and as it were reuerend'. E.K. adds, however, that archaisms must be used with discretion, and not 'stuffed in' everywhere. Used in moderation,

those rough and harsh termes enlumine and make more clearly to appeare the brightnesse of braue and glorious words.

That is, the archaisms act as a foil to the more elevated diction around them. There seems to be a contradiction between this view of archaisms as rough and harsh, and the earlier assertion that ancient solemn words make the style grave and reverend. Two different defences of archaisms have perhaps been juxtaposed.

E.K. knows that people will attack Spenser for using such words, and against them he invokes patriotic feeling:

for in my opinion it is one special prayse, of many whych are dew to this Poete, that he hath laboured to restore, as to theyr rightfull heritage such good and naturall English words, as haue ben long time out of vse and almost cleane disherited. Which is the onely cause, that our Mother tonge, which truely of it self is both ful enough for prose and stately enough for verse, hath long time ben counted most bare and barrein of both. Which default when as some endeuoured to salue and recure, they patched vp the holes with peces and rags of other languages, borrowing here of the french, there of the Italian, euery where of the Latine, not weighing how il, those tongues accorde with themselues, but much worse with ours: So now they haue made our English tongue, a gallimaufray or hodgepodge of al other speches.

The appeal is to national sentiment and to the concept of naturalness ('such good and naturall English words'). The attack on loan words relies heavily on metaphors ('patched vp', 'peces and rags', 'hodgepodge'), and produces no serious argument beyond the unsupported assertion that the other languages do not 'accord' well with English.

There are other critics, E.K. continues, who know less about English than about other languages, and if they meet an old word they immediately condemn it as gibberish. They ought to be ashamed, on three counts. First, because they are reckoned as aliens in their own mother tongue. Secondly because, if they fail to understand anything, they at once conclude that it is senseless. Thirdly, and most shameful of all, because:

> of their owne country and natural speach, which together with their
> Nources milk they sucked, they haue so base regard and bastard iudge-
> ment, that they will not onely themselues not labor to garnish and beau-
> tifie it, but also repine, that of other it shold be embellished.

The appeal once again is to patriotism and to naturalness, reinforced by the image of the nurse's milk. Spenser, E.K. believes, is beautifying the English language both by producing notable literature in it and also by extending its lexical resources.

In the seventeenth century, the main users of archaisms were poets influenced by Spenser, such as William Browne, John Davies of Hereford, Francis Davison, Michael Drayton, Edward Fairfax, Giles Fletcher the younger, Phineas Fletcher, and Henry More (the Cambridge Platonist). Their poetry contains many archaisms copied from Spenser, especially when they write in the pastoral mode. Examples of such words, all of which occur in *The Shepherd's Calendar*, and which also occur in the works of some or all of the above eight poets, are the following: *accoy* 'appease', *algate* 'always', *brag* 'proudly', *breme* 'fierce, raging', *eld* 'old age', *gar* 'cause, make', *hent* 'seized, took', *herdgroom* 'shepherd', *hery* (v.) 'praise', *queme* (v.) 'please', *sicker* 'certainly', *soote* 'sweetly', *stour* (n.) 'conflict', *underfong* 'deceive, entrap', *welked* 'withered, faded', *yblent* 'blinded, confused', *yfere* 'together', *yode* 'went', and *youngth* 'youth'.

Some of these words also existed in regional dialects, and Spenser was especially influenced by the dialects of northern England, as with the words *gar* 'cause' and *wimble* 'active, nimble'. Spenser is the first recorded user of *wimble*, but the word also existed in the dialects of Lancashire and Yorkshire. Spenser is also the first recorded user of the word *hask* 'a fisherman's basket', and presumably either took it from regional dialect or invented it himself. When archaisms and dialect words are found in seventeenth-century English poetry (English as opposed to Scots), they are usually imitated from Spenser, not taken direct from medieval literature or from regional speech. Sometimes such words occur in whole phrases closely modelled on those in Spenser's poetry.

Spenser's imitators sometimes misunderstood his archaisms, and used them in unhistorical senses. We find Spenserians using *breme* to mean 'cold', *gar* to mean 'ail, be amiss', and *stour* to mean 'time, occasion'. In his notes to *The Shepherd's Calendar*, E.K. glosses *breme* (in the phrase *breme winter*) as 'chill, bitter', and this probably misled later imitators. Spenser himself sometimes used his archaisms in unhistorical ways. The verb *welk* meant 'to wilt, wither, fade', but Spenser used it transitively in the sense 'to cause to wane or wither'. The past participle *behight* meant 'vowed, promised, warranted', but Spenser uses it with such meanings as 'delivered', 'given', 'commanded', 'called', and 'named' (perhaps through confusion with *hight*).

Even though the archaising movement was much influenced by Spenser, it would be a mistake to see it as due to the influence of a single poet. In the sixteenth century there were archaising poets before Spenser, like Thomas Phaer and Thomas Sackville: Spenser is part of a whole movement. In the seventeenth century, moreover, there were archaisers who had no particular connection with Spenser or with poetry – extremists like John Hare and Francis White, who advocated the use of archaisms for all purposes, and wanted loan words to be expelled from the language. In the later seventeenth century the movement waned, and there were attacks on the use of archaisms even in poetry. It became a standard criticism of Spenser that he had used obsolete language. As early as 1651, William Davenant, in the preface to *Gondibert*, says that among objections to Spenser he is constrained to mention his obsolete language, 'though it be grown the most vulgar accusation that is laid to his charge'. It was after 1660 that such attacks became most severe.

RHETORIC

The third feature that made a language eloquent was the fact that it was adorned with the devices of classical rhetoric. Rhetoric was the art of public speaking, but it was common for rhetorical theories to be applied to literature, and for the handbooks of rhetoric to be treated as instructions for poets. Elyot explains what qualities he expects from a good 'grammarian', i.e. a good humanist teacher:

> I call nat them gramariens / whiche only can teache or make rules / wherby a childe shall onely lerne to speake congrue ['grammatically correct'] latine / or to make sixe versis standyng in one fote / wherin perchance shal be neither sentence ['thought, meaning, substance'] nor eloquence. But I name hym a gramarien by the autoritie of Quintilian / that speakynge latine elegantly / can expounde good autours / expressynge the inuention and disposition of the mater / their stile or

fourme of eloquence / explicatyng the figures / as well of sentences as
wordes / leuyng nothyng / persone or place named by the autour / vn-
declared or hidde from his scholers.

The good teacher must be able to explain all the references in the classical
authors that he reads with his pupils, and must also be able to analyse the texts
in terms of a literary theory. This theory is a rhetorical one, as can be seen from
the technical terms used – *invention*, *disposition*, *the figures*. The rhetorical
basis of the literary explication is confirmed by the reference to Quintilian,
whose *Institutio Oratoria* was one of the standard handbooks.

The first three subjects of the traditional curriculum were grammar, rhetoric,
and logic (which together constituted the *trivium*). Grammar meant the grammar of Latin, the language of literature and scholarship: the pupil began by
learning the literary language. Logic taught him to argue in that language (*him*
because grammar schools were all-male institutions). And rhetoric gave him a
literary education, teaching him both style and the organisation of material.
The standard handbooks on rhetoric were those of Aristotle, Cicero, and Quintilian, together with the anonymous *Rhetorica ad Herennium*. In addition, a
number of continental texts were popular, especially those giving lists of the
figures, like Susenbrotus's *Epitome troporum ac schematum* (1541). Gram-
mar-school pupils would not necessarily read such texts themselves, but a
good teacher would have read them and would teach their theories.

In the middle of the sixteenth century, textbooks of rhetoric began to appear
in English. An influential one was Thomas Wilson's *Arte of Rhetorique*
(1553), which was reprinted many times up to about 1590, after which it went
out of fashion. Others took its place, however, for from about 1580 numerous
rhetorics were published in English. Moreover, these handbooks began to take
their illustrations from English literature instead of Latin: the techniques of
explication learnt for the classics were now applied to writings in the vernacular. Abraham Fraunce's *Arcadian Rhetorike* (1588) draws its illustrations
from Sidney's poetry and prose, as well as from continental poets. Alexander
Gil's *Logonomia Anglica* (1619) has a section on rhetoric. Although it is
written in Latin, it draws most of its illustrations from English poetry, nearly
all of them from Spenser's *Faerie Queene*. This was only possible because
English poets and dramatists were being influenced by classical rhetoric. In
the grammar schools, the pupils were not merely trained passively in rhetoric
as an aid to reading: they were also given intensive practice in applying the
techniques to their own (Latin) speech and writing. It is not surprising that
these techniques were then carried over into their writings in English.

Wilson's handbook is closely modelled on classical precedent. It talks all
the time about the orator, not the poet, and it deals with all five of the
traditional branches of rhetoric: *inventio*, *dispositio*, *elocutio*, *memoria*, and

pronuntiatio. Later English handbooks tend to be more selective, dealing with only part of the material, and often assume that they are concerned with poetry, or with writing in general, not with speechmaking.

Invention (*inventio*) was the methodical search for material. The orator took some set of categories ('topics' or 'places') and considered his subject from the point of view of each of these in turn. Especially favoured were sets of logical 'places'. One of these was Aristotle's set of ten 'predicaments' or logical categories. Another influential set was Cicero's, also based on logic: definition, division, the name, conjugates, genus, species, similarity, difference, contraries, adjuncts, consequences, antecedents, incompatibles, causes, effects, comparison. Cicero asserts that, when you have found arguments from these sixteen places, there is no topic of argument left to be discovered. The influence of such categories is pervasive in Renaissance writing, and anybody handling a subject is likely to begin by defining it, dividing it into its parts, discussing the significance of its name, and so on.

When the material has been found, it has to be arranged, and this is Disposition (*dispositio*). The aspect of the subject most influential in the Renaissance was the standard structure of a judicial oration. This was often treated as a pattern for all types of oration, and also got carried over into other types of writing. Basically it was a five-part structure: (1) Introduction (*introductio*, *exordium*, or *prooemium*), which aimed to gain the goodwill of the judge or the listeners. (2) Narration (*narratio*), a statement of the facts of the case. In non-judicial orations, it can be some other type of narrative, for example historical or legendary. (3) Proof (*probatio* or *confirmatio*), a statement of the positive arguments for your case. (4) Refutation (*refutatio* or *confutatio*), a destruction of your opponent's arguments. (5) Conclusion (*conclusio* or *peroratio*), which can summarise the arguments, or appeal to the emotions, or both.

The five-part structure is found in Quintilian, but some authorities, including the *Ad Herennium*, have a sixth main section, which comes after the Narration. This is the Division (*divisio* or *partitio*), which lays down the points at issue and gives a plan of the argument which is to follow. Quintilian in fact also has a Division, but he makes it part of the Proof. This five-part or six-part structure sometimes influences English prose writings, for example Sidney's *Defence of Poesie* (1595) and Milton's *Areopagitica* (1644).

When the material has been discovered and arranged, it has to be 'clothed' (to use a favourite Renaissance metaphor) in suitable language. This is the subject-matter of Elocution (*elocutio*), which covers style in all its aspects. From classical rhetoric comes the doctrine of the three styles (high, middle, and low), so influential in neo-classical theory. On the other hand, some things in the classical textbooks dropped into the background, notably their extensive discussion of prose rhythm. The technical terms for analysing prose rhythm became, in English, mere names for punctuation-marks, like *comma* and *colon*. But above all, the Elocution section of a rhetoric contained an account of the figures, defined as departures from normal usage for artistic effect.

Fourthly, the orator had to memorise his material, and so there was a branch of rhetoric called Memory (*memoria*), in which various mnemonic techniques were taught. And finally he had to deliver the speech, an art covered by the branch of rhetoric called Pronunciation (*pronuntiatio*). This covered not only voice production but also gesture, and also any theatrical business that the orator wished to introduce (like clinging to the knees of the judge, or bringing into the court the poor little children of his client).

When rhetoric came to be associated with literature rather than with oratory, the fourth and fifth branches, memory and pronunciation, fell into the background. Not that oratory was completely neglected. Public speaking was an art prized by gentlemen and noblemen in Renaissance England. Elyot points out the political usefulness of being able to speak well, which is learnt by studying the art of rhetoric in the classical handbooks, and by reading the orations of Demosthenes and Cicero. Even so, the English rhetorics tend to be concerned with poetry, and to give most prominence to elocution, the branch dealing with style. Within this branch, most prominence is usually given to the figures. Fraunce's *Arcadian Rhetoric* treats only elocution and pronunciation: 121 pages are given to elocution, and only 29 to pronunciation. Moreover, the section on elocution is devoted almost exclusively to the figures. Dudley Fenner's *Arte of Rhetorike* (1584) divides the art into elocution and pronunciation, but in fact treats only elocution, again with hardly anything except the figures. This does not mean, however, that invention and disposition disappeared from the scene, for they were often handled in textbooks of logic. Indeed, the followers of Ramus (among whom both Fraunce and Fenner are to be numbered) held as a point of principle that invention and disposition were not a part of rhetoric, but a part of logic. In general, elocution increasingly came to be seen as the principal branch of rhetoric, and elocution itself became almost exclusively concerned with the figures. Handbooks were written which dealt with nothing else, like Henry Peacham's *Garden of Eloquence* (1577), a book of 152 pages giving an account of 194 different figures. The aspect of rhetoric which made English eloquent was the extensive use in literature of the figures, which, from the time of Sidney and Spenser, were intensively cultivated in both verse and prose.

To the modern reader, a concept of style which confines itself to the figures of rhetoric sounds a limited one, but it was less narrow than it sounds. The figures covered a wide variety of different things, and could provide a theoretical justification for almost any kind of literary procedure. The broad division of figures is into Tropes and Schemes (though Quintilian uses the word *figurae* for the Schemes). Tropes are figures in which there is some kind of transfer of meaning or substitution, such as metaphor, metonymy, irony, pun, and allegory – devices which are *figurative* in the modern sense of the word. Schemes are figures in which there is no such transfer of meaning, and are divided into Grammatical Schemes and Rhetorical Schemes. Grammatical schemes are ones in which there is some departure from normal grammatical usage: abnormal word order, the use of an aberrant form of a single word, use of the 'wrong' part of speech, ellipsis, parenthesis, breaking off a sentence and leaving it unfinished, and so on. Rhetorical schemes involve no departure from normal morphology or syntax. They include the use of patterned language, achieved by various types of repetition; whole modes of procedure, like praising or cursing or consoling; and set pieces, like the elaborate description of a person or place. So the figures can cover everything from the smallest stylistic detail to the mode in which a whole work operates.

All types of figure were cultivated in Renaissance writings, but in the late sixteenth century, when English became eloquent, writers were particularly fond of rhetorical schemes involving repetition, which produce highly patterned language. Good examples of this very formal patterning can be found in the plays of Thomas Kyd and Christopher Marlowe, and in the early plays of Shakespeare. Round the turn of the century, however, this changed. Writers continued to make extensive use of the figures, but those producing formal patterning went out of fashion. The change can be seen by comparing Shakespeare's *Richard III*, which has long passages of patterned lament and execration, with *Macbeth*, which is in quite a different style. The change may partly reflect a change in social consciousness, as the Elizabethan sense of order and hierarchy gives way to the political and intellectual turmoil of the early Stuart period. Shakespeare often makes dramatic and thematic use of the contrast between patterned language and a more 'natural' style. Examples of this are discussed by Barber (1981a, 1981b, 1987).

The educated Elizabethan reader or playgoer, who had been drilled in the figures at grammar school, enjoyed the pleasures of recognition when they occurred in English works. In *The Shepherd's Calendar*, one of E.K.'s notes to the January eclogue is a comment on lines 61–2:

> I loue thilke lasse, (alas why doe I loue?)
> And am forlorne, (alas why am I lorne?).

E.K's note is as follows:

> a prety Epanorthosis in these two verses, and withall a Paronomasia or playing with the word, where he sayth (I loue thilke lasse (alas etc.

Such delight in technical details is difficult for us to recapture: we are unlikely to bounce up and down with exhilaration on recognising a pretty epanorthosis. But it is something we have to try to take into account when we read sixteenth-century literature.

The fourth feature that made a language eloquent, the fact that it was 'ruled' or regulated, had little weight in sixteenth-century England. It was only in the seventeenth century that pressure for regulation grew. A ruled language is one in which acceptable usage is explicitly laid down, for example by grammar-books and dictionaries, or by the rulings of an academy. Some people also believed that a properly ruled language would also be unchanging. Richard Bentley observed in 1699 that every language 'is in perpetual motion and alteration', but nevertheless believed that:

> it were no difficult contrivance, if the Publick had any regard to it, to make the *English* Tongue immutable; unless hereafter some Foreign Nation shall invade and over-run us.

He is perhaps thinking of the possible establishment of an official body to fix the language, for in the second half of the seventeenth century there was a movement in favour of an English Academy. Its functions would be to 'refine' or 'correct' the English language, to lay down correct usage, and perhaps to freeze the language in the desirable state thus obtained. The desire for an academy was encouraged by the examples of Italy and France. Especially influential was the *Académie française*, which began as an informal group in 1629 and was institutionalised by Cardinal Richelieu in 1635. Its statutes required it to lay down exact rules for the French language and to purge it of corruption. Its tasks were to include the production of a dictionary and a grammar.

In England, there were sporadic proposals for an academy in the first half of the seventeenth century, but the movement did not become strong until the Restoration period. From 1660 onwards, a number of influential people supported the idea, and for a short time in 1665 there was a committee for improving the language, set up by the Royal Society. One of its members was Dryden, who favoured an academy on French lines. Later supporters of the idea included Defoe and Swift.

Proposals for an academy came to nothing. In the seventeenth century, how-ever, grammars and dictionaries of English began to appear, and English spellings gradually became standardised, at any rate in printed books.

English Dictionaries

There were no dictionaries of the English language before the seventeenth century. The earliest, Robert Cawdrey's *A Table Alphabeticall*, was published in 1604. In 1582, Mulcaster had suggested that a dictionary was desirable: it would make known the correct spellings of words, their intrinsic or correct meaning ('natural force'), and the way they should be used ('proper vse').

75

Plainly, he envisaged a regulating function for the dictionary. He also envisaged a complete dictionary of English, but no dictionary before the eighteenth century even aimed at being this. All the seventeenth-century dictionaries explicitly aim at presenting only part of the English vocabulary.

In the sixteenth century, readers were perfectly familiar with dictionaries, but they were two-language ones, especially Latin–English and English–Latin. What they were not familiar with was the purely English dictionary, and it would not have occurred to most people that any such thing was needed. When they did come to feel the need, the bilingual dictionaries were there to provide a pattern. Starnes & Noyes (1946) have shown that the early English dictionaries were deeply influenced by Latin–English dictionaries, such as Thomas Thomas's *Dictionarium Linguae Latinae et Anglicanae* (c. 1588). Nearly half the words in Cawdrey's *Table* are lifted from Thomas. Cawdrey simply anglicises Latin words (*hemisphaerium* for example becoming *hemisphere*), and takes over Thomas's glosses of them.

People came to feel the need for English dictionaries because of the influx of new words into the language. Many of these, especially those from Latin and Greek, were incomprehensible to the unlearned reader. Without exception, the seventeenth-century English dictionaries are dictionaries of hard words, providing a selection of English words likely to be found obscure. Not all of the words selected are from the classical languages: some dictionaries include archaisms and words from specialised fields of discourse, and these may be Germanic words. But the majority of the words listed in the dictionaries are either from the classical languages or from French.

The history of the English dictionary in the seventeenth century is mainly one of increasing size and complexity. Robert Cawdrey's dictionary of 1604 contains about 2,500 words, while that of Elisha Coles in 1676 contains about 25,000. Cawdrey has very brief definitions. Later dictionaries often have more elaborate ones. They also introduce additional information, such as the etymology of the word, the field of discourse it comes from, and examples of authors who have used it.

Robert Cawdrey's title page ran as follows:

> A Table Alphabeticall, conteyning and teaching the true writing, and vnder-standing of hard vsuall English wordes, borrowed from the Hebrew, Greeke, Latine, or French, &c. With the interpretation thereof by plaine English words, gathered for the benefit and helpe of Ladies, Gentlewomen, or any other vnskilfull persons. Whereby they may the more easilie and better vnderstand many hard English wordes, which they shall heare or read in Scriptures, Sermons, or elswhere, and also be made able to vse the same aptly themselues.

The emphasis is on obscure words borrowed from the learned languages or from French. The dictionary will show the correct spelling ('true writing') and will explain the meaning in 'plaine English words'.

The next English dictionary was *An English Expositor* (1616), by John Bullokar, which claimed to teach 'the interpretation of the hardest words vsed in our Language'. It is larger than Cawdrey's, containing over 4,100 entries. It also gives more information. It sometimes indicates the field of discourse to which a word belongs, as in the two following consecutive entries:

Homonymie.   A terme in Logicke, when one word signifieth diuers things: as Hart: signifying a beast, and a principall member of the body.

Honour point.   In Herauldry the vpper part of a Scutcheon is so called, when the bredth thereof, is diuided into three euen parts.

Bullokar also marks archaic words, by means of an asterisk. Examples are *Bale* 'Sorrow: great miserie', *Eld* 'Old age', *Finance* 'An end', *Galoch* 'A kinde of shooe', *Golierdise* 'Hee that hath a fowle great mouth', *Ifere* 'Together', *Sweuen* 'A dreame', *Teene* 'Sorrow', *Thilke* 'The same', and *Welked* 'Withered'. Some of these, like *eld* and *thilke* and *welked*, may have been taken from the poetry of Spenser or his followers.

Most of the words, however, are loans from the learned languages or from French, though there are occasionally rather ordinary Germanic words, like *Hillock* 'A little hill' and *Hip* 'The red berry on the bryer'. The definitions tend to be longer than Cawdrey's. There are many brief ones, but there are numerous entries of fifty or a hundred words. The entry under the word *Diuination* occupies nearly three pages, and is appropriate to an encyclopedia rather than a dictionary.

Bullokar is concerned about spelling as well as meaning. For example, his entry for the word *Hipocrite* is 'See Hypocrite'. At the beginning of the book he has 'An Instruction to the Reader':

Haue care to search euery word according to the true Orthography thereof, as for Phoenix in the letter *P*. not in *F*. for Hypostaticall in *Hy*: not in *Hi*.

We see how the concept of correct spelling ('true Orthography') is encouraged by the making of dictionaries. In Bullokar's examples the criterion is an etymological one: *phoenix* has to be spelt with *ph-* because that is the spelling of the Latin word from which it is derived, and Greek upsilon has to be represented by *y*, as it is in Latin.

The next English dictionary was also the first to be given that title: *The English Dictionarie* (1623), by Henry Cockeram. Like the previous two, it proclaims itself on its title page to be 'An Interpreter of hard English words'. Its arrangement, however, is different from theirs. Instead of having one single body of words in alphabetical order, it is divided into three sections. The first contains 'the choicest words' with which the language has been enriched, meaning the inkhorn terms. The second section gives an alphabetical list of 'vulgar words', for which Cockeram gives 'more refined and elegant' equivalents. The third section is a short dictionary of mythology. Cockeram draws on both Cawdrey and Bullokar, and his book is nearly as long as their two put together.

Even larger was Thomas Blount's *Glossographia* (1656), an octavo volume of 688 pages. A sample count suggests that the number of entries is about 11,500. The title page claims that the work interprets all hard words from other languages that 'are now used in our refined English Tongue', and also the terms used in many arts and sciences. Like Bullokar, Blount often indicates the field of discourse from which a word comes. He also introduces two new features. His is the first English dictionary to give etymologies, which it does throughout. The etymology is usually given very briefly in brackets after the head word, for example *Antecede* (antecedo), *Antecursor* (Lat.), *Anthology* (Gr.), *Antichambre* (Fr.), *Aphelium* (Gr. *aphelion*), *Aporetique* (from *Aporia*), *Apparitor* (Lat.), *Appuyed* (from the Fr. *Appuyè*). Occasionally he expands into a longer discussion of the origin of a word. Not all his etymologies are good ones, but they do illustrate the growing interest in the history of English.

Blount's second innovation is the citing of sources: he sometimes indicates that a word has been used by a particular author or in a particular work. At the end of his entry on *climacterical* he gives a reference to Sir Thomas Browne's *Vulgar Errors*, complete with page number. Under *gildable* he refers to Camden, again with page number. And after defining *circumambient*, he adds 'Sir *Jo. Suckling* useth it thus'. With technical terms, for example legal ones, he often refers to standard textbooks. These innovations, together with its size, make *Glossographia* quite a landmark in English lexicography.

In 1658, only two years later, Edward Phillips (a nephew of Milton) produced *The New World of English Words*, a folio volume containing about the same number of entries as Blount's. Indeed, a great deal of *The New World* was plagiarised from *Glossographia*, as Blount pointed out in 1673. Even the phraseology of the title page is quite similar, and the very title of Phillips's work occurs in Blount's preface. Of the entries at least half are closely modelled on those of *Glossographia*. In his preface, however, Phillips has some material not found in Blount, including an outline history of the English language.

The plagiarising habit was continued by Elisha Coles. In *An English Dictionary* (1676) he borrowed extensively from Phillips. There is, however, a good deal of new material in his book, which contains about 25,000 entries, far more than any of its predecessors. Much of the increase is brought about by the introduction of many dialect words, cant terms, and archaisms. The cant terms are marked *c.*, and the archaisms *o.*, while for dialect words there is given either the county or a broad division into northern and southern. But Coles's dictionary is still not a general one. As its title page indicates, it is a dictionary of 'difficult Terms'. It was not until the eighteenth century that dictionaries began to include the ordinary everyday words of the language. The first to attempt this was *A New English Dictionary* (1702), perhaps by John Kersey. This was to be followed later in the century by the outstanding works of Nathan Bailey and Samuel Johnson.

All seventeenth-century English dictionaries, then, are limited in scope. Even so, the lexicographical activity of the century is both substantial and influential. The bulk is greater than appears from the number of titles, since all the dictionaries went through numerous editions, and some of them were extensively revised and enlarged, either by their original authors or by later editors. The dictionaries of Bullokar, Phillips, and Coles continued to be popular, in revised editions, until well into the eighteenth century. This lexicographical activity was a sign of the growing desire for regulation, and at the same time a contribution to it. In seventeenth-century dictionaries, English spelling and word meaning are gradually recorded and to some extent stabilised. In some of them, differences of style or acceptability are recorded. Elegant words are distinguished from vulgar ones, cant terms and dialect words from general educated usage, archaisms from current words. To record is not necessarily to prescribe. But, once dictionaries are established as normal works of reference, people inevitably begin to treat them as authorities, and they take on a regulating function. In the seventeenth century we see the beginnings of this process in English.

Grammars of English

English people of 1550 had no English dictionary. Similarly, they had no grammar of English. If they saw a book entitled 'Grammar' (like William Lily's *Short Introduction of Grammar* of 1549) they knew that it was a grammar of Latin. Even after grammars of English had come on to the market, it was still possible for a Latin grammar to be entitled simply 'Grammar', like Obadiah Walker's *Some Instruction in the Art of Grammar* (1691). Even the title *English Grammar* was ambiguous. It could mean either 'a grammar of English' or 'a grammar of Latin written in English'. It has the latter meaning in Edward Burles's *Grammatica Burlesa, or a new English Grammar* (1652).

In the late sixteenth century William Bullokar wrote a grammar of English. This was part of a larger project, described on the title page of his *Short Introduction or Guiding* (1580). The plan was to regulate English by means of three works: a book on spelling reform, a grammar, and a dictionary. *A Short Introduction* is a preliminary work on spelling reform. A 'ruled Grammar for Inglish', he says, has already been written but not yet published. The three works would facilitate the making of a 'perfite Dictionarie in time to come'. They would contribute to 'the perfite staie' of the language, presumably meaning that change would be arrested. Nothing more is known of the project for a dictionary, though one of the early dictionaries was by William's son John, over thirty years later. The English grammar has not survived, but in 1586 Bullokar published *Pamphlet for Grammar*, which he said was an abbreviation of it. This is a small quarto of about eighty pages, and is heavily dependent on the Latin grammar of William Lily.

Another English grammar was published before the turn of the century, the *Grammatica Anglicana* (1594), probably by Paul Greaves. It is a small book, with only thirty-six pages of grammar, padded out with a long word-index and a list of Chaucerian words. It is written in Latin, and much influenced by Lily.

In the seventeenth century the flow of substantial English grammars really begins. Alston (1965–87) gives in his first volume a list of English grammars written by native speakers in either English or Latin. In the first half of the seventeenth century there are five of them. They include Alexander Gil's *Logonomia Anglica* (1619), Charles Butler's *The English Grammar* (1633), and Ben Jonson's *The English Grammar* (1640). In the second half of the century there are nine. They include John Wallis's *Grammatica Linguae Anglicanae* (1653), Jeremiah Wharton's *The English-Grammar* (1654), and Christopher Cooper's *Grammatica Linguae Anglicanae* (1685). In addition, there were numerous works, some of them in English, designed for foreign learners of English.

These grammars of English were deeply influenced by the Latin grammars in which all educated people had been trained. There was a long and continuous Graeco-Latin grammatical tradition in Western Europe, and English grammarians found it hard to escape from the framework and the categories they had inherited. Many saw no necessity for any such escape. Others, like John Wallis, declared that an analysis suitable for the classical languages is not necessarily applicable to English, but were nevertheless unable to break completely free from traditional methods. Michael (1970) has shown that there was a surprisingly large amount of variability in the tradition, and that this continued in the English grammars. Despite this variation, none of the eModE grammarians manages to escape completely from the tradition. Even when they give an apparently new analysis, for example of the 'parts of speech' or of the tense system of the verb, they are merely reshuffling traditional material. Michael argues that the cause of the variability in the tradition is a confusion about the criteria to be used for establishing grammatical categories. Grammarians used a jumble of formal, semantic, and syntactical criteria. Consequently, their categories were seldom defined rigorously, and it was this that made variation possible.

Like their Latin models, the English grammars are rather narrow in scope, though this could hardly be guessed from the definition they give of their art. The opening sentence of Butler's grammar runs:

Grammar is the Art of writing and Speaking wel.

The identical sentence opens Wharton's grammar twenty years later. It is in fact a translation of the opening sentence of William Lily's *Brevissima Institutio*, the standard Latin grammar used in English schools. Lily himself, moreover, is merely giving his own version of a traditional definition.

A better idea of the actual content of a grammar is given by Butler's title page, which runs:

The English Grammar, or The Institution of Letters, Syllables, and Woords in the English tung. Whereunto is annexed An Index of woords Like and Unlike.

The grammar deals with letters, syllables, and words. No mention is made of any linguistic unit larger than the word. Some grammars, however, do have a section on syntax, Jonson's being one. Jonson's syntax section is almost exclusively concerned with concord, for example of gender and number. He does also make a few remarks on the use of the articles and on word order, for example the fact that an adjective normally precedes the noun that it qualifies. What is almost totally lacking is any consideration of the structure of clauses and of sentences. This limitation to the small-scale units is inherited from the grammars of Latin. There, most space was given to the paradigms the pupil had to learn, like the declension of the noun and of the adjective, and the conjugation of the verb. There was usually also a section on syntax, but it tended to be concerned very largely with concord and government, for example the cases governed by prepositions.

Spelling Reformers

The grammars and dictionaries contributed towards the standardisation of English spelling. There were also books concerned only or mainly with spelling, like *Orthoepia Anglicana* (1640), written by Simon Daines, a Suffolk schoolteacher. This claims on its title page to give 'exact rules of Orthography, and rules of spelling', and also rules for punctuation. In the preface, Daines laments the 'want of one uniforme and certain method' of speaking and writing English, and says that he has 'reduced' English orthoepy and orthography 'into a classical method'. It is clear from the preface that he intended the work for use in schools.

There is nothing startling about the spellings advocated by Daines: his work rests on traditional usage. But there are other books on spelling which advocate radical changes. Between about 1540 and 1640 there was a movement for spelling reform in England. Some of the reformers advocated sweeping changes, including the introduction of entirely new symbols. The earliest figures in the movement were Sir John Cheke and Sir Thomas Smith, whose interest in the subject arose from their attempt to introduce a reformed pronunciation of Greek at Cambridge in the 1530s. The prominent spelling reformers of the second half of the sixteenth century were John Hart and William Bullokar, while the most notable figures in the seventeenth century were Alexander Gil and Charles Butler. Some of them produced whole works in their proposed orthographies. Such works include the English grammars of Butler and Gil, Cheke's translation of St Matthew, Bullokar's *Aesops Fablz* (1585), and Butler's *The Principles of Musik* (1636).

As an example of the arguments used by spelling reformers, let us look at a work by John Hart. Hart wrote three such works, two of which were published, in 1569 and 1570. The third, *The opening of the unreasonable writing of our inglish toung*, was not published in Hart's own time. I shall give a brief account of this manuscript work, which is dated 1551.

Roughly the first third of the work deals with general principles. In the remainder, Hart considers English speech-sounds and spellings one by one, and makes his suggestions for reform. He takes the spoken language as primary. In speech, words consist of a certain number of 'voices' (i.e. speech-sounds). These are the minimum units ('elements' or 'least parts') of spoken discourse. In writing, letters are the marks corresponding to the 'voices' in speech. The writing system, therefore, should contain exactly as many symbols as there are 'voices' in the spoken language. Unfortunately this is not the case with the writing system of English, which is 'corrupt'. Hart considers that there are four main ways in which a writing system can be corrupt. These he calls diminution, superfluity, usurpation, and misplacing. English writing suffers from all these corruptions except the first. Diminution is the use of too few symbols in the written form for the number of speech-sounds to be represented. Superfluity is the use of more symbols in the written form than there are speech-sounds in the spoken form. As examples of this, Hart gives:

> the *b* in doubt, the *g* in eight, *h* in authoritie, *l* in souldiours, *o* in people, *p* in condempned, *s* in baptisme, and divers lyke.

He admits that there is some justification for silent letters in one particular case, namely when they are used to show that a preceding vowel is long, as in *feed* and *hope*. He thinks, however, that silent letters are undesirable, and proposes instead that some kind of accent should be used to indicate that a vowel is long.

The third corruption, usurpation, is the use of the wrong symbol. This arises because some symbols have 'double powers' (can be used to represent two different sounds). For example, *g* represents one sound in *gentle* but another sound in *together*, though in both cases it is followed by *e*. The fourth corruption consists in putting the written symbols in the wrong order: *fable* and *circle*, Hart says, would more reasonably be written *fabel* and *cirkel*, because we pronounce the *e* before the *l*, not after.

To remedy these 'corruptions', Hart proposes a writing system in which there is one symbol, and one only, for each 'voice'. (Since he is unaware of allophonic variation, this in effect means that he proposes one symbol for each phoneme of the language.) Pure vowels are to be represented by single symbols, never by digraphs, and an accent is used to show that a vowel is long. Diphthongs are represented by digraphs: the word 'side', for example, is written *seid*. The symbols *i* and *j* are given separate functions, *i* being used as a vowel symbol while *j* represents a consonant, and similarly with *u* and *v*; Hart seems to have been the first to propose these usages for English. He confuses things a little, however, by abolishing the symbol *w*, and using *u* for the semivowel /w/ as well as for the vowel. The symbol *g* is used for /g/ (never /dʒ/), and *k* always for /k/, releasing *c* for use as /tʃ/. The symbol *q* is abolished. The voiced and voiceless /s/ and /z/ are strictly distinguished as *s* and *z*, giving spellings like *iz* 'is' and *bodiz* 'bodies'. Similarly, the voiced and voiceless sounds represented by *th* are distinguished, and Hart invents two new symbols to represent them. He does retain the digraph *sh* for /ʃ/, but in his later works he invented a new symbol to represent this too. All 'silent letters' are abolished. The principle of correct order produces spellings like *huen* 'when'.

In the earlier part of the book, Hart spends a good deal of time answering possible objections to his reforms. It is clear from more than one passage that he had argued with people about them before he wrote the book. There are various practical objections to meet, like the expense of changing printers' fonts, and the difficulty of persuading people trained in one writing system to change over to another. Hart devotes most of his space, however, to answering three main justifications of the existing system. He labels them arguments from use, from derivation, and from difference.

The argument from use or custom rests on the value and importance of tradition. It is undesirable to change traditional ways. In reply, Hart pits reason against custom. If we accepted the argument from custom, we would be unable to speak against the usurped authority of the Pope. God has given us reason, which enables us to change things that are in need of reform. History shows that changes do take place in languages. Custom would require us to go on using an English spelling system which is corrupted. The reformed spelling would reduce the amount of paper in a book by about a quarter. It would make spelling easier to learn, and would make reading easier.

The argument from derivation says that it is desirable for the spelling to show the derivation of loan words, as in *doubt*, *people*, and *baptisme*. Hart rejects the idea that spelling should show the etymology of a word. We are under no obligation to the nations from whom we borrow words, and it is of no profit to us to use etymological spellings. Moreover, if there were any such rule, it ought to be applied to all borrowed words, not just a few. The function of orthography is to show the pronunciation of a word, not its derivation. Other written languages, such as Latin, do not use etymological spellings.

The third argument, from difference, is that variant spellings are necessary in order to distinguish between homophones.The words *sunne* and *sonne* are pronounced in the same way, but the spelling shows which is meant, and helps to avoid misunderstanding. If this were true, Hart says, it would be equally necessary for people to pronounce the two words differently, otherwise they might be misunderstood. If differentiation were necessary, it would be more necessary in speech than in writing, for speech 'passeth quickli away', whereas writing remains, and the reader can if necessary pause over it. The context usually tells us what the author means. There are homophones in English which are not distinguished in spelling, like *pale* 'fence' and *pale* 'pallid', and they cause no difficulty. Moreover, many superfluous letters in our spelling cannot be justified on such grounds, for example the final letters of *sadd* and *all*, and the final *-re* of *warre*.

A large part of *The Opening* is devoted to an examination of English speech sounds and the spellings used to represent them. Here Hart shows considerable powers of observation, and for his time he is a very good phonetician of English. His general competence is suggested by the opening of his section on the vowels:

> Necessarili is the distinktion made betuixt the voels and consonants, insomoch as a voel is a breath, with a ful simple sound commyng from the breast, which passeth into the eare clearly without any lett or stay of any part of the mouth: And the consonant (contrariwise) hath a necessari touching of some partes of the mouth to the lett and stay of the breath, and that other ['either'] with an inward sound, or an unsounded breath openyng or passing thorow the partes first touched.

That states well the phonetic difference between vowel and consonant, and also distinguishes voiced consonants ('with an inward sound') from voiceless ones ('[with] an unsounded breath'). Later, when he treats the consonants, Hart shows a clear understanding of the way they form voiced and voiceless pairs.

Hart considers the vowels in the manner of an articulatory phonetician. He recognises five *simple voels* ('pure vowels'), each of which can be either short or long. For each of the five, he attempts to describe the tongue position and the degree of lip rounding. He understands that the sequence of front vowels, /a/ /e/ /i/, is made by progressively raising and fronting the tongue. He also understands the effect on the back vowels of looser and tighter lip-rounding. He seems not to realise, however, that the tongue is raised and retracted for /o/

and /u:/ apparently he thinks that they are made with the same tongue position as /a/.

The pronunciations ascribed to words by many of the orthoepists were influenced by traditional spellings. Hart does not share this weakness to any great extent, and could obviously use his ears. He does share some traditional weaknesses with them, however. He tends to consider words in isolation, and therefore in their stressed or 'citation' form. This is one reason why he fails to identify the phoneme /ə/, which almost certainly existed in English in his time. Another reason for this failure is illustrated by a sentence at the end of his analyses of the pure vowels. He has, he says, described how the speech organs have:

> brought forth 5. divers full simple soundes of voels, which undoubtedli ar so many as euer any man could sound, of what toung or nation soever he were.

The five pure vowels he has described are the only ones that people can produce, whatever their language or nationality. Here we see the influence of traditional linguistic theories. Classical Latin has five vowel symbols, each representing a long and a short vowel. This pattern is universalised, made into a general rule of language. This rule had been enunciated long before Hart's time, for example in the thirteenth century by Roger Bacon, who asserted that there are only five vowels. That it should also be held by as competent a phonetician as Hart shows the strength of the classical tradition. This belief affects Hart's analysis of the high front rounded vowel [y:], which he has heard in French and in Scots. Since there are only five possible pure vowels, he analyses it as the diphthong [iu].

Spelling reformers like Hart throw interesting light on linguistic attitudes in the period. They also provide invaluable material for the reconstruction of eModE pronunciation, as by Dobson (1968). They had little effect, however, on English spelling. The proposals of radical reformers met no success. In the course of the seventeenth century, spelling did gradually become standardised, at least in printed books. What happened, however, was that certain traditional spellings triumphed at the expense of others. There were indeed a few innovations, such as the distinction between *i* and *j*, and between *u* and *v*, but these were exceptional.

Nor were arguments like those of Hart left unanswered. One notable answer is found in Mulcaster's *Elementary*. Richard Mulcaster (c. 1530–1611) was headmaster of the Merchant Taylors' School and later of St Paul's School. The *Elementary* is the first part of an incomplete work on the pre-grammar-school stage of education. In it, Mulcaster advocates a five-part syllabus for the elementary school. The extant work, however, is almost entirely concerned with spelling, 'the right writing of our English tung'. Before giving his own rules for spelling, Mulcaster has a long attack on the radical spelling reformers, and a justification of traditional spelling. He mentions no names, but it is clear that one of his targets is Hart: he deals, for example, with Hart's four ways in which a writing system can be corrupted. The main tenor of Mulcaster's argument is that sound should not be the sole criterion, in other words spelling should not be completely phonetic. He gives, in allegorical form, a schematic history of spelling, in which the main characters are Sound, Reason, and Custom. The history ends with the introduction of a fourth character, Art, who systematises and writes down the rules of spelling which have been hammered out by Custom. This final phase is the great age of a language, when it is 'fined' and regulated. Such was Greek in the age of Demosthenes, and Latin in the age of Cicero. And such, Mulcaster asserts, is English in his own day. He himself is the agent of Art, codifying the rules of English spelling.

Mulcaster has a long defence of custom, arguing that the attacks on it depend on a semantic ambiguity, a 'duble name'. Custom, properly so called, is 'a great and naturall gouernour' of language. The twenty-four letters of the traditional alphabet are sufficient for the spelling of English: they have been sufficient for 'the best, and brauest tungs'. All peoples have the same speech organs, so the same set of letters will serve for all languages. There are indeed some deficiencies in the existing system of English spelling, and some reformation is needed. But there is no need for radical change, like the introduction of new letters or the attempt to make spelling purely phonetic. Such change is undesirable.

Mulcaster then gives in detail his rules for English spelling, and an alphabetical word list containing about 8,500 items. His spellings differ from ours in several ways. He has no *j*, only *i*. He does not use *u* and *v* to distinguish vowel and consonant. Final *-ie* is used where we have *-y* (e.g. *hostilitie*). Final *-ll* is used in unstressed syllables, where we have *-l* (e.g. *equall*). Nevertheless, well over half the spellings in his list are identical with ours. If we disregard the conventions for *i/j* and *u/v*, the proportion becomes much higher.

THE CLASSICAL FALLACY

In examining the rise of English to eloquence, we have come across various different attitudes to language. Many of these exemplify what Lyons (1968) calls 'the classical fallacy'. Under this term, Lyons groups two misconceptions about language, which he traces back to the Greek scholars of the Alexandrian period. The first concerns the relation between written and spoken language: the written language is the centre of interest, and there is a tendency for it to be regarded as primary, and the spoken language as secondary and derivative. In any case, no consistent distinction is drawn between sounds and the letters used to represent them. The second misconception concerns 'purity', and the way languages change. It is assumed that the literary language of some earlier age is more 'correct' than the current colloquial language, and that the 'purity' of a language is maintained by the educated and 'corrupted' by the illiterate.

The second assumption is behind many of the Early Modern arguments about eloquence, and especially about regulation. The ideal literary languages looked back to as models are the Greek of Demosthenes and the Latin of Cicero. Later forms of Greek and Latin are regarded as corruptions, especially Medieval Latin, which is thought to be particularly barbarous. The hope was that a regulated English language could be produced, to vie with classical Greek and Latin. This would be a literary language based on the usage of the educated (usually meaning the gentry). Uneducated usage (often including that of the citizenry) was dismissed as 'vulgar' and 'barbarous'.

The other assumption, about the primacy of the written language, is also very common. It comes out in all sorts of ways. In rhetoric, there was a figure called paroemion. A typical definition of it is the one given by Henry Peacham:

> Parœmion, when many wordes beginninge with one letter, are set in one sentence, thus, this mischieuous Money make many men merueylous mad.

Peacham says 'letter', but he means 'speech sound'. He gives many further examples, and in all of them the letters in question represent the same phoneme. He has no examples like *cold/centre/child*, though these all begin with the same letter.

Another example of the confusion between sounds and letters is seen in Ben Jonson's English grammar. Its first section deals with 'Letters, and their powers'. He lists the twenty-four letters of the English alphabet, and continues:

> All *Letters* are either *Vowells* or *Consonants*: and, are principally
> knowne by their powers. The *Figure* is an Accident.
>
> A *Vowell* will be pronounced by it selfe: A *Consonant*, not without
> the helpe of a *Vowell*, either before, or after.
>
> The *receiued* Vowells *in our tongue, are a. e. i. o. u.*
>
> Consonants be either *Mutes*, and close the sound, as in
> *b.c.d.g.k.p.q.t.* Or, *Halfe Vowells*, and open it, as *f.l.m.n.r.s.x.z.*

Jonson acknowledges the difference between symbol and sound, in his distinction between 'figure' (shape of the written symbol) and 'power' (what the symbol stands for). In practice, however, he confuses the two. Characteristically, he starts from the written symbols, not from the sounds of the spoken language. He defines a vowel in terms of pronunciation (capable of being pronounced by itself), but immediately gives a list of the English vowels which is a list of alphabetical symbols, not of speech sounds (for the number of vowel phonemes in English in his time was much greater than five). Similarly, he divides the consonants into two groups according to their mode of articulation: they are either stops ('Mutes') or continuants ('Halfe Vowells'). But the lists which follow are of alphabetical symbols, not of phonemes. Among the stops, *c*, *k*, and *q* can all represent /k/. Among the continuants, there is nothing to represent /v/, its symbol *u* having already been listed under the vowels. The symbol *x* does not belong to either category, since it represents /ks/ or /gz/, a stop followed by a continuant. It could also be argued that *c* ought to be added to the first category, since it can represent /s/, and that *i* ought to be added to the first, since it can represent /dʒ/. In neither group is any provision made for the consonants normally represented by the digraphs *ch*, *sh*, and *th*.

There are two obvious ways of describing the relationship between sounds and symbols in a writing system. You can give a list of graphemes, and say what each can represent. Or you can give a list of phonemes, and say how each of them can be represented graphically. Jonson does neither of these things, but something which is a confusion of the two. It is a confusion typical of those under the spell of the classical fallacy.

The reformers who want to introduce phonetic spelling, like Hart, are less liable to this kind of confusion. But even Hart, as we have seen, is led astray by the five vowel symbols of the Latin alphabet. He is very insistent, too, on the 'auncient powers' of the letters, as if each letter had a 'proper' sound that it stood for, its original or traditional one. Moreover, although he distinguishes between sound and symbol, he does not develop a terminology to clarify this distinction. He uses *vowel* to mean both 'vowel' (speech sound) and 'vowel symbol' (letter), and *diphthong* to mean both 'diphthong' (glide vowel) and 'digraph' (group of two letter-symbols). The reader therefore has to make a constant effort of interpretation.

Nevertheless, the work of people like Hart did something to weaken the classical fallacy, by focusing interest on the spoken language. And in the seventeenth century there were some very good English phoneticians, like John Wallis and William Holder and Christopher Cooper. They were concerned, not with spelling reform, but with the mechanisms of speech production and with phonological theory, and they helped to lay the foundations for later linguistic science. There were other forces working against the classical fallacy: the rise of comparative linguistic studies; an increasing interest in the history of English; the spread of scientific ideas; and the influence of new philosophical ideas, as in the works of Descartes, Hobbes, Locke. They did not undermine the classical fallacy completely, for it still exists, but they did introduce some modifications in people's attitudes to language.

ATTITUDES TO ENGLISH

During the eModE period, the linguistic horizons of Western Europe were widened. During the Middle Ages, Latin had been not only the language of scholarship, but also the main subject of linguistic analysis, even Greek and Hebrew being relatively neglected. In the Early Modern period there was increased interest in Greek and Hebrew, partly because of the concern for biblical translation. Moreover, the Discoveries introduced Europeans to hitherto unknown languages, like those of America. Increased worldwide communication (by trade, missionary activity, colonisation) led to a closer knowledge of Chinese, Japanese, and the languages of India. Ultimately this was to lead to a knowledge of traditions of linguistic analysis different from the Graeco-Roman one, notably the traditions of Sanskrit and Chinese scholarship. At the same time, the prestige of the European vernaculars had risen, and attempts were made to describe and analyse them. English people in the seventeenth century, consequently, were in a position to know about a much greater variety of languages than their medieval ancestors.

This fact is illustrated by a book published in 1660, called *A Battle-Door for Teachers and Professors to Learn Singular and Plural*. It was written by George Fox, John Stubs, and Benjamin Furly. Its object was to justify the Quaker habit of invariably using *thou* as the singular pronoun of address, never *you*. Its method is to demonstrate that numerous languages make a distinction between singular and plural, and in particular between a singular second-person pronoun and a plural one. It is argued that the singular/plural distinction in the second-person pronouns is a natural and original one. Languages that have departed from it (like English, French, and Spanish) have degenerated through pride and ambition.

The number of languages mentioned in the book is enormous, and examples are given from about twenty-five of them. The languages exemplified include the classical languages, and most modern European languages, including Celtic ones. Languages from outside Europe include Turkish, Syriac, Arabic, Ethiopic, Coptic, Armenian, and 'the *East Indie* language'. No Dravidian language is quoted, nor is Chinese. The languages cited do, however, include a number of non-Indo-European ones (for example Arabic, Hungarian, Turkish). The book illustrates the expansion of linguistic horizons. Moreover, despite its sectarian argument, it is a comparative grammar of a kind.

In the long run, the knowledge of non-Indo-European languages was to undermine the central position of Latin in linguistic analysis. In the seventeenth century we see the beginnings of this process.

HISTORICAL STUDIES

The period also sees the rise of historical attitudes to language, and an interest in the history of the English language. This interest is exemplified in the brief histories of English which often appear in seventeenth-century grammars and dictionaries.

Historical philology arose in the Renaissance from the need of humanist scholars to establish satisfactory texts of the classics. Techniques were developed for distinguishing between texts of different periods and by different authors, and for explicating or emending obscure passages. In the fifteenth century a good deal of humanist energy was devoted to this basic work. Later, as the prestige of the vernaculars rose, these techniques were applied also to them.

In the Early Modern period, an awareness of linguistic change is normal among people who write about language. Their attitude to change, however, is not usually value-free. Change is often seen as corruption or degeneration, though a language could also improve, as English was thought to have done in the late sixteenth century. One common view was that change in languages (as in societies) was cyclical. There was a recurring cycle of improvement – perfection – decay. This is sometimes the significance, in eModE usage, of the word *revolution*. When people talked about 'the great revolutions of time', they were referring, not to cataclysmic events, but to circular processes of change. From the seventeenth century onwards, the cyclical view of history was increasingly challenged by the idea of progress. Bacon, for example, emphasised the improvements that had taken place in the mechanical arts, and looked forward to a world like that of his *New Atlantis* (1627), in which scientific research would be used to alleviate humankind's lot. But in the seventeenth century the doctrine of progress had little effect on people's views on language. English had improved, but it might degenerate again if care were not taken.

Views of cyclic change and of progress both involve evaluation: a language is in some sense better at one period than at another. One thing likely to undermine this kind of evaluation is a more detailed knowledge of the history of the language. In the Early Modern period, this kind of knowledge increased considerably. In particular, a good deal of attention was given to Old English, or 'Saxon' as it was then usually called. (Sometimes it was called 'English Saxon'. The term 'Anglo-Saxon', though it existed, was not common before the eighteenth century.) It was in the seventeenth century that the foundations of Old English studies were laid. Scholars like Sir Henry Spelman and William Lisle taught themselves to read the language. Manuscripts were collected, as in the library of Sir Robert Cotton, which contained nearly a thousand volumes of manuscripts of various periods. OE texts were published. Glossaries were built up, and led to the first OE dictionary, published by William Somner in 1659. In 1689, George Hickes published the first grammar of Old English. In the course of the century, a whole language and literature, that of pre-Conquest England, was recovered and made available to the modern world.

One of the impulses that led to the development of Old English studies was the rise in the Tudor period of an interest in history and in antiquarianism, partly motivated by the need to justify the Tudor state. The link is seen in Sir Thomas Smith's *De Republica Anglorum*, published posthumously in 1583. It is about the political institutions of Elizabethan England, but Smith has a sense of history, including linguistic history. He sometimes discusses the etymologies and earlier meanings of words that he uses, such as *king*, *knight*, and *yeoman*. He gives earlier English forms of such words, like OE *cyning*, and also the cognate forms in other languages. Mainly, however, it was the antiquarians of late Elizabethan and Jacobean times, like Camden and Spelman, who led the Saxon movement. Simply to understand the documents that they unearthed, they had to grapple with the earlier stages of the language.

The motives for studying Old English were therefore intertwined with the various motives behind the cultivation of historiography and antiquarianism. One of these motives was ecclesiastical. Archbishop Matthew Parker (1504–75), who more than any other single person initiated the study of Old English, wanted to demonstrate the continuity of the Church of England. This led him to study the records of the Anglo-Saxon church. Many of the antiquarians of the Jacobean and Caroline age, like John Selden, were motivated by the desire to support Parliament against the royal prerogative. The argument was that the English legal system was descended from Anglo-Saxon law, not from the laws of William the Conqueror. Thus the Saxon movement is linked with what Hill (1958) has called the 'Norman Yoke' theory of English history. Yet others were motivated by a protestant desire to vindicate biblical translation. One of these was William Lisle, who in his *Saxon Treatise* (1623) published a text by Ælfric.

In his preface, Lisle proclaims the doctrinal purpose of the book: to refute those who allow no Scripture in the vulgar tongues, or hold it but a 'new come doctrine'. He attacks both Catholics and puritans. He praises the 'Saxon' bibles for their clarity, which shows up the obscurity and 'fustian inkhorn terms' of some recent translations. He regrets the loss of the many native words which have been replaced by loans, but agrees that we cannot now revive the Old English words. He praises the excellence of the English language, which lacks only a grammar. He then gives six reasons for studying earlier forms of English: 1. To make known to the world that our Saxon ancestors had the Scriptures and books of divinity in the mother tongue. 2. So that when necessary we know the etymologies of words and names now used. False etymologies have been used in arguments about the antiquity of our universities. 3. To understand the right meaning of our old laws, which often shed light on the new. 4. So that we can declare to all people the true meaning of their titles, charters, privileges, territories, and precincts. 5. To understand the meaning of Christian names. 6. To decide controversies among heralds and antiquaries, for example about the meanings of words like *alderman*, *thane*, and *wapentake*.

This mix, including as it does the ecclesiastical, the political, the legal, the linguistic, the historical, and the antiquarian, probably gives a fair idea of the variety of drives behind the Saxon movement.

Lisle's book also illustrates the effort and devotion needed by the pioneers. He explains in his preface how by great labour he had taught himself to read Old English. First he had learnt High and Low German. Then he had read all the old books in English that he could find. At first it was very difficult, but gradually he managed to work backwards in time, until finally he was able to read Old English.

The Ælfric text that Lisle publishes is quite a substantial one. It is set in what must be a specially designed font, imitating Old English manuscript letters. Facing the text Lisle gives his own translation of it. The labour involved in producing this work, in the absence of such aids as grammars and dictionaries, must have been prodigious.

As the early texts were studied, people became clearer about the early history of the English and their language, and about the relationship of English to the other Germanic languages. A clear statement on these matters is found in Richard Verstegan's *Restitution of Decayed Intelligence* (1605). This is a work about the origins and early history of the English nation and the English language. Verstegan insists that the ancestors of the English are the Anglo-Saxons, and not, as so many people seem to imagine, the Britons. The descendants of the Britons are the Welsh. The Anglo-Saxons were just one branch of a Teutonic people who occupied a large part of northern Europe, and English is related to High and Low German, Dutch, and the Scandinavian languages. There was an ancestral Teutonic language from which all these languages evolved. This came about by divergent development. This was similar to the process by which regional dialects have arisen in English. By a similar process of change, Italian, French, and Spanish all evolved from Latin. Verstegan understands, moreover, that changes take place in a language even if there is no influence from outside. In Early Modern times, it is commonly assumed that the main cause of linguistic change is the influence of one language on another, especially when one people conquers another. This assumption is made by Bentley in 1699 when he discusses the possibility of making the English language immutable (p. 75 above). Verstegan is quite advanced in 1605 when he asserts that many changes in languages grow and increase 'within themselues'.

As we see in Verstegan, a study of the Old English records led to a denial that Britons had founded the English tradition. A critical examination of the early documents exploded the myths about Trojans, Brutus, King Arthur, and Celtic origins generally. But the Tudors had cultivated their Welsh ancestry and the Celtic legends as part of their mystique. James I continued this policy: it was no accident that Ancient British and Trojan material played a prominent part in the courtly masques and entertainments of Elizabeth I and James I. An attack on theories of Celtic origins for the English nation was an attack on part of the mythology of the ruling dynasty. Moreover, this tied in with parliamentarian arguments of the 'Norman Yoke' type. Verstegan himself seems to have had no political motives, but it is not surprising that his Saxonist ideas were taken up by other people, as the conflict between King and Parliament developed. As a consequence, there was a period in the first half of the seventeenth century during which the authorities tended to regard antiquarian and Anglo-Saxon studies as something subversive.

SCIENCE AND LANGUAGE

The seventeenth century saw the rise of modern science, the New Philosophy which, Donne says in a famous poem, 'calls all in doubt'. English science, with its empirical approach, its insistence on observation, its scepticism about traditional theories, and its use of mechanical and mathematical models, inevitably affected attitudes to language, though slowly.

In *The Advancement of Learning* (1605), the propagandist for the 'new philosophy', Francis Bacon, carried out a survey of all fields of knowledge. The object was to show where there were deficiencies, and so to provide a large-scale programme for research. He has a section on human communication, which he calls *Tradition* or *Delivery*. He points out that speech and writing are not the only means of human communication. Barbarous peoples who lack a common language often carry on commerce by means of gestures. There are cultures that, instead of letters and words, use ideographs, symbols that express 'notions' directly. Bacon calls these *characters real*, and thinks that Chinese writing provides an example. The study of such systems of symbols is one of the branches of learning which is deficient. So Bacon is advocating study which will lead to a general theory of signs. In the *De Augmentis Scientiarum* (1623), which is an expansion, in Latin, of the second part of the *Advancement*, Bacon has an additional passage (in the section on ciphers) which states that human communication can be carried on in any medium which permits of 'two differences', what today we call a binary contrast.

On speech and writing, Bacon is more complacent. The science concerning these is grammar, and it is not deficient. In any case, grammar is not very useful in a mother tongue: it is more useful for foreign languages, especially the learned ones. Grammar has two functions: 1. the popular, for the rapid learning of foreign languages and the understanding of authors, and 2. the philosophical, which deals with the relationship between words and reason. The latter has been handled in a rather scattered way, and needs to be brought together as a science in its own right, but it is not deficient. In the *De Augmentis*, Bacon adds that we need a study of the various properties of different languages, showing in what points each excels and each fails. In this way the various languages could be enriched by mutual exchanges, and moreover their different beauties could be combined (apparently in a perfect universal language). Bacon adds a passage remarking that nobody has studied the intonation of speech. And yet, he says, almost all humankind drop the voice at the end of a period, and raise it in asking a question.

Later in the century, as we have seen, the influence of the scientific movement appears in the work of the English phoneticians, and in the more empirical approach to grammar found in John Wallis, who was a founder-member of the Royal Society.

The scientific movement had another effect: it led to the cultivation of a plain style of writing, and a suspicion of the ornaments of rhetoric. After a hundred years or more had been spent in the pursuit of eloquence in English, there were people in the late seventeenth century who suggested that eloquence was a bad thing. Earlier, there had been an anti-rhetorical movement in some puritan circles. Preachers like William Perkins (1558–1602) cultivated a simple style of preaching, free from ornament. By contrast, anti-puritans like John Donne cultivated a high rhetorical style. But in the later seventeenth century it was above all the natural scientists who advocated plainness and led the attack on rhetoric.

The germ of the attitude can be seen in Bacon. One of the three kinds of learning that he attacks in the *Advancement* is 'delicate learning'. This, he says, consists in valuing style more than substance, a fault of the Renaissance humanists. But Bacon does not attack rhetoric: his own style is that of a writer trained in the rhetorical tradition, and he refers to rhetoric as 'A Science excellent, and excellently well laboured'. But the admirers of Bacon, the chemists and physicists and astronomers of the Restoration period, press the attack home.

The most famous expression of this anti-rhetorical spirit occurs in *The History of the Royal-Society of London*, by Bishop Thomas Sprat. It is a section on the manner of discourse of the members of the Royal Society, about which, Sprat says, they have been most solicitous. If they had not been watchful, the whole vigour and spirit of their design would have been eaten away by the luxury and redundance of speech.

> The ill effects of this superfluity of talking, have already overwhelm'd most other *Arts* and *Professions*; insomuch, that when I consider the means of *happy living*, and the causes of their corruption, I can hardly forbear recanting what I said before; and concluding that *eloquence*

ought to be banish'd out of all *civil Societies*, as a thing fatal to Peace and good Manners.

So much for eloquence! Sprat concedes, however, that we cannot abolish it entirely, otherwise the good would be at the mercy of the wicked, since the rhetorical arts are available to both. Originally, no doubt, the ornaments of speaking were an admirable instrument in the hands of the wise. Now, however, they have degenerated, and are in open defiance against reason, and in correspondence with the passions.

> Who can behold, without indignation, how many mists and uncertainties, these specious *Tropes* and *Figures* have brought on our Knowledge … Of all the Studies of men, nothing may be sooner obtain'd, than this vicious abundance of *Phrase*, this trick of *Metaphors*, this volubility of *Tongue*, which makes so great a noise in the world.

What Sprat wants is conciseness and an absence of ornament. His indignation is aroused by the devices of rhetoric, and above all by the figures: the arch-villain is metaphor. The evil has become so inveterate, he continues, that in most branches of learning he despairs of a cure. Only the members of the Royal Society have taken adequate safeguards against it:

> They have therefore been most rigorous in putting in execution, the only Remedy, that can be found for this *extravagance*: and that has been, a constant Resolution, to reject all the amplifications, digressions, and swellings of style: to return back to the primitive purity, and shortness, when men deliver'd so many *things*, almost in an equal number of *words*. They have exacted from all their members, a close, naked, natural way of speaking; positive expressions; clear senses; a native easiness: bringing all things as near the Mathematical plainness, as they can: and preferring the language of Artizans, Countrymen, and Merchants, before that, of Wits, or Scholars.

Sprat is concerned here with speech, but the same ideal held for the written language: simplicity, naturalness, clarity, conciseness, a rejection of all ornament. It is an admirable ideal for scientific prose, and indeed for many types of prose discourse. Sprat, however, seems to think that it is the ideal kind of language for all purposes. Not everybody agreed with him, and the rhetorical tradition continued to flourish in many kinds of writing. What we are witnessing is a bifurcation of the English literary tradition. Henceforth there will be a plain style for matters of fact and judgement, and a rhetorical style for matters of fiction and fancy. Increasingly, the plain style will come to be considered the norm.

FORM AND CONTENT

The attack on rhetoric is also, indirectly, an attack on another belief widely held in Early Modern times: the belief that form and content are separate and separable. People believed that there is a certain sense, or substance, independent of the words in which it is expressed. The same substance can be 'clothed' in various different sets of words. This theory is reflected in the neo-classical view of the function of poetry. The end of poetry is to teach and delight, or to teach by delighting. The teaching is done by the substance, the content of the poem. The delighting is done by its form, its beautiful words. Form and content are handled by different branches of rhetoric. The substance of a work is decided or discovered by the process of invention, and this substance is then given form by the procedures of disposition and elocution. An example of the way people thought of form and content as separable is seen in Sidney's *Defence of Poesie* (1595). Sidney refers to the traditional ballad of Chevy Chase:

> Certainly I must confesse mine owne barbarousnesse, I neuer heard the old Song of *Percy* and *Douglas*, that I found not my heart mooued more then with a Trumpet; and yet it is sung but by some blinde Crowder ['fiddler'], with no rougher voyce, then rude stile: which being so euill apparelled in the dust and Cobwebbes of that vnciuill age, what would it worke, trimmed in the gorgious eloquence of *Pindare*?

With admirable honesty, Sidney admits that the ballad moves him deeply. What moves him, he thinks, is the content of the ballad, despite the fact that it is 'apparelled' in such a 'rude stile'. How much more moving would it be if it were 'trimmed' in the eloquent language of Pindar.

The belief in the separability of form and content made people confident about translating from one language to another: it was simply a question of dressing the author's substance in a different set of words. This attitude is found in Dryden. In the preface to his *Fables* he defends himself for having translated Chaucer into modern English. He has not made this translation, he says, for 'some old *Saxon* Friends' who are capable of reading Chaucer in the original.

> I made it for their sakes who understand Sense and Poetry, as well as they; when that Poetry and Sense is put into Words which they understand.

The 'sense' and 'poetry' are an unchanged core, independent of the particular words they happen to be expressed in: Dryden has simply given them a new form. He does concede, however, that something is lost in all translation.

The demand for a plain style is not necessarily an attack on this theory of form and content. It might simply be a demand that one particular type of form should be used for apparelling the substance. In practice, however, those who attack rhetoric, like Sprat, tend to suggest that the substance becomes distorted, or even destroyed, when a figurative style is used. This implies that a change in form produces a change in content. Nevertheless, the neo-classical view of style remained dominant through most of the eighteenth century. From the late seventeenth century onwards, however, there was a tendency for literary devices to be thought of as decoration. The plain style gave the substance as it really was, whereas poetry added frills.

LANGUAGE AND THE PHILOSOPHERS

The English philosophers of the seventeenth century were influenced by the rise of modern science, and in general they encourage an empirical and naturalistic approach to language. Like the scientists, too, they are concerned about clarity of expression. One recurrent theme is the ambiguity of language, and the ways in which it can cause confused thinking. Bacon, Hobbes, and Locke all deal at some length with the traps set by language.

For Bacon, the misuse of words is one of the 'idols' that mislead people, the one he calls 'idols of the market place'. In the *Novum Organum*, he says that words mislead in two ways. There are names for things which do not exist, like *Fortune* and *the Prime Mover*. And there are words which are ambiguous without people realising the fact, ill-defined and shifting words. It would be prudent to reduce words to order by means of definitions, as mathematicians do, though this is not a complete cure, because the definitions themselves consist of words. The real cure lies in the method of forming notions and axioms. It is necessary to begin with particulars, and rise by gradual and unbroken ascent to the most general axioms of all, whereas the usually accepted method is just the opposite.

Thomas Hobbes was not much impressed by the scientists, and thought that the empirical method was extremely limited. Nevertheless his own world-view – determinist, materialist, mechanical – was influenced by the 'new philosophy'. His naturalist approach can be seen in what he says in *Leviathan* (1651) about the origin of language, which he calls 'the most noble and profitable invention of all other'. Language is not something God-given, but is one of the inventions of humankind. It is true that, in the Garden of Eden, God taught Adam how to name the creatures. But the rest of language was a human invention. Moreover, at the Tower of Babel people lost the power of language, and were obliged to invent it again gradually in different regions of the world under the pressure of their needs.

Hobbes lists four main functions of language, but corresponding to each function, he says, there is an abuse. The abuses are: 1. ambiguity of words, by which people deceive themselves; 2. the metaphorical use of words, by which they deceive others; 3. lying; and 4. the use of language to grieve another. The cure for ambiguity, Hobbes says, lies in clear and strict definition. Like Bacon, he is concerned about meaningless words: his examples include *entity*, *intentionality*, and *quiddity* (terms used by the scholastic philosophers). He is particularly scathing about what he claims are self-contradictory phrases, like *incorporeal substance*. This was an expression used by traditional philosophers, who said that body was corporeal substance, while spirit was incorporeal substance. But there is no place for spirit in Hobbes's universe, which by definition is entirely material.

> The Word *Body*, in the most generall acceptation, signifieth that which filleth, or occupyeth some certain room, or imagined place; and dependeth not on the imagination, but is a reall part of that we call the *Vniverse*. For the *Vniverse*, being the Aggregate of all Bodies, there is no reall part thereof that is not also *Body*; nor any thing properly a *Body*, that is not also part of (that Aggregate of all *Bodies*) the *Vniverse* ... And according to this acceptation of the word, *Substance* and *Body*, signifie the same thing; and therefore *Substance incorporeall* are words, which when they are joined together, destroy one another, as if a man should say, an *Incorporeall Body*.

Such expressions, Hobbes says, are usually made up from Greek and Latin names. If you translate them into plain English you see their absurdity. His technique, therefore, is often one of paraphrase, as when he here argues that *incorporeal substance* simply means 'bodiless body'. Here we see a link between the inkhorn controversy and the concern of the seventeenth-century scientists and philosophers with clarity of expression.

In *An Essay Concerning Human Understanding* (1690), John Locke argues that most of the disputes that agitate humankind are not about matters of substance, but are merely verbal, caused by the uncertain or mistaken signification of words.

> I am apt to imagine, that were the imperfections of Language, as the Instrument of Knowledge, more throughly weighed, a great many of the Controversies, that make such a noise in the World, would of themselves cease; and the way to Knowledge, and, perhaps, Peace too, lie a great deal opener than it does.

Like Hobbes, he discusses the abuses of language – the use of meaningless words, the use of words in shifting meanings, an affected obscurity, the mistaking of words for things, the failure to define terms clearly, the use of figurative language. But he also discusses, separately, the imperfections of language itself. It is not just that people misuse it: it also has certain inherent deficiencies. Language has two purposes: for recording our own thoughts, and for communicating our thoughts to others. It is in the second function that there are imperfections. These are unimportant for the ordinary everyday things of life. It is in the philosophical use of language that they are serious, when we try to arrive at certain and undoubted truths in our search after true knowledge. These imperfections are described in the framework of Locke's theory of Ideas, the mental representations which he believes constitute our knowledge, which words should correspond to. Since linguistic signs are arbitrary, they may not evoke exactly the same ideas in the hearer as in the speaker. This is especially likely in four cases: 1. where the ideas are very complex, as in moral words; 2. where the complex of ideas is manmade, without anything corresponding to it in nature, like *murder* and *sacrilege*; 3. where the thing referred to does exist in nature, but has many different qualities, so that its name signifies different things to different people; and 4. where the signification of a word, and the real essence of the thing, are not exactly the same. There are remedies for the deficiencies and abuses of language, though they are not easy. We must never use a word without an idea for which it stands, and this idea must be clear and distinct. We must as far as possible use words in conformity with normal usage, so that other people do not misunderstand us. If we are obliged to give a word a new meaning, or to invent a new technical term, we must declare its meaning plainly. Finally, we must be careful to use the same word constantly in the same sense.

A PHILOSOPHICAL LANGUAGE

The emphasis of seventeenth-century thinkers on the deficiencies of natural languages led to attempts to produce an artificial 'philosophical' language which would be free from these defects. There were other factors which encouraged such attempts. One was the development of mathematics, a subject often referred to by people who demanded clarity of definition and consistency of usage. Another was the gradual decline of Latin as an international language. Scientists felt the need for an international medium of communication. So did some protestant divines, who hoped that a philosophical language would end sectarian disputes by removing ambiguity from key terms. There may have been influence from Chinese, which became better-known in Western Europe during the century. Chinese writing was thought to be ideographic, and so to provide a model for an artificial language in which symbols would stand directly for ideas. There were other influences. Salmon (1966) calls attention to the part played by shorthand, by codes and ciphers (especially cultivated during the civil wars), by Cabbalistic ideas, and by the methods often used in grammars to classify lexical items. Perhaps we should add what Chomsky (1966) calls 'Cartesian Linguistics'. This was a school of thought which arose in France under the influence of Descartes, and which held the view that there is a universal grammar, a 'deep' grammar that underlies the surface grammar of all languages. This view is expressed in the so-called Port Royal Grammar, the *Grammaire générale et raisonnée* (1660). This emanated from a group of scholars connected with the Jansenist community at Port Royal des Champs. It was well known in England, the French text being published in London in 1664.

Bacon had mentioned the possibility of a universal language, called attention to Chinese writing, and advocated the development of a general theory of signs. But it was in the 1630s that widespread discussion of the idea began, both in England and on the continent, and the debate continued until about 1670. A number of people tried to produce a universal language, or at least a sketch of one, and in England the movement culminated in a work by John Wilkins, Dean of Ripon and a Fellow of the Royal Society. It was called *An Essay towards a Real Character, and a Philosophical Language* (1668), and was published under the auspices of the Royal Society. It is a large folio volume of over 600 pages, and is heroic in scope. It proposes nothing less than a complete categorisation of all possible notions or meanings, and the devising of a system of symbols to represent these meanings. The word *Character* in the title means 'set of written signs'. A *Real Character* is a set that refers directly to objects or notions, not to linguistic forms, a set of ideographs. The use of these ideographs must conform to a universal ('philosophical') grammar. This dictates the order in which the signs occur in a message, and provides additional signs to indicate grammatical relationships. If a phonological system is added, prescribing a pronunciation for each sign, the result is a 'Philosophical Language'.

The *Essay* contains four main sections. In the first, Wilkins considers natural languages, and discusses their deficiencies. In the second he gives his complete categorisation of objects and notions, in what he calls his 'philosophical tables'. In the third he sets out a philosophical grammar. In the fourth he presents a 'real character' and a 'philosophical language'. In a final chapter, he compares his universal language with natural languages, especially Latin, and argues that it is superior because of its greater regularity, clarity, and economy. At the end of the work is a substantial dictionary of English, in which each word is classified according to the principles of the philosophical tables in Section 2.

The longest section is the second, which gives a categorisation of 'notions'. It divides up meanings by a tree-structure. The first division is between General and Special, and by a continuing process of subdivision Wilkins arrives at forty Genera. These form the primary set of categories in the scheme, and include such things as discourse, world, metal, herb, fish, magnitude, manners, motion, possessions, and civil relation. Each of these genera is then divided into species, and the process of subdivision continues until provision has been made for all the distinctions required. The total number of terminal items is about 4,000, many of them being arranged in contrasting pairs. Most of the terminal items are given in the form of nouns, but they are intended as purely semantic units, independent of grammatical categories.

In the fourth section Wilkins proposes a real character, a set of written symbols corresponding to the categories of Section 2. He devises forty arbitrary symbols to represent the forty basic genera of the tables. These bear no resemblance to the traditional letters of the alphabet. Each consists of a long horizontal stroke with some distinguishing mark in the middle, for example a short line projecting above or below at some particular angle. The species within the genus is shown by a mark added at the left-hand end of the stroke, and the subspecies by one added at the right-hand end. If necessary, the sub-subspecies can be shown by a loop added at the right-hand end. In this way it is possible to represent all the 4,000 terminal items in the philosophical tables. Various other loops and hooks can be added to the symbol to indicate grammatical features (part of speech, plurality, active or passive, and so on). There is an additional set of symbols to represent grammatical words, such as pronouns and prepositions.

Having explained his real character, Wilkins proposes a phonological system for it. Each genus is represented by a consonant followed by a vowel. For example, the genus 'tree' is *go*. The species is shown by the addition of another consonant. For example, the fourth species of a genus is always represented by *t*. In the case of tree, the fourth species is 'glandiferous and coniferous trees', which are therefore represented by *got*. The subspecies is shown by the addition of another vowel: 'evergreen coniferous trees with large cones' is *goti*. In this particular case, the subspecies contains two terminal items, 'cedar' and 'pine'. The second is distinguished from the first by the repetition of the medial consonant at the end of the word, so that 'cedar' is *goti* and 'pine' is *gotit*. In this way, with various refinements and complications, phonetic values are assigned to all the elements of the real character, including the grammatical words. Thus is produced a speakable universal language, though Wilkins concedes that speakers of different languages will interpret his alphabetical symbols differently.

I must add that, for simplicity of presentation, I have departed slightly from Wilkins's own terminology. What I have called *species*, he calls *(subdivision according to peculiar) differences*. And what I have called *subspecies*, he calls *species*.

When we consider this remarkable book, we may be struck (as often in the seventeenth century) by the combination of modernity and antiquity. The whole enterprise is devoted to the advancement of learning, and is undertaken under the auspices of the Royal Society. Yet Wilkins's categorisation of knowledge somewhat reminds one both of Aristotelian logic and of medieval encyclopedism. To the modern reader, perhaps the most staggering thing is the assumption that the number of possible 'notions' in the universe is finite. To do Wilkins justice, he does say that there are some things that his philosophical tables cannot cover. They include things peculiar to one particular place or nation, such as titles of honour or of office, and legal terms, and also things which are continually changing, like fashions in clothes, games, foods, the tools of trades, and political and religious sects. But in spite of this qualification, he seems to think in terms of a universe in which there are certain fixed categories of objects and of notions, which are independent of the classificatory process carried out by language itself.

FURTHER READING

Many of the topics handled in this chapter are dealt with by Jones (1953), which rests on an admirable body of primary material. Useful anthologies of primary material are to be found in Craigie (1946), Tucker (1961), and Bolton & Crystal (1966–9).

On Caxton and the taste of his time, see Blake (1969). A detailed account of the curriculum of the Tudor grammar school will be found in Baldwin (1944). Sir Thomas Elyot's dispute with the physicians is discussed in Lehmberg (1960). The tastes, aspirations, and education of the citizen classes in the sixteenth century are examined by Wright (1935). For the sixteenth-century textbooks on the art of war, see Webb (1965). An account of the influence of the Reformers on the development of prose in the vernacular is given in Krapp (1915), the main interest of which is stylistic and literary. A good introduction to Renaissance rhetoric is provided by Vickers (1970); Joseph (1947) and Sonnino (1968) are more detailed.

On the early history of English dictionaries, see Starnes & Noyes (1946). An account of the Graeco-Latin grammatical tradition, and its development in England, is given by Michael (1970), while a general account of European linguistic theory in Early Modern times can be found in Chapter Five of Robins (1979). On the sixteenth-century antiquarians and historians, see McKisack (1971). The rise of medieval and Anglo-Saxon studies is described in Douglas (1939); this concentrates on the period 1660–1730, but has some material on the earlier period. On the 'Norman Yoke', and the political implications of Anglo-Saxon studies, see Hill (1958) and Brinkley (1967). On the puritan hostility to rhetoric, and the contrasting styles of puritan and High Anglican sermons, see Haller (1938). The motives behind a desire for a universal language are discussed by Salmon (1966).

Chapter Three

PHONOLOGY

In the Early Modern period, there was considerable variety of pronunciation, and probably more toleration of variety than in the couple of centuries that followed. Toleration was not complete, however, and disparaging references are often made to rustic, regional, and vulgar styles of pronunciation. Some people, clearly, were snobbish about class accents and regional accents. And, even though it was possible for members of the gentry to speak with a regional accent, there was one style of pronunciation that had especially high prestige. This, as we saw in Chapter One, was the accent of the court and of the 'better sort' in south-eastern England. This accent was sufficiently influential for us to regard it as a standard one, and it is this StE pronunciation that I shall be concerned with. It must be remembered, however, that this pronunciation was not universal among educated English people. Some poets, for example, use rhymes that depend on non-standard pronunciations. Moreover, there was considerable variety of pronunciation even within StE, and for many words there was more than one acceptable pronunciation.

It is impossible to have an exact knowledge of pronunciation in the pre-recording era, and we have to be content with reasonable approximations. For Early Modern English, however, we have quite strong evidence, which has been analysed in detail by numerous scholars, and notably by Dobson (1968). In addition to the various kinds of evidence which we have also for earlier periods, we have many descriptions of English pronunciation. In some cases these include accounts of articulatory movements, often with phonetic transcriptions of long passages of English. Such descriptions are found from the mid sixteenth century onwards, in the works of spelling reformers and phoneticians. These works are often marred by the influence of traditional spelling and traditional theories, but the best of them are of high quality.

Few people are in a position to study the primary evidence. Any educated person in the English-speaking world, however, has a large fund of information on the subject. We acquire this at school, when we learn how to spell. English spelling was not standardised until the end of the Early Modern period, but the spellings which then became accepted were ones which had taken shape a couple of centuries earlier. Modern spellings, therefore, are quite a good guide to StE pronunciations at the beginning of the Early Modern period. At school we learnt to distinguish in spelling between *ail* and *ale*, *laud* and *lord*, *meet* and *meat*, *write* and *right*. In doing so, we were learning about distinctions formerly made in pronunciation, if only we had the key to the code. Conversely, we learnt to use the same spelling for the vowels of *blood* and *food* and *good*, which did indeed formerly have the same vowel in pronunciation. The evidence of PresE spelling does, admittedly, fail us sometimes. A few of the distinctions of sixteenth-century English are not reflected in the spelling, and there are particular words which now have irregular pronunciations or unhistorical spellings. Nevertheless, it is surprising how often the present spelling of a word will lead us correctly to the eModE pronunciation, or at least to one common one.

THE VOWELS

I shall begin by considering the vowels. The starting point will be the situation in late Middle English, say about 1400. The variety of ME in question will be that which developed into the standard language of Early Modern times. In this language there were twenty vowel phonemes – seven long vowels, six short vowels, and seven diphthongs. I shall consider each of these phonemes in turn, tracing its development in eModE, and also indicating what it has become in present-day English. Unless the contrary is stated, the phonetic realisation postulated for a phoneme at any particular time refers to occurrences in stressed syllables.

The Long Vowels

The seven long-vowel phonemes of this form of ME were the following:

1. /i:/ 2. /e:/ 3. /ɛ:/ 4. /a:/ 5. /ɔ:/ 6. /o:/ 7. /u:/

ME /i:/ was a long close front vowel, with a quality like that of German *sie* or French *si*. ME /e:/ was a long half-close front vowel, like that of German *zehn*. ME /ɛ:/ was a long half-open front vowel, like that of French *faire* or German *fährt*. ME /a:/ was a long open front vowel, like that heard in Australian English *park*. ME /ɔ:/ was a long half-open back vowel, like that of PresE *law* (RP). ME /o:/ was a long half-close back vowel, like that of German *wo* or French *chose*. And ME /u:/ was a long close back vowel, like that of German *Uhr*. It will be understood that these suggested realisations of the seven ME phonemes are to be taken as approximations.

TABLE 3.1

The long-vowel phonemes of late Middle English

ME Phoneme	PresE Pronunciation	PresE Spellings	Examples
/iː/	/aɪ/	i, y, iCe, ie	child, fly, tide, pie
/eː/	/iː/	ee, ie	seed, field
/ɛː/	/iː/	ea, ei, eCe	heath, conceit, complete
/aː/	/eɪ/	aCe	make, dame
/ɔː/	/əʊ/	oa, oCe (o, oe)	boat, hope (so, both, foe)
/oː/	/uː/	oo (o, oCe)	food, goose (who, move)
/uː/	/aʊ/	ou, ow	house, how

We can usually tell what words these phonemes occurred in by consideration of the PresE pronunciation and spelling, as shown in Table 3.1. The first column lists the long-vowel phonemes of Middle English. The second column shows the regular development of each phoneme in Present-day English (RP). The third column shows the spellings normally found in Present-day English. Here the symbol C stands for 'any single consonant-symbol'. Spellings in brackets indicate less frequent forms.

Some spellings are found for more than one phoneme: *ie* is found for both ME /iː/ and ME /eː/, while the *o* and *oCe* spellings are found for both ME /ɔː/ and ME /oː/. In such cases the origin can be deduced from the PresE pronunciation. Often, the PresE pronunciation is not enough by itself to indicate the earlier pronunciation: *maid* and *say* did not have ME /aː/, nor did *soul* and *know* have ME /ɔː/, as we shall see later. In such cases the spelling provides a valuable clue. The spelling is also important for distinguishing between ME /ɛː/ and ME /eː/. Both have developed into PresE /iː/, but they were still separate phonemes until the late seventeenth century. In general, a consideration of both spelling and modern pronunciation provides the best guide to the earlier forms.

Of the seven long vowels of ME, four were front vowels, and three back, as shown in the vowel diagram in Figure 3.1. The diagram is somewhat schematic, the vowels being shown at exactly the close, half-close, half-open, and open positions, which is hardly likely to be exactly right. In the fifteenth, sixteenth and seventeenth centuries these vowels underwent a systematic change of realisation, often called the Great Vowel Shift, as indicated in the figure. They all moved into closer positions, except ME /iː/ and /uː/, which were already fully close: these became diphthongised. The process began with the close vowels. It was not a question of the open vowels becoming closer, and exerting pressure on those above. On the contrary, the first stage was

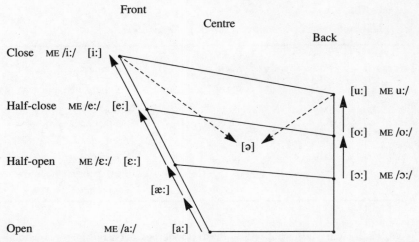

Figure 3.1. The Great Vowel Shift. The diagram shows the positions of the long vowels of late Middle English. The arrows show the way in which their realisations changed. In the case of the fully close vowels, the dotted lines show the changes in the starting-point of the diphthongs.

that /i:/ and /u:/ became diphthongs, which happened in the fifteenth century. This left spaces at the top of the diagram, into which the half-close vowels /e:/ and /o:/ drifted: this had happened by 1500. In the sixteenth and seventeenth centuries, the half-open and open vowels in their turn drifted into closer positions.

ME /i:/ and /u:/ probably became diphthongs quite early in the fifteenth century. At first the degree of diphthongisation was only slight, perhaps giving realisations like [ɪi] and [ʊu]. By 1500, however, it must have been quite considerable, because the two phonemes remained distinct from ME /e:/ and ME /o:/, which by this time had become realised as [i:] and [u:]. The exact quality of the diphthongs in the early sixteenth century is a matter of dispute. By the middle of the century, however, there is evidence to suggest that the starting-point of both diphthongs was the central vowel [ə], so that ME /i:/ was now [əɪ] and ME /u:/ was [əʊ] (or perhaps, as Dobson argues, [ʌʊ]). I shall assume that the normal sixteenth-century pronunciations were [əɪ] and [əʊ], so that *tide* and *fly* were pronounced [təɪd] and [fləɪ], while *house* and *now* were [həʊs] and [nəʊ]. Their later development to [aɪ] and [ɑʊ] took place in the second half of the seventeenth century.

After ME /i:/ and ME /u:/ had become diphthongs, ME /e:/ and /o:/ moved up into their places, and became realised as [i:] and [u:], which they remained. So *meet* was now [mi:t] and *food* was [fu:d]. As we shall see, some words with ME /o:/ underwent vowel-shortening in eModE, for example *good, flood*. The original vowel is indicated by the PresE spelling with *oo*.

At the beginning of the sixteenth century, ME /ɛ:/ and ME /ɔ:/ were still realised as half-open vowels, so that *meat* was [mɛːt] and *boat* was [bɔːt]. During the sixteenth century, however, they moved up to [eː] and [oː], and by 1600 pronunciations like [meːt] and [boːt] were common. In more conservative speech, however, the older pronunciations may have persisted well into the seventeenth century. The [oː] was subsequently diphthongised to [oʊ], but this did not happen until the late eighteenth century.

Until very late in the Early Modern period, ME /ɛː/ remained distinct from ME /eː/. In Shakespeare's time, *see* and *meet* were [siː] and [miːt], whereas *sea* and *meat* were [seː] and [meːt] (or, in conservative speech, [sɛː] and [mɛːt]). In some non-standard forms of English, however, probably including non-standard London speech, ME /ɛː/ had also developed into [iː], in late ME, so that *see* and *sea* were both [siː]. In the second half of the seventeenth century, the originally non-standard forms began to penetrate the standard language, so that some speakers pronounced *sea* and *meat* as [siː] and [miːt]. It is from this style of pronunciation that PresE pronunciation descends. Even at the end of the Early Modern period, however, there were still speakers who maintained the distinction between ME /ɛː/ and ME /eː/.

ME /aː/ was probably still realised as [aː] in 1500, but early in the sixteenth century it moved up to [æː], so that *make* and *dame* were pronounced [mæːk] and [dæːm] (with a vowel resembling the one often heard today in London speech in words like *bad* and *bag*). It continued to get closer, first becoming [ɛː] and later [eː]. By 1600, pronunciations like [mɛːk] and [dɛːm] were common, though the earlier pronunciation may have persisted for some time in conservative speech.

When ME /aː/ became [ɛː], it still remained distinct from ME /ɛː/, for the latter had by now moved up to [eː]. So in 1600, *mate* was [mɛːt] while *meat* was [meːt]. But ME /aː/ continued to get closer, and by the middle of the seventeenth century had become [eː], so that *make* and *dame* were commonly [meːk] and [deːm]. But for many speakers, ME /ɛː/ was still also [eː], so that the two phonemes coalesced. In this style of speech, therefore, *mate* and *meat* became homophones, both being pronounced [meːt]. This style of speech seems to have been common in StE in the late seventeenth and early eighteenth century. This is reflected in rhymes. For example, Dryden rhymes *make/speak* and *shame/dream*, Pope *shade/mead*, Swift *case/peace*.

Present-day pronunciation, however, is not descended from this style of speech. We have the same vowel in *meet* and *meat*, not in *meat* and *mate*. Our pronunciation comes down from the originally non-standard style in which ME /ɛː/ had coalesced with ME /eː/ in late Middle English, both being realised as [iː]. Between about 1650 and 1750, the two systems of pronunciation were competing. This is again reflected in rhymes. Besides having old-style rhymes, poets in the period also have 'modern' ones. For example, Dryden rhymes *speak/seek* and *dream/seem*, Pope *scene/green* and *conceive/believe*.

TABLE 3.2

Development of the Long Vowels

ME Phoneme	EARLY MODERN ENGLISH Stage 1	Stage 2	Stage 3	Pres E (RP)	Modern Spelling
/iː/	[təɪd]	[təɪd]	[taɪd]	/taɪd/	tide
/eː/	[griːn]	[griːn]	[griːn]	/griːn/	green
/ɛː/	[mɛːt]	[meːt]	[meːt], [miːt]	/miːt/	meat
/aː/	[mæːk]	[mɛːk]	[meːk]	/meɪk/	make
/ɔː/	[bɔːt]	[boːt]	[boːt]	/bəʊt/	boat
/oː/	[fuːd]	[fuːd]	[fuːd]	/fuːd/	food
/uː/	[həʊs]	[həʊs]	[haʊs]	/haʊs/	house

The change from one style of pronunciation to the other perhaps reflects social change. As merchants and aspiring citizens moved up into the gentry, they perhaps brought some of their pronunciations with them.

The 'new' style of pronunciation had become the standard one by about the middle of the eighteenth century, but we still have a few pronunciations from the earlier style: *break*, *great*, *steak*, *yea*. As their spellings suggest, these words all had ME /ɛː/, and were normally rhymed with other /ɛː/-words. For example, Surrey rhymes *great/beat*, Drayton *break/speak*, Dryden *great/seat*. The PresE pronunciation of these four words is perhaps a relic of the late seventeenth-century style of speech in which ME /ɛː/ had coalesced with ME /aː/, both being realised as [eː]. The [eː] from ME /aː/ has since become the diphthong [eɪ], but this did not happen until the end of the eighteenth century.

A summary of the development of the long vowels is given in Table 3.2, showing the pronunciation of specimen words. The changes in eModE are shown in three stages. Exact dates cannot be set for these stages, partly because different phonemes did not change at precisely the same time. Moreover, the times of the changes were different for different speakers, some having conservative pronunciations and others more advanced ones. It could be expected, too, that differences could occur even in the speech of a single speaker: more conservative pronunciations would be used in formal situations, and more advanced pronunciations in informal ones. Broadly speaking, however, Stage 1 pronunciations are normal sixteenth-century ones. Stage 2 pronunciations arise during the sixteenth century, and are common by about 1600. Stage 3 pronunciations arise in the seventeenth century, and are normal ones, even in conservative speech, by 1700.

Of the seven long vowels of late ME, two had become diphthongs before 1500, reducing the number to five. Yet another long vowel disappeared in the seventeenth century, when ME /ɛ:/ coalesced either with ME /a:/ or with ME /e:/. On the other hand, another long-vowel phoneme arose in eModE when the ME diphthong /ɑʊ/ developed into a pure long vowel. This was the fully open back rounded vowel [ɒ:], and fits neatly into the vowel diagram in Figure 3.1, making the pattern for the Great Vowel Shift more symmetrical. In accordance with that pattern, this vowel moved into a closer position, and has developed into PresE /ɔ:/, as in *law*, *laud*. In eModE there are no long vowels corresponding to PresE /ɑ:/ (as in *hard*, *father*) or to PresE /ɜ:/ (as in *bird*). These two phonemes did not arise in StE until the eighteenth century.

The Short Vowels

The six short-vowel phonemes of late ME were the following:

1. /ɪ/   2. /ɛ/   3. /a/   4. /ɔ/   5. /ʊ/   6. /ə/

Compared with the long vowels, these have changed little during the Modern English period.

ME /ɪ/ was probably a high front lax vowel, and has remained unchanged, giving PresE (RP) /ɪ/. Typical PresE spellings for words with ME /ɪ/ are *i* and *y*, as in *sit*, *pin*, *symbol*.

ME /ɛ/ has *e* as its usual present-day spelling, as in *set*, *bed*, *hedge*. In eModE it was realised as the half-open vowel [ɛ], similar to that heard in French *elle* or German *Bett*. This is opener than the vowel of present-day RP, which is between half-open and half-close, and commonly nearer to the latter. The change to a closer vowel probably began in the Early Modern period. The more open vowel [ɛ] is still heard, however, in much regional speech, for example in northern England. On the other hand some varieties of PresE, like those heard in Australia and New Zealand, now have a vowel even closer than that of RP.

When ME /ɛ/ moved to a closer position, this made it possible for the fully open front vowel also to drift upwards. This was ME /a/, which in the earlier part of our period was realised as [a], like the vowel heard in French *la* or German *Mann*. In the middle part of the period, however, it moved up to [æ], which was probably the normal pronunciation by the first half of the seventeenth century. It has developed into RP /æ/, though the opener pronunciation is still heard in much regional speech. The usual PresE spelling for ME /a/ is *a*, as in *hat*, *man*, *hand*.

ME /ɔ/ has present-day spellings with *o*, as in *dog*, *fox*, *top*. In the sixteenth century it was realised as the half-open back rounded vowel [ɔ], like that of French *donne* or German *von*. In the seventeenth century, however, it became much opener, approaching the position of the fully open vowel [ɒ]. It has developed into PresE /ɒ/, which in RP is an almost fully open back rounded vowel.

In some non-standard forms of English, the lowering of ME /ɔ/ took place much earlier, perhaps as early as the thirteenth century. In some forms of speech the vowel then became unrounded, and coalesced with ME /a/. Some forms with this vowel infiltrated the standard language: in eModE there are occasional forms like *Gad* 'God' and *plat* 'plot'. A few such forms have come down into the present-day standard language, for example *strap*, *sprat*, *nap* (of cloth), and *drat* (from *God rot*). In the later seventeenth century, it seems that the frequent use of ME /a/ in place of ME /ɔ/ was the mark of an affected style of speech. In Vanbrugh's comedy *The Relapse* there is an affected coxcomb, Lord Foppington, who regularly uses forms like *lard* 'lord', *marning* 'morning', *navelty* 'novelty', *packet* 'pocket', *rat* 'rot', *stap* 'stop', *Tam* 'Tom', and *tomarrow* 'tomorrow'. Much modern American speech also uses an unrounded vowel for ME /ɔ/, but in this case it is not a front vowel, but the unrounded open back vowel [ɑ], as in [dɑg] 'dog' and [hɑt] 'hot'.

ME /ʊ/ is usually spelt *u*, as in *cut* and *pull*, but occasionally *o*, as in *son* and *wolf*. In the sixteenth century it was realised as the close back lax vowel [ʊ], like that in present-day RP *pull* and *wolf*, but in Early Modern times it split into two distinct phonemes, which have developed into PresE /ʌ/ (as in *cut*, *son*), and PresE /ʊ/ (as in *pull*, *wolf*). This development took place in the seventeenth century. Round about 1600, and perhaps even earlier, the realisation of ME /ʊ/ became in many contexts unrounded, and perhaps also lowered, giving the realisation [ʌ]. But in some phonetic contexts it remained [ʊ], especially when followed by [l], or when preceded by [w], [p], [b], or [f], as in *bull*, *bush*, *full*, *pudding*, *put*, *wolf*. At this stage there was still only one phoneme: [ʊ] and [ʌ] were merely allophones, contextual variants.

During the seventeenth century, however, [ʊ] and [ʌ] appeared in some contexts in which they contrasted with each other, and then there were two separate phonemes, /ʊ/ and /ʌ/. One way in which this happened was by a late shortening of eModE [u:] (from ME /oː/). This shortening produced [ʊ], and sometimes this was in a context where it contrasted with [ʌ]. An example is provided by the words *look* and *luck*. The vowel of *luck* was ME /ʊ/, which in around 1600 quite regularly became realised as [ʌ]. The word *look*, as its spelling suggests, had ME /oː/, and in the sixteenth century was pronounced [luːk]. In the seventeenth century its vowel underwent shortening (a common feature in the period), producing the pronunciation [lʊk]. Now, therefore, there was a pair of words, /lʊk/ and /lʌk/, in which the two vowels contrasted with each other, and consequently they constituted two separate phonemes. This differentiation into two phonemes did not take place in all varieties of English. In some regional speech, like that of northern England, there is still only one phoneme, the exact realisation of which varies from area to area.

The split of ME /ʊ/ into two phonemes took place after the main conventions

TABLE 3.3

Development of the Short Vowels

ME Phoneme	EARLY MODERN ENGLISH Stage 1	Stage 2	Stage 3	Pres E (RP)	Modern Spelling
/ɪ/	[ʃɪp]	[ʃɪp]	[ʃɪp]	/ʃɪp/	ship
/ɛ/	[hɛdʒ]	[hɛdʒ]	[hɛdʒ]	/hedʒ/	hedge
/a/	[hat]	[hæt]	[hæt]	/hæt/	hat
/ɔ/	[dɔg]	[dɔg]	[dɒg]	/dɒg/	dog
/ʊ/	[pʊt]	[pʊt]	[pʊt]	/pʊt/	put
	[kʊt]	[kʊt]	[kʌt]	/kʌt/	cut
/ə/	['bɛtər]	['bɛtər]	['bɛtər]	/'betə/	better
	[-ɪd, -əd]	[-ɪd, -əd]	[-ɪd, -əd]	/-əd/	-ed

of English spelling had been firmly established. In consequence, the spelling system makes no provision for the differentiation between /ʊ/ and /ʌ/, which is why they are both represented by the same spellings.

ME /ə/ was a short unrounded central vowel, similar to that heard in the second syllable of PresE *father*. At the beginning of the Early Modern period it occurred only in unstressed syllables, for it had arisen from other short vowels when they were unstressed. In familiar speech, ME /a/, /ɛ/, /ɔ/, and /ʊ/, when unstressed, had all become /ə/ by the fifteenth century. This is why there is no regular spelling to represent /ə/. Through the influence of the traditional spelling, it continued to be represented by the symbols *a*, *e*, *o*, and *u*. Hence present-day spellings like *about, father, obey, submit*. Unstressed ME /ɪ/, however, did not become /ə/. Indeed, in the fifteenth century there was a tendency for /ə/ to become unstressed /ɪ/, as in the first syllables of *before, embark, eleven, select*. There was a good deal of variation in this matter between different speakers, and many words of this kind still have variant pronunciations with /ə/ and /ɪ/. Before the consonant /r/, however, /ə/ was always retained, as in *father, permit* v. In the course of the Early Modern period, as we shall see, it became possible for /ə/ to occur in stressed position.

A summary of the development of the short vowels is given in Table 3.3. It will be seen that the only change of any great significance since late Middle English times is the splitting of ME /ʊ/ into two different phonemes, which have become PresE /ʊ/ and /ʌ/. In reading eModE verse, we have to remember that, well into the seventeenth century, pairs of words like *cut* and *put* were exact rhymes. When Shakespeare, in one of his sonnets, rhymes *dullness* with *fullness*, this is exact. But when Rochester, in the late seventeenth century, rhymes *dull* with *full*, he is leaning on tradition, using an eye-rhyme, for in his speech the words almost certainly had different vowels.

111

TABLE 3.4

The diphthong phonemes of late Middle English

ME Phoneme	PresE Pronunciation	PresE Spellings	Examples
/iu/	/juː/, /uː/	ew, ue, u, uCe (ieu, iew)	new, blew, hue, true, truth, use, lute, suit (adieu, view)
/ɛʊ/	/juː/, /uː/	ew (eu, eau)	dew, shrewd (neuter, beauty)
/aʊ/	/ɔː/	au, aw	cause, law
/aɪ/	/eɪ/	ai, ay, ei, ey	nail, day, eight, whey
/ɔʊ/	/əʊ/	ou, ow	soul, know
/ɔɪ/	/ɔɪ/	oi, oy	noise, royal
/ʊɪ/	/ɔɪ/	oi, oy	boil, destroy

The ME Diphthongs

In late Middle English there were seven diphthong-phonemes:

1. ME /iu/ 2. ME /ɛʊ/ 3. ME /aʊ/ 4. ME /aɪ/ 5. ME /ɔʊ/
6. ME /ɔɪ/ 7. ME /ʊɪ/

We can often tell what words these occurred in from the PresE pronunciation and spelling, as shown in Table 3.4. The first column lists the diphthong-phonemes in the kind of late Middle English in question. The second column shows the regular development of each phoneme in Present-day English (RP). The third column shows the spellings normally found in PresE. Here the symbol C stands for 'any single consonant-symbol'. Spellings in brackets are less frequent forms.

ME /iu/ was probably a very close vowel, with its starting-point near to [iː] and its finishing-point near to [uː]. In the course of the Early Modern period it changed from being a falling diphthong to being the sequence of two phonemes [juː], rather like the present-day pronunciation of the word *you*. The change began in the sixteenth century, and was common in the early seventeenth. Sometimes, the sequence [sjuː] was assimilated to [ʃuː], and we occasionally find eModE spellings like *shue* 'sue', *shuter* 'suitor', and *ishu* 'issue'. The PresE pronunciations of *sure* and *sugar* go back to assimilations of this kind.

In some positions ME /iu/ developed into eModE [uː] instead of [juː]. This happened when it occurred after /tʃ/, /dʒ/, or /r/, as in *chew, June, rude*. Since 1700 there has been a tendency for [juː] to be supplanted by [uː] in other positions, and in PresE we often have alternative pronunciations, as in *lute, suit, enthusiasm*. In words where ME /iu/ has become [uː], the outcome is the same as for ME /oː/: the words *rude* and *rood* are now homophones, as also for many speakers are *lute* and *loot*. The original pronunciations, however, can be deduced from the spelling. Words which had ME /o:/ always have an *o* in the spelling (*food*, *who*, *move*, *shoe*), but words with ME /iu/ never do (*brew*, *true*, *juice*, *rule*). In the sixteenth century, *food* was [fu:d], but *fruit* was [friut].

ME /ɛʊ/ was a fairly open vowel, but it gradually became closer, and by the sixteenth century was probably realised as [eu]. At this stage it was still distinct from ME /iu/, but it continued to get closer, and eventually became [iu], at which point the two phonemes merged. Thereafter, of course, ME /ɛʊ/ shared the development of ME /iu/ to [ju:] or [u:]. In some regional speech, this coalescence of ME /ɛʊ/ and ME /iu/ may have taken place in late Middle English, but in StE it happened much later: even in advanced standard speech it appears not to have taken place until the late sixteenth century. During the first half of our period, the two phonemes were still kept distinct by many speakers: *due* was [diu], but *dew* was [deu].

With ME /iu/ and ME /ɛʊ/, there is a partial failure in our code for eModE pronunciation: both have the same pronunciation in PresE, and their spellings overlap. Some spellings are characteristic of ME /iu/ alone, but the spelling *ew* is commonly found for both phonemes. The commonest words with ME /ɛʊ/ are *beauty*, *dew*, *ewe*, *ewer*, *feud*, *few*, *hew*, *lewd*, *mew*, *neuter*, *newt*, *pewter*, *pleurisy*, *sew*, *sewer*, *shew* 'show', *shrew*, *shrewd*, and *strew*. The verbs *sew* and *shew* had variant pronunciations with ME /ɔʊ/, from which derive the PresE pronunciations. In the sixteenth century, some writers (or printers) distinguished ME /ɛʊ/ from ME /iu/ by spelling the former as *eau*, for example *deaw* 'dew'.

ME /aʊ/ perhaps had a starting-point near to [a], but by the sixteenth century it had been retracted, and the realisation was [ɑʊ] (similar to the vowel of PresE *how*). Round about 1600, ME /aʊ/ was monophthongised, its realisation becoming [ɒ:]. This was an open back rounded vowel, with a quality similar to that of PresE *dog*, but long. Subsequently it became closer, and has developed into PresE /ɔ:/, which is about half-open. The pronunciation [ɒ:] was the common one in StE in the seventeenth century.

Cases with PresE spellings like *cause* and *law* are straightforward, but ME /aʊ/ also occurred in a number of words with different PresE spellings. It occurred in words like *all*, *altar*, *always*, *chalk*, *malt*, and *salt*. These words originally had ME /a/, but before the consonant /l/ this developed into /aʊ/ in late Middle English. The change did not take place if a vowel followed, as in *balance*, *palace*, *valley*. Despite the PresE pronunciation, ME /aʊ/ also occurred in the words *almond*, *alms*, *calf*, *half*, and *psalm*. Here the normal development of ME /al/ to /aʊl/ had taken place, and then the /l/ lost in the fifteenth century. The sixteenth-century pronunciations were ['ɑʊmənd], [ɑʊmz], [kɑʊf], and so on. The PresE forms are descended from originally non-standard variants.

113

More complicated is a group of words of French origin in which, in some styles of speech, ME /a/ developed into /aʊ/ before the nasal consonants /m/ and /n/. These words have various outcomes in PresE:

1. PresE /ɔ:/, as in *haunch, haunt, launch, lawn, staunch, tawny, vaunt*.
2. PresE /eɪ/, as in *ancient, angel, chamber, change, danger, flame, grange, range, strange*.
3. PresE /ɑ:/, as in *aunt, chant, dance, demand, example, vantage*.
4. PresE /æ/, the same words as in 3.

Group 1 is regular in pronunciation and spelling, and presents no problems. The other three groups arose from various combinative changes in non-standard speech. In Group 2 the pronunciation [ɑʊ] was still normal in StE in the sixteenth century, but during the seventeenth century the other pronunciation, with ME /a:/, spread through the standard language. The pronunciations of Group 3, on the other hand, did not enter StE until the eighteenth century. The pronunciations of Group 4, with ME /a/, occur occasionally in StE in the Early Modern period, and have come down to many varieties of Present-day English, notably in North America and Australia. The fact that late ME /aʊ/ was the vowel in all four groups is often reflected in sixteenth-century spellings: very common are spellings like *auncient, chaunt, chaumber*, and *daunce*.

ME /aɪ/ was rather like the vowel of PresE *time*. In the fifteenth century, the starting-point of the diphthong was raised, and by 1500 the realisation was probably [æɪ], which then developed into [ɛɪ]. In the next stage the vowel was monophthongised, [ɛɪ] becoming [ɛ:]. This took place during the sixteenth century, and at the end of the century the two pronunciations were in circulation side by side, so that *day* could be either [dɛɪ] or [dɛ:].

When ME /aɪ/ became [ɛ:], it could become identical with either ME /ɛ:/ or ME /a:/, according to the date at which the change took place. When it became [ɛ:] early in the sixteenth century, the speakers in question were still using [ɛ:] for ME /ɛ:/, so that the two phonemes merged. This was the case with John Hart, in the middle of the century: his reformed spellings show that he used the same vowel in *way* as in *sea*, but a different vowel in *make*. His pronunciations were probably [wɛ:] and [sɛ:], but [mæ:k]. But if the development of ME /aɪ/ to [ɛ:] occurred later, it was likely that the speakers in question would now realise ME /ɛ:/ as [e:], and ME /a:/ as [ɛ:], so that the two phonemes that coalesced were ME /aɪ/ and ME /a:/. In this form of speech, *way* and *make* had the same vowels, which were different from that of *sea*. The pronunciations around 1600 would be [wɛ:] and [mɛ:k], but [se:]. It is this style of speech which has descended into present-day standard English, ME /a:/ and ME /aɪ/ both appearing as PresE /eɪ/. The original phoneme, however, is usually revealed by the spelling: compare *bate* with *bait*, *fate* with *eight*, *hale* with *hail*, *make* with *may*, *tale* with *tail*, *wake* with *whey*.

The different possibilities are reflected in the rhyming habits of different poets. Michael Drayton (1563–1631) commonly rhymes ME /aɪ/ with ME /ɛ:/, for example *way/sea*, *retain/mean/plain*. Edmund Spenser, on the other hand, although about ten years younger, frequently rhymes ME /aɪ/ with ME /a:/, for example *pain/bane*, *vain/bane*, *made/assayed*. This may seem a little early for such rhymes, but Spenser, although apparently born in London, often shows the influence of northern speech, and the merger of ME /aɪ/ with ME /a:/ took place earlier in the north than in the south.

In 1500, ME /ɔʊ/ was still a diphthong, probably realised as [ɔʊ]. During the sixteenth century, however, it became monophthongised to [ɔ:], which was a common pronunciation by 1600. As was often the case with such changes, the more advanced and the more conservative pronunciations probably co-existed for a considerable time. When ME /ɔʊ/ became [ɔ:], it was identical with ME /ɔ:/, and the two phonemes merged, the realisation subsequently moving up to [o:]. It is usually possible to tell which phoneme the PresE form goes back to by means of the spelling. Forms like *flow*, *soul*, *bowl* have their vowel from ME /ɔʊ/, while forms like *so*, *sole*, *boat* have their vowel from ME /ɔ:/. The spellings *ou* and *ow* are also used for ME /u:/, but in such cases the PresE pronunciation tells us whether the vowel goes back to ME /u:/ (*how*, *house*) or to ME /ɔʊ/ (*flow*, *soul*).

The monophthongal pronunciation of ME /ɔʊ/ developed earliest when the vowel occurred in word-final position. In poetry of the early sixteenth century, it is fairly common to find word-final ME /ɔʊ/ rhyming with ME /ɔ:/, as in *foe/low* (Wyatt) and *mo/row* (Surrey).

ME /ɔɪ/ was realised as [ɔɪ], and has been ever since, as in *noise*, *royal*, *coy*. Unfortunately, there are some words now spelt and pronounced in this way which did not have ME /ɔɪ/ but ME /ʊɪ/. In the sixteenth century this was [ʊɪ]. In the seventeenth century, and probably much earlier in some non-standard speech, it developed into [aɪ], and so became identical with ME /i:/. Regularly, this development would give a PresE pronunciation with [aɪ], like [baɪl] 'boil'. Many words with ME /ʊɪ/, however, had alternative forms with ME /ɔɪ/, and in the eighteenth century the latter forms displaced the former. Even forms which historically had only ME /ʊɪ/ became changed by analogy to conform with the /ɔɪ/ type, the process perhaps being helped by the influence of the spelling.

The earlier situation is sometimes reflected in rhymes. In the Restoration period and the early eighteenth century, words which today have /ɔɪ/ are often rhymed with words which today have /aɪ/. In Congreve's play *The Way of the World* (1700) we find the couplet:

> Love's but the frailty of the Mind,
> When 'tis not with Ambition join'd.

115

TABLE 3.5

Development of the Diphthongs

ME Phoneme	EARLY MODERN ENGLISH Stage 1	Stage 2	Stage 3	Pres E (RP)	Modern Spelling
/iu/	[viu]	[viu]	[vju:]	/vju:/	view
/ɛu/	[feu]	[fiu]	fju:]	/fju:/	few
/au/	[kɑuz]	[kɒ:z]	[kɒ:z]	/kɔ:z/	cause
/ai/	[dɛɪ]	[dɛ:]	[de:]	/deɪ/	day
/ɔu/	[lɔu]	[lɔ:]	[lo:]	/ləu/	low
/ɔi/	[ʤɔɪ]	[ʤɔɪ]	[ʤɔɪ]	/ʤɔɪ/	joy
/ui/	[buɪl]	[buɪl]	[baɪl]	/bɔɪl/	boil

The rhyme was exact, *join'd* having its vowel from ME /ui/, and being pronounced /ʤaɪnd/. Similarly, Pope rhymes *join/line*, Swift *child/spoil'd*, Dryden *toils/smiles*, Rochester *join/design*. Such rhymes are rare before the middle of the seventeenth century, but do occur occasionally. Waller rhymes *toil/isle*, Middleton *soiled/beguiled*, Spenser *spoil/beguile* and *I/destroy*. The earliest examples must represent a very advanced pronunciation, or possibly a dialectal one.

For ME /ui/, the evidence of PresE spelling and pronunciation fails us, since we cannot distinguish it from ME /ɔi/. In any case, however, many speakers did not distinguish between the two phonemes, but used [ɔi] for both. Even among those who used ME /ui/, the words in question varied to some extent. Words in which ME /ui/ was often used include *boil, coin, destroy, join, moist, point, poison, soil, spoil, Troy, turmoil*, and *voice*.

The development of the ME diphthongs is summarised in Table 3.5. In the course of the Early Modern period, it will be seen, all the ME diphthongs except /ɔi/ and /ui/ became monophthongs. On the other hand, two new diphthongs had arisen from ME /i:/ and /u:/. But, since ME /i:/ and ME /ui/ became identical, there were only three diphthong phonemes at the end of the period, realised as [aɪ], [ɑu] and [ɔi].

The influence of /r/

A powerful influence causing combinative changes in the Early Modern period was the consonant /r/. It affected many preceding vowels, causing changes of quality and of length, and in some cases causing an [ə] glide to develop after the vowel. The exact quality of the /r/ is uncertain. In Old and Middle English it was probably a 'rolled' or 'trilled' consonant, in which the tip of the tongue was vibrated rapidly against the teeth-ridge. By Early Modern times, however, its articulation had been weakened in the standard

116

language, and it was perhaps realised as a fricative, in which the sides of the tongue were pressed up against the teeth. It has since been weakened further, and in RP is now an approximant. In any case, in eModE it was pronounced before a consonant and in final position (i.e. before a pause). In these positions the /r/ was not lost in StE until the middle of the eighteenth century. In my transcriptions of eModE pronunciations, I shall not attempt to show the exact type of consonant, but shall simply use the symbol [r].

At the beginning of the Early Modern period, words with ME /ɛr/, /ɪr/, and /ʊr/, like *herb*, *birth,* and *curse*, not only had /r/ in the pronunciation, but also had vowels exactly like those in *bed*, *bid,* and *puss*: their pronunciations were [ɛrb], [bɪrθ], and [kʊrs]. In the course of the period, the three vowels were influenced by the following /r/, and all developed into [ə]. The pronunciations of the three words thus became [ərb], [bərθ], and [kərs]. At this stage, there-fore, [ə] was able to occur in stressed position. In the case of [ɛr] and [ɪr], the change took place in StE towards the end of the sixteenth century. In the case of [ʊr] it was a little later, but had taken place by the middle of the seventeenth century. The development took place earlier in some regional dialects, and this accounts for some rhymes and inverted spellings which are found in the six-teenth century. It also explains the words *cuss* and *bust*, which are variants of *curse* and *burst*: the [r] was lost early, before the vowel-change had taken place, and subsequently the two words have drifted into the standard language. But in careful StE, [ɛr] does not rhyme with [ɪr] until about 1600, and these do not rhyme with [ʊr] until well into the seventeenth century.

The change to [ə] took place when the [r] was pre-consonantal or final, but not when it was intervocalic. It occurred in words like *herb* and *stir* and *burn*, but not in words like *merry*, and *stirrup*, and *turret*. In PresE, words with seventeenth-century [ər] have instead the long vowel [ɜ:], as in /hɜ:b/, /bɜ:θ/, /kɜ:s/. There is no evidence to suggest, however, that the lengthening of the vowel took place in eModE: it probably occurred when the [r] was lost in the eighteenth century. Until the loss of final and pre-consonantal [r], there was no /ɜ:/ phoneme in English.

The /r/ phoneme has caused the lengthening of preceding vowels at various dates, and in eModE there were often alternative forms in circulation, some with lengthened vowels, some with short ones. Within the Early Modern period itself, lengthening before /r/ affected only ME /a/ and ME /ɔ/, and did not take place in StE until the second half of the seventeenth century. It did not occur when the vowel was intervocalic, so that it is found in *yarn* and *corn*, but not in *marry* or *borrow*.

The word *yarn* had ME /a/, and in the sixteenth century was pronounced [jarn]. When ME /a/ became eModE [æ] in free position, it seems likely that a following /r/ inhibited this change, so that the pronunciation remained [jarn]. At this stage, the [a] was simply an allophone of the /æ/ phoneme. In the second half of the seventeenth century, the [r] caused lengthening, producing the pronunciation [ja:rn]. In the middle of the eighteenth century, the [r] was lost, and the [a:] has developed into PresE /ɑ:/, giving the pronunciation /jɑ:n/. Not until the loss of /r/ was there an /a:/ phoneme contrasting with /æ/ (the vowel of *barn*, for example, contrasting with that of *ban*).

The word *corn* had ME /ɔ/, and in the sixteenth century was pronounced [kɔrn]. In the seventeenth century this regularly developed into [kɒrn]. Later in the century, the /r/ caused lengthening, giving the pronunciation [kɒ:rn]. At this date, [ɒ:] was also the reflex of ME /ɑu/. Consequently, the vowel of *corn* ceased to belong to the /ɒ/ phoneme of seventeenth-century English, and moved into the /ɒ:/ phoneme. This has become the /ɔ:/ phoneme of PresE, used both in *corn* and *cause*, in *lord* and *laud*.

Many words in eModE have alternative forms with ME /ɛr/ and ME /ar/. In late ME, /ɛr/ often became /ar/ in pre-consonantal and final position, but this did not happen in all varieties of speech, even in StE. Consequently, there was a good deal of variation in Early Modern times. The outcome in PresE would be /ɜ:/ in the one case, and /ɑ:/ in the other, and we have usually standardised one of the pronunciations for each word: for example, /ɜ:/ in *certain*, *err*, *herd*, *pert*, and *servant*, but /ɑ:/ in *clerk*, *farm*, *fart*, *harvest*, *marvel*, *sergeant*, and *star*. There is quite a good correlation between the PresE forms and the forms commonly used in eModE, but nevertheless we have to be prepared to encounter alternative forms. Surrey, in successive lines, has the words *sarue* 'serve' and *perched* 'parched'. Shakespeare, in his sonnets, rhymes *departest/conuertest*, *art/conuert*, and *parts/deserts* 'merits'. In a few cases we have doublets in PresE, like *person/parson* and *university/varsity*.

With long vowels, a following /r/ (including intervocalic /r/) inhibited the raising of open and half-open vowels. Normally, these vowels would have been raised as part of the Great Vowel Shift. Occasionally, too, a following /r/ caused the lowering of close vowels.

ME /ɔ:/ normally developed from [ɔ:] to [o:], so that *boat* was first [bɔ:t] and then [bo:t]. But before /r/ this change did not take place, so that *boar* remained [bɔ:r] throughout the period. Similarly with ME /ɛ:/: the word *meat* changed from [mɛ:t] to [me:t], but *bear* remained [bɛ:r] throughout the period. In the case of ME /a:/, the following /r/ prevented the raising going beyond [ɛ:]. So whereas *make* changed from [mæ:k] to [mɛ:k] and then to [me:k], the word *hare* changed from [hæ:r] to [hɛ:r], and stopped there.

The same applied to ME /ai/. When this was monophthongised, it too became [ɛ:], and a following /r/ prevented it from moving any closer. So *stair* developed from [stæir] to [stɛir] and then to [stɛ:r], at which it stayed. Before /r/, consequently, the contrast between ME /ɛ:/, ME /a:/, and ME /ai/ was neutralised. All three groups ended up as seventeenth-century [ɛ:r], so that *pear*, *pare*, and *pair* became homophones. In PresE the [ɛ:r] has become /ɛə/, as in *air*, *bear*, *care*, *fair*, *pear*, *share*. Some words with ME /ɛ:r/, however, appear in PresE with the diphthong /ɪə/, for example *beard*, *dear*, *ear*, *fear*, *gear*, *spear*. These pronunciations come from late ME non-standard variants, which later penetrated the standard language. This was already happening in Early Modern times, and many words had alternative pronunciations with [i:r] and [ɛ:r]. The word *spear*, for example, was pronounced by some speakers as [spi:r] and by others as [spɛ:r]. The spelling with *ea* gives a clue to the earlier standard form.

In StE, the only long vowel which frequently underwent lowering before /r/ was [u:]: in some styles of speech [u:r] changed to [ɔ:r]. Sixteenth-century [u:r] had two main sources. In part it was the regular development of ME /o:r/, as in *poor*, *floor*. Partly, however, it came from ME /u:r/, as in *court*, *pour*. Normally, ME /u:/ became eModE [əʊ] as part of the Great Vowel Shift. A following /r/, however, tended to inhibit the diphthongisation, especially if another consonant followed, so that in some words, or for some speakers, it remained [u:].

From about 1600 onwards, there was a strong tendency for [u:r], of whatever origin, to change to [ɔ:r], so that for example *poor* changed from [pu:r] to [pɔ:r]. Some speakers, however, continued to use the unlowered vowel, so that in the seventeenth century the two pronunciations existed side by side. In a few words, alternative pronunciations still exist in PresE: for example *poor* is pronounced by some people as [pʊə], by others as [pɔ:] or [pɔə], and similarly with *boor* and *moor*. In the majority of words, however, only the lowered vowel has survived, as in *door*, *floor*.

The spelling *oor* is a good indication that a word had sixteenth-century [u:r] from ME /o:r/. Words with sixteenth-century [u:r] from ME /u:r/ often have the spelling *our*, for example *bourn*, *course*, *court*, *courtier*, *fourth*, *gourd*, *mourn*, *pour*, and *source*. In some words, however, the spelling has been changed to represent the lowered vowel. For example, *hoard* and *coarse* were sixteenth-century [hu:rd] and [ku:rs], and common sixteenth-century spellings for them are *hoorde* and *course*. The spellings with *oa* are not found before the seventeenth century. Yet other words with sixteenth-century [u:r] now have the spelling *or*, for example *afford*, *form*, *forth*, *perform*, *sword*, and *whore*. In all these groups of words, the variants with the unlowered [u:] continue to be found right to the end of the seventeenth century. Christopher Cooper, writing in the 1680s, records the [u:r] pronunciation in *coarse*, *court*, *form*, *forth*, *mourn*, *source*, *sword*, and *whore*.

Long vowels followed by /r/ have resulted in the centring diphthongs of PresE. ME /e:r/ became eModE [i:r], which has become PresE [ɪə], as in *peer*, *pierce*. ME /ɛ:r/, /a:r/, and /aɪr/ all became eModE [ɛ:r], which has become PresE /ɛə/, as in *bear*, *dare*, *fair*. ME /o:r/ became eModE [u:r], which, if it escaped lowering, has become PresE /ʊə/, as in *poor*. And ME /ɔ:r/ became eModE [ɔ:r], which has developed into PresE /ɔə/, as in *more*, *soar* (though many speakers use /ɔ:/ in such words). These changes presumably took place in the eighteenth century, when final and pre-consonantal /r/ were lost. There is some evidence to suggest, however, that the process may have begun in the Early Modern period, with the development of an [ə]-glide between the long vowel and the /r/. This seems to have been especially frequent with [i:], so that *peer* changed from [pi:r] to ['pi:ər], which was dissyllabic.

In the Early Modern period, an [ə]-type glide often developed also between diphthongs and a following /r/. It is especially common after [əɪ] (from ME /i:/) and [əʊ] (from ME /u:/), in words like *fire* and *flour*. These became ['fəɪər] and ['fləʊər] (later ['faɪər] and ['flɑʊər]). Such words were then dissyllabic, and pronunciations of this kind explain some rhymes. In Samuel Daniel's *Delia* (1592), *desires* rhymes with *lyers*, and *fire* with *nye her* 'near her'. Waller, similarly, rhymes *higher* with *fire* and *admire*. The rhythm of poetry, too, often seems to demand a dissyllabic pronunciation for such words:

> 1. With greedy tallents gripe my bleeding hart,
>   And like a Harpye *tires* on my life.
>
>   (Marlowe, *Tamburlaine Part 1*)

> 2. Berowne they call him, but a merrier man,
>   Within the limit of becomming mirth,
>   I neuer spent an *houres* talk withall.
>
>   (Shakespeare, *Love's Labour's Lost*)

> 3. The wholsomness, the ingenuitie,
>   From rust, from soil, from *fire* euer free
>
>   (Donne, *Elegy XVIII*)

Alongside such dissyllabic pronunciations, the older monosyllabic ones continued to exist. In the vocal music of the time, such words were frequently set to a single note of music, though there are counter-examples: in John Wilbye's madrigal 'Flora gave me fairest flowers', the words *flowers* and *bowers* occur numerous times, and are invariably allotted two notes each (or more). When two pronunciations are in free variation, such things are to be expected.

For ME /i:r/, the PresE spelling does not usually suggest a dissyllabic pronunciation, the word *briar* being exceptional (cf. *fire*, *wire*, etc.). For ME /u:r/, on the other hand, there are spellings like *bower*, *flower*, and *tower*, alongside *flour* and *hour*. The words *flour* and *flower* illustrate in their spellings the earlier state of free variation, for originally they were the same word.

Table 3.6 summarises the effect of /r/ on a preceding vowel. In the case of the short vowels, it is to be understood that the /r/ is final or pre-consonantal, not intervocalic.

TABLE 3.6

The influence of /r/ on a preceding vowel

ME Phoneme	EARLY MODERN ENGLISH Stage 1	Stage 2	Stage 3	Pres E (RP)	Modern Spelling
/ɛr/	[ɛrb]	[ərb]	[ərb]	/hɜːb/	herb
/ɪr/	[bɪrθ]	[bərθ]	[bərθ]	/bɜːθ/	birth
/ʊr/	[kʊrs]	[kʊrs]	[kərs]	/kɜːs/	curse
/ar/	[jarn]	[jarn]	[jaːrn]	/jɑːn/	yarn
/ɔr/	[kɔrn]	[kɒrn]	[kɒːrn]	/kɔːn/	corn
/iːr/	[fəir]	['fəiər]	['faiər]	/'faiə/	fire
/eːr/	[piːr]	['piːər]	['piːər]	/piə/	peer
/ɛːr/	[bɛːr]	[bɛːr]	[bɛːr]	/bɛə/	bear
/aːr/	[fæːr]	[fɛːr]	[fɛːr]	/fɛə/	fare
/air/	[pɛir]	[pɛːr]	[pɛːr]	/pɛə/	pair
/ɔːr/	[mɔːr]	[mɔːr]	[mɔːr]	/mɔe, mɔː/	more
/oːr/	[muːr]	[muːr]	[muːr] [mɔːr]	/mʊə/ /mɔə, mɔː/	moor
/uːr/	[fləʊr]	['fləʊər]	['flaʊər]	/'flaʊə/	flower, flour

Other combinative changes

Two other combinative changes affecting vowels are worthy of mention: the rounding effect of /w/, and vowel-lengthening before voiceless fricatives.

For the first, we can begin with a stanza of Wyatt's:

> And here an end of all our mone!
> With sighing oft my brethe is skant,
> Sines of myshappe ours is alone –
> To lovve so well and yet to wantt.

The rhyme *scant/want* was an exact one. Both words, as the spelling suggests, had ME /a/, and their pronunciations were [skant], [want]. They no longer rhyme because the /w/ in *want* subsequently had a rounding effect on the following vowel, which became identical with ME /ɔ/. In some varieties of English, the change took place in Middle English, but in the standard language the new pronunciation did not begin to spread until the seventeenth century. Even then it made its way slowly, and for the greater part of the Early Modern period the unrounded vowel was normal. The modern spelling shows us which words had ME /a/, for example *quality*, *quarrel*, *swan*, *wan*, *warrant*, *was*, *watch*, *what*.

Rhymes like Wyatt's *scant/want* are common throughout the period. Spenser has *wan/can*, Shakespeare *watch/match*, Drayton *dash/wash*, Donne *watch/catch*, Milton *span/wan*, and Swift *wand/hand*. There can be little doubt that such rhymes were exact ones even late in the period, for some speakers were still using the unrounded vowel, at any rate in certain words, well through the eighteenth century.

If the vowel was followed by a velar consonant, the rounding did not take place, as in *quack*, *quagmire*, *twang*, *wag*, *wax*. The pronunciation of *quagmire* with a rounded vowel is a recent analogical one.

In words like *war* and *quart*, where [wa] was followed by final or pre-consonantal /r/, both rounding and lengthening took place, and the vowel became seventeenth-century [ɒ:]. It thus became identical with ME /ɑʊ/, and shared its development to PresE /ɔ:/. The earliest evidence for [ɒ:] in words like *war* is found in Simon Daines in 1640, but long after that date some speakers still used a short unrounded vowel. For the greater part of the period, *war* was pronounced [war], and not until the second half of the seventeenth century did [wɒ:r] become at all common in standard speech. Throughout the Early Modern period, we find rhymes like *reward/regard*, *swarms/arms*, *war/bar*, and *warble/marble*. Until the late seventeenth century, these were exact rhymes.

If the /r/ was intervocalic, the rounding took place, but the lengthening did not, as in *quarrel*, *warrant*.

There was no /ɑ:/ phoneme in eModE, and we have already seen how a phoneme of this kind arose in the eighteenth century from ME /ar/ (as in *yarn*) and from a non-standard development of ME /ɑʊ/ before nasals (as in *aunt*). There was, however, another source of PresE /ɑ:/, in words like *ask*, *pass*, *path*, and *staff*. These words had ME /a/, and in the sixteenth century were pronounced [ask], [pas], [paθ], and [staf]. It seems likely that this continued to be their pronunciation in the seventeenth century, the following consonant inhibiting the usual raising of [a] to [æ]. Then, in the later seventeenth century, the following consonant caused the vowel to be lengthened, and the pronunciations became [a:sk], [pa:s], [pa:θ], and [sta:f]. At this stage, the long vowel was merely an allophone of the /æ/ phoneme, but when an /a:/ phoneme came into existence in the eighteenth century, these long vowels became a part of it, and have regularly developed to PresE /ɑ:/.

The consonants that caused the lengthening were the voiceless fricatives, /s/, /f/, and /θ/. The lengthening did not take place if the consonant was inter-vocalic. Hence in PresE we have *class* with /ɑ:/, but *classical* with /æ/. And similarly with *pass* and *passenger*, *path* and *mathematical*.

The lengthening did not take place in all forms of English, and short [æ] or [a] can still be heard in such words in many varieties of the language. Indeed, short and long forms continued to exist side by side for a considerable time in StE, and a few words have retained a short vowel in the present-day language, for example *asp*, *bastard* (except as a term of abuse), *lass*, *masculine*, *mass*.

At one time, *ass* was commonly pronounced with the long vowel, but when pre-consonantal /r/ was lost in the eighteenth century, *ass* had the same pronunciation as *arse*. To prevent an embarrassing homophonic clash, the pronunciation of *ass* with /æ/ has been standardised, though the long vowel can still be heard in the playful expression *silly ass*.

ME /ɔ/ also underwent lengthening before voiceless fricatives at about the same time as ME /a/, and under the same conditions. The lengthened vowel was [ɒ:], which was identical with the reflex of ME /ɑʊ/, and has shared its development to PresE /ɔ:/. In the case of ME /ɔ/, however, the lengthened vowel was less generally accepted in educated speech, and short and long forms continued in use side by side. This is still true, and both PresE /ɒ/ and PresE /ɔ:/ can be heard in words like *broth*, *cost*, and *off*, though forms with the long vowel now sound old-fashioned.

Shortening of long vowels

Both in ME and in eModE there was sporadic shortening of vowels in words of one syllable, especially those ending in a single voiced consonant. In the Early Modern period, there were often long and short variants in free variation. One of the forms has since been standardised, though the other can often be heard in regional speech. In cases where we have standardised the shortened vowel, the spelling usually shows us that the vowel was originally long, provided that the long-vowel variant was still in circulation in eModE. We can tell from the spelling, therefore, that words like *good* and *blood* and *dead* and *gone* had long-vowel variants in the Early Modern period. On the other hand, if the vowel had been shortened in ME, and the long-vowel form did not exist in eModE, or was rare, the PresE spelling usually indicates a short vowel. Both *red* and *hot* originally had long vowels, but the shortened variants were the norm in eModE. It is true that in the sixteenth century there are sometimes spellings like *hote* or *hoat*, indicating a long vowel, but this was not the commonest pronunciation at that time.

The vowels that were especially subject to shortening in the Early Modern period were ME /ɛ:/ and ME /o:/. When ME /ɛ:/ was shortened, the outcome was [ɛ], which has regularly developed into PresE /e/, as in *bread*, *breath*, *sweat*, *spread*. In words of this kind, double forms were in circulation throughout the period.

ME /o:/ had become eModE [u:]. When this was shortened, the outcome was [ʊ]. If the change took place in the sixteenth century, before the regular development of ME /ʊ/ from [ʊ] to [ʌ], the new [ʊ] shared in this change, as in *blood*, *flood*. But if the shortening took place later, the [ʊ] remained, as in *look*, *foot*. In the second half of the seventeenth century, it was possible for three different forms of a word to be in circulation at the same time: one with unshortened [u:], one with [ʌ] by early shortening, and one with [ʊ] by later shortening. There is evidence, for example, for the existence of all three pronunciations of the word *foot*, namely [fu:t], [fʊt], and [fʌt], though the third was possibly vulgar.

Occasionally, other vowels were shortened. In *gone* and *shone*, there has been shortening of ME /ɔ:/. As the spellings suggest, these words had eModE variants with long vowels: in Sonnet 4, Shakespeare rhymes *gone/alone*, while in Sonnet 5 he rhymes *gon/on*. The word *broad*, as its spelling suggests, had ME /ɔ:/, and was pronounced [brɔ:d], later [bro:d], rhyming with *road*. Alongside this pronunciation was one with a shortened vowel, giving sixteenth-century [brɔd], seventeenth-century [brɒd]. Our present pronunciation comes from a relengthening of seventeenth-century [brɒd], resulting in [brɒ:d], which has regularly become PresE [brɔ:d]. The relengthened pronunciation is first recorded in the middle of the seventeenth century.

CONSONANTS

At the beginning of the Early Modern period, the consonant phonemes of English were as follows:

Stops:	/p/	/t/	/k/	/tʃ/
	/b/	/d/	/g/	/dʒ/
Fricatives:	/f/	/θ/	/s/	/ʃ/	/h/
	/v/	/ð/	/z/	
Sonants: Liquids:	/l/	/r/		
Nasals:	/m/	/n/		
Semivowels:	/j/	/w/		

In the course of the period, two new consonant phonemes arose, namely /ŋ/ and /ʒ/.

In the sixteenth century, words like *sing* and *thank* were pronounced [sɪŋg] and [θaŋk], but here the [ŋ] was merely an allophone of the /n/ phoneme, the contextual variant of /n/ which occurred before /k/ and /g/. At that stage, a phonemic transcription of *sing* would be /sɪŋg/. But round about 1600, the word-final cluster [-ŋg] was simplified to [-ŋ]. In other words, the final [g] was lost in words like *sing*, which was now pronounced [sɪŋ]. When this happened, /ŋ/ became a separate phoneme, for it could now contrast with /n/. For example, the words *sing* and *sin* were now /sɪŋ/ and /sɪn/, and were distinguished solely by the difference between /ŋ/ and /n/. In eastern dialects, and possibly in non-standard London speech, the change had taken place in late Middle English, but pronunciations like [sɪŋg] persisted in StE until the late sixteenth century. In some regional speech, for example in the Birmingham area, in Sheffield, and in south Lancashire, they persist to the present day.

Although the group [ŋg] was simplified to [ŋ] when it occurred in word-final position, this did not happen when it occurred in medial position before a vowel, as in words like *anger* and *finger* and *singular*. In such words, the [ŋg] pronunciation was retained. The PresE pronunciation of words like *singer* and *hanging*, with medial /ŋ/, is due to the influence of the forms from which they are derived, like *sing* and *hang*.

For final unstressed *-ing*, there was an alternative pronunciation [-ɪn], which had arisen in late ME. In the Early Modern period, however, this seems not to have been the usual standard pronunciation, and it was not until the eighteenth century that it became fashionable.

The other new consonant phoneme, /ʒ/, arose in the seventeenth century from the group /zj/. In the sixteenth century, *vision* was pronounced ['vɪzjən]. In the middle of the seventeenth century, the medial group [-zj-] coalesced into [-ʒ-], giving the pronunciation ['vɪʒən]. The new phoneme was easily accepted, since it fitted into the pattern of the English consonant system: it provided a voiced partner for the voiceless fricative /ʃ/, thus filling a gap in the pattern. It occurred in a number of words ending in *-sion*, like *derision* and *occasion*, and in a few words where /z/ was followed by [ju:] from ME /iu/, like *measure* and *pleasure*. The group /-zj-/ occurred only medially, so the new phoneme was restricted to this position. Subsequently, it has appeared in word-final position in loans from French, like *beige, garage, rouge*.

With the appearance of the /ŋ/ and /ʒ/ phonemes, the inventory of consonant phonemes became the same as in PresE. The other main changes in the consonant system since the sixteenth century have concerned the permissible clusters of consonants, and the use of the /h/ phoneme.

At the beginning of the Early Modern period, the /h/ phoneme had three allophones: [h], [ç], and [x]. The [h] allophone was the ordinary aspirate, and was used in syllable-initial position, as in *hat, behind*. The [ç] allophone resembled the consonant of Modern German *ich*, and the [x] allophone that of Modern German *ach*. They both occurred in word-final position and before /t/, the former being used after front vowels and the latter after back vowels. The former existence of /h/ in these positions is indicated by *gh* in the PresE spelling, as in *daughter, eight, high, rough, though, thought*.

In eastern dialects, [ç] and [x] had been lost as early as the fourteenth century, but in StE they continued to be used throughout the sixteenth century. Early in the century, therefore, *eight* could be pronounced as [ɛɪçt], and *though* as [ðɔux]. But alongside such pronunciations were alternative ones in which /h/ had been lost, and these gradually spread through the standard language, becoming normal by the seventeenth century. In late ME, in the form of the language in which /h/ was lost, the groups [ɪç] and [ʊx] developed into [iː] and [uː]. So [lɪçt] 'light' and [drʊxt] 'drought' became [liːt] and [druːt]. By the Great Vowel Shift, these regularly became sixteenth-century [ləɪt] and [drəʊt], leading to PresE /laɪt/ and /draʊt/.

In some words we now have /f/ where originally was /h/, as in *draught*, *enough, laugh.* These were dialectal pronunciations. In a number of ME dialects, [x] changed to [f], and often the preceding vowel was shortened. Some such forms made their way into StE in the middle of the Early Modern period, and by about 1625 the /f/ pronunciation was normal in all the words in which it is now used.

Some words have eModE spellings with initial *h-*, despite the fact that there was no /h/ in the pronunciation, and never had been. These were ME loans from French, in which initial [h] had been lost before the loan was made. Such words include *habit, harmony, hemisphere, herb, heritage, honour, host, hour,* and *humble.* In ME it is common for such words to be spelt without the *h* (*abit, armonye, emyspere,* etc.). Such spellings are also found in eModE, but commoner are spellings with *h.* The *h* is due to the influence of the Latin forms (*habitus, harmonia,* etc.). In the Early Modern period, however, the pronunciation without /h/ was still normal. Pronunciations with /h/ are due to the influence of the spelling, and are not common before the nineteenth century.

Simplification of consonant clusters

In the course of the Early Modern period, greater restrictions were placed on consonant combinations inherited from ME. In 1500, the initial clusters [wr-], [kn-], and [gn-] still existed, but during the period they were simplified to [r-], [n-], and [n-]. The earlier pronunciations are indicated by the spelling. For example *write, knee* and *gnat* were early sixteenth century [wrəɪt], [kniː], [gnat]. In some varieties of English, the simplification of [wr-] to [r-] had taken place in the fifteenth century, but in the standard language [wr-] was used until the middle of the Early Modern period. Initial [kn-] was more persistent, and continued in use throughout the period, though in the late seventeenth century it may have developed into [hn-]. The history of [gn-] is less clear: there were few words in which it occurred, and the evidence is sparse. It seems likely, however, that in StE it underwent two different developments: in some forms of speech it became [kn-] in the second half of the sixteenth century, while in others it developed directly to [n-] in about 1600. In the seventeenth century, therefore, *gnat* could be either [knæt] or [næt].

Throughout the Early Modern period, words now spelt with initial *wh* were pronounced with the cluster /hw-/. So *witch* and *which* were not homophones, the former being [wɪtʃ] and the latter [hwɪtʃ]. In StE, initial /hw-/ did not become /w-/ until the eighteenth century, though in non-standard speech the /w-/ pronunciation had been common in the south since ME times.

During the ME period, there was a tendency for some medial and final clusters to be simplified. In some cases, the earlier pronunciation probably continued to be heard in the Early Modern period, at any rate in conservative speech. The simplifications that took place can often be deduced from the PresE pronunciation and spelling. Among medial clusters, one such change took place in words like *bristle, chestnut, Christmas, listen,* and *often.* Changes in word-final clusters took place in words like *condemn, damn, dumb,* and *lamb.* On the other hand, the words *crumb, limb,* and *numb* never had a final [-b] in their pronunciation: their spellings are unetymological, and are due to analogy with such words as *dumb,* once final [-b] had been lost in these words. The new spellings are first recorded in the sixteenth century.

Changes that were probably still going on in the Early Modern period concern the loss of /w/ in some positions. It tended to be lost when preceded by another consonant followed by a rounded vowel. A good example is the word *who,* which developed from [hwu:] to [hu:]; the earlier pronunciation could be heard well into the seventeenth century. Other examples are the words *cwoth, swollen, swoon, sword, swore,* and *two.* In many such words, the [w] was often restored in pronunciation, either through the influence of the spelling, or by analogy with related words (*swore,* for example, being influenced by *swear*). In the Early Modern period there were often variant forms in free variation, one with [w] and one without. The verb *swoon,* for example, is found with such spelling variants as *swoon, soun(d),* and *swoun(d).* In the case of *sword,* the forms with [w] were normal until the middle of the seventeenth century, with such pronunciations as [swʊrd], [swu:rd], and [swɔrd]. On the other hand, the word *two* was normally [tu:].

The other position in which [w] was lost was when it occurred before an unstressed vowel, as in *answer, awkward, boatswain, conquer, forward, housewife,* and *pennyworth.* In some cases the [w] has since been restored in pronunciation, but forms without the [w] were common until the seventeenth century. In the case of *awkward,* the form without [w] persisted in StE until the end of the seventeenth century. The pronunciation was ['ɒ:kərd], and this was often reflected in spelling. For example, the spelling *auker'd* occurs in Wycherley's play *The Country-Wife* (1675).

Pre-consonantal and final /r/

In the eighteenth century, /r/ was lost in StE before a consonant and in final position. This produced an accent which is called *non-rhotic.* Nearly all varieties of speech in England today are non-rhotic, as are those of Australia and New Zealand. On the other hand, most American speech is rhotic, as also is much Irish and Scots speech.

Present-day speakers with non-rhotic accents need to remember that, throughout the Early Modern period, standard speech was rhotic, in other words /r/ was pronounced in all positions. The present-day spelling shows where there was an /r/ in eModE pronunciation, for example *barn, board, err, farmer, here, turf.* Since /r/ is no longer pronounced in such words by non-rhotic speakers, it is easy for them to overlook its existence in earlier forms of the language. For example, the present-day reader may detect puns and rhymes where these could not possibly have existed for the original readers. A present-day reader may imagine, for example, that an author is punning on *bawd* and *board*, but this is highly implausible: even in a style of speech in which the vowels of the two words had become identical, the presence of /r/ in one word makes it completely different from the other – as different, for example, as *sad* is from *sand*, or *kid* from *killed*. Similarly with rhymes: *sport* could not rhyme with *sought*, even in styles of speech in which [x] had been lost from the latter word.

There was one position where /r/ had been lost in some non-standard speech in late Middle English, namely when it occurred before /s/ or /ʃ/. This happened before the /r/ had changed the preceding vowel, and we have already encountered two examples of this: *cuss* and *bust*, originally non-standard variants of *curse* and *burst*. In Early Modern English, we occasionally find signs of such pronunciations, in spellings and rhymes. John Skelton, in his *Bouge of Court* (1568), rhymes *durste* with *trust*. In *Troilus and Cressida*, Shakespeare uses the word *tercell* 'a male hawk'. In *Romeo and Juliet*, the same word occurs with the spelling *tassel*. The latter form presumably arose by the common late ME change of [ɛr] to [ar], followed by the non-standard loss of /r/ before /s/. The spelling *tassel* is commonly found, alongside forms like *tercel* and *tarcel*, from the fifteenth century onwards: the pronunciation without /r/ perhaps drifted into StE from the language of professional falconers. Again, in Edward Sharpham's play *Cupids Whirligig* (1607), there are two occurrences of the spelling *accorst* for *accost*. This is obviously an inverted spelling, implying loss of /r/ before /s/. Examples like these, however, are not the norm, and loss of /r/ was not a feature of the standard language.

Strong and weak forms

Words which often occur in unstressed positions develop distinctive weak forms, because the sound changes occurring in such positions are different from those in stressed syllables. In unstressed position, long vowels are often shortened, short vowels reduced to [ə], and consonants lost. It often happens, however, that the weak form later comes to be used in stressed position, so that a new strong form arises. For example, in late Middle English the word *you* had the form [juː], which in unstressed position became [jʊ]. ME [juː] regularly became sixteenth-century [jəʊ], while [jʊ] remained unchanged. During the century, however, the weak form [jʊ] was restressed, and became [juː] (since in ModE a final stressed vowel is always long). So in the Early Modern period there were the strong forms [juː] and [jəʊ] (later [jɑʊ]), and the weak form [jʊ], from which developed a further weak form [jə]. Even in the sixteenth century, [jəʊ] was less common than [juː], but is nevertheless a well-attested variant, and accounts for rhymes like Thomas Dekker's *you/vow* in *The Shomakers Holiday* (1600). In the seventeenth century, the diphthongal variant fell out of use in polite speech, but as late as Waller (1645) we find *you* rhymed with *now*.

In the Early Modern period there were some weak forms that no longer exist, like [t] as a weak form of *it*. In the sixteenth century, the usual unstressed form of *it is* was *'tis*, and it was only in the seventeenth century that *it's* became common. More striking, however, is the fact that in eModE there are numerous *strong* forms which no longer exist: the general tendency is for old strong forms to die out, and to be replaced by restressed weak forms. The existence, and the pronunciation, of these obsolete strong forms can often be deduced from the PresE spelling. Consider the following rhymes:

1. Oh stay, three lives in one flea *spare*,
   Where wee almost, yea more then maryed *are*
   (Donne, 'The Flea')

2. Furnish and deck my soul that thou mayst *have*
   A better lodging, then a rack, or *grave*
   (Herbert, 'Christmas')

3. So should that beauty which you hold in lease
   Find no determination, then you *were*
   Your selfe again after your selfes decease,
   When your sweet issue your sweet forme should *beare*
   (Shakespeare, 'Sonnets')

4. But down, down, down, down I *fall*
   Down, and arise I never *shall*
   (Dowland, 'Sorrow Stay')

These are all exact rhymes, depending on the strong forms of *are*, *have*, *were*, and *shall*. These strong forms were in common use, and such rhymes occur frequently: Shakespeare, for example, habitually rhymes *are* with words like *care*, *prepare*, *rare*. In late ME, there was a strong form [a:r] and a weak form [ar]: the strong form became eModE [ɛ:r], rhyming with words like *care*, while the weak form was later restressed and has developed into PresE /ɑ:/. Similarly, *have* was strong [hɛ:v] alongside weak [hæv] and [əv], and so also with *hast* and *hath*. The word *shall* had a strong form [ʃɒ:l], with its vowel from ME /ɑʊ/, alongside a weak form [ʃæl]. By far the commonest form of *were* was the strong form [wɛ:r], with its vowel from ME /ɛ:/. A PresE pronunciation /wɛə/, descended from it, can still be heard occasionally, but the usual PresE forms come from the eModE weak form [wər], from earlier [wɛr]. Other words that often had strong forms in eModE are *should* and *would*, which retained /l/ in the strong forms, but lost it in the weak. Common pronunciations were strong [ʃu:ld] and [wu:ld], weak [ʃʊd] and [wʊd]. The mixed forms [ʃu:d] and [wu:d] also occurred.

One kind of contrast between strong and weak forms goes back to a consonant change of late Middle English. Words like *is*, *of*, and *with* originally ended in the voiceless fricatives [s], [f], and [θ]. In late ME, these fricatives became voiced to [z], [v], and [ð] when they were unstressed and in word-final position. In eModE, consequently, there were strong forms [ɪs], [ɔf], and [wɪθ], alongside weak [ɪz], [ɔv], and [wɪð]. Both pronunciations of *with* are still heard today, while *of* has been differentiated into two separate words, *of* and *off*. In most instances, however, we have retained one form and lost the other. Usually it is the weak form that has survived, as with *is*, *was*, *his*. In the case of *us*, PresE has the consonant of the old strong form, though pronunciations with [z] can still be heard in regional dialects. In eModE, however, there were still double forms for all such words: *is* could be [ɪs] or [ɪz], *was* could be [was] or [wəz] (or the mixed form [waz]), and *his* could be [hɪs] or [hɪz]. When such words occur in rhymes, they are usually stressed, and so, not surprisingly, the strong form tends to be used:

> 1. Heauen the Iudicious sharpe spectator *is*,
>   That sits and markes still who doth act *amisse*
>   (Ralegh, 'On the Life of Man')

> 2. Against that time when thou shalt strangely *passe*,
>   And scarcely greete me with that sunne thine eye,
>   When loue conuerted from the thing it *was*
>   Shall reasons find of setled grauitie
>   (Shakespeare, 'Sonnets')

These again are exact rhymes, depending on the strong forms of *is* and *was*, with voiceless [s]. In the case of 2., neither rounding after /w/ nor the lengthening before /s/ had yet taken place, and the pronunciations were [pas] and [was].

STRESS

Any attentive reader of the poetry of the Early Modern period notices that occasionally the rhythm of the verse seems to demand that a word shall be stressed in a way not heard in PresE, as in the following example:

> What may this meane?
> That thou dead Coarse againe in compleat steele,
> Reuisits thus the glimpses of the Moone,
> Making Night hidious?
> (Shakespeare, *Hamlet*)

Here the rhythm is odd unless *compleat* is stressed on the first syllable. In Shakespeare, the adjective *complete* usually has first-syllable stress when used attributively before a noun, but second-syllable stress when used predicatively. So we have:

> A thousand cómpleate courses of the Sunne
>> (*Troilus and Cressida*)

but:

> The one is filling still, neuer compléat
>> (*Timon of Athens*).

Another common word which has changed its stress pattern is *envy*. This had first-syllable stress as a noun, but second-syllable stress as a verb (rhyming with *cry*). The verb occurs in rhyming position in the following couplet from Thomas Middleton's play *A Trick to catch the Old-one* (1608):

> Who then can be so cruell, troth, not I,
> I rather pity now, then ought enuie.

This illustrates a general tendency in English in recent centuries, namely for stress to be moved to the first syllable, especially in two-syllable words. In many Shakespeare passages, it is necessary to give second-syllable stress to such words as *advertise, aspect, authorise, canonise, character, compact* n., *contents, demonstrate, essay* n., *increase* n., *instinct, nobody, obdurate, persever, precinct, protest* n., *record* n., *sinister*. Nevertheless, there are words in which the opposite change has taken place since Early Modern times. In some Shakespeare passages, it is necessary to give first-syllable stress to *chastise, commendable, consigned, corrosive, delectable, distinct, entire, extreme, forlorn, July, perfected, perspective, plebeian*. The first-syllable stressing of *July*, pronounced ['dʒiulɪ], is likely to strike anybody who sings the secular music of the period, such as Thomas Morley's madrigal 'April is in my mistress face' (1594).

Some words could be stressed either way, for example *character, distinct, entire, extreme, forlorn, nobody*: the verse sometimes calls for the one pronunciation, sometimes for the other. The fluctuation was not peculiar to Shakespeare, but was typical of the period. In part it was due to a conflict between the native system of accentuation, in which the stress was usually on the stem, and the French or Latin mode of accentuation in loan-words. Some seventeenth-century grammarians give accounts of the English stress system in their time. Charles Butler's *English Grammar* (1633) gives a set of rules for the accentuation of English, with many examples. The vast majority of these are stressed exactly as today. The exceptions are nearly all French or Latin loan-words, especially polysyllabic ones. He shows first-syllable stress in *acceptable, commune* v., *confessor, conventicle*, and *receptacle*; second-syllable stress in *confiscate* and *turmoil*; and third-syllable stress in *reconcile*.

He gives a list of words in which the verb has second-syllable stress, while the noun or adjective has first-syllable stress, like *accent* and *contract*. In this list he includes *direct* and *relapse*.

Butler observes that *contrary* can be accented on either the first or the second syllable. When accented on the first, it is following his general rule for polysyllabic words, which are, he says, accented on the antepenult. When it is accented on the second, it is following his exception to this rule, whereby loan-words 'commonly' have the accentuation of the word they are derived from, in this case Latin *contrárius*. So here Butler explicitly notes the conflicting native and foreign influences in English accentuation.

Secondary stress

There is, however, another factor in the variable stressing of eModE: the extensive survival, certainly until the middle of the period, of many secondary stresses now lost. In Middle English, many words, in addition to a main stress, had a syllable which carried secondary stress. In late ME, variants with single stressing arose alongside these, and in the sixteenth century the two types co-existed. In the seventeenth century, the forms with one main stress were normal in informal speech, but some of the forms with secondary stress continued to be used for quite a time, at any rate in formal or careful speech. When the forms with secondary stress had disappeared from speech, they continued to be used in poetry.

Secondary stress occurred in several types of word. It was normal in polysyllabic loan-words from French and Latin. In these, the syllable with secondary stress was separated from the main stress by one fully unstressed syllable, as in *cómmendàble*, *émperòur*, *mómentàry*. It also occurred in some disyllabic loans, like *empìre* and *cértàin*. In native words, it was especially common in compounds, the secondary stress falling on the second element of the compound: *hólidày*, *hóusewìfe*, *Shákespèare*. In native verbs, a prefix often had a secondary stress: *fòrbíd*. By analogy, a similar secondary stress could be given to verbs of French or Latin origin: *pròvíde*.

Where forms with and without secondary stress existed side by side, their phonetic development was different. Syllables with secondary stress developed in exactly the same way as ones with main stress. In fully unstressed syllables, on the other hand, long vowels were shortened, short vowels often changed to [ə], and some consonants lost. With secondary stress, the suffix *-able* retained a long vowel, rhyming with *table*: in 1600, *commendable* was perhaps ['kɔmənd,ɛ:bl]. With secondary stress, *emperour* had ME /-u:r/, which became eModE [-əʊr] (rhyming with *flour*), while *momentary* had the ending [-ɛ:rɪ] (rhyming with *Mary*). But without secondary stress, these endings were [-əbl], [-ər], and [-ərɪ]. With secondary stress, the second element of *housewife* remained identical with *wife*. But in the variant without secondary stress, the vowel was shortened in ME and the /w/ regularly lost before an unstressed vowel, leading to the forms *hussif*, *huzzif*, and *hussy*. The words *tempest* and *conquest* come from Old French words with similar phonetic structure, yet in the first we now have /ɪ/ in the second syllable, whereas in the latter we have /e/. This is because our pronunciation of *conquest* is descended from a form with secondary stress on the second syllable. This explains both the vowel /e/, and the retention of /w/, which would have been lost before an unstressed vowel (cf. *conquer*). Many variant pronunciations today go back to forms with and without secondary stress, for example the typical British and American pronunciations of the suffix -*ary*, and perhaps also of words like *fragile*.

When such variants were in circulation side by side, poets could choose one type or the other for the purposes of rhyme or rhythm. They continued to do this throughout the seventeenth century, after the forms with secondary stress had disappeared from the everyday spoken language. One type of word with secondary stress which was often used in poetry is illustrated in the following rhymes:

> 1. No, then I well perceiue you are not *nye*,
>   Either death or you Ile finde *immediately*
>   (Shakespeare, *A Midsummer Night's Dream*)

> 2. I wonder by my troth, what thou, and *I*
>   Did, till we lov'd, were we not wean'd till then?
>   But suck'd on countrey pleasures, *childishly*
>   (Donne, 'The good-morrow').

These are both exact rhymes, and depend on forms with secondary stress on final -*y*. In ME, final -*y* normally had secondary stress in words of more than two syllables, and was pronounced /iː/. If secondary stress was retained, it developed to eModE [əɪ] (rhyming with *die*). But if secondary stress was lost in ME, /iː/ was shortened to /ɪ/, which remained in eModE. In the sixteenth century, it occasionally happened that secondary stress was reimposed, causing a relengthening to [iː]. This accounts for rhymes like *these/faculties* (Donne) and *free/legacy* (Shakespeare). So in the sixteenth century there were three pronunciations of final -*y* in circulation: [-əɪ] with retained secondary stress, [-iː] with reimposed secondary stress, and [-ɪ] unstressed. There are several other types of rhyme which can be attributed to the retention of secondary stress, like *age/pilgrimage*, *date/temperate*, and *advance/ignorance* (all found in Shakespeare's sonnets).

Poets also made use of forms with secondary stress for metrical purposes, for in some cases the form with secondary stress had one more syllable than the form without. Endings like -*ia*, -*ian*, -*ient*, -*ier*, -*ion*, and -*ious* were originally disyllabic: the first syllable of the ending was [-ɪ-], and the second carried stress. But if this secondary stress was lost, the [-ɪ-] became [-j-], and the ending now consisted of only one syllable. So in the middle of the Early Modern period the word *nation* had alternative forms: ['nɛ:sɪˌʊn] with secondary stress, and ['nɛ:sjən] (later ['ne:ʃən]) without. Similar variants occurred in *ancient, Christian, collier, condition, glorious, ocean, profession,* and many others.

In poetry, forms with a secondary stress often occur at the end of a line:

> 1. Onely behold her rare *perfection,*
>   And blesse your fortunes fayre *election*
>
> (Spenser, *Amoretti*)

> 2. Holla, ye pampered Iades of *Asia*:
>   What, can ye draw but twenty miles a day?
>
> (Marlowe, *Tamburlaine Part 2*)

> 3. Sooner may one guesse, who shall beare away
>   The infant of London, Heire to an *India*
>
> (Donne, *Satire I*)

In each case, the rhythm seems to call for a disyllabic ending and a stress on the final syllable. When *India* and *Asia* had secondary stress, the vowel of the final syllable was ME /a:/: the pronunciations round about 1600 were ['ɪndɪˌɛ:] and ['ɛ:sɪˌɛ:]. Donne's satires are in rhymed couplets, and in (3.) *India* rhymes with *away*. That is, ME /a:/ here rhymes with ME /aɪ/, which was quite common by this date. On the other hand, *Tamburlaine* is in blank verse, and it is improbable that Marlowe intended a rhyme between *Asia* and *day*. It looks as though his pronunciation was more conservative than Donne's, at least in this feature, for he does not normally rhyme ME /a:/ with ME /aɪ/. In Marlowe's part of *Hero and Leander* (1598) there is not a single rhyme between ME /a:/ and ME /aɪ/, though there are numerous rhymes between /a:/ and /a:/, and between /aɪ/ and /aɪ/.

On the other hand, if the poet did not want the extra syllable or the stress, there was the alternative form of the word with a single main stress:

> That perfect blisse and sole felicitie,
> The sweet fruition of an earthly crown
>
> (Marlowe, *Tamburlaine Part 1*)

Here it looks as though *felicitie* has secondary stress on its last syllable, but *fruition* plainly has not. As in so many things, the 'unfixed' state of the language gave the writer alternative forms to choose from.

PHONOLOGY

The first substantial studies of English intonation were not made until the eighteenth century, and we know little about the intonation of eModE. What little is written about it in the period is consistent with a system much like that of PresE. Hart has a few sentences about it in his works on English orthography. In discussing marks of punctuation, he says that a falling tune is used in exclamations, and in questions beginning with words like *what, when, how*. Butler, in his *English Grammar*, refers to both a falling tune and a rising one. The falling tune is used at the end of a sentence, where we place a period. The rising tune is used at the end of a question, unless it is one that begins with an interrogative word like *what, how, where, when*. In this latter case the falling tune is used, and the interrogative word has high tone. In exclamations, the falling tune is used, but the exclamatory word in the utterance (*Oh, Alas*, etc.), or some other emphatic word, has high tone. Parenthetic phrases are uttered on a lower pitch, and usually end as a phrase does at a comma.

As for rhythm, it is probable that the language was stress-timed and isochronic, as it is today. In many languages, speakers try to space all syllables at equal intervals. In English this is not so: within a tone-group, speakers try to space the *stressed* syllables at equal intervals. The treatment of unstressed syllables suggests that this has been the basic rhythm of English for centuries.

If you read the poetry of the Early Modern period in the present-day manner, you find that, rhythmically speaking, it works. This is very noticeable with poets who depart from simple iambic rhythms to achieve particular effects, like the highlighting of single words or phrases. Wyatt and Donne are examples of such poets. The juxtaposition of stressed syllables slows the speed of the verse down, because the interval between stresses remains approximately the same, whether unstressed syllables occur in it or not. On the other hand, a sequence of unstressed syllables makes the verse move fast, because they all have to be fitted into the space between two stresses. As one small example, let us look at the final couplet of Andrew Marvell's poem 'To his Coy Mistress'. I have marked what seem to me to be the natural stressed syllables when you read the couplet, four in each line:

> Thús, thóugh we cannot máke our Sún
> Stánd stíll, yet we wíll make him rún.

The line-break, between subject and verb, practically forces the reader to use three successive stressed syllables, *Sun / Stand still*. The consequence is that the sun, while not actually stopping, certainly does go with a very measured tread. In the final line there are eight syllables, but there are stresses on the first two of them, taking up half the time-span of the line. That is why the remainder of the line really does run.

Numerous other examples of the use of stress-timing in English poetry are discussed in Barber (1983).

EXCEPTIONAL PRONUNCIATIONS

In this chapter I have tried to give a key to eModE pronunciation, using the PresE spelling and pronunciation as a guide. This works for a very large part of the vocabulary, but inevitably there are words where it fails. In some words, for various reasons, the modern spelling or pronunciation is not what would be expected.

One reason for such exceptional pronunciations is that words frequently drift into the standard language from regional or social dialects. A good example is the word *one*. This was OE *án*, with the same vowel as such words as *bán* 'bone' and *ác* 'oak'. The regular development of the vowel was to ME /ɔ:/, so that the eModE pronunciation was [ɔ:n], later [o:n], rhyming with *moan*. This was indeed the usual pronunciation in the standard language. The PresE pronunciation [wʌn] was adopted from a regional dialect, and did not enter StE until about 1700. One reason for its spread was probably that its adoption removed a homophonic clash between *one* and *own*, which could cause ambiguity in phrases like *my own/one brother*. The two words had become homophones when ME /ɔ:/ coalesced with ME /ɔʊ/ during the Early Modern period. The original pronunciation is reflected in *alone* and *atone*, which are derived from 'all one' and 'at one'.

Other common words where the PresE pronunciation is from a non-standard variant include *either*, *key*, *neither*, and *quay*.

Slightly different is the word *love*. In this case, the PresE /lʌv/ is the normal development from the OE and ME form. But in eModE there was a common variant [lu:v], which had arisen by a ME vowel-lengthening process in East Anglia and northern England. The form [lu:v] was especially cultivated by poets, because it enabled them to rhyme the word with *approve*, *move*, and *prove*. Other eModE words which had variants with [u:] include *above*, *come*, *dove*, and *Rome*.

Another cause of irregular development is analogy. For example, the verb *ache* was pronounced [ɛ:k], and usually spelt *ake*, while the noun was pronounced [ɛ:tʃ]. By analogy, the noun has adopted the pronunciation of the verb, though it is the noun's spelling which has been standardised. Another example is *lose* (v.) and its past participle *lost*. These were eModE [lo:z] and [lo:st], and the regular modern development would be /ləʊz/, /ləʊst/. The PresE pronunciation /lu:z/ is due to analogy with the word *loose*, and already existed as a variant in eModE.

Another factor is the influence of the spelling. Some spelling-pronunciations in fact restore an earlier pronunciation, as when people today insert /t/ in *often* and *waistcoat*. Frequently, however, the influence of the spelling produces pronunciations which are unhistorical. We have already seen how initial /h-/ has been inserted into words like *herb* and *host*. A group of words like *author* usually had [t] as the medial consonant: the PresE pronunciation with /θ/ is due to the influence of the spelling, itself a spelling variant from French. Other words which commonly had [t] include *authority*, *anthem*, and *orthography*, though [θ] was perhaps also heard. The word *schedule* had initial [s-], and was commonly spelt *sedule* or *cedule*. The PresE pronunciations, both British /ʃ-/ and American /sk-/, are due to the unhistorical spelling with *sch-*, which first appeared in the middle of the seventeenth century. Inverted spellings can also cause confusion. The words *wood* and *wool* have never had a long vowel, always [ʊ]. Their spellings are due to the influence of those like *good* and *look*, where eModE [u:] had been shortened to [ʊ].

There are, then, many exceptions to our rules for eModE pronunciation. To be certain about any word, we have to look at other evidence. One obvious source is the OED, which gives the etymology of a word, and also the spellings recorded in different centuries. To this needs to be added the evidence of the historical grammars of English, which traditionally have included large sections on historical phonology. But for the ordinary non-specialist reader of eModE texts, our key to the code will give the right answers most of the time.

PHONETIC TRANSCRIPTIONS

Let us end this chapter with phonetic transcriptions showing a possible pronunciation in StE of three poems from different dates. There is obviously scope for great variation. I have assumed that these lyrics would be spoken (or sung) in a fairly formal style. I have therefore given a somewhat conservative style of speech, and have often used strong forms where weak ones would have been possible. In particular, I have made sparing use of unstressed [ə]. The transcriptions are allophonic, as can be seen for example from the treatment of *thing* and *think*. Stress marks are used on words of more than one syllable, but this does not necessarily imply that the syllable thus marked was one of the main metrical stresses in the line.

The first extract is by Sir Thomas Wyatt (1503–42), three stanzas from his lyric 'My lute awake':

> As to be herd where ere ['ear'] is none,
>   [as tʊ biː hɛrd hwɛːr ɛːr iz nɔːn]
> As lede to grave in marbill stone,
>   [az lɛ(ː)d tʊ græːv ɪn 'marbɪl stɔːn]
> My song may perse her hert as sone;
>   [məɪ sɔŋg mɛɪ piːrs hər hɛrt az suːn]
> Should we then sigh, or syng, or mone?
>   [ʃuːld wiː ðen səɪç ɔr sɪŋg ɔr mɔːn]

No, no, my lute, for I have done.
    [nɔː nɔː məɪ liut fɔr əɪ hav duːn]

The Rokkes do not so cruelly
    [ðə rɔks duː nɔt sɔː ˈkriuəˌləɪ]
Repulse the waves continuelly,
    [rɪˈpʊls ðə wæːvz kɔnˈtɪniuəˌləɪ]
As she my suyte and affection,
    [az ʃiː məɪ siut and əˈfɛksɪˌʊn]
So that I ame past remedy,
    [sɔː ðat əɪ am past ˈrɛmɪˌdəɪ]
Whereby my lute and I have done.
    [hwɛːrˈbəɪ məɪ liut ənd əɪ hav dʊn]

– – – – – – – – – – – – – – – – – – – –

And then may chaunce the to repent
    [and ðɛn məɪ tʃɑuns ðiː tʊ rɪˈpɛnt]
The tyme that thou hast lost and spent,
    [ðə təɪm ðat ðəu hast lɔːst and spɛnt]
To cause thy lovers sigh and swoune;
    [tʊ kɑuz ðəɪ ˈluːvərz səɪç and swuːn]
Then shalt thou knowe beaultie but lent
    [ðɛn ʃalt ðəu knɔu ˈbɛutɪ bʊt lɛnt]
And wisshe and want as I have done.
    [and wɪʃ and want az əɪ hav duːn]

My second extract consists of three stanzas from a lute song by Thomas Ford
(c. 1580–1648), published in 1607:

There is a lady sweet and kind,
    [ðɛːr ɪz ə ˈlɛːdɪ swiːt ænd kəɪnd]
Was never face so pleased my mind,
    [wəz ˈnɛvər fɛːs sɔː pleːzd məɪ məɪnd]
I did but see her passing by,
    [əɪ dɪd bʌt siː hər ˈpasɪŋ bəɪ]
And yet I love her till I die.
    [ænd jɛt əɪ lʌv hər tɪl əɪ dəɪ]

Her gesture, motion and her smiles,
    [hər ˈdʒɛstiur ˈmoːsɪˌʊn ænd hər sməɪlz]
Her wit, her voice my heart beguiles,
    [hər wɪt hər vʊɪs məɪ hart bɪˈgəɪlz]
Beguiles my heart I know not why,
    [bɪˈgəɪlz məɪ hart əɪ knɔː nɔt hwəɪ]

And yet I love her till I die.

    [as before]

Cupid is winged and doth range,

    ['kiupɪd ɪz 'wɪŋgɪd ænd dʌθ rɒ:nʤ]

Her country so my love doth change,

    [hər 'kʌntrɪ so: məɪ lʌv dʌθ ʧɒ:nʤ]

But change she earth or change she sky,

    [bʌt ʧɒ:nʤ ʃi: ərθ ɔr ʧɒ:nʤ ʃi: skəɪ]

Yet will I love her till I die.

    [jɛt wɪl əɪ lʌv hər tɪl əɪ dəɪ]

The word *motion* is set to three notes of music, which suggests that it is tri-syllabic; if it is not, the pronunciation is perhaps ['mo:sjən]. I transcribe *love* as [lʌv] rather than [lu:v], since this seems to have been the common seventeenth-century pronunciation. The form [ərθ] 'earth' is from earlier [ɛrθ], but, as the spelling suggests, there was also a form with a long vowel, [ɛ:rθ]. Strong forms are again often used where weak ones would have been possible, since a singer would presumably prefer [ænd] to [ənd]. Similarly, loss of initial /h/ is not shown: in ME, /h/ had been lost at the beginning of unstressed words such as *him* and *her*, but I assume that the singer would prefer the form in which the /h/ had been re-inserted.

The final passage is the opening of 'To his Coy Mistress', by Andrew Marvell (1621–78). It was not published until 1681, but was perhaps written in the 1650s.

Had we but World enough, and Time,

    [hæd wi: bʌt wərld ɪ'nʌf ənd taɪm]

This coyness Lady were no crime.

    [ðɪs 'kɔɪnɪs 'lɛ:dɪ wɛ:r no: kraɪm]

We would sit down, and think which way

    [wi: wʊd sɪt dɑʊn ənd θɪŋk hwɪʧ wɛ:]

To walk, and pass our long Loves Day.

    [tʊ wɒ:k ænd pas ɑʊr lɒŋ lʌvz dɛ:]

Thou by the *Indian Ganges* side

    [ðɑʊ baɪ ðe: 'ɪndjən 'gænʤi:z saɪd]

Should'st Rubies find: I by the Tide

    [ʃʊdst 'ru:bɪz faɪnd aɪ baɪ ðe: taɪd]

Of *Humber* would complain. I would

    [əv 'hʌmbər wʊd kəm'plɛ:n aɪ wu:d]

Love you ten years before the Flood:

    [lʌv ju: tɛn jɛ:rz bɪ'fɔ:r ðe: flu:d]

And you should if you please refuse

    [ənd ju: ʃʊd ɪf ju: plɛ:z rɪ'fju:z]

Till the Conversion of the *Jews*.
[tɪl ðe: kən'vərsjən əv ðe: ʤu:z]
My vegetable Love should grow
[maɪ 'veʤə,tɛ:bl lʌv ʃʊd gro:]
Vaster then Empires, and more slow.
['vastər ðən 'ɛm,paɪrz ənd mɔ:r slo:]

Here I have used more weak forms than in the other two passages. I have, however, chosen forms with a long vowel for the rhyme *would/flood*, where the words are obviously stressed: possible alternative pronunciations are [wʊd] and [flʊd]. For the definite article *the*, I give the form [ðe:], which seems to have been fairly common, but there were other pronunciations in circulation, including [ði:], [ðɛ], and perhaps [ðə]. For the pronunciation of *Ganges* I have just guessed. I assume that the coalescence of ME /ɛ:/ with ME /a:/ (and /aɪ/) had not yet taken place, so that there are different vowels in *please* and *way*. The vowel of *pass* is an allophone of the /æ/ phoneme, but by this date /ʊ/ and /ʌ/ are separate phonemes.

FURTHER READING

The standard work on English phonology in the period is Dobson (1968), a work of prodigious scholarship. Dobson demonstrates the great variety of pronunciation that existed even in StE, and also has a good deal to say about non-standard pronunciations. He attaches great importance (rightly, in my view) to the evidence of the orthoepists of the period, and analyses it with great care. This kind of evidence, however, does tend to give prominence to formal and conservative styles of speech, and what Dobson presents as StE pronunciation at any given date is often a very conservative brand of it. In a subject so complex, and with evidence often susceptible to different interpretations, there are inevitably points of controversy, and Dobson's work has encountered criticisms: see for example the reviews (of the first edition of 1957) by Eilert Ekwall (*Review of English Studies* IX, 303–12), Herbert Koziol (*English Studies* XXXVIII, 138–41), and Martin Lehnert (*Anglia* LXXVI, 443–8). But, despite the points of controversy, the work will undoubtedly remain for many years the indispensable handbook on the subject.

Dobson's book, however, is a work for the specialist, not for the general reader: it is enormously detailed, and moreover presupposes in the reader a considerable knowledge of the phonology of Old English and Middle English. Other works in the field include Zachrisson (1913), Wyld (1923), Kökeritz (1953), and Cercignani (1981). Kökeritz's book has long been popular with students of English literature, but some of it rests on rather shaky evidence, and it should be treated with caution. The general reader would perhaps be advised to read shorter accounts, such as those found in histories of the English language.

Luick (1964) is a monumental historical phonology of English, too detailed for the ordinary reader. A study of the phonology of the period from 1400 to 1950 will be found in Horn (1954). More modern and more accessible is Jones (1989). The standard work on the pronunciation of present-day British English is Gimson (1989), while an account of present-day English accents worldwide is given by Wells (1982). On the intonation of present-day English, see O'Connor & Arnold (1973). A discussion of the use of stress-timing in English poetry can be found in Barber (1983).

In the past, the usual method of depicting the phonemes of Middle English has been to use ordinary alphabetical letters with various diacritics. For example, a macron shows that a vowel is long, a hook underneath that it is open, a dot underneath that it is close. I have abandoned this traditional system, and instead use standard phonetic symbols. Readers should have little difficulty, however, in correlating the two systems. Since I have abandoned the macron for Middle English, I have also abandoned it for Old English and for classical Latin. Here I have followed the OED, and mark long vowels with an acute accent, for example OE *bát* 'boat'.

Chapter Four

GRAMMAR:
(1) MORPHOLOGY

At one time it was common for books which called themselves historical grammars to handle phonology as well as grammar. It is however desirable to handle the two separately, and this is now normal practice. It is desirable because it reflects something in the nature of language itself. In human languages, there is a phonological system, and riding on this is a grammatical system. The phonological level has no direct link with meaning. Grammar, by contrast, deals with meaningful items, the smallest meaningful unit being the morpheme.

MORPHOLOGY AND SYNTAX

Grammar can be considered from two aspects, morphology and syntax. Morphology is concerned with the structure of words, and the way in which they change their form for grammatical purposes: for example, the way in which the inflections *-ed* and *-ing* can be added to verbs like *walk*. Syntax, on the other hand, deals with the permissible ways in which words can be strung together to make utterances – for example the structure of phrases and sentences.

Besides inflectional morphology, which deals with things like *-ed* and *-ing*, there is another branch of morphology which handles word-formation, for example the way in which *unhappy* is formed from *un-* and *happy*, or *quickly* from *quick* and *-ly*. This is called derivational morphology. It will not be discussed here, as it belongs to a later chapter, on vocabulary. Grammatical morphology, however, is not solely concerned with inflections: it also deals with paradigms like *he/him/his* and *give/gave/given*. In this chapter and the next, the separation of morphology from syntax will not be absolutely water-tight: to avoid repetition, it is sometimes desirable to take them together. For

142

example, it would be wasteful to list the relative pronoun *who/whom* under morphology, and then treat its use in relative clauses under syntax.

LEXICAL WORDS AND GRAMMATICAL WORDS

English words, both now and in Early Modern times, fall into a number of different grammatical categories. These were traditionally called the parts of speech, but are now usually called word-classes. They can be divided into two main types, lexical and grammatical. Grammatical words are ones that belong to a closed system: in PresE, for example, it is not difficult to make an exhaustive list of the personal pronouns (*he*, *she*, etc.) and of their oblique forms (*him*, *her*, etc.). But it is impossible to make an exhaustive list of nouns, because the category is open-ended: new ones are being formed all the time, and others falling out of use, and the number of nouns is indefinitely large. Nouns are lexical words.

In PresE, lexical words are nouns, verbs, and adjectives. Grammatical words include pronouns, auxiliaries, determiners, conjunctions, and prepositions. What were traditionally called adverbs must be subdivided, some of them being lexical and others grammatical.The exact number of word-classes depends on the analysis made: for example, I include demonstratives (*this*, *that*) in the determiner class, but it is possible to treat them as a separate category.

Anybody can invent a new noun, though with no guarantee that it will catch on and be used by other people. But no individual can successfully invent a new personal pronoun or auxiliary. The members of a grammatical class do indeed change: the system of personal pronouns has changed a good deal since the sixteenth century. But this is a gradual, long-term process.

NOUN INFLECTIONS

In eModE, most nouns have three forms: a base form, a plural form, and a possessive form. Usually the plural and the possessive are identical: base form *boy*, plural and possessive *boys*. In a few nouns, it is the base form and the plural which are identical: base form and plural *sheep*, possessive *sheeps*.

In PresE, we distinguish four forms by the spelling, even though only two forms are distinguished in pronunciation: *boy*, *boy's*, *boys*, *boys'*. This use of the apostrophe to mark the possessive is not a feature of eModE. Usually, both plural and possessive are spelt without an apostrophe. If an apostrophe is inserted, it is just as likely to be in a plural as in a possessive. The use of *'-s* as the spelling for the possessive singular is not common until the late seventeenth century. The regular use of *-s'* for the possessive plural is not common until the late eighteenth century. There are however a few words where eModE does have four distinct forms: base form *man*, possessive singular *mans*, plural *men*, possessive plural *mens*.

The vast majority of nouns formed their plural with the {-es} morpheme, represented in spelling by -s or -es: for example *boys*, *boyes*, *cats*, *catts*, *dogs*, *dogges*, *judges*, *lasses*. In speech, this morpheme had three allemorphs, that is, it was realised in three different forms. These were [-s], [-z], and [-ɪz] (or [-əz]). By the middle of the Early Modern period these were distributed as they are today. So [-ɪz] (or [-əz]) was used after /s/, /z/, /ʃ/, /tʃ/, and /dʒ/, as in *lasses*, *mazes*, *bushes*, *watches*, *judges*. After all other phonemes, [-s] or [-z] was used, the former occurring after voiceless consonants (*cats*, *hips*), the latter after voiced consonants and vowels (*dogs*, *flies*). To us this distribution seems so natural that we find it difficult to imagine any other, but in late Middle English there was a different distribution, from which the present-day one arose by a process of regulation during the sixteenth century. The modern distribution was probably not fully established until about 1600.

In EME the ending was [-əs]. Round about 1300, the [ə] was lost in some forms, especially words of three syllables. So *hunteres* ['hʊntərəs] became *hunters* ['hʊntərs] (still with voiceless [-s]). In the nouns which retained the full ending [-əs], this changed during the fourteenth century into [-əz], by the regular sound-change whereby final voiceless fricatives became voiced in unstressed syllables. So *kinges*, originally pronounced ['kɪŋgəs], became ['kɪŋgəz]. Then in the fifteenth century the [ə] was lost from most of these forms too, giving pronunciations like [kɪŋgz]. Thus in the late fifteenth century the situation was that forms with early syncope of [ə] had the ending [-s], and forms with late syncope had the ending [-z], whether the preceding phoneme was voiced or voiceless. In the sixteenth century a process of regulation took place, whereby [-s] was standardised after voiceless phonemes, and [-z] after voiced. There is evidence, notably from Hart, that this process was not completed until the second half of the century.

The [-ɪz] ending occurred in words in which syncope did not take place at all, being prevented by the preceding consonant. It arose from earlier [-əz], for in the fifteenth and sixteenth centuries it was quite common for unstressed [ə] to become [ɪ], though the positions in which this happened varied for different groups in the speech community. The plural ending [-ɪz] certainly existed in eModE, and is sometimes indicated by spellings like *horsis* or *horsys*, especially in the early sixteenth century. There is also evidence for [-əz], however, and both forms exist today in different varieties of English. In the earlier sixteenth century, the unsyncopated ending sometimes occurs with nouns which later have only [-s] or [-z]. In Sir Thomas Elyot, for example, there are spellings like *actis*, *beastis*, *magistratis*, and *spheris*. These too undergo the regulating process in the course of the century.

A few forms escaped this regulating process, probably because they were no longer apprehended as plurals. One example is *dice*, originally the plural of *die*. Another is *bodice*, originally *(a pair of) bodies*, where *body* means 'the upper part of a woman's dress'. A small number of nouns which in the singular ended in [s] or [z] suffered the opposite fate. They were mistakenly apprehended as plurals, and a new singular was formed from them. One example is *pease*, from which was formed the new singular *pea*, first recorded in the early seventeenth century: the older form of the word survives in *pease-pudding*. A similar case is *sherry*, from earlier *sherris*, also dating from the early seventeenth century.

Some nouns formed their plurals in other ways. There were a few plurals with the morpheme {-en}, represented by the spellings *-en, -n, -ne*. Some survive today: *children, oxen*, and (marginally) *brethren* and *kine*. A few additional ones sometimes occur in eModE: *eyen* or *eyne, peasen* 'peas', *housen, shoon*, and *hosen* 'leg-garments'. These, however, are not very common even in the sixteenth century, and are rare after 1600. The plural of *child* can be *childern* as well as *children*, and occasionally even *childer* or *childre*. These forms contain a relic of a late OE plural ending {-r-}, to which was added {-en} in Middle English. In the poetry of Spenser, and of people influenced by him, there are other nouns with {-en} plurals: Spenser himself, for example, has *foen* and *skyen*. Such forms, however, are archaisms or pseudo-archaisms.

There were also rather more nouns than today that formed their plural with the zero-morpheme. In addition to *sheep, deer, swine*, and similar familiar ones, we encounter plurals like *horse, lamb, winter, year*, alongside *horses, lambs*, and so on. Such uninflected plurals occur quite often in expressions of length and of monetary value, with words like *foot, mile, yard*, and *mark, pound, shilling*. Conversely, words where we now have the zero-morpheme plural are sometimes found with the {-es} plural. In *The Compleat Angler* (1653), Izaak Walton regularly uses forms like *carps, pikes, salmons, trouts*.

There were also 'mutated plurals', ones that indicated plurality by changing the vowel of the stem. These were the same as today: *feet, geese, men, lice*, and so on.

The possessive form of the noun, both singular and plural, is regularly formed with the {-es} morpheme: *my poore Fathers body, this Slaues Offall, the Lawes delay, Offences gilded hand, Dicers Oathes* (all from *Hamlet*). The allomorphs were the same as for the {-es} plural morpheme. Rather more often than in PresE, however, we find a possessive form with zero-morpheme. It often occurs when the noun ends in /s/, as in *poore Clarence death* (*Richard III*), *Frier Lawrence Cell* (*Romeo and Juliet*). It can also occur when the following word begins with /s/, and is particularly common before the word *sake* as in *for sport sake, for their owne Credit sake* (both from *Henry IV.1*). Such usages are by no means universal, however: there are also such examples as *the Princes Doome* (*Romeo and Juliet*) and *for Fames sake* (*Loves Labours Lost*).

A phrase from *Twelfth Night* illustrates an alternative to the use of the possessive inflection: *a sea-fight 'gainst the Count his gallies*. Here the *Count his gallies* means 'the Count's gallies'. Sometimes we find the same construction using *her*, as in *Lucilla hir company* 'Lucilla's company' (Lyly, *Euphues*). Less frequently it is found with *their*, as in *the vtopians their creditors* 'the Utopians' creditors' (Ralph Robinson's translation of More's *Utopia*). The construction with *their* is not found before the sixteenth century, but the constructions with *his* and *her* are very old, going back to OE. In eModE the construction with *his* is particularly common. This is probably because the unstressed form of *his* was [ɪz], and could therefore be identical with the {-es} possessive morpheme, with which it tended to be identified. This probably explains why *his* is occasionally used when the preceding noun requires *her*. The OED quotes an example from 1607, *Mrs Sands his maid*, which looks like an inverted spelling for *Mrs Sands's maid*. The *his* construction is therefore especially common after nouns which would require the [-ɪz] allomorph of the {-es} possessive inflection. In Shakespeare there are examples like *King Lewes his satisfaction* (*Henry V*) and *Mars his heart* (*Troilus and Cressida*). This is very striking in the later part of the period, when the construction is less common. In Joseph Glanvill's *Vanity of Dogmatizing* (1661) the {-es} possessive is overwhelmingly predominant: in 250 pages of text there are only eight examples of the *his* construction. All eight occur with proper names, and every one of these names ends in [-s] or [-z], like *Democritus his Well* and *Hercules his Pillars*. The tendency to use *his* after proper names is also noticeable earlier in the period, as in the examples from Shakespeare quoted above.

Adjectives

In Old English, the adjective was declined for number, case, and gender, but its inflections decayed in the course of Middle English, and by the fifteenth century it was indeclinable, as today.

There are, however, differences between eModE and PresE in the comparison of the adjective. We have two ways of comparing the adjective: 1. by using the inflections *-er*, *-est* (*bigger*, *biggest*), and 2. a periphrastic or analytic method using *more*, *most* (*more delightful*, *most delightful*). In accordance with the general development of English from a more synthetic type to a more analytic type of language, the *more/most* method of comparison spread a great deal in Middle English, and indeed is still spreading today.

The difference between eModE and PresE is that today there is a fairly strict regulation of the two methods. Things are indeed changing: there is a group of disyllabic adjectives (like *cloudy*, *common*, *cruel*, *pleasant*, *quiet*, *simple*) which a few years ago were normally compared with *-er/-est*, but which are now usually compared with *more/most*. Indeed, some speakers of the younger generation often use *more/most* even with monosyllabic adjectives. This does not mean, however, that there is no regulation of the two usages: it is just that the regulation is changing. In eModE, by contrast, the two methods of comparison were very nearly in free variation: as in so many things, the eModE speaker or writer had greater freedom of choice. There may indeed have been stylistic differences between them: for some adjectives, there is evidence suggesting that *-er/-est* was colloquial and *more/most* formal. But, broadly speaking, any adjective could be compared by either method, even by the same speaker or writer. So Ben Jonson uses both *fitter* and *more fit*, Shakespeare both *sweeter* and *more sweet*. Especially striking to the present-day reader is the use of *-er/-est* with polysyllabic words, the superlative being particularly common: *naturalest* (Sir Thomas Smith), *delicatest* (Lyly), *magnificentest* (Nash), *rascalliest* (Shakespeare), *notoriousest* (Archbishop Laud), *difficultest* (Milton), *ungratefull'st* (Otway). Also striking is the use of *-er/-est* with those disyllabic adjectives that now take *more/most* even in conservative speech. Such are *perfecter*, *perfectest* (Shakespeare), *learneder* (Jonson), *cursedst* (Shakespeare), *pacienter* (Gabriel Harvey), *auncientest* (Spenser), *frequentest* (Locke), *shamefuller* (Spenser), *careful'st* (Queen Elizabeth I), *willinger* (Ascham), *ragingest* (Nash), *greuouser* (Latimer), and *famousest* (Milton). In the superlative inflection there is often syncope of the vowel.

Another feature is that double comparison was acceptable: it was possible to use the inflectional and the periphrastic method together. There is a famous example in *Julius Caesar*:

> This was the most vnkindest cut of all.

Double comparatives are illustrated by Shakespeare's *more nearer* (*Hamlet*) and *more larger* (*Antony and Cleopatra*). But such usages are not confined to drama: they are common, in both verse and prose. An example from the King James Bible is *most straitest* 'strictest' (Acts 26:5). Its occurrence here shows that the usage was not just a colloquialism.

There are a few individual comparative and superlative forms which differ from those of PresE. In the sixteenth century, *lenger* and *lengest* are occasionally found as the comparative and superlative of *long*, and very early in the century *strenger* and *strengest* as those of *strong*. These are relics of a class of adjectives which in OE had mutated vowels in the comparative and superlative. The only such forms surviving today are *elder* and *eldest*, which we use only in a limited number of contexts. In eModE, on the other hand, they could be used instead of *older* and *oldest* in any kind of context. In *Julius Caesar*, Cassius says that he is an *Elder Souldier* than Brutus. In Congreve's *Way of the World* (1700), Mirabell says of a legal document:

> I suppose this Deed may bear an Elder Date than what you have obtain'd from your Lady.

The forms *more* and *most* could be used to mean 'larger, largest'. In *King John*

TABLE 4.1

Personal pronouns and pronoun-determiners c. 1500

Nominative	I	thou	he	she	hit, it		we	ye	they
Accusative	me	thee	him	her	hit, it, him		us	you	them, hem
Possessive	mine	thine	his	hers	his		ours	yours	theirs
Determiner	my, mine	thy, thine	his	her	his		our	your	their

we find *a more requitall* 'a larger recompense'. In his *Discouery of Guiana* (1596), Sir Walter Ralegh speaks of *the most ['largest'] and fairest houses*. Similarly, *less* and *least* could mean 'smaller, smallest', referring to physical size. In *Euery man out of his Humor* (1600), Ben Jonson uses the expression *less noses* 'smaller noses'. The words *later* and *latter* are used interchangeably, and so are *latest* and *last*: in *Henry IV Part 2*, the dying king gives to his son his *very latest Counsell* 'very last advice'.

PRONOUNS

Pronouns are grammatical (closed system) words. They fall into several subsets: personal, relative, interrogative, reflexive, intensive, demonstrative, and indefinite. The relative pronouns will be handled under Syntax, in the next chapter. The other pronouns will be handled here.

Personal pronouns

The personal pronouns of Modern English form a system in which there are distinctions of gender, number, case, and person. The cases distinguished are nominative, accusative, and possessive, for example nominative *I*, accusative *me*, and possessive *mine* (as in *the book is mine*). There is also a set of related pronoun-determiners, forms used as noun-adjuncts, like *my* (as in *my book*), and it is convenient to consider these along with the personal pronouns, since they pattern in the same way.

At the beginning of the eModE period, in 1500, the set of personal pronouns and related pronoun-determiners was as shown in Table 4.1. There were numerous variant spellings. For example, *thou/thee/thine* often appear as *thow/the/thyn*. For simplicity of presentation, I give a single spelling in each case, and have chosen the most modern form, which is not necessarily the one that was commonest in eModE. I give variant spellings only where these represent substantially different forms, like *them, hem*.

One striking thing about the system as compared with PresE is the fact that there are two different pronouns of the second person, *thou* and *ye*. Later we shall consider the ways in which these were used, but for the moment, for convenience, I shall refer to the *thou* group as the singular, and the *ye* group as the plural.

In the plural, the nominative is *ye* and the accusative *you*. In the course of the Early Modern period, however, *you* became the normal form for both nominative and accusative, and *ye* became just a minor variant. It is not entirely clear why it was the accusative form which became thus standardised, but it may have been by analogy with *thou*: the two forms usually had the same vowel in late Middle English, and, as we have already seen, the form [jəʊ], rhyming with *thou*, still existed in the sixteenth century.

The first examples of nominative *you* go back to the fourteenth century, but in the standard literary language its encroachment was not rapid until the 1540s. In the early sixteenth century, the *ye/you* distinction was preserved by many writers. It is maintained, for example, by Sir Thomas Elyot. It is also maintained in William Tyndale's translation of the New Testament, as in the following passage from Matthew (my italics):

> Blessed are *ye* when men reuyle *you* / and persecute *you* / and shall falsly say all manner of yvell saynges agaynst *you* for my sake … *ye* are the salt of the erthe … *ye* are the light of the worlde.

In the course of the sixteenth century, however, *you* was increasingly used as a nominative. Elyot, who was born in the 1490s, preserves the *ye/you* distinction. Roger Ascham, born in 1515, does not. In his *Toxophilus* (1545), the two forms are used indiscriminately for the nominative, while *you* is preferred for the accusative. This kind of usage is common in the third quarter of the century. By Shakespeare's time, *you* was the normal form for both nominative and accusative, and *ye* was a less common variant. By this time, moreover, *ye* too could be used as either a nominative or an accusative. Its use as an accusative is recorded as early as the fifteenth century, but in StE is not common until the later sixteenth century. In the seventeenth century, *ye* is just as likely to be used for the accusative as for the nominative, but is much rarer than *you* in both functions, and in the course of the century becomes increasingly archaic and literary. The way it is used in the plays of John Fletcher (d. 1625) suggests that in the Jacobean period it may have been considered more refined and courtly than everyday *you*.

It is possible, however, that the spelling *ye* sometimes represents the unstressed form [jə], which could have arisen from either *ye* or *you*. Such may be the case in the following sentence from Wycherley's *Country Wife* (1675):

> But what d'ye take ill, if he has done nothing?

In this kind of position, *ye* continued to be written, as in the formula 'How d'ye do?'. But in stressed position *ye* had fallen out of use by the end of the seventeenth century, except as a literary archaism.

There are also differences from PresE in the neuter pronoun *it*. The original form of the nominative and accusative was *hit*, which was still in use in the sixteenth century. The word *it* is an example of the restressing of a weak form: it arose in ME when intial /h-/ was regularly lost in unstressed syllables. Other forms like *he* and *her* similarly lost their /h-/ when unstressed, and we still have these forms, although they are not recognised in the written language. But in the case of *it*, we have lost the old strong form *hit*, and have generalised *it* for both stressed and unstressed positions. The disappearance of *hit* takes place during the sixteenth century, and by 1600 *it* is the normal form.

A further weak form /t/ arose from *it* in unstressed position. This is found in ME, but is not common until the late sixteenth century. In many positions, this /t/ was recognised by the literary language, in forms like *'tis*, *'twere*, *'twill*, *is't*, and *was't*. In plays which attempt to give the illusion of everyday speech, /t/ is even more frequent, and we find forms like *to't*, *by't*, *on't*, *give't*, and *bring't*.

In the accusative, we find *him* as well as *hit* and *it*. Originally, *hit* was accusative, while *him* was dative. The distinction between accusative and dative disappeared during the ME period, and in the other personal pronouns the modern accusative form (*me*, *you*, *her*, etc.) is desended from the OE dative. Only in the case of *it* does the modern accusative form go back to the OE accusative. Even here, the old dative form *him* was used as an alternative to accusative *it* all through the sixteenth century.

For the possessive and determiner of *it*, the traditional form was *his*. The word *its* was a new one, formed by adding the possessive ending {-es} to *it*. The first example of *its* recorded by the OED occurs in 1598, and it is rare in the opening years of the seventeenth century. The King James Bible of 1611 uses *his*, never *its*, as in the following sentence (Matthew 5:13):

> if the salt haue lost *his* sauour, wherewith shall *it* be salted?

There is a similar passage at Mark 9:50, where modern editions read *its salt-ness*, but where the original 1611 text has *his saltnesse*. The Shakespeare First Folio of 1623 has about ten examples of *its*, but not one of them occurs in the text of a play published in Shakespeare's lifetime. The usual form in Shake-speare is *his*, as when in *Hamlet* Polonius says:

> Giue thy thoughts no tongue,
> Nor any vnproportion'd thought *his* act.

The new word *its* spread rapidly, however. By the 1620s it was the normal form, and the use of *his* as a neuter was rare, though it lingered on until about 1670. The rapid success of *its* was probably due to the fact that it was incon-venient to have the same form *his* for the possessive of both *he* and *it*. Even before *its* was common, there was a tendency to avoid the use of *his* as a neuter: instead, writers often use *of it* or *thereof*. In the King James Bible we find *great was the fall of it* (Matthew 7:27), and *in Bethlehem, and in all the coasts thereof* (Matthew 2:16). For the latter phrase, the New English Bible of 1970 reads *in Bethlehem and its neighbourhood*.

Another alternative to neuter *his* was *it* used as a possessive. This was not infrequent in the later sixteenth century, and we have already encountered an example in George Pettie's *Civil Conversation* (1581): 'I marueile how our english tongue hath crackt *it* credite'. There is an example in the King James Bible, at Leviticus 25:5. There are a few examples in Shakespeare, a well-known passage being from the 1608 quarto of *King Lear*:

> the hedge sparrow fed the Cookow so long, that it had *it* head bit off be *it* young.

But once the form *its* had become firmly established, these other devices became unnecessary.

In the third-person plural, the Scandinavian forms *they*, *them*, *their*, and *theirs* are the normal ones by 1500. These had spread down from the north, but the nominative had spread faster than the others, and Chaucer uses nominative *they*, but English *hem* and *hir* for the accusative and possessive. In the sixteenth century, *hem* is still found as an alternative to *them*. In the course of the Early Modern period, *hem* becomes less frequent, and is rare in the seventeenth century, though it is still recorded as late as 1660. Its weak form was *em*, with the usual loss of initial /h-/ in unstressed syllables. This is found in ME, and must have existed in speech in the sixteenth century, though not recognised in the written language. It reappears in writing round about 1600, with spellings like *'em*, *em*, *am*, *um*, presumably representing a pronunciation [əm]. It is especially common in plays: Macbeth, for example, says 'Call *'em*, let me see *'em*'.

Another weak form which is common in plays round about 1600 is *'a* or *a*, an unstressed form of *he*, perhaps pronounced [ə]. It occurs in ME, and must have existed in speech in the sixteenth century, but is rarely recognised in the literary language in the early part of the century. It is common in the middle of the Early Modern period, however, in plays and in prose written in a colloquial style, like many of the cony-catching pamphlets of the 1590s. Shakespeare uses it, and not only in comic or low-life scenes: at one of the crises in *Hamlet*, when Hamlet finds the King praying, he says (according to the 'good' quarto of 1604):

> Now might I doe it, but now a is apraying,
> And now Ile doo't, and so a goes to heauen.

In both lines, the First Folio of 1623 changes the pronoun to *he*, perhaps because *a* 'he' was infrequent by this date. It is not found in the later part of the century.

TABLE 4.2

Personal pronouns and pronoun-determiners c. 1600

Nominative	I	thou	he, 'a	she	it, 't	we	you (ye)	they
Accusative	me	thee	him	her	it, 't	us	you (ye)	them, 'em
Possessive	mine	thine	his	hers	his	ours	yours	theirs
Determiner	my (mine)	thy (thine)	his	her	his, it	our	your	their

The pronoun-determiners of the first-person and second-person singular have alternative forms: *my* or *mine*, *thy* or *thine*. At the beginning of the Early Modern period, the distinction is the same as that between the two forms of the indefinite article: *my* and *thy* are used before consonants, while *mine* and *thine* are used before vowels (and sometimes before words beginning with /h-/). In the preface to Elyot's *Governor* we find *my duetie*, *my naturall contray*, *my faythe*, *my studie*, but *myne onely ... lord* and *myne owne experience*. As we have already seen, there is often an initial *h-* in the spelling which was not pronounced, and in such cases we of course find *mine* and *thine*, as in *mine honour*, *mine host*, *mine habit*. But *mine* and *thine* (and *an*) were also often used before initial /h-/, as in *mine heart*. This changed during the sixteenth century, however, and in the seventeenth century *my*, *thy*, and *a* are normal in this position: in Shakespeare, the word *heart* occurs very frequently, but almost without exception he uses *a heart*, *my heart*, *thy heart*.

In the earlier sixteenth century, the distinction between *my* and *mine*, and between *thy* and *thine*, is pretty consistently observed in the standard language. But in the course of the Early Modern period, *my* and *thy* spread at the expense of *mine* and *thine*. In other words, *my* and *thy* come more and more often to be used before vowels as well as before consonants. By 1600, *my* and *thy* are almost without exception the forms used before consonants, while before vowels *my* and *mine* are in free variation, as are *thy* and *thine*: Shakespeare has both *thine eyes* and *thy eye*, both *mine own* and *my own*. During the seventeenth century, *mine* and *thine* continue to recede, and by 1700 *my* and *thy* are the normal forms in standard literary prose (though the older forms continue to be used as poetic archaisms). In the preface to his *Fables* (1700), Dryden invariably uses *my* before vowels, as in *my Author*, *my only Difficulty*, *my Inadvertency*.

From what has been said, it will be seen that in 1600 the system of personal pronouns was as in Table 4.2. Less frequent forms are put in brackets.

'Thou' and 'You'

In 1600 there are still two different pronouns of the second person, *thou* and *you*. In the course of the seventeenth century, the *thou* forms fall into disuse, and by 1700 have disappeared from StE except as literary archaisms and in the special language used for liturgical purposes. For simplicity, I shall use *Thou* and *You* (with upper-case initial letter) to denote the whole group of related forms: *You* will mean 'one or more of *ye*, *you*, *yours*, *your*, *yourself*'. And similarly with *Thou*. Inevitably, most of the material will be drawn from literary sources, drama being especially useful. There is evidence, however, that change of usage took place more rapidly in speech than in writing (Hope 1993).

Originally, the difference between *You* and *Thou* was merely one of number: *Thou* was used in addressing one person, *You* in addressing more than one. But in ME the custom arose, under courtly French influence, of using *You* as a polite or deferential singular, and this was continued in eModE. For the plural, only *You* could be used: it has never been possible to use *Thou* as a plural. But in the singular the speaker or writer had a choice, *Thou* or *You*.

There are sometimes anomalies in the usage, things difficult to explain, but this is perhaps only to be expected in an age of great political and social change. And in any case, the broad outlines are clear enough. In the middle of the Early Modern period, *You* was the polite form used by inferiors to superiors: by servants to their master or mistress, by children to parents, by a citizen to a nobleman, by a nobleman to the sovereign. It was also used by the upper classes (and increasingly by the citizenry) as the neutral, unemotional form of address between social equals, the unmarked form. On the other hand, *Thou* was used for addressing a social inferior: by a master to a servant, by a parent to a child, by a nobleman to an ordinary gentleman, by a gentleman to an artisan, by any human being to an animal. In the polite classes, a husband sometimes addresses his wife as *Thou*, and she replies with *You*, in accordance with the traditional doctrine that he was her lord and master. This is not always the case, however, for sometimes husband and wife both use the polite *You*. The lower classes, however, normally use *Thou* to one another: two apprentices, or two artisans, or an artisan and his wife, usually address one another as *Thou*. In Shakespeare's *Richard III*, for example, there are only two obviously plebeian characters, the murderers of Clarence, and they address one another as *Thou*.

In addition to the use of *Thou* to indicate social relationships, there is another use: *Thou* is sometimes used, even in relationships where *You* would be normal, when the emotional temperature rises. There are two cases in which we find this emotional use of *Thou*. The first is to convey intimacy, affection, tenderness: members of the polite classes who are social equals may slip into *Thou* to express such feelings, and then return to the neutral *You*. The second case is just the opposite: *Thou* can be used to a stranger of equal social rank, and even to a social superior, to express anger, contempt, disgust. In the scene of Clarence's murder in *Richard III*, the two murderers usually address Clarence (who is a royal prince) as *You*, but at one point, when passions run high and they are making violent accusations against him, they switch to the hostile *Thou*, only to return to the expected *You* when the emotional temperature has fallen. Their use of *Thou* is violently insulting, and was presumably shocking to the original audience.

Since *Thou* is used to social inferiors, its use to a stranger of equal rank is also a deliberate insult. In *Twelfth Night*, when Sir Andrew Aguecheek is about to write a challenge, Sir Toby Belch advises him to use the insulting *Thou*:

> if thou thou'st him some thrice, it shall not be amisse.

Curiously enough, there are situations where the reverse can be true, and *You* becomes the hostile and insulting form: a master who normally addresses a servant as *Thou* may in anger switch to *You*. This is a kind of irony, and this use of *You* is especially common when the servant is addressed as *Sir* or *Sirrah*.

There is one apparent anomaly: in prayer, God is regularly addressed as *Thou*. In Christian thought, God is both our king and our father, and so should be addressed as *You*. Perhaps this is simply liturgical conservatism, reflecting the usage of Early Middle English, when *Thou* and *You* were simply singular and plural, with no social or emotional connotations. This would have been reinforced by biblical translations, in which the singular second-person pronouns of the original languages were regularly translated as *Thou*. This also means that it is pointless to look in such translations for examples of the social and emotional uses of *Thou* and *You*: in the King James Bible, for example, these pronouns are simply used as singular and plural.

Perhaps under the influence of the liturgical usage, *Thou* is also used for addressing other supernatural beings, such as pagan deities: in *King Lear*, for example, Edmund addresses the goddess Nature as *Thou*. But *Thou* is also used in apostrophes and invocations generally, even to inanimate objects and abstractions: at the opening of Jonson's *Volpone* (1607), Volpone addresses his gold as *Thou*. There are numerous such addresses in Shakespeare's *Richard III*, including ones to the earth, to outrage, to Pomfret Castle, to England, to night, and to conscience.

Apart from the liturgical usage, the trend during the Early Modern period is for *You* to supplant *Thou*. This may have been caused in part by the change from a hierarchical society to a more open society, as argued by Brown & Gilman (1960). But in any case it is an unsurprising development: if *You* is polite and respectful, it is the safer form to use, and will be chosen in cases of doubt. A servant will regularly address a master as *You*, but the master need not always address the servant as *Thou*: in the drama, there are scenes where a social inferior unswervingly addresses a superior as *You*, but where the superior in reply fluctuates between *You* and *Thou*, sometimes being more polite, and sometimes more patronising. Moreover, the use of *You* between equals of the upper classes was imitated by those below them, and the usage spread down the social hierarchy. By 1600, *You* was the normal unmarked form for all speakers with any pretension to politeness, while *Thou* was the marked form which carried special implications (emotional, social).

To the casual reader of Elizabethan and Jacobean drama, it often seems that *Thou* and *You* are used haphazardly, for sometimes a speaker switches from one to the other even within a single sentence. Closer examination, however, shows that many such switches are motivated: there is a change of tone or attitude in the speaker. For the present-day reader or audience, this is one of the nuances of eModE literature which it is difficult to respond to spontaneously. It perhaps helps if we compare the eModE usage with our own use of first names and titles. The big executive comes into his office, and says to his secretary 'Good morning, Gladys', and she replies 'Good morning, Mr Smith'. This is very much like eModE *Thou* and *You*.

There are two further complications. First, the choice of pronoun may have been influenced by the grammatical construction it occurred in: *Thou* tended to be favoured before auxiliaries, and *You* before lexical verbs. Secondly, as *Thou* retreats, at different rates for different speakers, it tends to become a purely literary form, with no social or emotional connotations. Such 'literary' uses of *Thou* seem to occur even in the middle of the Early Modern period, for example in apostrophes and invocations, and may explain some apparent anomalies. These usages were perhaps encouraged by the influence of classical Latin: an Early Modern writer could well have been influenced by the Latin text which was being translated or used as source material. The influence of the liturgical language and of biblical translations must have been in the same direction.

In the course of the seventeenth century, *You* steadily displaces *Thou* in educated usage. Even in the middle of the century, however, people were sufficiently sensitive to the implications of *Thou* to be shocked by its use in inappropriate situations. This can be seen in reactions to the Quakers, who insisted on using *Thou* as the second-person singular pronoun, whoever they were addressing. George Fox (1624–91), the founder of the Society of Friends, more than once recounts in his *Journal* how people reacted with hostility when he addressed them as *Thou*. Particularly likely to take offence were those of higher social rank than Fox, and especially those who claimed authority over him. Indeed, it is clear that his use of *Thou* was, in part, a subversive gesture, a refusal to accept the authority of secular jurisdiction. It was rather like refusing to take off your hat in the presence of a social superior, and indeed Fox himself links the two pieces of behaviour. He recounts how, in

1652, he was taken before a magistrate near Patrington, in the East Riding of Yorkshire:

> and when I was brought before him because I did not putt off my hatt and saide thou to him hee askt the man whether I was not Mased or fonde ['mad or imbecile']: and hee saide noe: itt was my principle.

Fox was of humble origins, the son of a Leicestershire weaver, and his preference for *Thou* tells us nothing about the usages of polite society. The revealing thing is the reaction of the polite when he used it to them.

In Restoration Comedy, which attempts to give the illusion of real speech, the normal second-person pronoun in smart London society is *You*, but *Thou* continues to occur right to the end of the century. Fine ladies almost invariably say *You* to one another even if they are close friends, or sisters, like Mrs Frail and Mrs Foresight in Congreve's *Love for Love* (1695). Fine gentlemen say *You* to fine ladies, even if they are lovers. But gentlemen sometimes say *Thou* to one another: gallants who are on friendly terms often slip out of *You* into *Thou*, and it seems to be a mark of male *camaraderie*.

There also continue to be a few examples of *Thou* used in situations of strong emotion. In *Love for Love*, Sir Sampson Legend's son Ben returns home after a long absence at sea. When he arrives, Sir Sampson for a time addresses him as *Thou*, but when the emotion of the moment has subsided he switches to *You*. Sir Sampson has another son, Valentine. He normally addresses him as *You*, but when he tries to wheedle him into signing away his heritage he uses *Thou*. When Sir Sampson converses with Foresight, another middle-aged gentleman, they both use *You*, but when Foresight becomes infuriated with Sir Sampson he bursts out for a moment with *Thou*:

> *Capricorn* in your Teeth, thou Modern *Mandevil*; *Ferdinand Mendez Pinto* was but a Type of thee, thou Lyar of the first Magnitude.

In attempting to mollify him, Sir Sampson himself changes for a short time to *Thou*, presumably to suggest friendly intimacy.

One striking thing in Restoration Comedy is that *Thou* is not normally used to social inferiors. Gallants and fine ladies usually address their servants as *You*, and also use *You* to orange-girls, shoemakers, and other members of the lower classes, who a century earlier would have been addressed as *Thou*. There are exceptions: some ladies use *Thou* to their waiting-women, for example Harriet in Etherege's *Man of Mode* (1676) and Lady Wishfort in Congreve's *Way of the World* (1700). It is possible that this is meant to tell us something about the characters of these two ladies. But, generally speaking, *Thou* is no longer used to mark social distinctions, and occurs among polite speakers only as an occasional indicator of emotional attitude – anger, male *camaraderie*, wheedling.

TABLE 4.3

Personal pronouns and pronoun-determiners c. 1700

Nominative	I	he	she	it	we	you	they
Accusative	me	him	her	it	us	you	them, 'em
Possessive	mine	his	hers	its	ours	yours	theirs
Determiner	my	his	her	its	our	your	their

In literary prose, *Thou* is rare in the later part of the century. One place where it continues to be found is in addresses to the reader. Locke uses it in this way in his *Essay*. He has a dedication to the Earl of Pembroke, whom he addresses as *You*. Then he has a long 'Epistle to the Reader', in which he consistently uses *Thou*. This usage continued in the eighteenth century. In poetry, *Thou* continued to be used with great regularity, but was clearly a literary archaism. It also continued to be used in regional speech, and in some local dialects has persisted to the present day.

In the standard literary language, however, and in everyday speech, *Thou* existed only marginally by 1700, and the system of personal pronouns was in effect the same as today, as shown in Table 4.3. The *Thou* forms have disappeared, as have *hit*, *'t*, *'a*, *hem* and *ye*. The pronoun-determiner of the first person singular is *my*, before both vowels and consonants, and *its* has supplanted *his* as the possessive and the determiner of the neuter pronoun.

Other pronouns

The interrogative pronoun *what?* can be used to mean 'why?', as in the following sentence from *As You Like It*:

But *what* talke wee of Fathers, when there is such a man as Orlando?

There is also an interrogative pronoun which we no longer use, namely *whether?*, meaning 'which of two?' The following example is from *All's Well that Ends Well*:

Whether doest thou professe thy selfe, a knaue or a foole?

This means 'Which of the two do you set up to be, a knave or a fool?' *Whether* is also used in a similar sense as an indefinite pronoun, and to introduce indirect questions. These uses continue throughout the period, being found for example in Bentley's *Dissertation* (1699). The following example from Bentley illustrates the indefinite use:

Whether of these our Author made bold with, I cannot determin.

This occurs in a context where Bentley is discussing two different possibilities.

Who and *whoso* can be used as indefinite pronouns, where we say 'whoso-ever' or 'anyone who', and *that* where we say 'what':

1. *Who* steales my purse, steales trash   *(Othello)*
2. Now followes *that* you know   *(Hamlet)*

In both of these, the pronoun introduces a noun clause which is the subject of the main clause.

The demonstrative pronouns *that* and *those* are often used where we say 'the one(s)', for the latter usage did not then exist. So in *All's Well* we find the following piece of dialogue:

Helena. Which is the Frenchman?
Diana. Hee, / *That* with the plume

The demonstrative pronouns are also used freely to refer to persons, where we say 'this man', 'these people', and so on:

they are both hang'd, and so would *this* be, if hee durst steale any thing
aduenturously   *(Henry V)*

Here, *this* refers to Ancient Pistol. On the other hand, *one* was often used where we say 'somebody', as in the following example from *Julius Caesar*:

Stand close a while, for heere comes *one* in haste.

The pronoun *other* is used both as a singular and as a plural. The plural *others* is recorded from the late fourteenth century, but only slowly supplants plural *other*, which is still common in the sixteenth century, and persists right through the seventeenth. The following example is from *A Midsummer Night's Dream*:

That he awaking when the *other* doe,
May all to Athens backe againe repaire.

Here *other* refers to the four lovers. On the other hand, *some* can be used as a singular, meaning 'somebody, something'. The OED quotes an example from Thomas Lodge, dated about 1581:

I feare me *some* will blushe that readeth this, if he be bitten.

The fact that *some* is singular is clear from the {-eth} inflection and from the pronoun *he*. Forms like *somebody* and *something* also existed, but singular *some* occurs alongside them throughout the period.

There are also occasional differences from PresE in the emphatic and reflexive pronouns. We use the same forms (*myself, himself, ourselves*, etc.) for both the emphatic and the reflexive functions. Originally this was not so: in OE, *self* was used as the emphatic pronoun, while for the reflexive function the ordinary personal pronouns were used, without any *self* added. Forms like *myself*, used for both functions, arose in EME, but in the Early Modern period we still find the older usage alongside the new. The following examples from Shakespeare show the use of the ordinary personal pronouns in reflexive function:

1. Ile go hide *me*   (*Merry Wives*)
2. If you submit *you* to the peoples voices   (*Coriolanus*)

The use of *self* alone as an emphatic pronoun is less common, but nevertheless continues to be found. The following extract from E.K.'s glosses on Spenser's *Shepherd's Calendar* (1579) contains both the older *self* and the more usual *himself*:

> This is no poetical fiction, but vnfeynedly spoken of the Poete *selfe*, who for speciall occasion of priuate affayres (as I haue bene partly of *himselfe* informed) and for his more preferment remouing out of the North-parts came into the South.

Forms with the plural *-selves* are not found until about 1500. Earlier we find forms like *them self*, and these are still found in the sixteenth century, as when Elyot talks of oligarchs who rule by terror and cruelty:

> thinking therby / to kepe *them selfe* in suertie ['keep themselves safe'].

The forms with *-selves* are however the normal usage by the middle of the six-teenth century. They can also be used in a reciprocal sense, meaning 'each other'. In *Much Ado about Nothing*, Leonato says of Beatrice and Benedick:

> if they were but a weeke married, they would talke *themselues* madde ['talk one another mad'].

The relative pronouns were *who* (and its oblique forms), *which*, *that*, and (less commonly) *the which* and *as*. Their uses will be discussed under syntax, in the next chapter.

DETERMINERS

I use *determiner* in a wide sense, to cover all grammatical (closed system) forms which act as adjuncts to nouns. The use of determiners in the structure of the Noun Phrase will be discussed under syntax, in the next chapter, but here we can consider a few ways in which the system of determiners differed from that of PresE.

Before vowels, the definite article is sometimes written *th* or *th'*, represent-ing a pronunciation [ð], as in *themperour* (Elyot) and *th'Oke* (Milton). In the seventeenth century this form is found mainly in dramatic dialogue and in poetry, where it is used for metrical purposes, but in the sixteenth century it is found in all kinds of writing, including formal prose. In dramatic dialogue there are also forms like *ith* 'in the' and *ath* 'of the, on the'. These can occur before consonants as well as before vowels, as in King Lear's *i'th' clout* 'in the target'.

The definite article is sometimes inserted in positions where we omit it. It is occasionally used before titles, like *the Lord Northumberland*. It can be used before vocative expressions like *The Gods!* 'You Gods!': in *Julius Caesar* Brutus addresses the dead Cassius:

The last of all the Romans, far thee well.

It is often inserted before the names of branches of learning, arts, crafts, games, and pursuits: *the chess*, *the mathematics*, *the metaphysics*. It is commonly used with the names of diseases: people suffer from *the stone* or *the gout*. Before the names of parts of the body, it is sometimes used where we say *my*, *his*, and so on:

1. The king is angrie, see, he bites *the* lip   *(Richard III)*
2. Come, come, no longer will I be a foole,
   To put *the* finger in *the* eie and weepe   *(Comedy of Errors)*

But we also find the PresE usage: in 1. 'bites the lip' is the reading of the First Quarto (1597), while the First Folio (1623) reads 'gnawes his Lippe'. We also find expressions like *the death*, *the life*, *the heaven*, and phrases like *at the last*, *at the least*, *at the length*.

Conversely, the definite article is sometimes omitted in positions where we insert it. It is sometimes omitted before river names: in *Henry V*, a character says 'hee could wish himselfe in Thames vp to the Neck'. It can also be omitted in a number of preposition phrases, like *at door*, *at gate*, *at mercy of*, *at town's end*, *by help of*, *in manner of*, *in name of*, *in presence of*.

The use of the indefinite article was much as today. Originally, it was the unstressed form of the numeral *one*, and in eModE there are occasional uses that remind us of this: in the following examples, the indefinite article means 'one' or 'the same':

1. my selfe, and a sister, both borne in *an* houre   *(Twelfth Night)*
2. and ['if'] two men ride of *a* horse, one must ride behinde

                                                  (Much Ado)
3. These Foyles haue all *a* length   *(Hamlet)*

Sometimes the indefinite article is omitted where we insert it, as in expressions like *it is pity* (*fact*, *shame*, etc.). This is seen in the title of John Ford's play *'Tis Pitty Shee's a Whore* (1633).

At the beginning of the Early Modern period, the negative article *no* had an alternative form *none*. Their distribution was the same as for *a* and *an*. In the

160

early sixteenth century the distinction is well preserved: it is regularly made, for example, in Elyot's *Governor*, as in the following excerpt:

> *none* industrie auayled / *no* strength defended / *no* riches profited.

During the sixteenth century, *no* spreads at the expense of *none*, and by 1600 is the normal form before both vowels and consonants. The process is parallel to the one that took place with *my/mine* and *thy/thine*, but happened more quickly. Shakespeare often uses *mine* and *thine* before vowels, but even in his early works he regularly uses *no* before vowels as well as before consonants, as in *no eyes, no impression, no vnwelcome newes*. The word *none* does indeed occur frequently in Shakespeare, but as a pronoun, with such meanings as 'nobody', 'nothing', not as a determiner. Attributive *none* does continue to exist in the seventeenth century, but is rare except in the expression *of none effect*.

The demonstratives, *this/these* and *that/those*, were already established in their present form when the Early Modern period opened. There was also a form *tho*, used as an alternative to *those*, but it was infrequent, and was already dying out. Nevertheless, the system of demonstratives was different from ours. We have a binary system, in which *this/these* contrasts with *that/those*. But in eModE there was another demonstrative, *yon*, with variants *yond* and *yonder* used in the same way. There was thus a ternary system, the components of which we can call {this}, {that}, and {yon}. The demonstratives involve a pointing-out or singling-out process, either literal or figurative. When they are used in their simple local sense, to point to physical objects around the speaker, they have different implications about the position of the object referred to: {this} implies 'near the speaker', {that} implies 'remote from the speaker', while {yon} implies 'remote from both speaker and hearer'. Demonstrative {that} carries no implications about position relative to the hearer. The thing referred to can be close to the hearer, as when, in Jonson's *Alchemist* (1611), the puritan Ananias says to a supposed Spanish nobleman:

> Thou look'st like Antichrist, in *that* leud hat.

But it can be remote from the hearer: in *The Comedy of Errors*, the Merchant and the Goldsmith see Antipholus of Syracuse walking in the distance, and the Goldsmith says:

> 'Tis so: and *that* selfe chaine about his necke,
> Which he forswore most monstrously to haue.

These possible alternative uses of {that} are used to effect in Thomas Middleton's play *The Reuengers Tragœdie* (1607). The mother of the chaste Castiza is trying to persuade her to prostitute herself, and Castiza says:

Mother, come from *that* poysonous woman there.

The 'poysonous woman' is the mother herself (or her worse self), and the doubleness of that enables Castiza to imply that the woman behaving badly both is and is not her mother.

On the other hand, {yon} always implies 'remote from both speaker and hearer'. Moreover, it carries the additional implication 'visible, in sight'. Almost invariably, therefore, it accompanies (or replaces) a pointing gesture: the speaker is saying 'Look, that one over there'. This is clear in the drama: {yon} is used to refer to some other character on the stage, but remote from the interlocutors, or to some object visible to them:

1. *yon* grey Lines,
   That fret the Clouds, are Messengers of Day.   (*Julius Caesar*)
2. Nerrissa, cheere *yond* stranger, bid her welcome
                                                  (*Merchant of Venice*)
3. But soft, what light through *yonder* window breaks?
                                                  (*Romeo and Juliet*)

In 1., the conspirators are arguing about the direction of the east, and Cinna indicates a part of the sky where he thinks he sees signs of dawn. In 2., Gratiano is speaking to Nerissa about Jessica, who has just entered with Lorenzo, and who is obviously on the other side of the stage. In 3., Romeo, in the Capulets' garden, sees Juliet appear on her balcony.

The visual implications of {yon} are used to effect in a scene in *King Lear*, when the mad Lear meets the blind Gloucester:

What, art mad? A man may see how this world goes, with no eyes. Looke with thine eares: See how *yond* Iustice railes vpon *yond* simple theefe. Harke in thine eare: Change places, and handy-dandy, which is the Iustice, which is the theefe.

Lear's *yond* invites Gloucester to look, reinforcing the argument that a person may be able to see although blind. It is an invitation to him to use his visual imagination.

Just occasionally we meet examples of {yon} where the thing referred to is not in fact visible. In such cases, the thing is being imagined vividly, so that it is visible to the mind. There is an example in *Twelfth Night*, when Maria tells her cronies about the behaviour of Malvolio:

If you desire the spleene, and will laughe your selues into stitches, fol-low me; *yond* gull Maluolio is turned Heathen, a verie Renegatho ... Hee's in yellow stockings.

Malvolio is not in sight, otherwise Maria would not need to tell the others about the yellow stockings, or to describe his behaviour, as she goes on to do. But she is full of the story. She has just seen Malvolio, and is remembering him vividly, and she points with her *yond* at the thing thus vividly imagined. There is another example in the same play, when the Duke, sending Viola to Olivia, tells her to go 'to *yond* same soueraigne crueltie'. But the usage is rare: an examination of the great Harvard concordance shows that there are only three further examples in the whole of Shakespeare, and one of these may be a textual error. Overwhelmingly, {yon} is used for things which are visible.

Both {yon} and {that} can be used of things remote from the hearer, but {yon} has stronger implications of singling-out and pointing. This can be illustrated by a passage from the first scene of *Hamlet*, when the characters are waiting for the Ghost to appear:

> Last night of all,
> When *yond* same Starre that's Westward from the Pole
> Had made his course t'illume *that* part of Heauen
> Where now it burnes …

The finer focus is on *yond same Starre*, while *that part of Heauen* is a larger area 'over there' within which the star is located.

Because of its limitation to the visible, {yon} has a more restricted usage than {this} and {that}, and occurs much less frequently. For example, {this} and {that} can be used of things which are only figuratively close to or remote from the speaker. In the same scene of *Hamlet*, Marcellus makes the first reference to the Ghost:

> What, ha's *this* thing appear'd againe to night.

By *this*, Marcellus means 'the one we are all thinking about, the one that's on our minds'. Moreover, {this} and {that} are not restricted to physical referents, but can be used of abstract things. Macbeth talks about '*This* supernaturall solliciting', and Lady Macbeth about '*those* Honors' which Duncan has bestowed on their house. Such non-local uses are not found with {yon}.

The demonstrative {yon} is found throughout the Early Modern period, but by the late seventeenth century it is becoming a literary word, largely confined to poetry. Characters in Restoration Comedy sometimes use the adverb *yonder*, but rarely the determiner {yon}. When it does occur, it is not usually in the mouths of fine ladies and gentlemen, but of non-standard speakers, like the sailor Ben Legend in *Love for Love*. It is used by Bunyan (1628–88), who was the son of a tinker, and continued to be used by the lower classes after it had disappeared from the speech of polite society. It also continued to be used in Scots, and in some rural dialects of England.

There is a group of determiners which cannot collocate with the articles (*any*, *each*, *every*, etc.). In eModE there is in this group a determiner which no longer exists, *mo*. It is used in some contexts where we use *more*. The following are examples:

1. by declaring the vertue in a fewe *mo* wordes ...   (Elyot, *Governor*)
2. *moe* things, then there are words ...   (Lever, *Art of Reason*)
3. an hundred Ladies *moe*   (Spenser, *Faerie Queene*)
4. Send out *moe* Horses   (Shakespeare, *Macbeth*)

As the examples suggest, *mo* is most often used with plural nouns, to mean 'more in number'. Indeed, in the sixteenth century, *mo* is the normal determiner for 'more in number': *more* is not used in this way until late in the century. On the other hand, even in the sixteenth century, *more* is the usual determiner with uncountable nouns to mean 'greater in quantity', as in *more art*, *more love*, *more money*. In the sixteenth century, as we have already seen, *more* was also used as a comparative adjective meaning 'larger, bigger'. In the first half of the seventeenth century this use dies out, and at the same time *more* as a determiner gradually displaces *mo*. In other words, *more* comes increasingly to be used before plural nouns in the sense 'greater in number'. So *mo* gradually dies out, and has disappeared by about 1650. In the period in which *mo* is used as a determiner, it can also be used as a pronoun: *the mo* means 'the majority', and *mo of* means 'a greater number of'.

THE VERB

At the beginning of the Early Modern period, the verb has seven forms, as shown in Table 4.4. The spellings given are common ones in the period, but there are many variants, for example *cutte, cutt, cut.*

Form 1 is the base-form of the verb, completely unmarked. Form 2 is the second-person singular, marked for concord with *thou* ('thou bearst', 'thou giuest', etc.). Form 3 is the third-person singular ('he beareth', 'she giueth', etc.). Form 4 is used in conjunction with an auxiliary to produce the progressive forms ('he was walking', etc.). Form 5 is marked for pastness or unreality, while Form 6 has the additional marking for concord with *thou*. Form 7 is the past participle, used in conjunction with auxiliaries to produce the perfect and the passive ('he hath giuen', 'it is giuen', etc.).

Of the seven forms, four are always finite (2, 3, 5, 6) and two non-finite (4, 7). The base-form can be either finite ('they beare') or non-finite ('to beare'). Of the finite forms, two are past tenses (5, 6). The finite forms which are not marked for pastness I shall call *present-tense* forms, in accordance with traditional usage, even though it is not a very satisfactory name.

Not all verbs have seven distinct forms: in four of the verbs cited, Forms 5 and 7 are identical, and in one of them (*cutte*), Forms 1, 5, and 7 are identical. The verbs with seven distinct forms are in fact a minority, but they are a substantial minority. Moreover, the seven forms have seven clearly distinct

TABLE 4.4

Verb forms c. 1500

1.	beare	giue	walke	cutte	meete	haue
2.	bear(e)st	giu(e)st	walk(e)st	cutt(e)st	meet(e)st	hast
3.	beareth	giueth	walketh	cutteth	meeteth	hath
4.	bearing	giuing	walking	cutting	meeting	hauing
5.	bare	gaue	walked	cutte	mette	hadde
6.	bar(e)st	gau(e)st	walkedst	cutt(e)st	mett(e)st	hadst
7.	borne	giuen	walked	cutte	mette	hadde

functions. It is therefore desirable to adopt a general seven-form system of classification.

There is however one verb which is anomalous, and does not fit the pattern, namely the verb *to be*. This can function either as an auxiliary or as a main verb, but even when it is a main verb it behaves differently from normal lexical verbs, and has to be considered as something *sui generis*. Among other things, it has more than seven distinct forms. In addition to the base-form *be*, it has a present-plural form *are* (in the early sixteenth century also *arne*). It has a first-person singular form *am*. It has two alternative forms corresponding to Form 2, namely *art* and *beest*. There are two different past-tense forms, singular *was* and plural *were*. And there are two alternative forms corresponding to Form 6, namely *wast* and *wert*.

The second-person singular

Forms 2 and 6 are used throughout the period, though naturally they become rarer as the pronoun *thou* falls into disuse during the seventeenth century. The {-est} morpheme appears both in its full form (*thou giuest, gauest*) and with syncope of the vowel (*thou giu'st, gau'st*). The syncopated forms are common, and almost the rule when {-est} follows the past-tense {-ed} inflection, as in *thou walkedst, promisedst, pretermittedst* (examples from Nash). The verb *to haue* normally has the contracted form *hast*, though *hauest* is occasionally found in the sixteenth century.

Occasionally, the ending {-es} occurs instead of {-est}. It was the earlier form of the second-person inflection, and had been retained in northern dialect. An example of its use can be seen in these lines from *Hamlet*:

> What may this meane?
> That thou dead Coarse againe in compleat steele,
> *Reuisits* thus the glimpses of the Moone,
> Making Night hidious?

The use of this second-person ending is especially common when, as here, the verb ends in /t/. It is perhaps motivated by considerations of euphony, avoiding the awkward final consonant cluster /-tst/.

For the verb *to be*, the usual present-tense form is *thou art*. The variant *thou beest* is found especially in conditional and concessive clauses, perhaps through the influence of the subjunctive *thou be*.

The third-person singular

In the third-person singular of the present tense, the {-eth} morpheme does not usually have syncope of the vowel, but appears in its full form: *giueth*, *walketh*, and so on. Exceptions are the verbs *do* and *say*, which often have the syncopated forms *doth* and *saith*, and the verb *have*, which has the contracted form *hath*. The pronunciation of the full form was usually [-ɪθ] or [-əθ], but rhymes sometimes require [-ɛθ].

Alongside the third-person {-eth} inflection was an alternative one, namely {-es}. This had three allomorphs, [-s], [-z], and [-ɪz] (or [-əz]), which had a distribution similar to that of the noun plural ending. Originally, the difference between {-es} and {-eth} was one of region: {-es} was originally northern, but in the course of ME it spread down over part of the Midlands. When the new standard literary language took shape, {-eth} was still normal in the south, and so became the standard written form. But {-es} continued to move southwards, and when the Early Modern period opened was probably common in southern speech.

In the early Tudor period, {-eth} is normal in formal prose, though {-es} is sometimes found in less formal documents like private letters and diaries. It is also found in poetry: it was convenient for poets to have the choice between the two endings, because {-eth} nearly always constituted a syllable, whereas {-es} most often did not. The poet could therefore select the ending according to the needs of rhyme or rhythm. This can be seen in a sonnet by Henry Howard, Earl of Surrey (1517–47), 'The soote season'. In this, there are seven examples of {-es} at the end of a line, all in words which rhyme with the noun *things*. Within the line, there are four examples of {-eth} and only one of {-es}, and this one is necessary for the rhythm of the line.

In the course of the Early Modern period, {-es} gradually supplants {-eth}. In formal prose the change is rather slow. For example, {-es} does not occur at all in Ralph Robinson's translation of *Utopia* (1551) and occurs very infrequently in Roger Ascham's *Schoolmaster* (1570) (Bambas 1947). From about 1590, however, it occurs freely in most kinds of writing, alongside {-eth}, though {-eth} continues to be favoured in highly formal things like sermons. In the 1590s, {-es} is very common in poetry, in journalistic prose (like the pamphlets of Greene and Nash), and above all in the drama. In the plays of Marlowe (1564–93), {-es} is overwhelmingly predominant. In those of

Shakespeare, {-es} is decidedly more frequent than {-eth}, though the latter is preferred in the forms *hath* and *doth*.

Almost certainly, {-es} spread much more rapidly in speech than in writing. As early as 1500 there is evidence for its use in familiar speech even in the London area, and in the course of the sixteenth century it became the normal spoken form. The continued use of the spelling *-eth* after about 1590 is an example of the conservatism of the written language. By about 1600, there is evidence that people often used the spelling *-eth*, but expected it to be pronounced as though it were *-es*. William Camden, in his *Remaines of a Greater Worke* (1605), gives an account of Sir Thomas Smith's proposed spelling reforms. In this occurs the following sentence:

> Z; he would haue vsed for the softer S, or eth, and es, as *dîz* for dieth, *lîz* for lies.

In other words, Smith wanted the letter *z* to be used as the regular spelling for /z/. Camden himself, however, clearly uses the spellings *eth* and *es* indifferently to represent the allomorph [-z] (*dieth*, *lies*). His spelling *dieth* obviously represents the pronunciation [dəɪz].

This does not necessarily mean, however, that {-eth} was never heard in the spoken language. It was probably used in highly formal and solemn speech. Moreover, poets continued to use it for rhythmical purposes, obviously expecting their readers to pronounce the {-eth} ending. There is an example of both motivations in a line from the first scene of *Hamlet*:

> The Bird of Dawning singeth all night long.

The rhythm requires the actor to pronounce *singeth* as two syllables. Moreover, the use of {-eth} reinforces the solemn and reverent tone of the line, which is referring to the belief that the cock sings continuously on the night of Christ's nativity. Elsewhere in the scene, Shakespeare uses only {-es}, except for his usual *hath* and *doth*.

In the writings of the first half of the seventeenth century, {-eth} continues to occur quite frequently, mainly in formal styles. Shakespeare rarely uses {-eth} in comic or low-life prose scenes. In Jonson, {-es} predominates in the plays, but {-eth} is common in dedications, prefatory arguments, and stage directions (Partridge 1953a). In Middletons's city comedies, in which the dialogue tries to give the illusion of contemporary London speech, {-eth} hardly occurs at all, and even *has* and *does* are normal. On the other hand, the King James Bible invariably uses {-eth}. This is partly because of its dependence on earlier translations, but partly too, no doubt, because {-eth} was more formal amd dignified.

By the middle of the seventeenth century, {-eth} has become a good deal less frequent, but usage varies from author to author. Milton is fairly typical in showing a strong preference for {-es}, in both verse and prose. He does indeed prefer *hath* to *has*, but otherwise he seldom uses {-eth}. Even after the middle of the century, however, there are authors who prefer {-eth}: in Hobbes's *Leviathan* (1651), {-eth} is twice as frequent as {-es}. In the Restoration period, {-eth} is rare except in poetry. In Locke's *Essay* (1690), {-es} is normal, with just a few occurrences of {-eth}, mainly in *hath* and *doth*. In Dryden's preface to his *Fables* (1700), there are about 120 examples of {-es}, including numerous occurrences of *has*, but not a single example of {-eth}.

When {-eth} and {-es} are both in common use, they often appear to be selected haphazardly. Hobbes has *implies* and *implyeth* in successive sentences. Shakespeare uses *hath* and *has* in a single line of *Macbeth*: 'The Earth hath bubbles, as the Water ha's'. Nevertheless, there are certain cases where an author is especially likely to choose {-eth}, and this becomes clearer as the seventeenth century wears on, and {-eth} becomes rarer. There are two cases where {-eth} tends to be preferred. The first is with the forms *doth*, *hath*, and *saith*, which persist quite strongly. Glanvill's *Vanity of Dogmatizing* (1661) normally uses {-es}, but invariably has {-eth} in *doth*, *hath*, and *saith*. Some authors favour one or two of these forms, but not all three. Shakespeare has a preference for *doth* and *hath*, but not for *saith*. Hobbes has a preference for *saith*, which in *Leviathan* (judging from a sample count) occurs about eight times more frequently than *says*. On the other hand, he does not use *doth* and *hath* any more frequently than other {-eth}-forms. It is possible that these three forms continued to have a pronunciation with [θ] until late in the seventeenth century.

The other case in which {-eth} is often favoured is when the {-es} morpheme would be syllabic, in other words would be realised as [-ɪz] or [-əz]. So we often encounter forms like *ariseth*, *engageth*, *passeth*, *teacheth*, *wisheth*. It is almost as though the spelling *-eth* had come to be thought of as representing [-ɪz]. Partridge (1953a) has pointed out that such forms are common in Shakespeare and Jonson. They continue to be common throughout the seventeenth century. In Glanvill's *Vanity of Dogmatizing* (if we exclude *doth*, *hath*, and *saith*), {-eth} occurs only thirty-nine times in 250 pages: of these thirty-nine, no fewer than thirty-six are of the type in question (*advanceth*, *judgeth*, etc.), leaving only three 'unpredictable' forms in the whole book. In Locke, similarly, the rare examples of {-eth} (apart from *doth* and *hath*) are almost invariably of this type. And in *Leviathan*, where the general ratio of {-eth} to {-es} is about two to one, the ratio for this particular type is about five to one.

The present plural

The normal form for the present-tense plural is the base-form of the verb, as today:

they both *socour* other artificers	(Elyot, *Governor*)
the Norweyan Banners *flout* the Skie	(Shakespeare, *Macbeth*)
All things that *exist*	(Locke, *Essay*)

In a few cases, however, we encounter other forms: there are plurals with the inflections {-eth} or {-es} or {-en}. Originally, these were present-plural endings in different regions: in ME, broadly speaking, {-es} was Northern, {-en} Midland, and {-eth} Southern. There was an alternative Midland plural form in which the final /-n/ had been lost, and from this descends the normal plural of Modern English. In the Early Modern period, however, the other three forms also crop up occasionally.

The old southern {-eth} plural appears sporadically throughout the sixteenth century, possibly encouraged by the analogy of the third-person singular. Elyot normally uses the base-form for the plural, but occasionally {-eth}, as in the following passage from *The Governor*, where he is discussing order:

> And that haue we in dayly experience: for the pannes and pottes / *garnissheth* wel the ketchyn / and yet shulde they be to the chambre none ornament. Also the beddes / testars / and pillowes *besemeth* nat the halle / no more than the carpettes and kusshyns *becometh* the stable.

Elyot probably came from Wiltshire, a county which had the ME {-eth} plural. In the later sixteenth century, plural {-eth} is very rare. Even Spenser, who cultivated archaisms and dialect forms, seldom used it. On the other hand, it is as likely to occur in his prose as in his verse.

In ME, the use of {-es} as a plural inflection is found in Scots, in Northern England, and in part of the North-East Midlands. Its occasional use in the standard southern language may be due to the influence of these northern forms. Alternatively, it may be due to the analogy of the third-person singular {-es} inflection. This is suggested by the fact that plural {-es} is seldom found in the early sixteenth century, and is commonest around 1600, when {-es} had displaced {-eth} as the singular ending.

In the early Tudor period, the rare examples of the {-es} plural usually occur in poetry, often in rhyme position. It is found occasionally, for example, in the poetry of John Skelton (d. 1529), who was not a northerner. It occurs more frequently in the late sixteenth and early seventeenth century, and there are quite a number of examples in Shakespeare. Some of these can be explained away, like the following:

1. The venome clamors of a iealous woman,
   Poisons more deadly then a mad dogges tooth   (*Comedy of Errors*)
2. reason and respect,
   Makes Liuers pale, and lustyhood deiect   (*Troilus and Cressida*)
3. But stay, here *comes* the Gardiners   (*Richard II*)

It could be argued that in all three cases the verb is really singular: that in 1. it is influenced by the proximity of the singular noun *woman*, that in 2. the expression 'reason and respect' is notionally singular, and that 3. is a special case because the verb precedes the subject, and in such constructions a speaker often chooses a singular verb irrespective of the number of the subject.

There are, however, a considerable number of {-es} plurals which cannot be explained away like this, as in the following:

1. By'r lakin, I can goe no further, Sir,
   My old bones *akes*   *(The Tempest)*
2. His teares *runs* down his beard like winters drops   *(The Tempest)*
3. These high wilde hilles, and rough vneeuen waies,
   Drawes out our miles, and *makes* them wearisome   *(Richard II)*
4. Vntimely stormes, *makes* men expect a Dearth   *(Richard III)*
5. The great man downe, you marke his fauourites *flies*,
   The poore aduanc'd, makes Friends of Enemies   *(Hamlet)*

As can be seen, the usage is not confined to vulgar or dialectal speakers. Moreover, such forms occur too frequently for them to be dismissed as printers' or copyists' errors.

Other writers in Shakespeare's time sometimes use the {-es} plural, but in the first half of the seventeenth century it falls out of use quite quickly. This can be seen if you compare the Shakespeare First Folio of 1623 with the later Folios of 1632, 1663 and 1685. These later Folios have no independent authority for Shakespeare's text. They do, however, attempt to correct mistakes in the text, and one common type of 'correction' is the replacement of {-es} plurals by base-forms. In the quotations from *The Tempest* in 1. and 2. above, all the later Folios emend *akes* to *ake*, and *runs* to *run*. In the *Hamlet* quotation in 5., such a change is impossible, because of the rhyme, so instead they emend *fauourites* to *fauourite*. So as early as the Second Folio of 1632 we see plural {-es} being treated as a grammatical error. Later seventeenth-century writers like Milton and Dryden do not use it, but it continues to occur in dialogue representing vulgar or dialectal speech.

The old Midland plural inflection {-en} was normal in London in late Middle English, but by 1500 it had largely been displaced in the standard language by the use of the base-form. It occurs occasionally in early Tudor poetry, as in the following example from Surrey:

Wherwith the heauy cares that heapt are in my brest,
Breake forth, and me *dischargen* clene of all my huge vnrest.

Even at this date, however, {-en} is probably an archaism. Surrey perhaps selects it for metrical reasons: the poem is in Poulter's Measure, in which twelve-syllable and fourteen-syllable lines alternate. It is rare in prose. In the later sixteenth century, it is found only in poetry, and especially in the archaising Spenser. He is particularly likely to use it to suggest rustic speech, as in the February eclogue of *The Shepherd's Calendar*:

> And when the shining sunne laugheth once,
> You *deemen*, the Spring is come attonce.
> Tho gynne you, fond flyes, the cold to scorne,
> And crowing in pypes made of greene corne,
> You *thinken* to be Lords of the yeare.

In Shakespeare, the {-en} plural is used very rarely, and only when an archaic or rustic effect is desired. In *Pericles* we find the forms *perishen* and *escapen*: they are put in the mouth of the fourteenth-century poet Gower, who acts as Chorus, and who regularly speaks in an archaic style. There is also an example in *A Midsummer Night's Dream*:

> And then the whole quire hold their hips, and loffe,
> And *waxen* in their mirth, and neeze, and sweare,
> A merrier houre was neuer wasted there.

The speaker is Robin Goodfellow, and the {-en} inflection is probably meant to suggest a rustic style of speech, a style which is also indicated by *loffe* 'laugh' and perhaps by *neeze* 'sneeze'. In the seventeenth century, {-en} is very rare, and is hardly found outside the imitators of Spenser.

In summary, it can be said that, in the present plural, {-eth} occurs occasionally in the early sixteenth century, {-es} occurs as a variant in the middle years of the Early Modern period, and {-en} occurs as a literary archaism, mainly in the sixteenth century. These, however, are all decidedly minority usages. The normal and overwhelmingly predominant form of the present plural throughout the Early Modern period is the uninflected one, the base-form.

The subjunctive

In the second- and third-person singular, we often find the base-form of the verb used, instead of the usual inflected forms. There are several examples in the following passage from Tyndale's New Testament:

> Agre with thyne adversary quicklie / whyles thou arte in the waye with hym / lest that adversary *deliver* the to the iudge / and the iudge *delivre* the to the minister / and then thou *be* cast into preson. I say vnto the verely: thou shalt not come out thence till thou *have* payed the vtmost farthinge.

There we have the base-forms *delivre* and *deliver*, instead of *delivereth* or *delivers*, and similarly *thou be* and *thou have* instead of *thou art* and *thou hast*.

171

These are examples of the subjunctive, which was still a feature of English in the Early Modern period.

In OE there were two sets of verb inflections, in both present tense and past tense, which we can call the indicative and the subjunctive. The indicative was the normal or unmarked form. The subjunctive was the form selected when certain constructions were used, especially in contexts suggesting doubt, hypothesis, or volition. In the course of English history, the subjunctive has gradually died out, and now only survives vestigially in a few usages, like *if need be*, and *if he were*. It was still in use, however, in the Early Modern period.

In eModE, if we disregard the verb *to be*, the subjunctive-indicative contrast is shown in only two forms: the second-person singular and the third-person singular of the present tense. So we find indicative *thou comest* and *he cometh* (or *comes*), but subjunctive *thou come* and *he come*.

With the verb *to be*, there are more distinctions. In the first-person singular, we find indicative *I am*, subjunctive *I be*. In the present plural, we often find indicative *are* and subjunctive *be*, but some writers use *be* for both, especially early in the period. Indicative *be* is also common in the construction 'There be'. The distinction also survives in the past tense singular: indicative *I was*, *he was*, subjunctive *I were*, *he were*. The second-person singular in the past tense is less clear-cut: the traditional form was *thou were*, both indicative and subjunctive, but in eModE this is increasingly displaced by the analogical forms *thou wast* and *thou wert*. Sometimes *wast* is used for the indicative and *wert* for the subjunctive, but *wert* is also used as an indicative, for example by Shakespeare.

The subjunctive is sometimes used in a main clause, and its force is then optative, as in this passage from *Richard III*:

> Though not by Warre, by Surfet *dye* your King,
> As ours by Murther, to make him a King.
> Edward thy Sonne, that now is Prince of Wales,
> For Edward our Sonne, that was Prince of Wales,
> *Dye* in his youth, by like vntimely violence.
> Thy selfe a Queene, for me that was a Queene,
> *Out-liue* thy glory, like my wretched selfe.

This is part of a curse uttered by Queen Margaret to her enemies, and the meaning is 'May your king die ... may Edward your son die ... may you yourself outlive your glory'. This use of the subjunctive survives today in the set phrase 'Long live ...'.

More often, however, the subjunctive is found in subordinate clauses:

1. it may nat be called ordre / excepte it *do* contayne in it degrees

(Elyot, *Governor*)

172

2. Tell him from me (as he will win my loue)
   He *beare* himselfe with honourable action

   (Shakespeare, *Taming of the Shrew*)
3. though it [the Earth] *move*, its motion must needs be as insensible, as
   if it *were* quiescent   (Glanvill, *Vanity*)
4. If any one *take* the like Offence at the Entrance of this Treatise, I shall
   desire him to read it through   (Locke, *Essay*)

The subjunctive is particularly frequent in clauses introduced by *if*, and is
quite common in ones introduced by *except* 'unless', *though*, *till*, and *whether*.
In none of these types of clause, however, is the subjunctive invariably used:
sometimes we find the subjunctive ('if he take'), sometimes the indicative ('if
he takes'). The selection of the subjunctive signals doubt, hypothesis, or
incredulity. It is also found in clauses expressing purpose, and so occurs in
noun clauses after verbs of commanding and entreating, as in example 2.
above.

Today, when the subjunctive is only vestigial, we feel that it is a somewhat
literary usage. In eModE, however, it was part of everyday familiar speech,
even among lower-class characters. In the drama, the subjunctive comes regularly from the lips of tradesmen, apprentices, artisans, peasants, people with
no social pretensions. In *Richard III*, an obviously plebeian character, one of
the murderers of Clarence, says to his mate 'What if it *come* to thee againe?'
So when we encounter the subjunctive in dramatic dialogue, we have to be
prepared to react to it, not as something literary or pretentious, but as a normal
feature of everyday speech.

The imperative

The base-form of the verb is also used for the imperative, both singular and
plural:

1. Well, Ile goe with thee, *prouide* vs all things necessary, and *meete* me
   tomorrow night in Eastcheape   (*Henry IV Part 1*)
2. *Send* me your Prisoners with the speediest meanes

   (*Henry IV Part 1*)

Constructions involving the imperative will be discussed under syntax, in the
next chapter.

Past tenses and past participles

The past-tense and past-participle forms of the verb functioned very much as
today. Quite often, however, the actual forms for any given verb are different
from the ones we use today, as in the following:

173

1. the name ones brought in custome / shall be as facile to vnderstande as other wordes late *commen* out of Italy and Fraunce

(Elyot, *Governor*)

2. How canst thou vrge Gods dreadfull Law to vs,
   When thou hast *broke* it in such deere degree?

(Shakespeare, *Richard III*)

3. The frame and huge foundation of the Earth
   Shak'd like a Coward   (Shakespeare, *Henry IV Part 1*)

4. how was it possible to be decided who *writ* the best Plays, before we know what a Play should be?   (Dryden, *Essay of Dramatic Poesy*)

In 1. and 2., *commen* and *broke* are past participles, corresponding to PresE *come* and *broken*. The other two examples have the past tenses *Shak'd* and *writ*, corresponding to PresE *shook* and *wrote*. These forms, however, are not the only possible ones in eModE. Shakespeare uses a past participle *broken* as well as b*roke*, and a past tense *shook* as well as *shaked*. As often, variant forms circulated side by side, where we have standardised one of them.

Regular weak verbs

As today, the regular weak verbs formed their past tense and past participle by adding the {-ed} morpheme to the base form. Today, {-ed} has three allomorphs, /-ɪd/, /-d/, and /-t/. The first occurs when the verb-stem ends in /t/ or /d/, as in *waited*, *heeded*. Otherwise, /-d/ and /-t/ occur, the former when the verb-stem ends in a vowel or a voiced consonant (*died*, *begged*), the latter when it ends in a voiceless consonant (*looked*, *wished*). The three allomorphs arose from a late ME ending [-əd], by a process of syncopation, assimilation, and regulation similar to that for the ending {-es}. The process of regulation was still going on in the sixteenth century, and the [-ɪd] pronunciation was often used in more positions than today. This pronunciation is sometimes indicated by the spelling *-id* or *-yd*, as in the following lines from a poem by Sir Thomas Wyatt (1503–42):

> Fforget not then thyn owne *aprovyd*,
> The whyche so long hathe the so *lovyd*,
> Whose stedfast faythe yet neuer *movyd*,
>   Fforget not thys.

By 1600 the present-day regulation was well established in speech. Poets, however, continued to use the [-ɪd] form in all positions when the metre required it, and it was familiar as a literary or archaic form all through the seventeenth century. In the middle of the Early Modern period, syncope is often indicated by the spelling, in forms like *begd*, *lookte*, *placst*. During the seventeenth century there is a tendency to standardise the spelling *-ed*, but in

174

the later part of the century the spelling -'*d* is often used to indicate syncope, especially in poetry. Dryden regularly uses spellings like *chang'd*, *confess'd*, and *disdain'd*, to show that the ending is not syllabic, and this practice is continued in the eighteenth century.

Strong verbs and weak verbs as alternatives

In the course of English history, there has been a tendency for strong verbs to become weak: *brew*, *fare*, *fold*, *help*, *melt*, *seethe*, *starve*, *suck*, and *sup*, which are now weak, were all strong in OE. New verbs introduced into the language, whether by borrowing or by word-formation, are almost invariably weak. There are also a few examples of weak verbs becoming strong: *dig*, *spit*, and *stick* 'pierce' were originally weak, and the past tenses *digged*, *spitted*, and *sticked* are common in eModE. The strong forms *dug*, *spat*, and *stuck* arose in the sixteenth century.

In eModE there are numerous verbs with alternative strong and weak forms in circulation. Verbs which are strong in OE but weak in PresE often have both forms as alternatives in eModE. Examples are *climb* (p.t. *clamb*, *clomb*, *climbed*), *delve* (p.t. *dolve*, *delved*), *help* (p.t. *holp*, *helped*), *melt* (p.t. *molte*, *melted*), and swell (p.t. *swole*, *swelled*). Some verbs that are strong in both OE and PresE nevertheless have double forms in eModE. An example already cited is *shake*, which has p.t. *shaked* or *shook*. Others include *cling* (p.t. *clung*, *clinged*), *drive* (p.t. *drave*, *drove*, *drived*), *grind* (p.t. *groond*, *ground*, *grinded*), *run* (p.t. *ran*, *ron*, *run*, *runned*), and *shine* (p.t. *shoon*, *shone*, *shined*). Past participles, similarly, fluctuate between strong and weak: *help* has strong p.p. *holp* or *holpen*, and weak *helped* or *holped*.

The past tense of strong verbs

From the examples already cited, it can be seen that there were also variant forms in the past tenses of individual strong verbs. Such variants arose partly through the effects of analogy, and partly from the fact that in OE there were two different p.t. stems in strong verbs. There was one stem for the first- and third-person past indicative singular, like *rád* 'I/he/she/it rode' and *sang* 'I/he/she/it sang'. The other stem was used for all other p.t. forms, including plural ones, like *ridon* 'they rode' and *sungen* 'they sang'. In ME there was a tendency for one or other of the p.t. stems to be generalised, but even in Chaucer we sometimes find both, as in *he rood* 'he rode' and *they riden* 'they rode'. In PresE the distinction is preserved only in *was/were*. For all other verbs we have generalised a single stem, sometimes the old singular (*rode*, *sang*), sometimes the old plural (*slid*, *clung*). But in eModE we often find both stems used side by side, as alternatives: sometimes people say *he rode*, *he sang*, sometimes *he rid*, *he sung*.

Moreover, some of our strong verbs derive their p.t. vowel from neither of the old past-tense forms, but from the past participle. This is the case with the verb *to bear*, in which p.t. *bore* has its vowel from the p.p. *born(e)*. The normal sixteenth-century p.t. is *bare*. The analogical p.t. *bore* is not found before the fifteenth century, and is rare until about 1600. During the seventeenth century it becomes the dominant form, but *bare* is in use alongside it as late as the eighteenth century. Similar cases (though with some differences of chronology) are *brake/broke*, *spake/spoke*, *stale/stole*, *tare/tore*, and *ware/wore*.

Variant forms are also produced by the analogy of other verbs. The regular p.t. of *swear* was *swore*, but under the influence of verbs like *bear*, a new p.t. *sware* was formed in the fifteenth century, and is found as a variant throughout the Early Modern period. In the sixteenth century, similarly, we find past tense forms like *drave*, *rade*, *smate*, *strade*, *strave*, and *wrate*, under the influence of past tenses like *brake* and *spake*.

The past participle

In OE, the prefix *ge-* was usually added to past participles: *gewriten* 'written', *gelufod* 'loved'. In ME, the *ge-* became *y-* or *i-*: *ywriten*, *yloved*. In the course of ME the prefix was lost, and is hardly found after the middle of the fifteenth century. When it occurs in the Early Modern period, it is a literary archaism: Spenser, for example, often uses forms like *ybound*, *ycarud*, *yslaine*. Such forms are not found in prose, and even in poetry they are rare except with archaising poets.

Strong past participles originally had the ending {-en}. In some verbs this still survives (*ridden*, *slain*), but in others it has been lost (*bound*, *begun*). In eModE many verbs have alternative forms, so that for example it is possible to say 'I had forgotten' or 'I had forgot'. Other such variants are *arose/arisen*, *broke/broken*, *chose/chosen*, *come/comen*, *held/holden*, *rode/rid/ridden*, *smote/smot/smit/smitten*, *swore/sworn*, and *took/taken*. Some of these, like *come* and *rid*, are the old past participle with loss of {-en}. Others have been influenced by the past tense, with which they are identical, for example *rode*, *smote*, *took*: such forms are common in eModE, and continue to be found throughout the eighteenth century.

The past participles of weak verbs usually have the ending {-ed}, but sometimes we encounter one without an ending. In *Richard III* we find 'Before I be *conuict* by course of Law', and in *Macbeth* 'this report / Hath so *exasperate* their King ...'. The regular forms would be *convicted* and *exasperated*. Forms without {-ed} are common with verbs ending in /-t/, such as *acquit*, *addict*, *articulate*, *confiscate*, *consecrate*, *contract*, *create*, *dedicate*, *degenerate*, *deject*, *infect*, and *suffocate*. In part, such forms may be due to the analogy of verbs like *cut*, *met*, and *shut*: historically, these are weak verbs, but the final {-ed} had been lost by sound changes going right back to OE times. Probably more important, however, is the fact that verbs like *convict* and *exasperate* are

176

derived from Latin past participles (*convictus*, *exasperátus*). In an age when every educated English person knew Latin, it was natural for forms like *convict* to be used as past participles or participial adjectives. This is especially common with forms in *-ate*, and sometimes the participial use is recorded in English earlier than the use as a finite verb: the OED records *enumerate* as a participle meaning 'listed' from 1646, but not as a finite verb 'to list' until 1647.

The modal auxiliaries

The auxiliaries can be divided into two groups, the 'modal', and the 'non-modal' or 'primary'. The primary auxiliaries, *be*, *do*, and *have*, will be discussed under syntax, in the next chapter.

When the Early Modern period opened, there were twelve modal auxiliaries:

can	dare	may	mote	shall	will
couth	durst	might	must	should	would

There are numerous variant spellings. In particular, the form *couth* or *couthe* also appears as *coud* or *coude*. The PresE spelling *could* arises in the first half of the sixteenth century. The *l* in *could* is unetymological, and has never been pronounced: it was inserted through the influence of *should* and *would*: these both had /l/, but this was lost in their weak forms. In 1500, *couth* was already old-fashioned, and the normal sixteenth-century form is *coud*. When *couth* is found in the later sixteenth century, as sometimes in Sidney and Spenser, it is an archaism. Auxiliary *might* has an alternative form *mought*, which occurs commonly throughout the period in texts of all kinds. Auxiliary *will* has the alternative forms *woll* and *wull*. There are also weak forms of *will* and *would*, found especially in dramatic dialogue, as in *Ile* 'I will', and *heed* 'he would'.

For most of the Early Modern period, one of the marks of a modal auxiliary is that, in a verb phrase, it is used in conjunction with a lexical verb without any linking *to*. So in 'I ought crave pardon', *ought* could be a modal auxiliary, but in 'as he ought to do' it could not. This however changes in the seventeenth century, for reasons which will appear later, and by the end of the period *ought to* can be classified as a modal auxiliary.

The other distinguishing mark of a modal auxiliary is that it lacks the {-eth} or {-es} inflection in the third-person singular: *he can*, *he shall*. We sometimes meet expressions like 'he dares' and 'he willeth', but this simply means that there are lexical verbs *to dare* and *to will* alongside the auxiliaries *dare* and *will*. The auxiliaries do, however, have the {-est} inflection in the second-person singular: *thou canst*, *coud(e)st*, *may(e)st*, and so on. It does not occur, however, with *durst* and *must*. Auxiliary *shall* and *will* do not take the {-est} inflection, but instead have the second-person singular forms *shalt* and *wilt*.

The modal auxiliaries lack an infinitive and an -*ing* form: we find *he shall*, but not *to shall* or *shalling*. Very early in the period we do indeed occasionally find participles like *maying* 'being able', and infinitives like *to can* 'to know' and *to mow* 'to be able', but these we can consider to be relics of old lexical verbs, already obsolescent in eModE.

At the beginning of the Early Modern period the twelve modal auxiliaries form six pairs. In each pair, the members bear a present/past relationship, *should* for example being a past-tense equivalent of *shall*. During the sixteenth century, this symmetry disappears. For one thing, *mote* falls out of use, leaving *must* unpaired. Even in 1500, the link between *mote* and *must* had become tenuous, for *must* was often used without any past-tense connotations. Auxiliary *mote* was used to indicate permission or possibility. It therefore overlapped with *may*, which is perhaps one of the reasons why it fell out of use. It is still found in Early Tudor prose. Later in the period, however, it is not found in prose (except in Scots), and when it occurs in poetry it is an archaism. Spenser, for example, uses it, as in the following lines from *The Faerie Queene*:

> Now *mote* ye vnderstand that to this groue
> Sir Calepine by chaunce, more then by choyce,
> The selfe same euening fortune hether droue.

After about 1550, however, it cannot be considered a part of the standard southern language.

Auxiliary *must* was thus left unpaired. It signalled necessity or obligation, normally without any implication of pastness, and this had been a common way of using it since late ME times. Occasionally, however, it is used as a past-tense form, as in Macduff's exclamation in *Macbeth*:

> And I *must* be from thence? My wife kill'd too?

He is reproaching himself for not having been at home when his wife and children were murdered, and he means 'And I had to be away!'

In the sixteenth century, another unpaired auxiliary arose, namely *need*. At the beginning of the period, it was an ordinary lexical verb, with a third-person singular form *needs* or *needeth*. It could be followed by a noun-object, by an infinitive preceded by *to*, or, from the late fifteenth century, by a base-form without *to*. In the sixteenth century it became fairly common to use *need*, followed by the base-form, without the {-eth} or {-es} inflection of the third-person singular. When used in this way, it had become a modal auxiliary. The first clear example in the OED is dated 1538: 'he nede commaunde non other'. Probably, forms like *he need* were originally subjunctive. Then, because this particular verb occurred very frequently in the subjunctive, it was generalised, and *need* was used in constructions usually requiring the indicative. Auxiliary

178

need has been quite common since the middle of the sixteenth century. The following examples are from the later part of the century:

> 1. Such selfe assurance *need* not feare the spight
>   Of grudging foes   (Spenser, *Amoretti*)
> 2. Be secret false: what *need* she be acquainted?
>   (Shakespeare, *Comedy of Errors*)

In 2., *what* means 'why'.

To *need* and *must*, we can perhaps add *ought* as an unpaired auxiliary in the sixteenth century. Originally, it was the past tense of the lexical verb *to owe*, and meant 'owed' or 'possessed'. It can still be used in this way in eModE, as in this extract from *Henry IV Part 1*:

> *Prince:*   Thou say'st true, Hostesse, and he slanders thee most grossely.
> *Hostess:* So he doth you, my Lord, and sayde this other day,
>   You *ought* him a thousand pound.
> *Prince:*   Sirrah, do I *owe* you a thousand pound?
> *Falstaff:* A thousand pound Hal? A Million. Thy loue is worth a Million: thou *ow'st* me thy loue.

This use of *ought* survives throughout the Early Modern period, alongside the new formation *owed*, which had arisen in the fifteenth century. Already in ME, however, *ought* was also used without any connotation of pastness, to signal duty or obligation. Usually it was followed by *to*, but sometimes by the base-form without *to*, and in such cases it conforms to the criteria I have suggested for sixteenth-century modal auxiliaries:

> 1. For what tyme thy Lorde, vnto his hors is prest,
>   Then *ought* no seruaunt, lye in his bed at rest.   (Barclay, *Egloges*)
> 2. In princes hartes gods scourge imprinted depe,
>   *Ought* them awake, out of their sinfull slepe.
>   (Surrey, *Songs and Sonnets*)
> 3. (Being Mechanicall) you *ought* not walke
>   Vpon a labouring day   (Shakespeare, *Julius Caesar*)

This construction, however, is not as common as *ought to*, and is very rare in the seventeenth century. The example from *Julius Caesar* is the only one of its kind in Shakespeare. It perhaps occurs sufficiently often, however, for us to classify *ought* as a sixteenth-century modal auxiliary.

In the central part of the Early Modern period, then, we can classify the following as modal auxiliaries:

> can, could; dare, durst; may, might; shall, should; will, would; must; need; ought.

At this stage there are ten paired auxiliaries and three unpaired ones.

I have excluded two marginal cases, *mun* 'must' and *list* 'please'. The former behaves like a modal auxiliary, but is a regional dialect form, not StE. The latter very occasionally behaves like an auxiliary, usually in poetry. I have also excluded *used*, which is always followed by *to*. In eModE, *used* is simply the p.t. of the lexical verb *to use*, which can mean (among other things) 'to be in the habit (of)'. Even at the end of the seventeenth century it is still normal to say such things as 'he uses to do it' and 'he did not use to do it'. On the other hand, in the second half of the seventeenth century it seems reasonable to classify *ought to* as a modal auxiliary. By that time, the criteria for classifying a form as an auxiliary have changed. In part, this is due to the emergence of /nt/ as a weak form of *not*: it then becomes possible to classify a form as an auxiliary if it can be immediately followed by /-nt/ (often with some change of form, as with *shan't* and *won't*). In part, the change is made possible by the regulation of auxiliary do (see next chapter).

Adverbs

The words traditionally called adverbs include several different types, with more than one function, in eModE as in PresE. The following are examples of the ways in which they are most often used in eModE:

1. Books will speake *plaine*, when Counsellors blanch (Bacon, *Essays*)
2. Thou art *right* welcome, as thy master is

(Shakespeare, *As You Like It*)
3. Infaith, it is *exceedingly* well aym'd (Shakespeare, *Henry IV Part 1*)
4. *Assuredly* the thing is to be sold   (Shakespeare, *As You Like It*)

In 1., the adverb is a verb-modifier. In 2., it modifies an adjective. In 3., it modifies another adverb. And in 4. it is a sentence-modifier. When used as in 2. and 3., adverbs have traditionally been called 'adverbs of degree', and are now sometimes called 'intensifiers'. Some adverbs, like *very*, cannot be used as verb-modifiers or sentence-modifiers. Others, like *there*, cannot be used as intensifiers. Many adverbs, however, can be used in all four ways, and it is convenient to treat them all together.

Some adverbs are grammatical words, belonging to a closed set, while others are lexical words. The latter group obviously includes adverbs formed from adjectives by means of the suffix -*ly*, such as *certainly* and *heartily*. These adverbs can be compared: *more heartily*, *most heartily*. The closed set includes a considerable number of words like *abroad*, *along*, *always*, *down*, *everywhere*, *forwards*, *now*, *often*, *once*, *somehow*, *then*, *there*, *very*, *well*.

In eModE, there were quite a few adverbs in the closed class which have since fallen out of everyday use. They include *afore* 'before', *anon* 'immediately, soon', *anything* 'in any way', *belike* 'perhaps', *haply* 'by chance, perhaps', *inly* 'inwardly', *nothing* 'not at all', *passing* 'exceedingly', *per-*

adventure 'by chance, perhaps', *something* 'rather, somewhat', *thrice* 'three times', *toward(s)* 'at hand, in preparation', *whilom* 'at times, formerly', and *withal* 'moreover, in addition'.

There are other adverbs which were in common use in the early part of the period, but which later became literary archaisms. Such is *uneath* 'with difficulty, scarcely', which is common in Early Tudor times. It is used frequently by Elyot, as in the following extract from *The Governor*:

> his shippe and men were perisshed in the see / and he *vneth* escaped / and was caste on lande.

It continues in quite common use until the end of the sixteenth century, but then becomes much rarer, and after about 1650 survives only as an archaism. Somewhat similar is the case of *algates* 'always, in any case'. This is found in prose texts until about 1580, but after that date is rarely encountered outside poetry. It is especially likely to occur in Spenserian poetry, and is very rare after about 1625. Other adverbs which are normal only in the earlier part of the Early Modern period include *eft* 'again, back, afterwards', *eftsoon(s)* 'again, afterwards', *eke* 'also', *erst* 'earlier, at first', and *othergates* 'otherwise, differently'. We could perhaps add *tho* 'then', but it seems more probable that this was already a literary archaism when the period opened.

There are other adverbs which are still in common use, but which in eModE could be used in senses different from their present ones. The following are examples from Shakespeare:

1. And then (they say) no Spirit can walke *abroad* ('at large, outdoors')
   (*Hamlet*)
2. This is to giue a dogge, and in recompence desire my dogge *againe* ('back') (*Twelfth Night*)
3. What Ostler, come *away* ('along, here') (*Henry IV Part 1*)
4. That trusted *home* ('completely, to the utmost'),
   Might yet enkindle you vnto the Crowne (*Macbeth*)
5. Yet if this seruile vsage *once* ('at all, in any way') offend,
   Go, and be free againe, as Suffolkes friend (*Henry VI Part 1*)
6. *Ariel:*   *Presently* ('immediately')?
   Prospero: I: with a twincke (*The Tempest*)
7. 'Tis like you'll proue a iolly surly groome,
   That take it on you at the first so *roundly* ('plainly, bluntly, without ceremony') (*The Taming of the Shrew*)
8. As Hectors leysure, and your bounties shall
   Concurre together, *seuerally* ('separately, individually') intreat him
   (*Troilus and Cressida*)
9. Thou *still* ('continually, always') hast bin the Father of good Newes
   (*Hamlet*)

181

These could also be used in most of their present-day meanings.

Sometimes, an open-class adverb lacks the ending *-ly*, and is identical with the related adjective:

1. Therwith enrag'd she loudly gan to bray,
   And turning *fierce* her speckled taile aduaunst
   (Spenser, Faerie Queene)
2. A *maruellous* witty fellow I assure you   (Shakespeare, *Much Ado*)
3. Me thinkes the ground is eeuen. – *Horrible* steepe
   (Shakespeare, King Lear)
4. To shew an vnfelt Sorrow, is an Office
   Which the false man do's *easie*   (Shakespeare, *Macbeth*)
5. Speake *free*   (Jonson, *Volpone*)
6. Books will speake *plaine*, when Counsellors Blanch (Bacon, *Essays*)

Such forms arose by analogy with adverbs like *fast* 'firmly, quickly', *hard* 'vigorously', and *soft* 'softly, comfortably'. These derive from the OE adverbs *fæste*, *hearde*, and *softe*, in which the adverbial ending *-e* had been added direct to the stem. In ME, this final *-e* was lost, so that we now have a number of adverbs like *fast* which are identical in form with the corresponding adjective. There were quite a few such forms in eModE, and this may have led to the adverbial use of adjectives like *fierce* and *easy*, alongside the regular forms *fiercely* and *easily*.

Other form-classes

The consideration of conjunctions, interjections, prepositions, and relative pronouns will be deferred to the next chapter, on syntax.

FURTHER READING

Historical grammars covering the whole of the Modern English period include Sweet (1892–1903) and Jespersen (1961), though neither of these works devotes much space to Early Modern English. Books covering morphology in the works of individual authors include Sugden (1936, Spenser), Franz (1939, Shakespeare), Partridge (1953a, Jonson), and Emma (1964, Milton). Abbott (1870, Shakespeare) is old-fashioned, but contains useful material. On *you* and *thou*, see Brown & Gilman (1960, 1989), Mulholland (1967), Barber (1981c), Wales (1983), Calvo (1992) and Hope (1993).

Chapter Five

GRAMMAR: (2) SYNTAX

Syntax deals with the rules for combining words and phrases into utterances. We say 'A beautiful young German girl', not 'A German young beautiful girl'. We say 'The dog bit John', not 'John dog the bit'. Obviously there are complicated rules for the ways in which we organise such structures, rules which we have internalised, even if we cannot formulate them. The basic unit for the study of syntax is the Sentence.

In eModE, as today, the commonest type of sentence, at any rate in writing, is what Bloomfield (1935) calls 'the full sentence'. A full sentence is one that consists of a Subject and a Predicate. But in both periods, other kinds of sentence are found, especially in speech. Bloomfield calls these 'minor sentences', which he classifies as completive, exclamatory, and aphoristic. In eModE they occur frequently in plays which attempt to give the illusion of everyday speech. There are numerous examples in Falstaff's speech about honour in *Henry IV Part 1*, as in the following brief extract:

> What is Honour? A word. What is that word Honour? Ayre: A trim reckoning. Who hath it? He that dy'de a Wednesday. Doth he feele it? No. Doth hee heare it? No. Is it insensible then? yea, to the dead.

There, Falstaff's questions are all full sentences, but the answers are minor sentences of the completive type: 'A word', 'Ayre', 'He that dy'de a Wednesday', 'No', 'yea, to the dead'. It is true that 'He that dy'de a Wednesday' contains a subject and a predicate, but these are in a subordinate clause dependent on *He*, and there is no main clause. The extract also contains a minor sentence of the exclamatory type: 'A trim reckoning'. There are no examples of the aphoristic type: it can be illustrated by an utterance of Shylock's in *The Merchant of Venice*: 'fast binde, fast finde'.

In most kinds of writing, however, the normal type is the full sentence, with subject and predicate, and it is this kind of sentence which I shall discuss in what follows. The subject always contains a noun or something noun-like, while the predicate must contain a lexical verb, or an auxiliary, or both. The irreducible minimum of the subject is a Noun Phrase (NP), while that of the predicate is a Verb Phrase (VP). Other things can occur in both subject and predicate: for example, a noun phrase can occur in the predicate, as a direct object or a complement, but in that case it is a subordinate part of the verb phrase.

THE NOUN PHRASE

The essential element in a noun phrase is the head, which can be either a noun or a pronoun. The head can constitute the whole NP: '*Thou* turn'st mine eyes into my very soule', '*Honor* prickes me on'. To the head can be added adjuncts – determiners, adjectives, other nouns, preposition phrases, subordinate clauses. One common pattern is determiner (D), adjective(s) (A), and noun (N). In eModE, as today, the normal order in the NP is D-A-N, as in 'these sweet thoughts' (*The Tempest*). There are numerous possible variations on this pattern or expansions of it. For example, in addition to the adjectives, or in place of them, there can be numerals, noun-adjuncts, and participles, while the noun can be followed by a preposition phrase as adjunct. Most of these structures are the same in eModE as in PresE. Not that any particular pattern is as frequent in one period as in the other. Potter (1975) has pointed out that expressions like 'the Marriage Tables' (*Hamlet*) are relatively infrequent in eModE: today it is very common for nouns to be used as adjuncts, but eModE prefers the construction where the adjunct is in the possessive case, as in 'our deere Brothers death' (also from *Hamlet*). Moreover, some of the eModE variants on the D-A-N pattern are no longer normal usage. We can consider these divergences under three headings: 1. the type of elements that can occur in the NP; 2. the order in which they can occur, and 3. the rules about the co-occurrence of elements.

In the basic D-A-N pattern, the head, in PresE, must be a noun. In eModE, however, we sometimes find a personal pronoun used instead. In other words, the pronoun sometimes has determiner and adjective adjuncts:

1. But to *the highest him*, that is behight
   Father of Gods and men by equall might;
   To weet, the God of Nature, I appeale   (Spenser, *Faerie Queene*)
2. Lady, you are *the cruell'st shee* aliue   (Shakespeare, *Twelfth Night*)
3.   and to *poore we*
   Thine enmities most capitall   (Shakespeare, *Coriolanus*)
4. Who ere shee bee,

That not impossible shee
That shall command my heart and mee

(Crashaw, *Steps to the Temple*)

In 1., the pronoun is given the appropriate case after the preposition, but in 3. it is not: the nominative form of the pronoun is in effect being converted into a noun. Sometimes this process is carried further, and the pronoun given a noun inflection: a character in *Cymbeline* talks of 'The Shees of Italy'. The examples given above are all in poetry, but the usage is not confined to this kind of context. In the Putney Debates of 1647, Colonel Rainborough is reported to have said:

for really I thinke that *the poorest hee* in England hath a life to live as *the greatest hee*.

The construction often occurs with superlative adjectives.

We also find personal pronouns followed by preposition phrases as adjuncts:

1. and *hee of Wales*, that gaue Amamon the Bastinado

(*Henry IV Part 1*)
2. *he in the red face* had it (*Merry Wives*)
3. *they of Rome* are entred in our Counsailes (*Coriolanus*)

In PresE we avoid this construction, and instead say things like 'the one with the red face' and 'the people of Rome'.

Occasionally, we find closed-system adverbs used in the noun phrase, as adjunct or even as head. We can use *then* as an adjunct ('his then employer'), but hardly *here*, as Shakespeare does in 'thy heere approach' (*Macbeth*). The usage is not confined to poetry: in Glanvill's *Vanity of Dogmatizing* there are expressions like 'our now Reasons'. The use of an adverb as the head of a noun phrase is rarer, but we do sometimes come across phrases like:

Thou loosest here *a better where* to finde (*King Lear*)

In the order of the elements of the NP, there are a few variants which are not usual today. Occasionally, we find an order influenced by French, the adjective following the noun instead of preceding it. This is found mainly in set expressions, especially legal and administrative ones, like *armour defensive*, *captain general*, *Court Christian* 'ecclesiastical court', *cousin german* 'first cousin', *fee simple*, *heir male*, *lords temporal*. We still have a few such expressions in everyday use, like *proof positive*, but there are more in eModE. Apart from such set expressions, the noun-adjective order is uncommon in prose texts. When it does occur, it is perhaps a result of legal training: Elyot and Bacon were both lawyers, and both use the construction occasionally, for example *other beastes sauage* (Elyot), *the languages originall* 'the original languages' (Bacon). In poetry, on the other hand, the construction is common. Here it is a rhetorical device, a deliberate departure from normal usage for stylistic effect: the rhetoricians would have classified it as the grammatical scheme called hyperbaton. Milton hardly ever uses noun-adjective order in his prose, but it occurs quite often in his verse, in phrases like *Regions milde* and *A Dungeon horrible* (Emma 1964).

Occasionally we find the order adjective-determiner-noun. It occurs especially in vocative expressions, like 'good my Brother' (*Hamlet*), 'Ah poore our sexe' (*Troilus and Cressida*), 'Deare my Lorde' (*Julius Caesar*). Rarely, it occurs in other kinds of utterance, as in 'bequeathed me by will, but *poore a thousand Crownes*' (*As You Like It*).

Another pattern which is not uncommon in eModE is illustrated in the following sentence from Elyot's *Governor*:

> But the moste honourable exercise in myne opinion / and that besemeth the astate of euery noble persone / is to ryde suerly and clene / on *a great horse and a roughe.*

This construction would not come naturally to a present-day writer, who would want to place both adjectives before the noun. Variations on the pattern can be seen in the following examples from Shakespeare:

1. *A goodly portly man* yfaith, *and a corpulent*, of a Chearefull Looke
(*Henry IV Part 1*)
2. *An honest mind and plaine* (*King Lear*)

In 1., the asseveration *yfaith* is placed between the head and the following adjunct, and then follows another adjunct of the usual kind, a preposition phrase. In 2., there is no indefinite article before the second adjective.

In phrases like 'the two greatest men' (or 'the greatest two men'), it is possible in eModE to put the cardinal numeral before the article:

1. In *eight the first yeeres* of his empire (Elyot, *Governor*)
2. Prethee stay, and behold *two the most prodigious rascals* that euer slipt into the shape of men
(Middleton, *A Trick to Catch the Old One*)

The meanings are 'the first eight years' and 'the two most prodigious rascals'. Apart from this construction, the numerals occur in the same position as in PresE, namely after the determiner but before the adjectives (as in 'the seven deadly sins'). The rather complicated rules for the order in which the adjectives occur are usually the same as in PresE, though there are occasional differences, as when a character in *Richard III* speaks of 'a Christian faithfull man'. As in PresE, a noun used as an adjunct is placed after the adjectives, immediately before the head, for example 'a little *wicker* basket' (Spenser, *Prothalamion*).

As far as the co-occurrence of elements is concerned, there is one clear difference from today. In PresE, certain determiners are mutually exclusive: one, and no more than one, can occur in the same structure. There are four groups of such determiners: 1. the articles (*the*, *a/an*, *no*), 2. the demonstratives (*this/these*, *that/those*), 3. the pronoun-determiners (*my*, *our*, etc.), and 4. a group of invariable determiners including *any*, *each*, *every*, *much* and *some*. The members inside each group are mutually exclusive. Moreover, the members of 1., 2. and 3. cannot collocate with one another, while the members of group 4. cannot collocate with the articles. In eModE, however, some such collocations are possible: the pronoun-determiners frequently collocate with the demonstratives, and occasionally with the invariable determiners (but not with the articles). The following are examples:

1. *this your* moste noble realme   (Elyot, *Governor*)
2. all *those his* Lands   (Shakespeare, *Hamlet*)
3. At *each his* needlesse heauings   (Shakespeare, *Winter's Tale*)
4. of *euery These* happend accidents   (Shakespeare, *The Tempest*)
5. Art thou *that my* Lord Eliiah?   (*King James Bible*)
6. *this our* mansion   (Locke, *Essay*)

The forms with the demonstratives are very common, the others less so. Today we replace such constructions by ones like 'all those lands of his' and 'each of its needless heavings': such constructions were also in use throughout the Early Modern period.

We also find the pronoun-determiners after *other* and *the same*:

1. imploye all the powers of theyr wittes and theyr diligence / to the only preseruation of *other theyr* inferiours   (Elyot, *Governor*)
2. *the same their* deuises   (Mulcaster, *Elementary*)
3. because it aduanceth any *other their* ends   (Bacon, *Advancement*)

Notice that *other their* does not mean the same as *their other*: in 3., the meaning is 'other ends of theirs'. Similarly, 2. means 'the same devices of theirs'. Perhaps 1. is different, since *other* could be interpreted as a pronoun ('other people') in apposition to *theyr inferiours*. But in any case, the phrase does not mean 'their other inferiors', but 'others, who are inferior to them'.

THE VERB PHRASE

In the predicate of a sentence, the irreducible minimum part is a verb phrase (VP). The essential minimum part of a verb phrase, its head, is a lexical verb or an auxiliary. It is possible for either of these to form the whole of the VP: 'I *go*, I *go*' (*Midsummer Night's Dream*), 'No, thou *shalt*' (*Henry IV Part 1*). When an auxiliary is used, however, it is normally in conjunction with a lexical verb, which is then the head of the VP. To the head can be added various subordinate parts, such as an NP as object or complement, preposition phrases, and adverbs or adverb clauses modifying the head.

THE TENSE SYSTEM

The VP had a tense system which made use of the primary auxiliaries. As today, there were three of these: *be, have*, and *do*. Unlike the modal auxiliaries, they have a distinct form for the third-person singular: *is, hath* or *has, doth* or *does*. Auxiliary *be* and auxiliary *have* are used in conjunction with parts of the lexical verb to form the tense system. The use of auxiliary *do* will be discussed later.

Without the aid of an auxiliary, the verb can be unmarked (the base-form) or can be marked for pastness or unreality (the past-tense form). With the aid of the auxiliaries, it can be marked as perfect, progressive, and passive. Examples of these markings are given in Table 5.1.

Today, we can combine any two or three of the markings, for example *he had eaten* (past and perfect), *he has been eating* (perfect and progressive), *it had been eaten* (past and perfect and passive), and so on. In eModE, however, this was not the case: there was one combination which was impossible, namely that of the progressive with the passive. We do not find sentences like 'the meal was being eaten' or 'the house is being built'. In eModE, the writer either omitted the progressive marking and wrote 'the meal was eaten', or used constructions like 'the meal was eating', 'the house is (a)building'. The combination of the passive and the progressive is not found until the late eighteenth century.

At the beginning of the Early Modern period, the progressive tenses were already a well-established part of the verbal system. As today, they signalled continuous or repeated action in a limited period of time. They were, however, used less frequently than today. Often, where in PresE we use a progressive, in eModE we find an unmarked form. In the scene of Clarence's murder in *Richard III*, the two murderers discuss the best way of killing Clarence, who is asleep. Then one of them says, 'Soft, he wakes'. In PresE we use a progressive in this kind of situation: our equivalent would be something like 'Sh! He's waking up'.

TABLE 5.1

The markings of the lexical verb

Unmarked	Past	Perfect	Progressive	Passive
he eats	he ate	he has eaten	he is eating	he is eaten
they eat	they ate	they have eaten	they are eating	they are eaten

The perfect marking was also well established when the period opened. One way of forming it was with auxiliary *have* plus the past participle of the lexical verb, just as today: 'men *haue died* from time to time, and wormes *haue eaten* them' (*As You Like It*). With intransitive verbs, however, auxiliary *be* is sometimes used instead:

1. Thinke not that I *am come* to destroye the lawe

(Tyndale, *New Testament*)

2. Worcester *is stolne* away by Night: thy Fathers Beard *is turn'd* white with the Newes (Shakespeare, *Henry IV Part 1*)

3. The King himselfe *is rode* to view their Battaile

(Shakespeare, *Henry V*)

4. Now I saw in my Dream, that by this time Pliable *was got* home to his House again (Bunyan, *Pilgrim's Progress*)

5. If there happen to be found an irreverent Expression, or a Thought too wanton, they *are crept* into my Verses through my Inadvertency

(Dryden, Preface to *Fables*)

This form of the perfect is very common with verbs of motion, like *come*, *creep*, *depart*, *descend*, *enter*, *go*, *meet*, *pass*, *return*, *ride*, *run*, and *wander*. It is found even more frequently with verbs denoting a change of state, like *become*, *change*, *grow*, *melt*, *turn*, and *wax*. In verbs of these two types, *be* is much more frequent than *have*. Perfects with *have* do occur, however, as in the following examples:

1. Since when, my watch hath told me, toward my graue I *haue trauail'd* but two houres (*Twelfth Night*)

2. Let me embrace thee good old Chronicle,
That *hast* so long *walk'd* hand in hand with time

(*Troilus and Cressida*)

3. I *haue gone* ['walked'] all night: 'Faith Ile lye down, and sleepe

(*Cymbeline*)

A comparison of these two groups of examples shows that there is a difference between them. In the examples with auxiliary *have*, the concern of the sentence is with the action of the verb as a continuing process. In those with auxiliary *be*, the concern is rather with a state, the situation that has arisen as a result of the action. This is the main principle behind the choice of *have* or *be* for the perfect with verbs of this type. There are, however, several other factors which influence the choice, as has been shown by Fridén (1948).

The perfect marking is very common in the Early Modern period, but perhaps not quite as common as it is today: occasionally a writer uses a past tense where we use a perfect. In *Henry VI Part 2*, a scene opens with the King and Queen entering with their attendants and 'Faulkners hallowing'. Clearly, they are engaged in the sport of falconry, and have just been flying their birds. The opening words of the scene are spoken by the Queen:

> Beleeue me Lords, for flying at the Brooke,
> I *saw* not better sport these seuen yeeres day.

In this situation, a present-day speaker uses the perfect, and says something like 'I *haven't seen* better sport for years'. For the present-day reader, the absence of the perfect marking is especially striking in constructions involving *never* or *since*, as when a character in *King Lear* says 'You *spoke* not with her since?' The PresE equivalent would be 'You *haven't spoken* with her since then?'

THE SENTENCE

The usual order of the subject and verb in the sentence is S-V. Transitive verbs also have a direct object, which normally comes after the verb, giving the very common pattern S-V-O, as today. This is sometimes called 'straight word order'. If there is an auxiliary, its position in straight word order is before the lexical verb, giving the pattern S-Aux-V. Transitive verbs can also have an indirect object, but intransitive verbs have no object. If the main verb is a copula (like *be* or *become*), there is no direct object, but some kind of complement, which can for example be a noun phrase, an adjective, or a preposition phrase. The following are examples of these common sentence patterns:

1. Betweene them they will kill the Coniurer   *(Comedy of Errors)*
2. I gaue him gentle lookes   *(Two Gentlemen)*
3. I go, I go   *(A Midsummer Night's Dream)*
4. I was then Frugall of my mirth   *(Merry Wives)*

In 1. there is the order S-Aux-V-O. In 2. there is both a direct object ('gentle lookes') and an indirect object ('him'). In 3. there is an intransitive verb. In 4. there is a copula, with an adjective phrase as complement ('Frugall of my mirth'). I shall use the expression 'straight word order' to refer to all these types.

In eModE, however, it is not uncommon to encounter the order V-S, or, if there is an auxiliary, Aux-S-V, as in the following examples:

1. Now comes in the sweetest Morsell of the night.   *(Henry IV Part 2)*
2. Now would I giue a thousand furlongs of Sea, for an Acre of barren ground.   *(The Tempest)*

Both these patterns, V-S and Aux-S-V, are sometimes called 'inverted word order', and the phenomenon is called 'inversion'.

In PresE, the order Aux-S-V is normal in questions, but inverted word order

190

is rare in declarative sentences. Straight word order has always been important in English, but in earlier periods of the language there were also other common patterns, including the inverted one. In the course of ME, straight word order spread at the expense of other patterns, and by the opening of the Early Modern period it was the predominant one for declarative sentences. Inverted word order is still quite common in eModE, however, and is often used where we use straight word order. It is particularly likely to occur when the sentence begins with an adverb or adverbial phrase. If the object of the sentence is placed at the beginning, either for emphasis or to provide a link with what has gone before, this too can cause inversion.

In verse, a writer often departs from normal word-order for reasons of rhythm or emphasis or rhyme. For this reason, I take the following examples of inversion exclusively from prose works:

1. For so *persecuted they* the Prophetes which were before youre dayes
   (Tyndale, *New Testament*)
2. He was of a meane stature, and though stricken in age, yet *bare he* his bodye vpright
   (Robinson, *Utopia*)
3. now *shal I* be openly discyphred, and that in the sight of euery man: now *shal it* openly be knowen, whether I be Erostrato the gentleman, or Dulipo the seruaunt: we haue hitherto played our partes in abusing others, but now *commeth the man* that wil not be abused
   (Gascoigne, *Supposes*)
4. Then *doo they* vaunt themselues ouer the common multitude
   (Nash, *Pierce Penniless*)
5. The same day *arriued Captaine George Gifford* with your Lordships ship
   (Ralegh, *Guiana*)
6. And this s*hall you* neuer so wel doe
   (Robinson, *Utopia*)

In 1., 3. and 4., there is inversion after the adverbs *so*, *now*, and *then*. Other adverbs which commonly cause inversion are *also*, *here*, *therefore*, and *thus*. In 5. there is inversion after the adverb phrase 'The same day'. In 6., the object of the sentence, *this*, is thrown to the beginning, and is followed by inversion. As the examples suggest, pronoun subjects are especially liable to inversion, though it does happen with nouns too.

All the above examples are from the sixteenth century, a period in which they occur freely. During the seventeenth century, however, such constructions become progressively rarer. Jacobsson (1951) gives statistics for sentences beginning with a number of adverbs like *then* and *now*. In late ME, he finds that inversion occurs in 44 per cent of such sentences. For the sixteenth century, the figure is lower, but still substantial, at 34 per cent. But for the period 1600 to 1712, the figure is only 7 per cent. Inversion persisted most strongly with the verbs *have* and *say*, and with a number of intransitive verbs such as *come* and *stand*. It persisted more strongly in sentences with auxiliaries than in ones without.

There are some cases, however, where inversion is normal in PresE, but where eModE can have straight word order. The most frequent type of inversion in PresE occurs in sentences which begin with a negative or restrictive expression, such as *never, nor, only, rarely, seldom,* and so on. In such sentences an auxiliary must be used, and inversion takes place ('Seldom have I heard such nonsense', 'Not once did he pause to consider ...'). Such constructions also occurred in eModE, but it was also possible to use straight order in sentences of this kind. The following passage from *The Governor* contains two examples of straight order where PresE would use inversion:

> An other publique weale was amonge the Atheniensis / where equalitie was of astate amonge the people / and only by theyr holle consent *theyr citie and dominions were gouerned*: whiche mought well be called a Monstre with many heedes: nor neuer *it was* certeyne nor stable.

After *nor*, indeed, inversion is not found until about 1590, but then quickly becomes the predominant construction (Jacobsson 1951). After other negative and restrictive expressions, we find that in the sixteenth century the two types of word-order are in free variation.

In the course of the seventeenth century, there is a tendency for inverted order to be standardised in sentences beginning with a negative or restrictive expression. At the same time, there is a tendency for straight order to be standardised in sentences beginning with a non-negative adverbial expression, or with the object of the sentence. In the sixteenth century there is free variation, while in PresE there is regulation, and to a considerable extent the process of regulation takes place in the seventeenth century.

In eModE, there is another characteristic construction with inverted order: conditional clauses can be formed without the use of a subordinator (*if, unless,* and so on): instead, inverted order is used, and the verb (where possible) put in the subjunctive:

1. *Goe* not *my Horse* the better,
   I must become a borrower of the Night   (Shakespeare, *Macbeth*)
2. *Spoyle thou* his subiects, thou despoylest me;
   Touch thou his brest, thou doest attaint this heart

(Greene, *James IV*)

These mean 'Unless my horse ...', 'If you spoil ...', 'If you touch ...'. In PresE the construction survives in a few usages, such as 'Did you but know' and 'Were he to ...', but in eModE it has a much more general currency.

SYNTAX

In eModE, as in PresE, the primary auxiliary *do* is semantically empty. It can be used with the base-form of a lexical verb to make a verb phrase, but only if no other auxiliary is being used. Possible sentences are 'he does know' and 'he did know', but auxiliary *do* cannot be inserted in sentences like 'he may know' or 'he has known'. There is, however, one big difference between eModE and PresE: today, the insertion or omission of auxiliary *do* is strictly regulated, whereas in eModE its use was optional, and it could be inserted or omitted at will. Today, if there is no other auxiliary in the VP, we must insert *do* in negative sentences ('I do not know'). We must also insert it in most types of interrogative sentence ('Did you know him?'). In affirmative declarative sentences, we insert it only if we want sentence emphasis, in which case *do* is given nuclear tone, which makes it the most prominent word in the sentence ('I DO know him').

In eModE, by contrast, negative and interrogative sentences can be formed either with or without *do*. Moreover, *do* can be inserted in affirmative declarative sentences without necessarily giving sentence emphasis. This free variation between sentences with and without *do* can be illustrated from a scene we have drawn on before, that of Clarence's murder in *Richard III*. There we find questions formed with do, just as today:

1. How do'st thou feele thy selfe now?
2. Wherefore do you come?

But alongside these there are questions formed by placing the subject after the lexical verb:

3. Why lookes your Grace so heauily to day?
4. how cam'st thou hither?

Similarly, there are negative sentences where *do* is used:

5. O do not slander him.

But there are also many negative sentences formed without do:

6. He sends you not to murther me for this
7. beleeue him not.

There is only one example in the scene of a negative interrogative sentence, and this is formed without *do*:

8. Awak'd you not in this sore Agony?

In other texts, however, there are examples with *do*, like the following from *Henry IV Part 2*:

193

9. Did not goodwife Keech the Butchers wife come in then, and cal me gossip Quickly?

In the *Richard III* scene, the affirmative declarative sentences are mostly formed without *do*, like the following:

10. Who from my Cabin tempted me to walk
11. it makes a man a Coward ... it accuseth him ... it Checkes him ... it detects him.

There is however a substantial minority of cases where do is inserted, as in the following:

12. Where eyes did once inhabit
13. Your eyes do menace me
14. And that same Vengeance doth he hurle on thee
15. Thou didst receiue the Sacrament.

In these cases, it is highly improbable that *do* is inserted to give emphasis: Clarence is not saying 'Your eyes DO menace me'. His sentence is just an alternative way of saying 'Your eyes menace me', and the *do* is probably quite unstressed.

It is of course difficult to be certain in a particular case whether *do* is being used for sentence emphasis, but there are occasional occurrences where it seems probable, as in the following piece of dialogue from Jonson's *Silent Woman*:

Daw. ... do's she refuse me?
Cler. No, Sir, doe not take it so to heart; shee do's not refuse you, but a little neglect you. Good faith, Tru-Wit, you were too blame to put it into his head, that shee do's refuse him.
True. She do's refuse him, Sir, palpably; how euer you mince it.

There it is pretty clear that Clerimont's 'shee do's refuse him' has the usual unemphatic use of *do*. On the other hand, in Truewit's repetition of the same sentence, *do's* must surely be emphatic, since he is denying the truth of what Clerimont has said. Presumably the actor was expected to stress the word *do's*, and perhaps use intonation to make it the most prominent word in the sentence. The evidence suggests, however, that this was not the most usual type, and that in affirmative declarative sentences auxiliary *do* was normally unemphatic.

In the course of the Early Modern period, the use of auxiliary *do* gradually became regulated as it is today: it became increasingly normal to insert *do* in negative and interrogative sentences, and to omit it from affirmative declarative ones (except when sentence-emphasis was required). The regulating

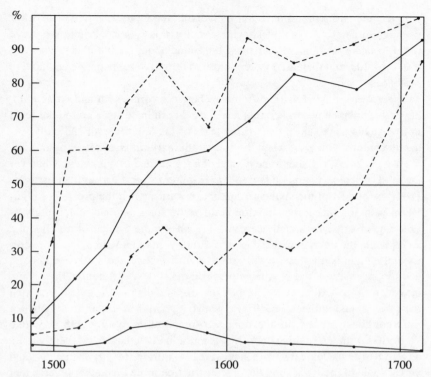

Figure 5.1. Auxiliary *do*. Percentage of *do* forms in different types of sentence, 1500–1700. Upper broken line: negative questions. Upper solid line: affirmative questions. Lower broken line: negative declarative sentences. Lower solid line: affirmative declarative sentences. (Adapted from Ellegård 1953)

process began in the middle of the sixteenth century, and was very nearly complete by 1700. This is shown by the graph in Figure 5.1, adapted from Ellegård (1953), which is based on a large body of prose texts. It shows the number of *do* forms in different types of sentence, as a percentage of the number of possible occurrences. When the Early Modern period opens, the frequency of *do* is rather low, but is already rising steeply in negative and interrogative sentences, and continues to rise fairly steadily throughout the period. Some of the humps in the curves are probably due to chance variations in the sample. The percentage of *do* is always highest in negative questions, followed by affirmative questions, and then by negative declarative sentences. In the early part of the period, the percentage also rises in affirmative declarative sentences, but in the middle of the sixteenth century the curve begins to fall, and continues to do so for the rest of the period. At no time, however, is *do* found in more than 10 per cent of affirmative declarative sentences. By 1700, the affirmative declarative curve is approaching zero, while the other three curves are all above 75

195

per cent and still rising. I have not included in the figure Ellegård's curve for negative imperatives. In the sixteenth century, this is very close to the curve for affirmative declarative sentences, but round about 1600 it makes a sudden leap upwards, and thereafter is very close to the curve for negative declarative sentences.

There were some stylistic differences between forms with and without *do*. Several scholars have argued that auxiliary *do* originated as a colloquial form in low status contexts. In the written texts of the late fifteenth and early sixteenth century, however, when the use of auxiliary *do* was spreading rapidly, the use of *do* seems rather to be typical of a formal and literary style, whatever the kind of sentence; and, in late ME, *do* is found in verse earlier than in prose. From the middle of the sixteenth century onwards, when the process of regulation is taking place, the situation is different. It seems that, increasingly as time goes by, the regulated use of *do* becomes more typical of a colloquial style, while the unregulated use is more literary. In other words, the more colloquial a style is, the less it will use *do* in affirmative declarative sentences, and the more it will use it in negatives and questions. Different authors vary, however, in the extent to which they use *do*, and also in the extent to which their use is the regulated one. There is also a good deal of variation between different constructions. In questions, *do* spread more rapidly with transitive verbs than with intransitive ones. It was more likely to be used if there was an adverb before the lexical verb. There were also differences between individual verbs, some of them resisting the *do* construction more than others. Verbs that resisted the use of *do* in negative sentences include *care*, *come*, *doubt*, *know*, *mistake*, *speak*, and *trow*: even in the late seventeenth century it is common to find expressions like 'I know not', 'if I mistake not'. Verbs that resist the *do* construction in questions include *come*, *dare*, *do*, *have*, *hear*, *mean*, *need*, *say*, and *think*: in the late seventeenth century we still find expressions like 'Say you so?', 'What think you?'.

Just occasionally, in the sixteenth century, there is a different use of *do*, in which it is not a semantically empty auxiliary, but a causative. Spenser sometimes uses it thus, as in the following lines from *The Faerie Queene*:

So matter did she make of nought,
To stirre vp strife, and *do* them disagree ['cause them to disagree'].

Causative *do* had been quite common in Middle English, but had almost died out by the beginning of the Early Modern period, and is rare, even in archaising poets like Spenser.

MODAL AUXILIARIES

In eModE there were a few constructions with modal auxiliaries that are no longer possible. An auxiliary could be followed by a past participle:

1. I would haue sworne the puling girle,
   Would willingly *accepted* Hammons loue

   (Dekker, *Shoemaker's Holiday*)
2.   her death was doubtfull,
   And but that great commaund oreswayes the order,
   She *should* in ground vnsanctified *been* lodg'd

   (Shakespeare, *Hamlet*)

Today we say 'would have accepted', 'should have been lodged'. This was also possible in eModE, as in 'I would haue sworne' in 1. The text of 2. is taken from the good Quarto of 1604: the First Folio of 1623 reads 'She should in ground vnsanctified haue lodg'd'. The construction with the past participle alone is not very common, but occurs often enough to show that it is not a mistake or abnormality, but part of accepted usage in the period.

Normally, the modal auxiliary is followed by a lexical verb, but this can be dispensed with in sentences indicating motion, even though no relevant verb has occurred in the immediately preceding context. The following are examples from Shakespeare:

1. I *must* to Couentree   (*Richard II*)
2. I *will* after straight
   And tell him so   (*Henry IV Part 1*)
3.   thou *shalt* not from this groue,
   Till I torment thee for this iniury   (*A Midsummer Night's Dream*)

These mean 'I must go to Coventry', and so on.

There are also differences from PresE in the meanings of the modal auxiliaries. Auxiliary *can*, as today, most often indicates capacity or capability, but it sometimes carries its earlier sense of 'know' or 'know how to'. It is not used, however, to give permission: *you can go* means 'you have the physical ability to walk', not 'I give you permission to go'.

Auxiliary *may*, as today, is used for permission, wish, and possibility. It is also used, however, to signal capability or physical power, where today we prefer *can*. The following is an example from *The Governor*:

in thynges subiecte to Nature / nothyng of hym selfe onely *may* be norisshed.

This means 'Nothing in Nature can (has the capability to) be autonomous and self-nourishing'. In negative sentences with *may not*, the *not* negates the auxiliary, whereas in PresE it negates the following lexical verb. In eModE, *he may not go* means 'he is not permitted to go', whereas today it usually means 'it is possible that he will not go'. This can be seen in the following examples from Skelton's *Bouge of Court*:

1. Naye naye be sure whiles I am on your syde
   Ye *may not* fall truste me, ye *maye not* fayle
2. For nowe am I plenarely dysposed
   To shewe you thyngs that *may not* be disclosed.

In 1., *ye maye not fayle* means 'it is not possible for you to fail' (as against PresE 'it's possible you'll not fail'). In 2., *that may not be disclosed* means 'that are not permitted to be disclosed'.

Auxiliary *will*, as today, could signal prediction, or promise, or resolve, but it could also signal wish or desire. Auxiliary *would*, similarly, could mean 'wished to, desired to', and also 'would like to', as in the proverbial expression 'Jack would be a gentleman'. Auxiliary *shall* could be used throughout the Early Modern period to signal obligation or necessity, as in the following:

1. thou *shalt* love thyne neghbour   (Tyndale, *New Testament*)
2. He that parts vs, *shall* bring a Brand from Heauen,
   And fire vs hence, like Foxes   (Shakespeare, *King Lear*)

In 2., we should today say *must* or *will have to*. The meaning is that in order to separate them it would be necessary to bring a brand.

The past-tense auxiliaries *could*, *durst*, *might*, *should*, and *would* were more closely linked semantically to their present-tense partners than they are today. As today, the choice of the past-tense form often signalled hypothesis or un-reality, or was a mark of polite obliquity. But, more often than today, the past-tense auxiliary simply signalled the same thing as its present-tense partner, plus the implication of pastness. So *would* often meant 'wished, was willing to' and *could* 'had the capacity to, knew how to'. Auxiliary *might* often meant 'was able to', as in a well-known passage from *A Midsummer Night's Dream*:

> But I *might* see young Cupids fiery shaft
> Quencht in the chaste beames of the watry Moone.

SENTENCE NEGATION

We have already seen one way in which eModE sentence-negation differs from that of PresE, namely that it can take place without the use of an auxiliary: 'I know not', beside 'I do not know'. Occasionally, too, we find expressions of the type 'I not know' (which occurs in Jonson's *Volpone*).

Another feature of eModE negation is illustrated in the following examples:

1. *Ne* they be *nat* in commune ... *nor* one man hath *nat* al vertues
                                        (Elyot, *Governor*)
2. withstand *not* the knowen trueth *no* longer   (Martin Marprelate)
3. I can*not* goe *no* further   (Shakespeare, *As You Like It*)

4. I haue one heart, one bosome, and one truth,
   And that *no* woman has, *nor neuer none*
   Shall mistris be of it, saue I alone   (Shakespeare, *Twelfth Night*)

The phenomenon is that of multiple (or cumulative) negation, which is common in OE and ME. Two or more negative words are used to negate the sentence. These negatives do not cancel one another out, but reinforce one another: the more negatives there are, the more emphatic the negation is. In late ME, negation is often achieved by putting *ne* early in the sentence, and *nat* after the verb. This is still found in the early sixteenth century, as in example 1. As *ne* fell into disuse, it became common to negate a sentence with *nat* (or *not*) alone. Nevertheless, multiple negation continues to be found alongside simple *not* throughout the sixteenth century, as in 2., 3., and 4. It was already dying out in the middle of the Early Modern period, however. It is rarely found in StE after the time of Shakespeare, except that it continues to be possible to use a second negative after initial *nor*, as in the following extract from Congreve's *Love for Love* (1695):

> *Foresight:*   Why, if I was born to be a Cuckold, there's no more to be said –
> *Sir Sampson: Nor no* more to be done, Old Boy.

In any case, multiple negation continued to be well-enough known for it to become one of the targets of the eighteenth-century prescriptionists, who condemned it on mathematical-logical grounds.

REPETITION OF THE SUBJECT

In eModE we sometimes find a double subject, a normal subject with a noun as its head being followed by a personal pronoun:

> The skipping *King hee* ambled vp and downe   (*Henry IV Part 1*)

This is particularly likely to happen when a long modifier is inserted between the noun-subject and the verb:

> 1. *Kynge Philip* / whan he harde that his sonne Alexander dyd singe swetely and properly / *he* rebuked him   (Elyot, *Governor*)
> 2.   my two *Schoolefellowes*,
>   Whom I will trust as I will Adders fang'd,
>   *They* beare the mandat   (Shakespeare, *Hamlet*)

In 1., an adverb clause is inserted between subject and verb, in 2. a relative clause dependent on the subject. In both cases, the pronoun acts as a reminder to the reader about the subject, helping to keep the structure of the sentence clear.

If the subject of the sentence is a clause, or a phrase with an infinitive as its head, it can be duplicated by the pronoun *it*:

1. to recouer himselfe *it* wilbe verie harde (Nash, *Have with you*)
2. That I haue tane away this old mans Daughter,
   It is most true (Shakespeare, *Othello*)

In PresE in such cases we can use *it* as an anticipatory subject, and place the true subject after the verb ('It is most true that I have ...'), but we do not usually place both *it* and the true subject before the verb. In eModE both constructions were possible.

OMISSION OF THE SUBJECT

The core of a full sentence is S-V, but in a colloquial style we sometimes find that a personal pronoun is omitted when it is the sole subject of the sentence. This is most likely to happen when the pronoun is *thou*, perhaps because in this case the inflection of the verb or of the auxiliary shows that the subject is second-person singular. The omission is also most likely to occur in questions:

1. canst [thou] not heare, and twere not as good deede as drinke to break the pate on thee, I am a very villaine, come and be hangd, hast [thou] no faith in thee? (Shakespeare, *Henry IV Part 1*)
2. As I remember Adam, it was vpon this fashion[: he] bequeathed me by will, but poore a thousand Crownes (Shakespeare, *As You Like It*)
3. Ha! what art [thou], who thus maliciously hast awakned me?
   (Congreve, *The Old Batchelor*)

Sometimes the subject-pronoun is omitted even though the style is not a colloquial one:

Nor do we finde him forward to be sounded,
But with a crafty Madnesse [he] keepes aloofe (Shakespeare, *Hamlet*)

In PresE we can omit the second subject when two clauses are co-ordinated, but only if the two subjects are identical. In eModE, the second subject is sometimes omitted even though it is different from the first, provided there is some word in the first clause from which it can be extracted. In the example above, this function is performed by the word *him*.

There are also a few relics of impersonal verbs. In OE and ME there had been a number of such verbs. They have no subject expressed, and are usually accompanied by a pronoun in the dative or accusative case. Examples are *me mette* 'dreamed to me' ('I dreamed'), *him hungreth* 'hungers to him' ('he is hungry'), *me thinketh* '(it) seems to me', *her listed* '(it) pleased her'. Such usages largely die out in late ME, but a few vestiges remain in eModE, like the following:

200

1. And then may *chaunce the* to repent,
   The tyme that thou hast lost and spent   (Wyatt, *Poems*)
2. *Me nede* not long for to beseche
   Her that hath power me to commaunde   (Wyatt, *Poems*)
3. *Me thought* that Glouster stumbled   (Shakespeare, *Richard III*)

These had to compete with alternative constructions, which ultimately replaced them. One was a construction with *it* as subject ('It repents me ...', 'It chanced him that ...'). There was an even stronger tendency for the verbs to be made personal, with a pronoun subject: beside 'me need' we find 'I need', and beside 'her listed' (which occurs in Spenser) we find 'she listed'. In the course of the Early Modern period, the personal construction supplants the impersonal one. Personal uses, like *I list* 'I desire, wish', are found as early as the fourteenth century. In the sixteenth century, forms like *I list* and *me list* occur side by side, but in the early seventeenth century the impersonal use disappears: the last example in the OED (apart from archaic ones in the nineteenth century) is dated 1633.

Exceptionally, the forms *methinks* 'it seems to me' and *methought* 'it seemed to me' survive throughout the Early Modern period. We do not, however, find seventeenth-century forms like **him thinks* or **them thought*: the two forms that do survive are isolated fragments of a paradigm. For this reason, they are sometimes misapprehended, and people try to make them conform to some other pattern in the language. Even in the sixteenth century, we sometimes meet them in such forms as *my thinks*, *my thought* or *my thoughts*, where the second element is apparently treated as a noun. In the seventeenth century, and later, we sometimes encounter the form *methoughts*. In this case, the final *-s* is perhaps due to analogy with *methinks*, or perhaps it is an adverbial ending (as in *needs* 'necessarily', *betimes* 'early', and so on). In either case, *thought* is no longer apprehended as the past tense of an impersonal verb.

THE IMPERATIVE

There is one case where the omission of the pronoun-subject is not exceptional, but the normal rule, both in eModE and in PresE: this is when the sentence is an imperative one. In eModE, the base-form of the verb, without accompanying pronoun, is the usual form of the imperative, both singular and plural:

1. Well, Ile goe with thee, *prouide* vs all things necessary, and *meete* me
   to morrow night in Eastcheape   (Shakespeare, *Henry IV Part 1*)
2. *Send* me your Prisoners with the speediest meanes
                                             (Shakespeare, *Henry IV Part 1*)

In PresE, we sometimes insert the second-person pronoun before such imperative forms. This can be done for contrastive emphasis: 'No, *you* go, and I'll wait here'. It can also be used to signal a particular emotional tone: 'Just you do as you're told!' This use of the pronoun-subject before an imperative is found in OE and ME, but is practically unknown in eModE: it disappears in the fifteenth century, and is not found again until the 1690s (Visser 1963).

In eModE, a different construction is found: the pronoun is often inserted, but is placed *after* the verb. The following two examples come from *Richard III*, the scene of Clarence's murder once again:

1. Take thou the Fee, and tell him what I say.
2. Go you to him from me.

An examination of the context suggests that in 1. the pronoun is probably emphatic: '*You* take the fee, I won't'. No such contrast, however, seems to be implied in 2., which is simply another way of saying 'Go to him from me'.

It seems likely that the imperatives without the pronoun were somewhat more peremptory, and that the more polite forms were ones like 'Go you', 'Go thou'. The construction goes back to OE, and is found throughout the Early Modern period. An example from late in the period can be found on the first page of Congreve's *Love for Love*, where Valentine says to his servant Jeremy:

And d'ye hear, go you to Breakfast.

Today it survives only in a few stock phrases, like 'Mind you', 'Mark you', 'Look you'. These are merely used parenthetically, almost as if they were interjections (Yamakawa 1966).

PREPOSITION PHRASES

In eModE, as today, preposition phrases play a considerable part in sentence structure. They can for example act as noun-adjuncts, as adverbials modifying a verb, or as complements in the predicate of a sentence. These three functions are illustrated in the following examples, which also use eModE prepositions no longer current:

1. in the bataile *againe ['against'] Cataline*   (Elyot, *Governor*)
2. I charge thee waft me safely *crosse ['across'] the Channell*
                                                (Shakespeare, *Henry VI Part 2*)
3. You Mistris, all this coyle ['turmoil'] is *long of ['because of'] you*
                                        (Shakespeare, *Midsummer Night's Dream*)

Usually, as in those examples, the preposition governs a noun or something noun-like – a pronoun, a noun phrase. Occasionally, however, the preposition governs a closed-system adverb:

1. I come to tell you things *sith ['since'] then* befalne

                                                        (*Henry VI Part 3*)

2. And I must be *from thence* (*Macbeth*)

3. I neuer saw him so grosse in his iealousie *till now* (*Merry Wives*)

Prepositions can be classed as grammatical words, even though, in Modern English, their number is rather large. Both in Middle English and in Modern English, the use of prepositions, and also the number of prepositions in the language, increased considerably. This was part of the movement of the language from a more synthetic to a more analytic state: as the old case-systems decayed, their function was often taken over by prepositions. Not all prepositions consist of a single word: there are groups like *cross of* 'across' and *out of* 'beyond, except', which can be classed as prepositions. New prepositions which arose during the Early Modern period include *concerning*, *in advance of*, *on account of*, *owing to*, *pending*, and *touching*.

In eModE there were a number of prepositions which are no longer in use in the everyday language. We have already seen *again* 'against', *cross* 'across', *long of* 'because of', and *sith* 'since'. The following are further examples:

1. Thy wyt and counsell, hath ryd me *fro* ['from'] great payne

(Barclay, *Egloges*)

2.   he saw me, *maugre* ['in spite of'] all his powre,
That glorious spoyle of beautie with me lead

(Spenser, *Faerie Queene*)

3. My loue to thee is sound, *sans* ['without'] cracke or flaw

(Shakespeare, *Love's Labour's Lost*)

4. You are contented to be led in Triumph
Thorow ['through'] the streets of Rome

(Shakespeare, *Julius Caesar*)

The prepositions *again*, *fro*, and *sith* are not uncommon in the sixteenth century, but fall out of use in the seventeenth. The preposition *thorow* or *thorough* is an alternative form of *through* which developed in stressed position: it is found throughout the Early Modern period, even in prose texts.

The majority of eModE prepositions are still in everyday use, but the way they were used often differs from present-day usage. These differences are too numerous to be listed here: Franz (1939) devotes seventy pages to Shakespeare's usage alone. The following examples merely call attention to a few of the commoner differences:

1. Fit to decke maydens bowres,
And crowne their Paramours,
Against ['in preparation for'] the Brydale day

(Spenser, *Prothalamion*)

2. Then speake the truth *by* ['about, concerning'] her

(Shakespeare, *Two Gentlemen of Verona*)

3. almost continually now, *by* ['for'] the space of Six-score yeeres
(Bacon, *Essays*)

4. but *for* ['as for, as regards'] these foolish Officers, I beseech you, I may haue redresse against them   (Shakespeare, *Henry IV Part 1*)

5. the wordes publike and commune / which be borowed *of* ['from'] the latin tonge *for* ['because of'] the insufficiencie of our owne langage
(Elyot, *Governor*)

6. But this is *from* ['not in, absent from'] my Commission
(Shakespeare, *Twelfth Night*)

7. I haue bin told so *of* ['by'] many   (Shakespeare, *As You Like It*)

8. some secret Art of the Soul, which to us is utterly occult, and *without* ['outside, beyond'] the ken of our Intellects   (Glanvill, *Vanity*)

COMPLEX SENTENCES

So far we have been considering the construction of single sentences. Frequently, however, two or more sentences are combined. They can be combined at the same rank in the linguistic hierarchy, producing what have traditionally been called 'compound sentences'. Or they can be combined with one sentence as a subordinate part of another, embedded in it, producing what have traditionally been called 'complex sentences'. The embedded sentences have traditionally been called 'subordinate clauses'. The complex and the compound can be used together to produce complicated sentences, traditionally called 'compound-complex sentences'. I shall use the term 'complex sentences' for all three possibilities – compound, complex, compound-complex.

Examples of complex sentences can be seen in the following extract from *The Merchant of Venice*:

> *Duke.* Go one, and cal the Iew into the Court.
> *Sal.*   He is ready at the door, he comes my Lord.
> *Enter Shylocke.*
> *Duke.* Make roome, and let him stand before our face.
> *Shylocke* the world thinkes, and I thinke so to
> That thou but leadest this fashion of thy mallice   5
> To the last houre of act, and then 'tis thought
> Thou'lt shew thy mercy and remorse more strange,
> Than is thy strange apparant cruelty;
> And where thou now exact'st the penalty,
> Which is a pound of this poore Merchants flesh,   10
> Thou wilt not only loose the forfeiture,
> But touch'd with humane gentlenesse and loue:
> Forgiue a moytie of the principall.

In line 1, there are two co-ordinate imperative sentences, linked by the conjunction *and*. Line 2 is an example of parataxis: two sentences are simply put side by side, with no conjunction: it is to be assumed that they are co-ordinate. In line 3, there are two co-ordinate imperatives ('Make ...', 'let ...'), and the second of these has as complement a noun clause ('stand ... face'). In line 4, there are two co-ordinate sentences ('the world thinkes', 'I thinke'), and the first of these has a noun clause as direct object ('That thou ... act'). There follows another sentence co-ordinate with those of line 4 ('tis thought ...'), which has as complement a noun clause ('Thou'lt shew ... remorse'), which contains a sub-subordinate clause modifying the noun *remorse* ('more strange ... cruelty'). The remainder of the extract consists of a pair of co-ordinate clauses ('Thou ... forfeiture', 'But ... Forgiue ... principall') which are further complements of 'tis thought'. The first of these has a subordinate clause dependent on its verb ('where ... flesh'), and this itself contains a sub-subordinate relative clause modifying 'penalty' ('which ... flesh').

It will be seen that, even in this relatively straightforward passage from Shakespeare, the sentence structure is quite complicated. This is typical of the age. In the course of the sixteenth century, there is a tendency for increasingly complicated sentence structures to be used, perhaps through the influence of classical Latin texts. We have already seen (pp. 36–37 above) that an extract from a sermon by John Donne in the early seventeenth century constitutes an extremely complex sentence. By contrast, the extract from Latimer's sermon of 1549 (pp. 37–38 above) has relatively simple sentence structures. Even allowing for the difference of style (populist Protestant as against high-church Anglican), the contrast between the sentence structures is striking. In the earlier sixteenth century, even a sophisticated writer like Sir Thomas Elyot does not use sentence structures as complicated as that seen in the Donne passage. The use of parataxis, as in line 2 above, similarly becomes rarer. In Middle English writing, it was quite common, but in the passage from Celia Fiennes in the late seventeenth century (pp. 38–39 above) parataxis is a mark of artlessness.

CONJUNCTIONS

A major part in the structure of complex sentences is played by conjunctions. These are of two types, co-ordinators and subordinators. Co-ordinators link items of the same type – noun phrases with noun phrases, adverb phrases with adverb phrases, sentences with sentences, and so on. The items linked, moreover, are at the same hierarchical level in the grammatical structure. Subordinators, on the other hand, link items which are on different levels in the hierarchy: they signal that the item joined is a component of the item it is joined to.

The central co-ordinators of eModE are *and*, *but*, *or*, and *nor*. In addition there are correlatives like *both … and*, *either … or*, and *neither … nor*. In the sixteenth century, *other* and *nother* occur as alternative forms of *either* and *neither*.

The co-ordinator *and* is sometimes inserted in positions where we omit it. It is often inserted for emphasis, especially at the beginning of a question or a negative sentence, and it is also used to join a declarative sentence and an imperative one:

> 1. *And* wylt thow leve me thus?
>   Say nay, say nay, ffor shame   (Wyatt, *Poems*)
> 2. Thou art inclinde to sleepe: 'tis a good dulness
>   *And* giue it way   (Shakespeare, *The Tempest*)

Among the correlatives, there is some variation. Instead of *both … and*, we sometimes find *both … and both*, and sometimes even structures of the form 'X and Y both'. We frequently meet *nor … nor* and *or … or*. Much less common are *either … either* and *neither … neither*, but they do occur. Sometimes, especially early in the period, we meet *neither … ne*, and occasionally even *ne … ne* 'neither … nor'. Throughout the period, we also find *neither … or*. In sentences where we use *neither … nor*, an eModE writer sometimes omits the *neither*, despite the fact that the first of the items correlated is intended to be negated. Examples:

> 1. *Both* goodly Castle, *and both* goodly Towne
>   (Spenser, *Faerie Queene*)
> 2. to auoid the Scandall, *and* the Danger *both*   (Bacon, *Essays*)
> 3. Thou hast *nor* youth, *nor* age   (Shakespeare, *Measure for Measure*)
> 4. All Husbands must, *or* pain, *or* shame, endure
>   (Congreve, *Way of the World*)
> 5. do *neither* to moche *ne* to litle: to soone *ne* to late: to swiftly *nor*
>   slowely   (Elyot, *Governor*)
> 6. Yet *neither* thus disheartn'd, *or* dismay'd,
>   The time prefixt I waited   (Milton, *Paradise Regained*)
> 7. But /ø/ my fiue wits, *nor* my fiue sences can
>   Diswade one foolish heart from seruing thee   (Shakespeare, *Sonnets*)

In Early Tudor times, *ne* was still in use in prose, as in 5. above. Besides being used as a correlative, it occurred by itself as an adverb of negation, as an alternative to *nat* or *not*. By Spenser's time, however, *ne* had become an archaism.

Subordinators introduce dependent clauses, especially adverbial ones, but sometimes also noun clauses or relative clauses. In eModE, it is very common to use a compound subordinator, with *that* as its second element, for example *when that* 'when', *after that* 'after', and many others. Examples:

1. Alexander retayned with hym the poete Cherilus honorably / for writing his historie *all though that* ['although'] the poete was but of small estimation (Elyot, *Governor*)
2. He lettes me to pursue a conquest welnere wonne,
   To folow where my paines were lost *ere that* ['before'] my suite begonne (Surrey, *Songs and Sonnets*)
3. Where goodly solace was vnto them made,
    And dayly feasting both in bowre and hall,
   Vntill that ['until'] they their wounds well healed had
   (Spenser, *Faerie Queene*)
4. The reason is, *for that* ['because, that'] there is no sense without some stay of the Object on the faculty (Glanvill, *Vanity*)

When there are two parallel dependent clauses which require the same subordinator, the second subordinator is sometimes replaced by *that*:

> *Though* yet of Hamlet our deere Brothers death
> The memory be greene: and *that* it vs befitted
> To beare our hearts in greefe ... (Shakespeare, *Hamlet*).

Sometimes a compound subordinator has *as* for its second element, as with *when as* 'when', *where as* 'where', and others:

1. But *while as* ['while'] Astrofell did liue and raine,
   Amongst all these was none his Paragone (Spenser, *Colin Clout*)
2. *Like as* ['as, just as'] the waues make towards the pibled shore,
   So do our minuites hasten to their end (Shakespeare, *Sonnets*)
3. The Visions, Voyces, Revelations of the Enthusiast ... are judged exterior Realities; *when as* ['when, whereas'] they are but motions within the Cranium (Glanvill, *Vanity*)

The word *as* is also used to mean 'as if', and is often used after *so* and *such*, where today we use *that*:

1. You looke *as* ['as if'] you had something more to say
   (Shakespeare, *King Lear*)
2. the Motion of a Bullet in the Ayre, which flyeth *so* swift, *as* ['that'] it out-runs the Eye (Bacon, *Essays*)

Very common is the use of the subordinator *and*, meaning 'if'. The form *if* also existed, and sometimes the two were combined, giving *and if* 'if'. There was a variant form *an*, which had arisen in unstressed position, but this is much less frequent than *and*, especially in the sixteenth century. After 1650, however, *an* is more usual than *and*. Examples:

1. What *and* he slyde downe, who shall hym saue? (Skelton, *Bouge*)

2. ye are the salt of the erthe: but *and yf* the salt haue lost hir saltnes /
   what can be salted ther with?   (Tyndale, *New Testament*)
3. I see a voyce; now will I to the chinke,
   To spy *and* I can heare my Thisbies face
                              (Shakespeare, *A Midsummer Night's Dream*)
4. 'Sheart, *an* you grutch me your Liquor, make a Bill
                              (Congreve, *Way of the World*)

By Congreve's time, however, this usage had become old-fashioned. In *The Way of the World*, all the examples of *an* 'if' occur in the speech of Sir Wilfull Witwoud, the unpolished country squire. The smart ladies and gentlemen of London, and their servants, invariably use *if*, and even Sir Wilfull himself uses *if* more often than *an*.

Another subordinator now out of use, or found only as a literary archaism, is *ere* 'before'. In eModE, we also encounter the alternative form *or* 'before'. The two are in fact cognates, *ere* being the native English form and *or* a loan from Old Norse. Occasionally we find *or ere*, as in King Lear's:

No, Ile not weepe, I haue full cause of weeping,
But this heart shal break into a hundred thousand flawes
Or ere Ile weepe.

In *or ere*, however, the *ere* is not the subordinator, but an alternative form of the adverb *ever*. The same expression, but with the full form of *ever*, is found in a speech of Hamlet's:

Would I had met my dearest foe in heauen
Or euer ['before ever'] I had seene that day Horatio.

Thus the good quarto. The First Folio reads:

Ere I had *euer* seene that day Horatio.

The following are examples of other subordinators which are now obsolete or archaic:

1. And *but* ['unless'] thou loue me, let them finde me here
                              (Shakespeare, *Romeo and Juliet*)
2. All this is but a Sheep in a Lions Skin, *except* ['unless'] the Breed and
   disposition of the People, be stout and warlike   (Bacon, *Essays*)
3. And *for* ['because'] the morning now is something worne,
   Our purpos'd hunting shall be set aside
                              (Shakespeare, *A Midsummer Night's Dream*)
4. Ile play the Cooke,
   And see them ready, *gainst* ['by the time that'] their Mother comes
                              (Shakespeare, *Titus Andronicus*)

5. Fare thee well King, *sith* ['seeing that, since'] thus thou wilt appeare,
   Freedome liues hence, and banishment is here

   (Shakespeare, *King Lear*)

6. When he the loue of fayre Oenone sought,
   What time ['when'] the golden apple was vnto him brought

   (Spenser, *Faerie Queene*)

7. *Whiles* ['while'] I threat, he liues   (Shakespeare, *Macbeth*)

8. What should provoke her to be your Enemy, *without* ['unless'] she
   has made you Advances, which you have slighted?

   (Congreve, *Way of the World*)

Most subordinating conjunctions are identical in form with prepositions. Historically, there has been a good deal of mutual influence and interchange between the two groups, prepositions developing into conjunctions and vice versa.

RELATIVE CLAUSES

Among subordinate clauses ('embedded sentences'), relative clauses constitute a large and important group. They are usually introduced by a relative pronoun, and are dependent on a noun or something noun-like. There are two main types of relative clause, the restrictive (or defining) and the non-restrictive (or continuative). The two different types are illustrated in the following quotations from Shakespeare:

1. The man that hath no musicke in himselfe,
   Nor is not moued with concord of sweet sounds,
   Is fit for treasons, stratagems, and spoyles   (*Merchant of Venice*)
2. Wee'll visit Caliban, my slaue, who neuer
   Yeelds vs kinde answere   (*The Tempest*)

In 1., the relative clause ('that hath no musicke in himselfe') is restrictive (defining): it tells us what man we are concerned with. In 2., the relative clause ('who neuer / Yeelds vs kinde answere') is non-restrictive (or continuative): it simply adds information about how Caliban behaves. In PresE we distinguish the two types in speech by intonation: the non-restrictive clause forms a separate tone-group, the restrictive does not. It is likely that some such form of distinction was also made in eModE speech. In writing, we distinguish the two types by putting commas before and after the non-restrictive type, but not the restrictive type. Unfortunately, this distinction in punctuation is not always made in eModE writings, and there are a few occasions when it is doubtful whether a relative clause should be classified as restrictive or non-restrictive.

The relative pronouns commonly used in the Early Modern period are *who* (and its oblique forms), *which*, and *that*. Rather less common is *the which*: this had been fashionable in the fifteenth century, but in eModE is much rarer than *which*. These relative pronouns are often used in ways that still seem normal to us. Sometimes, however, they are used in ways no longer possible, or at least no longer ordinary, as in the following examples from Shakespeare:

1. The mistris *which* I serue (*The Tempest*)
2. The party gainst *the which* he doth contriue,
   Shall seaze one halfe his goods (*Merchant of Venice*)
3.   A braue vessell
   (*Who* had no doubt some noble creature in her)
   Dash'd all to peeces (*The Tempest*)
4. My foolish Riuall *that* her Father likes,
   (Onely for his possessions are so huge) (*Two Gentlemen*)

In 1., *which* is used with a personal antecedent ('mistris'), where today we should say *whom* or *that*. In 2., similarly, *the which* is used with a personal antecedent, for the context shows that *party* means 'person'. In 3., conversely, *Who* is used with a non-personal antecedent ('vessell'). In 4., the wider context shows that, despite the absence of a comma after *Riuall*, the relative clause is a non-restrictive one. The construction is not impossible today, but would not be the favoured one: in PresE we hesitate to use relative *that* unless the clause is restrictive (Quirk 1957, Quirk, Greenbaum, Leech & Svartvik 1985). It will be noticed that relative clauses do not necessarily have straight word-order, since the relative pronoun is placed at the beginning of the clause even if it is the object or complement.

As today, there were several factors influencing the choice of relative pronoun, such as the grammatical function of the relative pronoun within the clause, the type of antecedent, and the distance between the relative and its antecedent. Two ways in which eModE differed from PresE have been illustrated above: *which* was freely used with personal antecedents while *who* was occasionally used with non-personal antecedents, and *that* was quite often used to introduce non-restrictive relative clauses. In the course of the Early Modern period, there is a steady move in the direction of PresE usage: *which* and *who* become increasingly confined to non-personal and personal antecedents respectively, and *that* becomes increasingly confined to restrictive clauses. By 1700 these two limitations were almost as fully operative as they are today.

In ME, the common relative pronouns were *that* and *which*, but not *who*. The accusative *whom* was sometimes used as a relative, but the nominative *who* usually only as an interrogative or indefinite pronoun. So when the Early Modern period opened, the normal relative pronouns were *that* and *which* (less often *the which*), and in the accusative *whom*. In the first half of the sixteenth century, *who* also became firmly established as a relative, but was still much less frequent than *that* or *which*. The situation in the early decades of the century can be illustrated from Elyot's *Governor*. Statistics given by Rydén (1966) show that, when the relative pronoun is in subject position and has a personal antecedent, *who* occurs less than half as often as *which*, and less than a quarter as often as *that*. On the other hand, when the relative pronoun is in object position and has a personal antecedent, the usual form is *whom*, occurring many more times as often as *which* or *that*. Relative *whom* is also very common after prepositions. When *who* does occur, it is most often after a personal antecedent, and nearly always in non-restrictive clauses, as in the following examples:

1. Artaxerxes the noble kynge of Persia: *who* reiected nat the pore husbond man
2. the reders of this warke / *who* perchance for the more parte haue nat ben trayned in lernyng
3. appointed to them Saul to be theyr kynge / *who* exceded all other in stature

It is very common, as in 1. and 3., for *who* to have a proper name as its antecedent. It is also common, as in all three examples, for the antecedent (or its head) to be separated from the *who*. Occasionally, however, *who* is found with a non-personal antecedent, as in the following examples:

4. Bucephal / the horse of great kynge Alexander / *who* suffred none on his backe saulfe onely his maister
5. a vice very vgly and monstruouse / *who* vnder the pleasaunt habite of frendshippe and good counsaile with a breeth pestilenciall infecteth the wittes

These illustrate the two common cases where, in Elyot, *who* is found with a non-personal antecedent: in 4. the antecedent is the name of an animal, and in 5. there is an element of personification.

Even in this early period, then, there is a strong tendency for *who* to be limited to personal antecedents. There is no corresponding limitation on *which*, which is freely used with both personal and non-personal antecedents, especially in non-restrictive clauses, but quite often also in restrictive ones. The following are examples of *which* with personal antecedent:

6. men / *which* wil be studious about the weale publike
7. the pore husbond man / *whiche* offred to hym his homely handes full of clene water
8. they *which* do suppose it so to be called
9. the best and most sure gouernaunce / is by one kynge or prince: *whiche* ruleth onely for the weale of his people

211

The antecedents include both nouns and pronouns. As the examples suggest, personal *which* usually occurs in subject position. In object position, and after prepositions, the normal personal relative is *whom*, as in

> 10. a hundred senatours / *whom* Romulus did sette in autoritie

But by far the commonest relative pronoun in the early part of the sixteenth century is *that*, which occurs more frequently than *which*, *who*, and *whom* put together. It occurs freely with both personal and non-personal antecedents, and after both nouns and pronouns, though seldom after proper names. In most cases it occurs in restrictive clauses, but there is a substantial minority of examples in non-restrictive ones. The following are examples of relative *that*:

> 11. they *that* be gouernours
> 12. Also Ouidius / *that* semeth to be moste of all poetes lasciuious / in his mooste wanton bokes hath righte commendable and noble sentences
> 13. the hede of an enemie *that* he had slayne

There we see *that* in both subject and object position, and with both noun and pronoun antecedents. In 12. it occurs in a non-restrictive clause, and with a proper name as antecedent.

In the central part of the Early Modern period, relative *who* becomes more frequent. Figures given by Sugden (1936) suggest that, in Spenser's *Faerie Queene*, relative *who* is more frequent than *which* when the antecedent is personal. Relative *who* is also common in many other writers of the time, including Sidney, Shakespeare, Bacon, Jonson, and Donne. It is not common in the King James Bible, but this is just part of the linguistic conservatism of that work. The spread of *who* takes place especially in non-restrictive clauses with personal antecedents, where it competes with *which*. It does not displace *which* completely, however, and the use of *which* with a personal antecedent continues to be acceptable.

The position in literary prose in the middle of the period can be illustrated from Book 1 of Bacon's *Advancement of Learning* (1605). Here, *who* is the commonest relative in non-restrictive clauses with personal antecedents, occurring a little more often than *which* and *that* put together. In restrictive clauses, *who* does not occur at all. In object position, *whom* is invariably used in non-restrictive clauses with personal antecedents. Relative *which* still occurs fairly often with personal antecedents, as in the following examples:

> 1. there hath not beene since Christs time any King or temporall Monarch *which* hath ben so learned
> 2. the ignorance of second causes should make a more deuoute dependance vppon God, *which* is the first cause

3. such Popes doe greater thinges, and proceed vpon truer principles of Estate, than those *which* haue ascended to the Papacie from an education & breeding in affaires of Estate, and Courts of Princes

4. the first two Cæsars, *which* had the art of gouernement in greatest perfection, ...

Of these, 1. and 3. are restrictive, the other two non-restrictive. The antecedents are of various grammatical types – noun, pronoun, proper name.

In the Bacon chapter, on the other hand, there are no examples at all of *who* being used with a non-personal antecedent. In other authors of the period, however, there are occasional instances of this kind. The following are from Shakespeare:

1. All wound with Adders, *who* with clouen tongues
   Doe hisse me into madnesse   (*The Tempest*)
2.   the Windes,
   Who take the Ruffian Billowes by the top   (*Henry IV Part 2*)
3. The first of gold, *who* this inscription beares   (*Merchant of Venice*)

As in Elyot, such examples tend to occur either when the antecedent refers to an animal, as in 1., or when personification is possible, as in 2. But there are also occasional examples like 3., where *The first* refers to a casket, so that we have to recognise that relative *who* can be used, albeit infrequently, with completely non-personal antecedents.

While, in the course of the sixteenth century, *who* becomes more frequent, *that* becomes less so, at any rate in formal prose. In Early Tudor times, *that* had occurred more frequently than *who* and *which* combined. In the Bacon sample, by contrast, *which* occurs twice as often as *that*, and even outnumbers it in restrictive clauses. When *that* does occur in Bacon, it is usually in restrictive clauses, but there is still a substantial minority of cases in non-restrictive ones, like the following:

1. his aduersarie Æschynes, *that* was a man giuen to pleasure
2. it was the fault of Dionisius, *that* had his eares in his feete
3. such is their methode, *that* rests not so much vpon euidence ... as vpon particular confutations

We have to take account, however, of stylistic differences. The spread of *who* and *which*, and the recession of *that*, are especially characteristic of a formal style of writing. In informal and colloquial styles, *that* remains the commonest relative pronoun. This can be seen in Elizabethan and Jacobean plays that try to give the illusion of contemporary speech, and especially in those that are remote from courtliness. This dominance of relative *that* is seen in the city comedies of Thomas Middleton, like *A Trick to Catch the Old One* (1608).

In this play, relative *that* occurs sixty-two times, *which* eighteen, *who* three, and *whom* five. Most of the examples of *that* are in restrictive clauses; but, even in non-restrictive clauses with personal antecedents, *that* is as frequent in subject position as *who*. It seems likely, then, that the growing dominance of *who* and *which* is typical of a formal literary style. In informal style, and probably in speech, *that* remained the dominant relative pronoun.

The same trends continue in the seventeenth century as in the sixteenth. In the Restoration period, *who* is even more frequent than before, and is quite often found in restrictive clauses as well as non-restrictive ones; *who* and *which* are almost entirely confined to personal and non-personal antecedents respectively; and *that* is largely confined to restrictive clauses.

The situation towards the end of the century can be illustrated from Book 1 of Locke's *Essay* (1690), in which there are slightly more than 400 examples of relative pronouns. Here, *who* is by far the commonest relative pronoun when the antecedent is personal. There are no examples of *whom* in object or complement position, but there are several examples of *whom* after prepositions. With non-personal antecedents, *which* is by far the most frequent form, even in restrictive clauses. Relative *that* is virtually confined to restrictive clauses, with only one instance in a non-restrictive one. The limitation of *who* and *which* to personal and non-personal antecedents respectively is almost absolute, but not quite: there are just two examples of *which* with a personal antecedent, both in the same sentence:

> And Garcilasso de la Vega tells us of a People in Peru, *which* were wont to fat and eat their Children they got on their female Captives, *which* they kept as Concubines for that Purpose.

The antecedents are *People* 'nation' and *Captives*, and even today it is not impossible to use *which* with antecedents of this type. There is just one example of *who* with a non-personal antecedent:

> Whosoever does so, will have reason to think hundreds of Propositions, innate Principles, since there are many *who* have as good a title as this to be received for such ...

Here the antecedent of *who* is *many*, meaning 'many propositions'.

As before, however, we have to distinguish different styles. The dominance of *who* and *which* is characteristic of a formal style. In Restoration Comedy, which tries to mirror speech, the dominant relative pronoun is still *that*. In Congreve's *Love for Love* (1695), there are one hundred examples of relative *that*, and only eighteen of *which*, eight of *who*, and six of *whom*. Relative *who* occurs in both restrictive and non-restrictive clauses with personal antecedents, but in both it is heavily outnumbered by *that*. As could be expected, *that* is much more frequent in restrictive clauses than in non-restrictive ones, but even in the latter it occurs more frequently than any other relative pronoun. Bately (1964) has shown that Dryden similarly uses relative *that* in the prose of his plays, but avoids it in his poetry and non-dramatic prose. It seems likely, then, that in an informal style, and presumably also in speech, *that* was the dominant relative pronoun throughout the Early Modern period.

There is yet another form used occasionally in eModE to introduce relative clauses, namely the word *as*. The following are examples from Shakespeare:

1. those *as* sleepe, and thinke not on their sins   (*Merry Wives*)
2. And wish his Mistresse were that kind of Fruite,
   As Maides call Medlers when they laugh alone   (*Romeo and Juliet*)
3. I could not answer in that course of Honour
   As she had made the ouerture   (*All's Well*)

When used in this way, *as* should be classified as a relative pronoun, for it has a pronominal function in the relative clause: in 1. it is subject, in 2. it is object, and in 3. it is equivalent to 'in which'. Today such usages are non-standard, but in eModE, though infrequent, they are quite respectable, and occur in formal literary prose. The following are from Bacon's *Advancement*:

1. there hath not beene that choise and iudgement vsed, *as* ought to haue beene
2. in a sort, *as* may be soonest beleeued

There is, however, yet another relative construction which is quite common in eModE. This is the use of the zero relative: in the position where there could be a relative pronoun there is a blank, and the relative clause simply follows the antecedent, without the use of any linking word. In the following examples from *Hamlet*, I mark the juncture of the two clauses (the position occupied by the zero relative) with the symbol /ø/:

1. The friends /ø/ thou hast, and their adoption tride,
   Grapple them to thy Soule …
2.   it went hand in hand, euen with the Vow /ø/
   I made to her in Marriage.

In these sentences, it would be possible to insert *that* or *whom* or *which* at the point marked /ø/. In both cases, the zero relative is in object position: the 'missing' relative pronoun is the object of the verbs *hast* and *made*. This is also a familiar construction in PresE. In eModE, however, it is also normal to use a zero relative in subject position, as in the following examples from Shakespeare:

1. My Father had a daughter /ø/ lou'd a man   (*Twelfth Night*)
2. I haue a brother /ø/ is condemn'd to die   (*Measure for Measure*)

3. heere's a night /ø/ pitties neither Wisemen, nor Fooles   (*King Lear*)
4. there is a Noble man of the Court at doore /ø/ would speake with you
(*Henry IV Part 1*)

In these, the zero relative is the subject of the subordinate clause. This construction occurs in PresE in informal speech, but not in formal literary style. In eModE, by contrast, it could occur in formal literary prose. The following examples are from Locke:

1. 'Tis not that I think any Name, how great soever, set at the beginning of a Book, will be able to cover the Faults /ø/ are to be found in it
2. 'Tis Trial and Examination /ø/ must give it price
3. Men worship the Idols /ø/ have been set up in their Minds

If anything, the use of zero relative in subject position becomes more frequent in the course of the Early Modern period, for it is very rare in Early Tudor times. Throughout the Early Modern period, it is as likely to occur in formal as in colloquial style, but it is always much less frequent than zero relative in object position.

One further point about relative constructions in eModE. The antecedent of a relative pronoun is sometimes not a head, but an adjunct. It may, for example, be a noun in the possessive case, as in the following example from *Hamlet*:

how the knaue iowles it to th' grownd, as if it were Caines Iaw-bone, *that* did the first murther.

The antecedent of *that* is not 'Iaw-bone', but 'Caines': it means 'the jawbone of Cain, who did the first murder'. The antecedent can also be a pronoun-determiner, like *my*, *her*, *our*. The following example is from *Julius Caesar*:

And do you now strew Flowers in his way,
That comes in Triumph ouer Pompeyes blood?

The antecedent of *That* is 'his': 'in the way of him who comes'. Such usages are found throughout the Early Modern period, and are not confined to dialogue: Locke uses the construction, as in the following:

which ... make no considerable addition to his stock, *who* gathers them.

This means 'to the stock of him who gathers them'.

UTTERANCES OUTSIDE THE SENTENCE STRUCTURE

So far, we have been considering the structure of a sentence. There can be parts of an utterance, however, which do not enter into syntactic relations, but stand as independent items outside the sentence structure. Some of these, interjections, can function as entire utterances by themselves, expressing some mood or attitude. Some are particularly used as utterance-initiators, the preliminary noises that speakers make before they embark on the utterance proper. Some can function as pause-fillers, the noises that speakers insert in their sentences to fill in the gaps while they hesitate or think what to say next. These categories are not mutually exclusive: oaths and asseverations, for example, are often used in all three ways.

Interjections are common in dramatic dialogue. The attitude conveyed by an interjection no doubt varied according to the intonation with which it was spoken, and also the particular context. The following usages, however, are common ones in the Early Modern period: *Alack!* (deprecation, regret), *Ay me* (sorrow, pity), *Fie!* (disgust, reproach), *Ha!* (triumph, indignation, surprise), *Helas!* (grief, sorrow), *Heyday!* (surprise, wonder), *Out!* (indignation, reproach), *Pish!* (impatience, contempt), *Welladay!* (sorrow, lamentation).

Among utterance-initiators, the use of *Well* goes right back to OE, and is common in eModE. The use of *Why* in this function dates from the early sixteenth century. Perhaps we should count *Peace!* and *Soft!* as utterance-initiators, though it could be argued that they are imperative sentences, the first meaning 'Be quiet!' and the second 'Not so fast!', 'Wait a moment!' The word *la* is used both as utterance-initiator and as pause-filler.

Numerous oaths and asseverations occur in dramatic dialogue. Very common are aphetic forms like *sblood* '(by) God's blood', *slight* '(by) God's light', *zounds* '(by) God's wounds'. There are also variants in which *God* is replaced by euphemisms like *cock* or *gog*, as in *cocks bodikins, gogswounds*. From about 1600, the form *od* came into use, and we find expressions like *odsbobs, odsbud, ods pittikins*. The use of such disguised forms of *God* was probably encouraged by official hostility to profanity, reinforced in the seventeenth century by the increasing influence of the Puritans. The second element in such expletives is also often transmogrified, as with *bud* 'blood'. Some such elements, like *pittikins* and *bodikins* (diminutives of *pity* and *body*), occur only in oaths. Some, like those in *odsnigs* and *Godsookers*, seem to be meaningless.

The exclamation *marry* had originally meant '(by the Virgin) Mary'. By the sixteenth century, its origin had perhaps been forgotten, and it was often used as an utterance-initiator, especially in replies to questions. From the second half of the sixteenth century, we also find the form *birlady* 'by our lady'. Since this was used by Protestants, its original meaning too had perhaps been forgotten. Readers of the drama will encounter many other exclamations current in the period, including many mild ones like *forsooth, ifaith* and *troth*.

FURTHER READING

A good introduction to syntax is Burton-Roberts (1986). Works on historical English syntax include Visser (1963–73) and Denison (1993). Particular points of eModE syntax in everyday speech are discussed in Salmon (1965) and Wright (1995). For the early part of the period, relative clauses have been very fully studied by Rydén (1966). On the use of *have* and *be* for forming perfect tenses, see Fridén (1948). On the spread and regulation of auxiliary *do*, see Ellegård (1953). On sentences in which the verb precedes the subject, see Jacobsson (1951), which concentrates on the Early Modern period.

Chapter Six

THE EXPANDING VOCABULARY

We have seen that, during the Early Modern period, there was considerable debate about the desirability of expanding the lexicon of English, and about the methods to be used for doing this. An examination of the language itself shows that the period was indeed one of great vocabulary expansion, and that substantial use was made both of borrowing (especially from Latin) and of word-formation (especially by affixation). For the original (1976) version of this book, I took a 2 per cent sample of the OED, scrutinised every word in the sample for its etymology, and used this body of material both for the conclusions drawn and for the words cited as examples.

Since that time, the second edition of the OED has appeared (1989). This, moreover, is available on CD-ROM, and I had hoped to use this to take a second similar sample to supplement the first. This, unfortunately, proved more difficult than I had expected. It is indeed possible to use the date filter on the CD-ROM, and obtain a list of words which entered the language in any year, or any period of years. It does not seem possible, however, to have the words in such a list sorted according to etymology, mainly because there is no standard format for the etymology entries in the OED. I have therefore taken a smaller sample from the CD-ROM, to supplement the original one. The earlier sample will be called 'the main sample', and the new one 'the supplementary sample'.

The supplementary sample was taken from the OED entries for seven different dates: 1511, 1541, 1571, 1601, 1631, 1661, and 1691. The date filter was used to produce a list of words which entered the language in each of these years. A 10 per cent sample was then taken from the list for each year, and the etymology of each word examined and recorded. As with the main sample, some words were excluded from the lists, namely those recorded as having been used only in Scots or in regional English dialects. Words with unknown or obscure etymologies were not excluded, but were classified as 'obscure'. For some words, the OED editors consider more than one possible etymology: if they consider one particular etymology as the likeliest, that etymology is accepted for the sample.

The number of words thus obtained was 334, compared with 1,911 in the main sample. The findings of the supplementary sample broadly support those of the main one. The two have not however been amalgamated, partly because they were compiled by different methods, and partly because there is a slight overlap between them. In what follows, the figures given will refer to the main sample alone, unless the contrary is stated. If the findings of the supplementary sample show any considerable departure from these, this fact will be stated and discussed. In one matter, however, the two samples will be silently combined: this will be when words are given as illustrations, for example of fields of discourse or methods of word formation. But if any words are cited which do not appear in either corpus, this fact will be stated.

The fact that the main sample comprises no fewer than 1,911 words suggests that in the Early Modern period the expansion of the lexicon was indeed very great. In this 2 per cent sample, the number of new words arising in ME runs to about 17 per decade, whereas the number arising in eModE is about 95 per decade. These figures must be interpreted with caution: the total number of texts is greater in eModE than in ME, as can be seen from the OED bibliography. Even so, the figure for eModE is remarkable. Indeed, it is almost as great as that for the period 1701–1900, despite the fact that the latter group includes many highly specialised terms which can hardly be said to belong to the general vocabulary of the language.

Many of the new words of the Early Modern period, however, were short-lived. Nearly one-third of the words in the corpus are not recorded after 1700. Some others are recorded only in dictionaries or word-lists, not in texts, and a few are marked by the OED editors as having been found only once in their material. This is only to be expected in a period of hectic expansion, when new words are competing with one another both for 'necessity' and for 'bravery'.

Of the 1,911 words in the main sample, 63 are of obscure or uncertain etymology, leaving us with 1,848 words of reasonably certain etymology. The methods by which these words were acquired is shown in Table 6.1. Slightly more than one-third of the new words are loans. By far the most frequent method of acquiring words is by affixation, especially suffixation: there are very nearly as many words formed by suffixation as are borrowed from all languages. Curiously enough, this appears not to have been noticed by contemporaries, despite all the arguments about expanding the vocabulary. Purists advocate compounding, and the giving of new meanings to existing words, but they rarely mention affixation. This is perhaps because the process is so common that people fail to notice it, or fail to think of it as a source of new words.

TABLE 6.1

New Words in Early Modern English: Methods of Acquisition

Word-formation	No.	Loan-words	No.
Suffixation	607	Latin	393
Prefixation	261	French	121
Compounding	217	French or Latin	20
Zero-morpheme derivation	99	Greek	35
Others	39	Spanish/Portuguese	16
		Italian	16
		Low German/Dutch	9
		Other languages	15
Total	1,223	Total	625

The supplementary sample gives a similar picture to that in Table 6.1, but has a higher proportion of loans, about 43 per cent compared with about 33 per cent in the main material. In part this is due to the different methods of sampling. In the supplementary sample, only the headword of each entry was taken into the corpus. In the main sample, on the other hand, the combinations and derivatives in each entry were also scanned, to see if any of them should be included. None of these, obviously, would be loan-words, so that the proportion of loan-words is smaller than in the supplementary sample. There is another factor which works in the same direction: the chance inclusion in the supplementary sample of a work which contains an enormous number of loans. This is *The questyonary of cyrurgens*, a medical work by Robert Copland, published in 1541. The 10 per cent sample for 1541 produced forty-eight words: no fewer than forty-one of them come from Copland's book. Of these, sixteen are from Latin, nine from French, and two are obscure, leaving only four produced by affixation. This freak inclusion obviously increases the relative bias towards loan-words in the supplementary sample.

Apart from the proportion of loan-words, there is little difference between the two samples. Moreover, the ranking orders in the two samples are identical, except for some small differences at the bottom of the loan-word column: Italian moves to the bottom of the table, no examples at all having been found, and Spanish/Portuguese drops down to the penultimate position. The numbers involved, however, are extremely small, Low German/Dutch being represented by only three examples, and Spanish/Portuguese by two. These changes in ranking, therefore, have no statistical significance.

LOAN-WORDS

The heading 'Other languages' conceals no fewer than eleven different ones, so that altogether there are loans from eighteen different languages. By contrast, the ME part of the main sample contains loans from only five languages: Latin, French, Old Norse, Low German, and a Celtic language. The horizons have widened by Early Modern times, and in the seventeenth century there are loans from Arabic, Malay, the languages of India, and Amerindian languages.

The balance has also changed between the different donor-languages. In the ME material, the loans are overwhelmingly from French: French loans outnumber Latin ones by nearly four to one. The proportion of Latin loans increases in the fifteenth century, but French loans still outnumber them by well over two to one. In eModE the situation is reversed: Latin loans outnumber French ones by more than three to one. Indeed, after suffixation, Latin loans provide the largest single source of new words in the period.

LOANS FROM LATIN

In the main sample, Latin loans are found throughout the Early Modern period, but are not evenly distributed in it. There are rather few loans in the early sixteenth century, but the number rises steadily throughout the century, and is very high between 1590 and 1660. After 1660 it falls sharply, and the decline continues throughout the Restoration period. This drop is made more striking by the fact that the period 1651–60 is the most prolific decade of all. A very similar pattern is found in the supplementary sample, except that there is a secondary peak in 1541: this is to be explained by the publication in that year of Robert Coplan's book referred to earlier.

The Latin loans tend to be bookish words rather than popular or colloquial ones. Most of them belong to the general vocabulary, but more than one-third belong to specialised fields of discourse. Among these, by far the largest group consists of scientific words, especially medical and biological ones. The large medical group includes adjectives like *paregoric* (1684) and *sporadic* (1689), and nouns like *rheumatism* (1601), *deligation* 'bandaging' (1661), and *paresis* 'partial paralysis' (1693). The anatomical terms include *uvea* (1525), *molar* (1541), *ulna* (1541), and *metacarpus* (1676). The medical words cluster in the later part of the period, a very large number of them being first recorded after 1650. As we have seen, there is a sharp drop in Latin loans after 1660. It seems, therefore, that in the Restoration period, Latin was relatively unfashionable for general words, but extensively used for technical terms like those of medicine and anatomy.

The biological words are mostly plant names, mainly from the sixteenth century, like *pinaster* (1562) and *Britannic* 'water dock' (1567). Late in the period there are also two technical descriptive terms of botany and zoology, the adjectives *muricate* 'furnished with sharp points' (1661) and *imbricate* 'with scales overlapping like roof tiles' (1656). The words from the physical sciences are almost entirely from the seventeenth century, and are mainly from chemistry, like *aquafortis* (1601), *deliquate* v. (1669), and *muriatic* adj. (1675), or from astronomy, like *lunistice* (1650). Notable is the absence of words from physics or mechanics. There is a small group of mathematical words, like *commensurable* (1557), *subduct* v. (1571), and *quadrable* (1695). The paucity of words from mathematics and physics is surprising, in view of the advances which were made in these subjects in the seventeenth century.

Two other sizeable groups of Latin loans are in the fields of religion and of the liberal arts, each of which contains roughly half as many words as the scientific-medical group. In the case of religious words, the tendency to borrow from Latin was probably strengthened by the Reformation, with the consequent change-over from Latin to English in church services, and the adoption of the *Book of Common Prayer* (1549). As could then be expected, the peak period for religious loans is earlier than that for Latin loans in general, well over half being introduced between 1526 and 1600. They include many theological terms, like *invinate* 'embodied in wine' (1550), *trans-accidentation* (1581), and *piaculum* 'expiation' (1601). There are also words to do with church seasons, like *quadragesima* (1604), and with ecclesiastical organisation, like *commendam* 'the custody of a benefice in the absence of the regular incumbent' (1563). There are also a few ordinary words, like *relapse* v. (1568). In the later part of the period, the sample includes the political-sectarian term *latitudinarian* (1662).

Under the heading of liberal arts I have included the traditional subjects of school and university education, except those already covered in the scientific group. These subjects were the trivium, the quadrivium, and the three philosophies (natural, moral, metaphysical). Natural philosophy falls in the scientific group, as do three subjects of the quadrivium: astronomy, arithmetic, and geometry. The fourth subject of the quadrivium, music, is not represented in the sample. That leaves us with the trivium (grammar, rhetoric, logic), and with philosophy in the modern sense. To these I have added words concerned with the educational process itself, and words to do with the fine arts. Examples are *frequentative* (1530, grammar), *metabasis* (1657, rhetoric), *pyrrhicius* (1586, prosody), *relate* n. (1633, logic), *transcendental* (1668, philosophy), *prelector* (1586, education), and *depict* v. (1601, fine arts). Words from the fine arts were more likely to be borrowed from modern European languages than from Latin. On the other hand, words connected with the useful or mechanical arts were more likely to be coined from native elements. The sample contains only three examples from Latin: two from architecture, *transept* (1542) and *quadra* (1664), and the adjective *prelal* 'to do with printing' (1659).

There are two yet smaller groups, one dealing with classical civilisation, and one with public affairs. Each of these groups is about two-thirds the size

223

of the liberal arts group. The words to do with classical civilisation are the kind needed for writing about Ancient Roman history, customs, religion, mythology, and culture. Such are *lupercal* (1513), *gorgon* (1529), *gladiator* (1541), *murra* (1598, the name of a substance from which precious vessels were made), and *rostrum* (1579). The early examples in English of this last word are all in the plural form *rostra*, and are used to refer specifically to the platform for public speakers in the forum in Ancient Rome, which was decorated with the beaks of warships (*rostra*). The use of the word for any kind of stage or platform for public speaking is not found until the eighteenth century.

Of the words connected with the world of public affairs, the majority, while not necessarily technical legal terms, are to do with the law and its enforcement. Such are *delict* 'a violation of law or right' (1523) and *prehension* 'arrest' (1534). The remainder are from commerce or accountancy, like *anatocism* 'compound interest' (1656), or from the world of officialdom or administration, like *imbreviate* v. 'enrol, register' (1609).

There is a group of words, about half the size of the liberal arts group, dealing with geography and travel. Many of them are the names of places and peoples, like *Britany* 'Britain' (1579) and *Muscovite* (1555), and the adjective *Lesbian* (1601). There are a few words which are more technical, like *fret(e)* n. 'strait' (1576), *transalpine* (1590), and *isthmian* (1601).

Since so many of the loans are from traditional fields of scholarship, it is not surprising that a fair number of them are from post-classical Latin. Nearly a quarter of all Latin loans are marked by the OED editors as being from Late, Medieval, or Modern Latin, the largest group being that from Medieval Latin. A few of the loans are not recorded in any form of Latin, but were assembled by their inventors from Latin morphemes.

More on Latin loans

We have been considering Latin loans in specialised fields of discourse. Nearly two thirds of the loans, however, are less specialised and belong to the general vocabulary. Many have survived to the present day, and are quite ordinary words. There are nouns like *relaxation* (1526), *immaturity* (1540), *frequency* (1553), *relegation* (1586), and *invitation* (1598). There are adjectives like *involuntary* (1531), *offensive* (1548), *relevant* (1560), *susceptible* (1605), and *invidious* (1606). And verbs like *investigate* (1510), *transcribe* (1552), *imbue* (1555), and *officiate* (1641). There are many others which have not survived, like *parility* 'equality' (1610). Some strike the present-day reader as rather ridiculous: such are *latron* 'a robber' (1613) and *latration* 'a barking' (1623). These probably come under Mulcaster's heading of 'mere bravery'.

Most of the loans are either nouns or adjectives, the nouns being a little more frequent. The verbs number only about a half of either of these groups.

The number of adverbs is negligible. They vary in form. In some, the form of the Latin original was retained in full: that is, the English word was spelt in exactly the same way as the Latin original, and was given a corresponding pronunciation in accordance with the current method of pronouncing Latin in England. This method was used to produce a number of nouns, like *delirium* (1599), but was not used for adjectives or verbs. In some words the Latin inflection was dropped, and the English form taken from the stem alone, as with *fret(e)* (1576) from *fretum*, and *immature* (1548) from *immátúrus*. In yet other cases, the ending of the word was adapted, Latin *-ábilis* for example being made into English *-able* (*inviolable, commensurable*): here we see the influence of earlier French loans into English. In addition, analogy sometimes affected the form of a Latin loan: *delinquish* v. 'to fail in duty' (1606) is from Latin *délinquere* but has been modelled on *relinquish*, while *latitudinarian* (1662) is derived from the Latin noun *látitúdo*, on the analogy of *trinitarian*.

Of the nouns, about a third appear in unchanged nominative form, like *gladiator* (1541), *investigator* (1552), *lupus* (1583), *murex* (1589), *pinaster* (1562), *quadragesima* (1604), *rostrum, -a* (1579), and *ulna* (1541). The majority of Greek nouns that have come into English via Latin belong to this category: such are *aegilops* 'a fistula in the eye' (1601), *metabole* 'change in medical state' (1693), *parelcon* (1678, a figure of rhetoric), *parenthesis* (1568), and *parergon* 'ornamental accessary (in painting)' (1601).

A small group of nouns has the ending adapted. The common types have *-ity* (Latin *-itás*), or *-ence, -ency, -ance, -ancy* (Latin *-entia, -antia*). Examples are *immaturity* (1540), *transcendence* (1601), delinquency (1636), and *relevancy* (1561). The remaining nouns, just over half in all, are formed from the Latin stem, the inflection being dropped. They divide almost equally between those formed from the Latin nominative stem, and those from the oblique stem (when the two differ). Those formed on the nominative stem are of several types, including nouns in *-ic, -ism, -ian*, and *-ine*, but the largest group consists of nouns in *-y* (Latin *-ius, -ia, -ium*). Such are *commentary* (1531), *prelaty* 'prelacy' (1641), and *deliry* 'delirium' (1669). Those formed on the oblique stem are nearly all nouns in *-ion* (mostly *-ation*), like *prelusion* (1597), *invitation* (1598), and *relaxation* (1526). There are also a few in *-ent*, like *delineament* (1593).

Most of the adjectives are formed on the Latin nominative stem. The two big groups are adjectives in *-ate*, from Latin past participles, like *inveterate* (1528) and *immediate* (1533), and adjectives in *-al* (Latin *-ális*), like *official* (1533) and *transcendental* (1668). Other common types are illustrated in the words *offensive* (1548), *utopian* (1551), *laudatory* (1555), *transalpine* (1590), *lunar* (1626), *ancillary* (1667), and *sporadic* (1689). Adjectives formed on the oblique stem all end in *-ent* or *-ant*, like *frequent* (1531) and *relevant* (1560). Those with an adapted ending are nearly all in *-able, -ible* (Latin *-ábilis*,

-ibilis), like *inviolable* (1530) and *susceptible* (1605), or in *-ous* (Latin *-us*, *-ósus*), as in *auspicious* (1601).

Of the verbs, two-thirds are in *-ate*, from the past participle stem of the Latin first conjugation, like *imitate* (1534), *commemorate* (1599). A small number are formed on other past participle stems, like *relapse* (1568), *transact* (1584), and *immerse* (1605). Alongside this last form, however, there is also *immerge* (1611), from the Latin present stem: about one-fifth of the verbs are of this type, including *imbue* (1555), *imburse* (1530), and *transcribe* (1552). It is clear, however, that the normal way of taking a verb from Latin was to form it on the past participle stem, and that the great majority were in *-ate*.

LOANS FROM GREEK AND HEBREW

Compared with Latin, the other learned languages are very sparsely represented among the loans. In the main sample, there is only one word from Hebrew, the biblical place-name *Goshen* (1611), used allusively to mean 'a place of plenty or light'. In the supplementary sample, there are no Hebrew loans at all. In the main sample, there are only thirty-five loans from Greek (twenty-three nouns, ten adjectives, two verbs). They occur more frequently in the seventeenth century than in the sixteenth. Very striking is the almost total absence of words from the general vocabulary: almost without exception, the Greek loans belong to specialised fields of discourse. The largest group is in the field of religion: theological terms like *anathematism* (1565), words from ecclesiastical history like *Messalian* (1591). There are words connected with classical civilisation and mythology, like *Pyrrhic* 'the war-dance of the ancient Greeks' (1597), and *trilogy* (1661). Words to do with Greek philosophy include *Pythagorism* (1653). There is a group relating to style and rhetoric, like *parison* 'even balance in the parts of a sentence' (1586) and *decastich* 'poem of ten lines' (1601). The words from the scientific field are all to do with medicine, anatomy, and the life-sciences: such are *metacarpion* (1597), *parenchyma* (1651), and *drastic* adj. (1591).

In addition to the words borrowed direct from Greek, the sample contains about an equal number of Greek words which came into English via Latin. These, however, are not classified as Greek loans, but as Latin ones, since the classification is according to the proximate source, not the ultimate one. A smaller number of Greek words have come into English via French, and these similarly are classified as French loans. Both these groups show the same kind of restriction in fields of discourse as the words borrowed direct from Greek.

LOANS FROM FRENCH

The only large group of loans, apart from the Latin ones, is that of words borrowed from French. In the main sample, about 68 per cent of these are nouns, while the remainder are equally divided between adjectives and verbs. The peak period is earlier than that for Latin loans: the number of French loans per decade is rather small until about 1520, but then trebles until about 1620, after which it falls back to its earlier level. It is surprising that the number of French loans is relatively small in the Restoration period, when French was such a fashionable language.

More than half the French loans are from the general vocabulary. Many have not survived, or are now rare, but there are quite a few familiar ones, like the nouns *entrance* (1526), *docility* (1560), and *prelude* (1561), and the verbs *invite* (1533) and *prejudge* (1561). Among the general words there is, as could be expected, a sprinkling of words to do with clothes, like *chapeau* (1523), and with food and drink, like *muscat* (1578) and *carbonade* (1631). There are also what might be called 'social words', like *messieurs* (1624), *entregent* 'social intercourse' (1651), and *delicatesse* (1698).

Among the words from more specialised fields of discourse, the biggest groups are military and scientific. The military words include *counterscarp* (1571), *bayonet* (1611), *pike* (1621), and *commandant* (1687). The scientific words are all from medicine and the life sciences, and mainly from anatomy, like *muscle* (1533), *cauterise* (1541), *parietal* (1597), *pineal* (1681), and indeed the word *anatomy* itself (1528).

There are several smaller groups, containing such words as *anathematise* (1566) and *chapelry* (1591, religion), *enurny* (1562) and *brisure* (1623, heraldry), *pargeter* 'plasterer' (1538) and *smalt* 'a kind of coloured glass' (1558, mechanical arts). There are a few words from commerce, including *invoice* n. (1560), and it is possible that a number of other French loans arose in this way, for example the names of materials, like *gossampine* (1533), and of other objects of trade, like *muscat* (1578). There are a few legal and administrative words, like *forjure* v. (1601) and *counter-roll* (1603). Music is represented by *counterpoint* n. (1530) and *chanson* (1603), and there is a similar small sprinkling from architecture, geography, and philosophy. Literature, which one might have expected to be well represented, appears in the sample in only one word, *pindarise* v. 'to imitate Pindar' (1607).

In form, the loans do not depart much from their French originals. They were given the French spelling, or one very similar to it, and a pronunciation in which each French phoneme was represented by the English phoneme which seemed to the speakers most like it. There were, however, cases where the form of a loan was affected by the analogy of existing English words, especially ones borrowed from French in the Middle English period. For example, the French prefix *contre-* was anglicised to *counter-*, as in *counter-point*, *counterscarp*. The form *counter-* had developed in ME from Anglo-French *countre-*, corresponding to Parisian French *contre-*. Again, *docility* (1560) is from French *docilité*, but has been given the ending found in similar

227

words borrowed from French in Middle English. And the verbal ending *-ise*, as in *cauterise* (1541), was anglicised in pronunciation, on analogy with verbs borrowed in Middle English, like *solemnise* (1382), in which the vowel of the ending had subsequently been changed in the Great Vowel Shift.

In addition to the French and Latin loans, there is a small group classified as either French or Latin. These words could be added to either the Latin group or the French group without changing the patterns that have been found, either of chronology or of fields of discourse.

LOANS FROM OTHER MODERN EUROPEAN LANGUAGES

The loans from other modern European languages are relatively few, not much more than one-third of the number from French. Most are from Romance languages. In some cases it is impossible to be sure which Romance language is the source: for the word *rosmarine* 'walrus' (1590) the OED gives the language of origin as 'Modern Latin or Italian or Spanish or Portuguese'. Moreover, the English borrowers sometimes took over a word from one language but gave it a form appropriate to another. The Italian word *imbroccato* 'brocade' came into English as *imbrocado* (1656), under the influence of Spanish and Portuguese *brocado* (or of its English derivatives *brocado*, *brocade*). Nevertheless, two groups stand out clearly among the Romance loans, an Italian group and a Spanish/Portuguese group, each of sixteen words.

The Italian loans occur especially in the Elizabethan age, eight of the sixteen being between 1560 and 1600. Half of them come from specialised fields of discourse: from commerce come *bazaar* (1599) and *premio* 'insurance premium', and the names of two materials, *gossipine* (1565) and *imbrocado* (1656). There is a word from fencing, *imbroccata* (1595), a military word, *imboscata* 'ambush' (1595), a word from the visual arts, *fresco* (1598), and one from the world of public affairs, *entrate* 'revenue' (1670). Of the more general words, no fewer than five out of the eight are verbs, like *imbosk* 'to conceal oneself' (1562).

Since the sample is small, we can well supplement it from the findings of Serjeantson (1935). She confirms that many of the Italian loans were to do with trade, warfare, or the arts. The military words in her lists include *squadron* (1562), *generalissimo* (1621), and *fuse* (1644). With these can be grouped terms of horsemanship (for which the Italians were famous), like *curvet* (1575). Words to do with trade include *trafigo* (1506, later modified, under French influence, to *traffic*), *artichoke* (1531), and *felucca* (1628). Her words from the arts include musical terms, like *madrigal* (1588) and *opera* (1644), literary terms like *stanza* (1588), and words from the visual arts, like *cameo* (1561) and *chiaroscuro* (1686). Her lists also include types not found in our sample: architectural terms, like *cupola* (1549) and *balcony* (1619), names of ranks, offices, and people, like *magnifico* (1573) and *bravo* 'villain' (1597), words to do with Italian customs and social activities, like *gondola* (1549) and *carnival* (1549), and two food-names, *macaroni* (1599) and *vermicelli* (1669).

Altogether, the loans, though so much less numerous than those from French, testify to the great cultural influence of Renaissance Italy, her commercial importance, the high reputation of Italians as soldiers and horsemen, and the interest of English people in Italian life and customs. Moreover, there were many additional words of Italian origin which came into English via French.

The sixteen words in the Spanish/Portuguese group are mainly from Spanish, but two are from Portuguese, and a few could have come from either language. They cluster in the centre of the period, and no fewer than twelve of the sixteen entered the language between 1580 and 1625. The Spaniards and the Portuguese were the first European nations to explore and colonise in the New World, and many words concerned with the Americas came via their languages. This is illustrated by the sample, which includes *pina* 'pineapple' (1577), *mestizo* (1588), and the corresponding feminine form *mestiza* (1582). According to Hakluyt, a mestizo is 'one which hath a Spaniard to his father and an Indian to his mother'. There are two words connected with trade, the second of which has American associations: *anchovy* (1598) and *muscovado* 'unrefined sugar' (1642). The Portuguese, besides having a stake in the New World, had also rounded the Cape and opened up oceanic trade-routes to the Far East, and the two Portuguese loans in the sample are concerned with India: *balliadera* 'Hindu dancing-girl' (1598) and *berenjaw* 'fruit of the egg-plant' (1611). The first of these was later modified to the French form *bayadère*. The second occurs from the eighteenth century onwards as *brinjawl* or *brinjal*, but many different spellings are found in the Early Modern period. Portuguese had borrowed the word from Arabic, which had it from Persian, and the earliest form recorded in the OED, the plural *pallingenies*, is perhaps direct from Arabic. The sample also includes a naval word, *launch* 'the largest boat of a man-of-war' (1697), and a military title, *commendador* (1580). The Spaniards were noted for their formality and ceremoniousness, and one of the general words in the sample is *entrada* 'ceremonial entry' (1618).

Serjeantson's material shows that many of the loans were indeed to do with the Americas, and that naval and military terms were also quite prominent. She lists large numbers of Spanish loans to do with the New World, such as *cannibal* (1553), *lagarto* 'alligator' (1568), *potato* (1565, Spanish *patata*, from Haitian *batata*), and *vaynilla* (1662, later modified, under Latin influence, to *vanilla*). The word *cannibal* was formed from a dialectal variant of *Carib*, the name of a people in the West Indies. Alongside the word *lagarto* there were such sixteenth-century forms as *alligato*, which incorporated the definite article, being from Spanish *al lagarto* 'the lizard'. There are also words that stem from Africa rather than America, like *negro* (1555) and *banana* (1597). This last word probably came into Spanish or Portuguese from a West African language. There are also further Portuguese loans relating to India: *caste* (1555) and *tank* 'artificial reservoir' (1616).

The military and naval group is a good deal smaller. It includes *armada* (1533), *bilbo* 'a high-quality sword' (1592, from the place-name *Bilbao*), *comrado* 'room-mate, fellow-soldier' (1598), and *embargo* (1602). There is also a small group to do with trade and its products, like *sherris* (1597, later *sherry*), *cargo* (1657), and *port* (1691, the wine, from the place-name *Oporto*). Serjeantson also has some groups unrepresented in our sample: persons and titles, such as *don* (1523), grandee (1598), *renegado* 'renegade' (1599), and *duenna* (1668); card-games, like *primero* (1533) and *ombre* (1660); and dancing, like *guitar* (1621) and *castanet* (1647). Miscellaneous words include *sombrero* 'Oriental parasol' (1598) and *plaza* (1683).

Some Spanish words came into English via French, like *casque* (1580) and *corvette* (1636). More often, however, Spanish and Portuguese loans came into English direct. By contrast, large numbers of Italian words came into English through the medium of French. If such indirect loans are taken into account, it can be seen that the linguistic influence of Italian on English was considerably greater than that of Spanish.

In our main sample, the remaining loans from Modern European languages are, with one exception, from Germanic languages. The exception is a Celtic loan, *bawn* 'a fortified enclosure', from Irish *bábhun*. It was used only in Irish contexts, and was obviously picked up by soldiers and administrators engaged in England's colonial wars against Ireland. Of the Germanic words, one is probably from Scandinavian, and two from German, while nine are from Dutch or Low German (often indistinguishable). The Dutch/Low German loans are thus the only group of any size in the sample outside Latin, Greek, and the Romance languages.

The Dutch were a great maritime and trading nation, and many of the loans into English have been nautical. This is reflected in the sample, which includes the word *dock* 'the bed in which a ship lies at low water' (1513). There are also two fish names, *lump* (1545) and *quab* (1617). A few military words were borrowed, because of the wars in the Low Countries, and one word in the sample falls into this category: *lunt* 'a slow match' (1550). In later use this was Scots, but in the sixteenth century occurs also in the southern language. Among the miscellaneous words is *quacksalver* (1579), and in the supplementary sample *waggon* (1511), cognate with English *wain*.

Serjeantson lists a number of nautical, commercial, and military loans. The nautical ones include *yacht* (1557, originally a fast pursuit vessel), *riffe* 'a narrow ridge of rocks' (1584, the variant *reef* not being found until the eighteenth century), *smack* (1611), *sloop* (1629), and *yawl* (1670). The commercial words include *cambric* (1530), *brandwine* or *brandy-wine* (1622), and *smuggle*

(1687). The word *cambric* was from *Kameryk*, the Flemish name of the town which in French is called *Cambrai*. The word *brand(y)wine* (later shortened to *brandy*) literally meant 'burnt wine, distilled wine'. Among the military words are *forlorn hope* (1539), *knapsack* (1603), and *furlough* (1625). A 'forlorn hope' was a picked body of men sent to the front to begin the attack, a kind of suicide squad, the expression coming from Dutch *verloren hoop*, literally 'lost troop'.

The Dutch school of painting was famous, but no words from this field occur in our small sample. Serjeantson, however, lists a number of loans from the field of art, including *manikin* 'artist's lay-figure', *landscape* (1598), and *easel* (1634). There were also a fair number of miscellaneous words, including quite a few verbs, such as *foist* (1545), *snip* (1586), *rant* (1598), *drill* (1622, both in the military sense and in the sense 'to pierce, bore'), and *hustle* (1684).

As can be seen from the examples, the Dutch/Low German loans, in contrast to the Latin and French ones, tend to be popular rather than learned or polite. The sixteenth century was the time when they came into English in the greatest numbers.

LOANS FROM NON-EUROPEAN LANGUAGES

There were very few loans from non-European languages in Middle English, or even in the sixteenth century. It is in the seventeenth century, with the great expansion of British oceanic trade, exploration, and colonisation, that we begin to get that trickle of loan-words from all over the world which has gone on ever since. As we have seen, early loans from the New World and the Far East often came via Spanish or Portuguese. There are also, however, loans direct into English, and the sample contains eight of them. Four of them are from the Indian sub-continent. From southern India there is a loan from Tamil, *pariah* 'member of a low caste' (1613). From the Hindi dialects of northern India come *lungi* 'loin-cloth' (1634) and *chank* 'kind of large shell' (1698). From Sri Lanka there is a loan from Sinhalese, *wanderoo* 'a species of monkey' (1681). Three of the loans are from America, but two of them are merely variant forms of the same word. From the Algonquin languages, then spoken in large areas of eastern North America, come *wampumpeag* 'string of beads (often used as money)' (1631), and a shortened form of the same word, *wampum* (1636), which arose from the fact that Europeans mistakenly divided *wampumpeag* into two words. The other American word is *anatta* (1682), the name of an orange-red dye, which is perhaps a native word from Central America. The remaining non-European loan is from Malay, *pinang* 'areca tree, betel nut' (1662). All eight are concerned with local customs or local flora and fauna. The main sample contains no loans from Arabic, but there is just one in the supplementary sample: *Druse(an)* 'member of a Muslim sect' (1601).

There were also sources unrepresented in our samples, for example Persian, with *dervish* (1585) and *caravan* (1599); Turkish, with *coffee* (1598) and *pasha* (1646); Japanese, with *shogun* 'hereditary commander-in-chief of the Japanese army' (1615) and *saké* 'an alcoholic liquor made from rice' (1687); and African languages, with *zebra* (1600) and *drill* 'species of baboon' (1644). Once again the words are concerned with local culture and local fauna, or with trade and the objects of trade.

AFFIXATION

As we saw in Table 6.1, most of the new words in eModE were not loans, but were produced by various methods of word-formation from existing English words and morphemes. These 'existing English words and morphemes' are taken to include loan-words which had been taken into English and naturalised before the process of word-formation took place. For example, the adjective *implacable* (1522) had been borrowed from French. From it was formed the adverb *implacably* (1631), and this is classified as an example of suffixation, not as a loan-word. Similarly, prefixes and suffixes such as *re-* and *-ist*, which had entered the language from Latin or Romance languages, are counted as English morphemes, since they had long been a productive part of the language.

In the Early Modern period, affixation is by far the most usual method of word-formation. The chronological distribution of words thus produced bears a general resemblance to that for French and Latin loans: there are few examples before about 1520; the number rises until about 1590; there is a peak period between about 1590 and 1660; and then a decline in the later part of the seventeenth century. The patterns are not identical: for French loans, the decline begins round about 1620, and for Latin loans quite sharply soon after 1660, while for affixes the number remains moderately high until about 1670. Nevertheless, the resemblances are striking, and suggest that, unless there is some in-built bias in the OED material, there was a great peak of vocabulary expansion between about 1590 and 1660, which then died away.

Compared with loans, the words produced by affixation show no marked preferences for certain fields of discourse, and a high proportion of them belong to the general vocabulary. There are indeed words from many of the fields favoured by the loans, since it is quite common for further words to be derived from the loan-words by means of affixation. The material contains such words as *relapser* (1625) and *anathemise* v. (1674, religion), *parisonal* (1652, rhetoric), *commensurableness* (1557, mathematics), *parenchymatic* (1651, biology), *anatomically* (1646, anatomy), and *transalpiner* (1599, geography). All of these are derived by affixation from loan-words which have been encountered earlier in this chapter. In such fields there are also words formed by affixation from older elements, such as *spoon-billed* (1668, natural history), *straight-lined* (1571, geometry), *entrenchment* (1591, military), *counter-opening* (1611, surgery), and *uncoated* (1663, chemistry and physics). Their number, however, is relatively small.

There were some practical fields where loan-words were rare, and in these we find a number of words formed by affixation: in mechanical arts, like *spooler* (1554), *uncloy* 'unnail' (1611), and *counterweight* (1693), in horticulture, like *imbranch* v. 'to graft' (1577), and in farming, like *uncocked* (1641). But even these are not very numerous. Overall, the words formed by affixation have a very wide scatter, with small groups of words from many different fields, and large numbers of unspecialised words.

SUFFIXES

Suffixation is the commonest method of word-formation in the sample. The largest group is of nouns, fairly closely followed by adjectives. The group of adverbs is only about one-third the size of either of these, and the number of verbs is very small.

Among the nouns, over thirty different suffixes are found. Those that occur ten times or more in the sample are shown in Table 6.2. Two suffixes, *-ness* and *-er*, are clearly predominant, and account for nearly half of all the forms. The former is used for forming abstract nouns from adjectives, while the latter is used to form agent and instrument nouns from verbs.

The supplementary sample gives a similar picture, except that it has a higher position for *-ist*, as in *Yorkist* (1601). This is one of three suffixes in the main sample which just miss the cut-off point, but the supplementary material suggests that *-ist* might well be pushed up. The suffix *-ism*, as in *utopianism* (1661), also just misses the cut, but all nine examples occur in the seventeenth century, seven of them in the second half of the century, so it

TABLE 6.2

Suffixes used to form nouns

Suffix	Number of occurrences	Examples
-ness	70	bawdiness, briskness, straightness
-er	59	frequenter, gormandiser, murmurer
-ment	19	entrenchment, investment
-(a)tion	16	invigoration
-ship	13	tribuneship
-ess	11	commandress 'female commander'

TABLE 6.3

Suffixes used to form adjectives

Suffix	Number of occurrences	Examples
-ed	37	latticed, lunged 'having lungs', muscled, rose-cheeked, rosy-bottomed
-y	22	bawdy, heathery, brittly 'fairly brittle'
-ical	19	prelatical
-less	16	heatless, relentless
-able	15	laughable, transferable
-ish	12	brinish, straightish
-(i)al	12	parishional, ancestorial
-like	11	sheep-like
-ous	10	murmurous
-ive	10	commemorative, sportive

would seem that this suffix was just rising to prominence in the later part of the Early Modern period. The table excludes the *-ing* forms of verbs used nominally, since there are often problems of categorisation and of dating. Many of them, however, are clearly nouns, such as *engraving*, when used in the concrete sense 'that which is engraved, an engraved figure or inscription' (1611).

Nouns are often formed by suffixation even though there is already a noun in existence with a similar meaning. Examples are *delicateness* (1530), *frequentness* (1664), *immatureness* (1665), *immediateness* (1633), and *immenseness* (1610). With these compare *delicacy* (1374), *frequency* (1553), *immaturity* (1540), *immediacy* (1605), and *immensity* (1450), which had been formed direct from French or Latin.

For the formation of adjectives, over twenty-five suffixes are found in the sample, and there is a more even spread among different suffixes than with the nouns. Those that occur ten times or more are shown in Table 6.3. The *-ing* and *-ed* forms of verbs used attributively are not included in the table, once again because of uncertainties of categorisation and dating. Despite the omission of these verbal forms, the suffix *-ed* is easily top of the table, being frequently attached to nouns. The suffix *-y* is normally affixed to nouns, but occasionally to adjectives. Among the suffixes I have included what Marchand (1969) calls 'semi-suffixes', one of which is *-like*.

The adverbs in the sample are almost without exception formed with the suffix *-ly*, for example *anatomically* (1646), *bawdily* (1628), *commandingly* (1603). A very small number are formed from *-s* and from the semi-suffixes *-wise* and *-like*, for example *heavenwards* (1650), *sporting-wise* (1579), *gospel-like* (1576).

The number of verbs in the sample is very small. Most of them are formed with *-ise*, for example *anathemise* (1674), *tranquillise* (1623). There are a few formed from *-ate*, *-en*, *-ify*, or *-le*, for example *deliriate* 'make delerious' (1658), *freshen* (1697), *tranquillify* (1683), *quackle* 1622).

PREFIXES

No league table will be given for the prefixes. The sample was based on *pages* of the OED, and, while this should not affect the overall figures for prefixation, it means that some particular prefixes may be over-represented in the sample, and others under-represented. Here the supplementary sample may help, since the sampling method was different: for each of the chosen years, every tenth word was chosen from the alphabetical list.

One finding of the main sample, however, is certainly correct. By far the commonest prefix is *un-*, with 40 per cent of the examples. It is used freely before nouns, adjectives, participles, verbs, and adverbs, and with words of foreign origin as well as native ones. A few examples: *uncircumcision* (1526), *unclasp* v. (1530), *unclimbable* (1533), *uncircumspectly* (1535), *uncloaked* (1540), *uncivil* adj. (1553), *uncited* (1581), *uncomfortable* (1592), *uncivility* (1598), *unclog* v. (1607), *uncivilised* (1607), *uncircumscribed* (1610), *un-coalcarrying* 'unwilling to submit to insult' (1611), *uncity* v. (1661), *un-come-at-able* (1694). The word *uncivility* was coined (and persisted) despite the fact that the French loan *incivility* (1584) was already in the language. The form *un-coalcarrying* is recorded only once, in a play by George Chapman, and illustrates the ease with which the prefix was used for nonce-formations. The dominance of *un-* is confirmed by the supplementary sample, in which it forms 39 per cent of the examples.

Other prefixes which occur quite often in the main sample, and are also found in the supplementary sample, are (in order of frequency): *counter-*, as in *counterstroke* n. (1596) and *counterprove* v. (1679); *im-*, especially in verbs like *imbranch* 'graft' (1577) and adjectives like *immalleable* (1675); *pre-*, as in *prelimitation* (1637) and *pre-instruct* v. (1646); *in-*, as in *involatile* 'wing-less' (1659); and *re-*, as in *re-lay* v. 'lay again' (1590).

There are three prefixes of moderately frequent occurrence which are found in the main sample, but not in the supplementary one: *trans-*, mainly with verbs, like *transcolour* 'change the colour of' (1664); *en-*, all the examples being verbs, like *entrust* (1602); and *com-*, as in *commeasurable* 'commen-surable' (1670). The prefix *trans-* does not appear in the early part of the period: the earliest of the thirteen examples is in 1598, and the majority of them come from the second half of the seventeenth century.

On the other hand, there are twelve prefixes in the supplementary sample which are not found in the main sample. Each of them is found only once, so that it is impossible to say anything about their relative frequency. These prefixes occur in the following words: *antecourt* n. 'entrance court' (1691), *antifebrile* n. 'substance efficacious against fever' (1661), *byfall* n. 'incidental accessory' (1571), *dissort* v. 'be incongruous' (1631), *exordinary* adj. 'extra-ordinary' (1601), *forestated* 'mentioned previously' (1691), *interplanetary* (1691), *non-consenter* n. 'dissenter' (1661), *out-villain* v. (1601), *over-indul-gence* (1631), *supernumerous* 'too numerous' (1661), and *under-proposition* 'minor premise' (1691).

There were many other productive prefixes in eModE: Marchand (1969) discusses more than sixty prefixes found in Present-day English, and the vast majority of these were productive in the Early Modern period. This section just gives a taste of some of the things going on in the period.

COMPOUNDING

In affixation, a bound morpheme is attached to a free morpheme. In compounding, two free morphemes are joined. This causes some difficulties of categorisation, since it is not always easy to distinguish between a compound and a syntactic group, especially when the forms are rare and obsolete. I have been fairly generous in admitting borderline cases into the group, and there are probably some forms which should not be there. Their omission, however, would make no significant difference to the findings.

The compounds in the main sample form a substantial group of 217 words, representing 18 per cent of all words produced by word-formation. The corresponding figure for the supplementary sample is 17 per cent. The compounds fall into a wide range of different fields. There is a large group connected with farming, like *sheep-brand* (1586) and *pin-fallow* 'winter fallow' (1668). A medium-sized group has to do with nautical matters and fishing, like *heaving-net* (1584) and *anchor-tow* (1637). A substantial group is concerned with the mechanical arts, like *pin-dust* (1552) and *spool-knave* (1688). Among these are names of tools, like *pinching-iron* (1519) and *spoon-hammer* (1688). A fair-sized group has to do with commerce, like *transfer-book* (1694), or the commodities it handles, like *Bristol-diamond* 'a kind of transparent rock-crystal' (1596).

A very large group is formed by the names of trees, plants, and birds, especially plants, like *rose-campion* (1530), *waterdock* (1548), *wych hazel* (1561), *spoonwort* (1578), and *rot-grass* (1631). These are especially common in the sixteenth century, and tend to be popular names, or the names used in herbals, rather than scientific ones. The distinction is not a sharp one, however, and some compounds do occur in works of natural history, for example bird names like *spoonbill* (1678) and botanical terms like *pine-cone* (1695). Otherwise there are not many scientific words: a couple from anatomy, like *pine-glandule* 'pineal gland' (1515), a few medical words, like *lung-sick* 'suffering from a pulmonary complaint' (1520), and one arithmetical word, *offcome* 'product' (1542).

A fairly large group consists of words for people, such as *bawdy-basket* 'hawker of indecent literature' (1567) and *Frenchwoman* (1593). A number of these are popular and opprobrious terms like *pinchback* (1600) and *scrape-penny* (1584), both meaning 'miser'. There is a small group of military words, including *murdering shot* (1628), *commander-in-chief* (1650), and *hand-grenade* (1661). There is quite a large group of religious words. These are not theological or official terms, but popular and practical ones, often showing the influence of the Puritan movement. Such are *will-work* 'a work performed without divine grace' (1538), *church-papist* 'a Roman Catholic who conformed outwardly to the Church of England' (1601), *gospel-lad* 'Covenanter' (1679), and *church-warden* (1688). They are nearly all from the seventeenth century. Early in the period, however, there are a small number of biblical words, like *heave-offering* 'an offering elevated by the priest' (1530), coined by Tyndale in imitation of the Hebrew, and adopted by later translators.

The overwhelming majority of the compounds in the sample are nouns, amounting to 89 per cent. There are a few adjectives (8 per cent), and a negligible number of adverbs and verbs. There are several different types of compound in English, which have been discussed in detail by Marchand (1969). In the sample, three-quarters of the nouns are of the form Noun + Noun. Most of these are of the straightforward type like *pincushion*, *rosewood*, *spoonbill*, and *water-dock*. A dozen are of the type that have an agent-noun as their second element, like *gorget-maker* and *copyholder*. Another dozen have a verbal substantive as their first element, like *heaving-net* and *laughing-stock*, and a couple have a verbal noun as their second element, like *sheep-stealing*. Various other methods of noun-formation are exemplified, but none in very great numbers: there are fifteen of the type Verb + Object, like *do-all* and *pinchback*; ten in which a noun is premodified by an adjective, like *Frenchwoman* and *freshman*; ten in which a noun is premodified by the possessive form of a noun, like *sheep's foot* 'a kind of claw-hammer'; and ten other types each represented by one or two examples.

Half of the adjectives are formed from a noun followed by a past participle, like *chap-fallen* and *heaven-sent*. There are three examples of Noun + Adjective, like *brink-full*, and half a dozen other types each represented once. The few verbs are borderline cases, verbal phrases of the type *do up* 'repair'. The few adverbs include *heaven-wide* and *straightforth*.

ZERO-MORPHEME DERIVATION

The only other group of any size is that of words produced by zero-morpheme derivation. There are ninety-nine of these, representing 8 per cent of the words coined by word-formation. The supplementary sample yields a similar percentage.

Zero-morpheme derivation, sometimes called 'conversion', is the process by which one word is derived from another without any change of form, as when the verb *channel* (1596) was derived from the noun *channel* (a ME loan from French). This particular verb is first exemplified in the opening speech of Shakespeare's *Henry IV Part 1*:

> No more shall trenching Warre channell her fields.

In the main sample, the vast majority of words formed by zero-morpheme derivation are either nouns or verbs. There are slightly more nouns than verbs, but in the supplementary sample the reverse is true, and overall the two groups are about equal in size. The main sample also contains a few adjectives and one adverb, neither of which occurs in the supplementary sample.

Three types of derivation are far commoner than all others. The commonest is the formation of verbs from nouns, for example *apprentice* (1631), *barbecue* (1661), *gormandise* (1548), *gossip* (1590), *label* (1601), *launder* (1610), and *spool* 'wind on to a spool' (1603). In the case of *gormandise* and *launder*, we have subsequently lost the original nouns from which the verbs were formed. The noun *gormandise*, a fifteenth-century loan from French, meant 'gluttony', and its conversion to a verb was no doubt encouraged by the *-ise* ending. The noun *launder*, a variant form of *lavender* recorded from the fourteenth century, meant 'person who washes linen, launderer'.

The second common type is the formation of nouns from adjectives, for example *ancient* 'an aged person, one who lived in ancient times' (1502), *brisk* 'a gallant, fop' (1621), *commendatory* 'commendation' (1555), *fresh* 'stream of fresh water' (1538), and *invincible* 'one who is invincible' (1640).

The third is the formation of nouns from verbs, for example *heave* (1571), *invite* 'invitation' (1659), *laugh* (1690), *scramble* (1674), *scratch* (1586), and *transfer* (1674).

The only other types represented in the sample by more than one word are the forming of adjectives from nouns, and the forming of verbs from adjectives. The former is seen in the adjectives *Briton* 'British' (1547) and *murrain* 'ill-conditioned, plaguy' (1571), while the latter is illustrated by the verb *dizzy* 'to make dizzy' (1501).

OTHER TYPES OF WORD-FORMATION

The remaining thirty-nine words were produced by various minor methods of word-formation. None of these is represented by more than nine words in the sample, and several by only one. Nine words were produced by clipping, or shortening. In most of these it is the end of the word that has been dropped, as with *quack* 'one who falsely pretends to medical skill' (1638, from *quack-*

salver) and *chap* 'purchaser, customer' (1577, from *chapman*). The present-day meaning of the latter, 'fellow, lad', is not recorded until the eighteenth century. A few words were produced by back-formation, like *dizz* v. 'to make dizzy' (1632), from the adjective *dizzy*, on the analogy of pairs like *craze/crazy*. Another group, nearly all verbs, are described by the OED as being 'imitative', 'of symbolic sound', 'echoic', or 'onomatopoeic'. A small group of words were produced by the reshaping of existing words by popular etymology. Such are *ancient* 'a flag, standard-bearer' (1554, from *ensign*), and *frenne* 'foreign' (1553) from *fremd* (which goes back to OE), under the influence of *foreign* (a ME loan from French). The remaining words are miscellaneous oddities: an invented mnemonic word from logic, a pseudo-archaism invented by Spenser, a proper name made into a common noun, the plural of a word misapprehended as a singular, a word produced by misdivision, and a few irregular nonce-formations.

TYPES AND TOKENS

We have seen that large numbers of new words entered the language in the Early Modern period, but that many of them were of rare occurrence or were short-lived. Here we need to distinguish between *types* and *tokens*. If you wish to count the number of words in a passage, this can mean several different things, but there are two broad divisions. 1. You can count every graphic unit on the page as one occurrence, so that if, for example, the form *and* occurs a hundred times, this adds a hundred to your total count. Here you are counting tokens. 2. You can count many occurrences of the same form as only one occurrence, so that if the word *and* occurs a hundred times, this adds only one to your total count. Here you are counting types. There are complications: are *love* v. and *love* n. to be counted as one type or as two? And similarly with *ask/asked* and *swim/swam*. Even so, there are still two main methods, counting tokens and counting types.

I am suggesting, then, that in the Early Modern period many new types entered the vocabulary, but that in actual passages of writing (or of speech) they were represented by relatively few tokens. This can be conveniently illustrated from the complete works of Shakespeare. He himself produced many new words: we have already seen that he coined the verb *channel* from the noun, and the OED entries show that he is the first recorded user of no fewer than 164 words beginning with the prefix *un-*. Moreover, his oeuvre is large, as is his vocabulary: the great Harvard concordance (Spevack 1968–80, 1973) contains more than 29,000 head-words (types) and more than 800,000 citations (tokens). It can be assumed, therefore, that Shakespeare was as likely as anybody in his age to make free use of new words.

The Harvard concordance, used in conjunction with the OED, can give us some idea of the number of recently coined words he uses (types), and the frequency of their occurrence in his works (tokens). In the present chapter up to this point, more than 220 words have been cited which entered the language in the period 1500–1600, and which would therefore have been available to Shakespeare. Of these, almost exactly a quarter are recorded in Shakespeare. Most of them, however, occur infrequently: twenty-three occur only once, eleven occur twice, and seven occur three times. Only five occur more than ten times. This infrequency of occurrence applies even to words which Shakespeare himself coined: for eleven of the words, Shakespeare is the first recorded user, and ten of the eleven occur only once or twice in his works. The eleventh, which occurs five times, is *sportive* adj. (1590).

The five words which occur more than ten times each in Shakespeare are mainly ones which entered the language quite early in the sixteenth century, and which are rather ordinary words. Such are *entrance* n. (1526), *imitate* v. (1534), and *invite* v. (1533). The remaining two words are *ancient* 'ensign' (1554) and *Don*, the Spanish title (1523). The former was clearly an established military word by Shakespeare's time. The latter is often used in the plays with the names of Spanish characters, and is the word of most frequent occurrence, with twenty-four tokens.

Overall, then, it is clear that Shakespeare made considerable use of new words (types), but that their frequency of occurrence (tokens) was rather low. This can be seen by comparing these words with commonly used ones which had entered the language before 1500. Going back to Old English are such words as *lady* (265 occurrences), *wife* (476), *love* (2,259), and *lord* (2,705). Middle English loans from French include *mercy* (193 occurrences), *majesty* (262), *grace* (601), and *noble* (657). Of course, many words from OE and ME occurred infrequently, but the above figures put the matter into perspective: even the most frequent of the new words, with twenty-four occurrences, can hardly be said to be used by Shakespeare very often.

NEW WORDS AND THE MODERN READER

As we have seen, an enormous number of new words entered the language in Early Modern times, and this sets problems for the present-day reader, especially the reader of literature. In any work of the period, we are likely to meet unfamiliar words, and it is often difficult to know whether they were also unfamiliar to the original reader. Some words which have since died out were nevertheless quite common in the sixteenth and seventeenth centuries, but others were rare, and probably seemed as surprising to the original readers as they do to us. Moreover, many words now quite familiar did not come into the language until Early Modern times, and when first used may have had all the shock and dazzle of novelty. When we read or hear Shakespeare, it is difficult to remember that he is the first recorded user of such ordinary words as *Frenchwoman, investment, invitation, laughable, rant* v., *uncomfortable, undress* v., and *unhelpful*. But equally, he is the first recorded user of *lune* 'fit of lunacy', which for us is archaic, and of *chanson*, which seems as French to us as it must have done to the original audience. Moreover, he is the first known user of some words which have never been recorded since, like *chapeless* 'without a sheath' and *invised* 'unseen'.

FURTHER READING

Accessible to the general reader are Sheard (1954, a general history of the English vocabulary) and Serjeantson (1935, loan-words in English). On methods of word-formation, Marchand (1969) is a major work for the student; Bauer (1983) and Adams (1973) are shorter works, more suitable for the general reader. A brief account of the history of the scientific vocabulary in English is given by Savory (1967).

Chapter Seven

CHANGES OF MEANING

We shall be concerned in this chapter, not with the theory of meaning or of semantic change, but with some of the substantial changes of meaning which have taken place in particular lexical words since the year 1500. There have been an enormous number of such changes, and there is no point in trying to make this chapter into a dictionary. What I shall do, therefore, is to suggest the kinds of change that a modern reader needs to look out for, and give examples.

LEXICAL SETS

We shall confine ourselves to the meanings of single words. Meaning is also carried by bound morphemes (such as *un-*, *-ed*, and *-able*), and by units larger than the word, but I shall not deal with these. Even when we discuss the meaning of a single word, however, we may not be able to treat it in isolation. Lexical items form sets, the members of which may be mutually defining, or may overlap in meaning, so that a change in one member of a set may affect the meaning of all the others.

An example of a lexical set is the group of words for colours. Different languages divide up the spectrum differently, and so have different sets. In English, one substantial change in the colour-set took place in the Early Modern period. The common English garden bird, the robin (*Erithacus rubecula*), is often known as a *redbreast*, or *robin redbreast*. In December, the shops display numerous Christmas cards with pictures of robins, and these robins are almost invariably depicted with vivid red breasts. But anybody who actually looks at a robin knows that its breast is not red, but orange. Why the discrepancy? The answer is that when the word *redbreast* was coined, *orange* did not exist in English as a colour-word, and what we call 'orange' was then included in 'red'. The noun *orange* as the name of the fruit goes back to

Middle English, but the adjective *orange* meaning 'orange coloured' is not recorded until 1542, and the noun *orange* meaning 'orange colour' until about 1600. But the word *redbreast* as the name of a robin was coined much earlier, the first example in the OED being about 1400, and at that date the colour of a robin's breast fell into that part of the spectrum covered by the word *red*.

Two other new colour-words arose in eModE, *indigo* (1622) and *olive* (1634), but these are usually felt simply as shades of established colours. In his *Opticks* (1704), Newton reckoned indigo as one of the primary or prismatic colours, but in general usage it seems to be treated just as a shade of blue. Olive, similarly, is usually treated as a dull yellowish brown, or a dull yellowish green. Since Early Modern times, numerous other colour-words have arisen, especially in the fashion and decorating industries, but these again are just shades of established colours.

MILITARY RANKS

Another example of a lexical set is provided by the names for military ranks. In the late sixteenth century, the infantry-officer two degrees below a captain was called an ensign (or ancient). In the British army in the nineteenth century, *ensign* was still the name for the rank two degrees below a captain, though it was being displaced by *sub-lieutenant* or *second-lieutenant*, which in some branches of the service were used in the eighteenth century. It would not, however, be accurate to say that sixteenth-century *ensign* or *ancient* could be translated by nineteenth-century *ensign* or *sub-lieutenant*, for the total number of ranks in the hierarchy had changed. Typically, the sixteenth-century ensign was the fifth rank in an eight-rank system, whereas the nineteenth-century ensign was the eleventh rank in a sixteen-rank system. Moreover, in the nineteenth century there was a sharp division between commissioned and non-commissioned officers, and the ensign was the lowest officer of commissioned rank. In the sixteenth century, there was no such clear-cut division.

Indeed, the whole hierarchy was less clearly defined in the sixteenth century, when there was no standing army and no Army List. In the late sixteenth century, the soldier without rank was called a *common soldier*, or sometimes a *private soldier*. Above him, there was commonly a hierarchy of seven ranks, which in the infantry were called *corporal*, *sergeant*, *ensign* (or *ancient*), *lieutenant*, *captain*, *colonel* (or *coronel*), and *general*. The general commanded an army, or a large section of it, the colonel commanded a regiment, and the captain a company. The four lower grades were company officers, appointed by the captain. Of these, the lieutenant was the captain's deputy, and the ensign was originally the *ensign-bearer* 'standard-bearer'. There was only one lieutenant and one ensign in a company, but a sergeant to every hundred men or so, and a corporal to every twenty or twenty-five. A company (sometimes also called an *ensign*) could consist of anything from a hundred to three hundred men. But the terminology was not cut and dried. The word *captain* was also used to mean 'commander, general'. The word *lieutenant* was freely used to mean 'deputy', and *lieutenant-general* is recorded from 1618, *lieutenant-colonel* from 1598. The adjective *general* could be added after a title to indicate a wider command than usual for the rank, and *captain-general* could mean 'commander-in-chief'.

Moreover, no consistent distinction was made between ranks and functions. Elizabethan military theorists, like Thomas Digges and Barnaby Rich and Robert Barrett, give long accounts of the various officers and their duties, but they lump together indiscriminately ranks (like general, captain, and sergeant), and functionaries (like trench-master, muster-master, scout-master, forage-master, company clerk, surgeon, chaplain, and drummer). In some cases it is difficult to be sure whether a title belongs to what we should consider a rank, or whether it simply refers to a function or office (like twentieth-century *adjutant*). In each regiment, we are told, there is a sergeant-major, who is responsible for the deployment and marching-order of the whole regiment, but it is not clear whether he is a captain who has this particular regimental function, or whether sergeant-major is a rank between captain and colonel. In the ensign we see a transitional phase between function and rank: it is clear from Elizabethan military treatises that he still carried the company's colours, but it is also explicitly stated that he is third-in-command of the company, and takes command in the absence of the captain and the lieutenant. In my postulated eight-rank hierarchy, I have included the ensign, but have excluded the sergeant-major, treating him as a functionary. Whether or not this is correct is arguable, but the fact that it is arguable shows that the concept of military rank has changed since the sixteenth century.

Despite these complications, the normal Elizabethan chain of command is probably well represented by my eight-stage hierarchy. Since then, the distinction between ranks and functions has been made clearer, and the number of ranks in the hierarchy has increased: *lieutenant-general* and *lieutenant-colonel* date from the middle of the Early Modern period, *major* and *major-general* from the Civil Wars, *brigadier* from the later seventeenth century, *field marshal* in its modern military sense from the eighteenth century, *sergeant-major* in its modern sense from about 1800, and *lance-corporal* from about the same date (though *lance-pesade*, meaning 'experienced and trustworthy private soldier', is recorded from the later sixteenth century onwards). As the number of ranks has increased, the meaning of each title has changed, since the terms in a system of this kind are mutually defining.

OVERLAPPING FIELDS OF REFERENCE

With military ranks, the terms are mutually exclusive: you can be a lieutenant or a captain, but not both at once. Often, however, sets of related lexical items have fields of reference that overlap. An example in the Early Modern period is a group of words designating human faculties, which includes *conscience*, *curiosity*, *ingenuity*, *intellect*, *intelligence*, *memory*, *mind*, *sense*, and *wit*. Each of these nine words overlaps in meaning with at least one other, yet each of them has at least one meaning found in none of the others. The pattern of overlaps can be illustrated by the word *wit*, for this overlaps in meaning with nearly all the other eight.

The following were the main meanings of the noun *wit* in the middle of the Early Modern period:

1. 'the seat of consciousness, the mind'. The overlap is with *mind* and *conscience*. The latter already had its present meaning of 'consciousness of right and wrong, moral sense', but could still be used in a more general sense of 'consciousness', and occasionally 'mind'.

2. 'the faculty of thinking and reasoning'. The overlap is with *mind*, *intellect*, and *intelligence*. Occasionally, *wit* was used for other specific mental faculties, including memory, and here it overlapped with *mind* and *memory*.

3. 'the faculties of perception'. Here it overlaps with *sense*: it was possible to talk about 'the five wits', where today we say 'the five senses'. Contemporary theory indeed recognised ten wits or senses: in addition to the five 'external' senses (sight, hearing, smell, taste, touch), there were five 'internal' senses (common sense, imagination, fancy, estimation, memory). Either *wit* or *sense* could be used for both groups, though sometimes *the five wits* was used for the internal, and *the five senses* for the external. By 1600, this use of *wit* was old-fashioned, and it did not last long into the seventeenth century.

4. 'right mind, sanity'. This usage survives in phrases like 'out of one's wits'. In eModE, the singular *wit* could also be used in this way. The overlap was with *mind* and with the plural *senses*.

5. 'great mental capacity, intellectual ability'. Here *wit* overlapped with *intelligence* and *ingenuity*. The latter meant (among other things) 'great intellectual capacity'. Its present meaning 'capacity for invention or construction' is not recorded until 1649. Moreover, both *wit* and *ingenuity* were also used to mean something much stronger than 'intelligence', suggesting rather 'outstanding intellectual and creative ability, genius'. The word *genius* also existed, but did not take on this meaning until the late seventeenth century; it supplanted *wit* and *ingenuity* in this sense during the eighteenth century.

6. 'a person of great intellectual ability, a genius'. For this usage, *wit* was supplanted by *genius* in the eighteenth century. Here there is no overlap between *wit* and other words in the group. Both *intelligence* and *intellect* could indeed be used to mean 'an intelligent being', but only when the reference was to a spirit or supernatural being.

7. 'practical talent, constructive or mechanical ability'. Here *wit* overlapped with *curiosity*. The latter had many meanings which have since disappeared,

including 'carefulness', 'attention to detail', 'fastidiousness', 'careful or elaborate workmanship', 'a nicety of argument', and 'a matter on which undue care is bestowed'. In the sense 'practical talent', *curiosity* and *wit* were supplanted by *ingenuity* during the eighteenth century.

8. 'good judgment, discretion'. This is perhaps Polonius's meaning when he says that *Breuitie is the Soule of Wit*. It overlapped with *sense*.

9. 'apt, agile, or entertaining use of language; the capacity for this'. This is a group of meanings from which the PresE senses of *wit* are descended. The use of *wit* to mean 'a person with this kind of ability' is not clearly recorded until the late seventeenth century. In these senses, *wit* does not overlap with the other words in our group.

This brief account of the overlaps of *wit* is by no means complete. It also overlapped with other words outside the group, like *discretion*, *reason*, and *understanding*. The other words in the group, similarly, overlapped in varying degrees with one another, and also with words outside the group: *sense*, for example, overlapped with *feeling*, *intention*, *judgment*, *meaning*, *opinion*, and *signification*. There was, plainly, a great complex of overlapping semantic fields. What has happened since the sixteenth century is that many of the boundaries have changed: *wit* has contracted its field of reference, having been supplanted for some usages by other words like *genius*, *ingenuity*, *mind*, and *sense*; by contrast, *sense* has expanded its field of reference, having developed a number of new meanings, such as 'practical soundness of judgment', 'consciousness (of one's own motives, weaknesses, etc.)', and 'direction of motion', though at the same time it has lost a few of its earlier meanings, like 'liability to feel pain or irritation'.

GAIN AND LOSS OF MEANINGS

Words like *wit* and *sense* have narrowed or widened their field of reference by losing or gaining meanings. Changes of this kind are going on all the time, and the case that the present-day reader perhaps needs to be especially alert for is the one where a meaning has been lost since Early Modern times. A few examples follow.

In 1600, *addition* could mean 'the process of adding', but also 'an additional name, a title of rank', as when, in *Macbeth*, Ross and Angus greet Macbeth with the *addition* 'Thane of Cawdor'. The noun *back* had several meanings still in use, including the basic anatomical one, but could also mean 'body of followers, support'. Moreover, *a back* could also carry the connotation 'virility, male sexual prowess', perhaps even 'penile erection'. This use can be found in seventeenth-century comedy, and there is an example in Jonson's *Alchemist* (1612), when Sir Epicure Mammon is contemplating the advantages he will have from possessing the Philosopher's Stone:

I doe meane
To haue a list of Wiues, and Concubines,
Æquall with *Salomon*; who had the *Stone*
Alike, with me: and I will make me, a back
With the *Elixir*, that shall be as tough
As *Hercules*, to encounter fifty a night.

The adjective *brave* could mean 'courageous', but also 'splendid, excellent', and more specifically 'finely dressed', and even 'showy, ostentatious'. The noun *commodity* could mean 'an article of commerce', but also 'opportunity, occasion', 'expediency', and 'self-interest' (as in a well-known speech by the Bastard in Shakespeare's *King John*). The adjective *foul* could mean 'offensive', 'polluted', and 'wicked, detestable', as it can today, but also 'dirty, muddy' (for example of a road) and 'ugly' (of a person). The adjective *secure* could mean 'safe', but also 'over-confident, rash'. This meaning is seen in *Hamlet*, when the Ghost tells Hamlet about the murder:

Sleeping within mine Orchard,
My custome alwayes in the afternoone;
Vpon my secure hower thy Vncle stole
With iuyce of cursed Hebenon in a Violl.

The context shows clearly that it was not a safe hour, but a carefree or over-confident one.

GENERALISATION AND SPECIALISATION

When a word gains or loses a meaning, its field of reference expands or contracts. There is, however, a somewhat different sense in which the field of reference can become wider or narrower: the meaning can become more general or more specialised. When the word *gambit* entered the language in the seventeenth century, it had only its technical meaning in the game of chess, 'opening in which White offers a pawn sacrifice'. It was not until the middle of the nineteenth century that it was generalised to mean 'opening move(s) in any kind of transaction'. Conversely, in eModE the word *pollen* meant 'fine flour, fine powder', which has subsequently been specialised to mean 'the powdery substance on the anther of a flower'. This specialised botanical sense is recorded from the middle of the eighteenth century. These two words, *gambit* and *pollen*, illustrate the fact that specialisation of meaning is likely to take place when a word moves into a restricted field of discourse, and generalisation to take place when it moves out of a restricted field into the general vocabulary.

Sometimes the more general and more specific meanings of a word continue to exist side by side: in eModE, *meat* can mean both 'food in general' and 'flesh of animals used as food', while *disease* can mean both 'lack of ease, discomfort, trouble', and the more specialised 'morbid physical condition'. In both words, the earlier and more general meaning has since been lost.

If a word has several meanings, just one of them may undergo generalisation or specialisation. In eModE, the word *conceit* had a wide range of meanings, including 'idea, conception', 'mental capacity', 'opinion', 'favourable opinion', 'fanciful notion', and 'fanciful or ingenious expression'. The most usual present-day meaning, 'excessively high opinion of oneself', is a specialisation of 'favourable opinion', itself a specialisation of 'opinion'. The present meaning arose via the expression *self-conceit* '(favourable) opinion of oneself', which is the normal seventeenth-century word. Since then, *conceit* has slowly supplanted *self-conceit*, and at the same time lost most of its other meanings.

TITLES AND TERMS OF ADDRESS

An area where generalisation has often taken place is in titles and polite terms of address: words which at one time were restricted to small groups in the speech-community come to be used much more widely. The title *Mr* is now used of any male above school-leaving age, but formerly this was not so. *Mr* is an unstressed form of *master*, from which it was not distinguished in eModE. Abbreviations like *Mr.* and *M.* are found, but they can be used for *master* in any of its senses, and are not restricted to its use as a prefixed title. The OED gives examples like the following, dated 1597:

> But tell mee, art thou put away for whippinge thy yonge M^r?

Its last example of this type is dated 1674: after this date, *master* and *Mr* were presumably apprehended as two separate words.

As a title, the word was usually only accorded to the gentry, that group of perhaps 5–10 per cent of the population which constituted the ruling class. Sir Thomas Smith, in *De Republica Anglorum* (1583), refers explicitly to this use of the word:

> as for gentlemen, they be made good cheape in England. For whosoeuer studieth the lawes of the realme, who studieth in the vniuersities, who professeth liberall sciences, and to be shorte, who can liue idly and without manuall labour, and will beare the port, charge and countenance of a gentleman, he shall be called master, for that is the title which men giue to esquires and other gentlemen, and shall be taken for a gentleman.

As Smith's phrasing suggests, the title was most often used of the two lowest ranks of the gentry, the simple gentleman and the esquire. Occasionally, however, it is used of people higher up the social scale, especially knights and bishops: John Foxe, in his account of the martyrdom of a Bishop of London and a former Bishop of Worcester, refers to them as *Maister Ridley* and *Maister Latymer*. Nevertheless, the title is most often given to gentlemen below the rank of knight, as when the Shakespeare First Folio is called *Mr. William Shakespeares Comedies, Histories, & Tragedies*: the poet's father had successfully applied for a coat of arms. A man below gentle rank who was nevertheless of some substance and respectability was often given the title *Goodman*. This usage died out in the eighteenth century, presumably because the title *Mr* was now accorded to such people.

The spread of *Mr* down the social scale began during the Early Modern period: the word is sometimes used of people of some substance, such as prosperous citizens, despite the fact that they are not gentle. A fictional example is perhaps provided by Master Ford and Master Page in *The Merry Wives of Windsor*. On the other hand, people like this often had pretensions to gentility, and, as the quotation from Sir Thomas Smith suggests, it was not difficult for the wealthy citizen or yeoman to cross the class boundary. But, although *Mr* was now accorded as a title to men below the rank of gentleman, it was still confined to men of some substance, and was not used for artisans.

A similar extension has taken place with *lady* and *gentleman*. Today, the notices *Ladies* and *Gentlemen* on doors are taken as invitations to all members of the appropriate sex, but in eModE the words were normally restricted to members of the gentry. In Philip Rosseter's *Book of Ayres* (1601), there is an amusing lute-song by Thomas Campion, which begins as follows:

> I care not for these Ladies
> That must be woode and praide,
> Giue me kind Amarillis
> The wanton country maide,
> Nature art disdaineth,
> Her beautie is her owne,
> Her when we court and kisse,
> She cries forsooth let go,
> But when we come where comfort is
> She neuer will say no.

And so it continues, comparing 'these Ladies' unfavourably with Amaryllis, later called the 'Nutbrowne lasse'. The contrast is not only between town and country, or between art and nature, but is also one of class: the upper-class women are cold and pernickety, while the lower-class country girl is warm-hearted.

By this date, however, *lady* was beginning to spread down the social scale. The motives of politeness (or of flattery) which encouraged the change are illustrated by an incident in Middleton's comedy *A Chaste Maid in Cheapside*, probably written in about 1613. A christening celebration is going on in a middle-class London household. To the party enters Sir Walter Whorehound, the godfather, who is elsewhere described as a 'braue Court Spirit'.

2nd Gossip.   O here comes the chiefe Gossip Neighbours.

Sir Walter.   The fatnesse of your wishes to you all Ladyes.

3rd Gossip.   O deer sweet gentleman, what fine words he has,
                The fatnesse of our wishes.

2nd Gossip.   Calles vs all Ladyes.

4th Gossip.   I promise you a fine Gentleman, and a courteous.

The gossips (baptismal sponsors) are of modest citizen rank: the second is an apothecary's wife, and the third is the wife of a maker of sweetmeats. Their reactions show that they are flattered by Sir Walter's use of the word *ladies*.

CONNOTATIONS OF APPROVAL AND DISAPPROVAL

Some words carry connotations of approval or of disapproval. In some cases, such connotations have been gained or lost since Early Modern times. Changes of this kind are sometimes called 'amelioration' and 'pejoration'. In fact, however, we need to distinguish four different possibilities: a word can gain the implication of approval, or it can lose it, and similarly it can gain the implication of disapproval, or can lose it. It may happen that, when a word loses the implication of disapproval, it gains the implication of approval, but this is not necessarily so: it may simply become neutral with respect to such implications.

To the present-day reader, the most striking group is the one where the implication of disapproval has been gained since Early Modern times. Examples, with typical eModE meanings, are *addicted* 'devoted, inclined, attached', *artful* 'learned, skilful, artistic', *cunning* 'skill, dexterity, art', *gaudy* 'gay, ornate', *mediocrity* 'moderation, temperance, average ability', *obsequious* 'compliant, obedient', *ringleader* 'leader, head', and *unctuous* 'oily, greasy'. Some of these, especially *mediocrity* and *obsequious*, are sometimes used in the seventeenth century in what looks like the present-day way, with implications of disapproval. Many examples can be found, however, where such implications are clearly absent. For example, in his poem on the death of Lady Rich, Waller says that Lady Rich's mother:

> Mov'd with just grief expostulates with Heaven,
> Urging that promise to th'obsequious given,
> Of longer life, for nere was pious soul
> More apt t'obey, more worthy to controul.

Here *obsequious* cannot have implications of disapproval, for it must mean either 'obedient to the will of God', or (more probably) 'obedient to parents', the reference being to Exodus 20:12.

Examples of words which had the implication of disapproval but have since lost it include *enthusiasm*, which in the later seventeenth century was an anti-Puritan word, meaning 'imagined divine inspiration, intemperate religious emotion'; *politician*, which often meant 'crafty schemer, intriguer'; *precise* 'excessively scrupulous, puritanical'; *shrewd* 'malicious, hurtful, cunning'; and *sophisticated* 'adulterated, lacking naturalness'. Of these, *shrewd* and *sophisticated* have moreover gained implications of approval.

Words which have lost former implications of approval include *artificial* 'skilfully made, artistic' and *curious* 'careful, fastidious, skilful, exquisitely made'. Both words, however, also had meanings which on the contrary carried implications of disapproval, such as 'affected in manners' (*artificial*) and 'inquisitive, prying' (*curious*).

METAPHOR

So far, many of the changes we have looked at involve a change at the periphery of the field of reference. Sometimes, however, there is a leap to an apparently remote semantic area, rather than a simple expansion or contraction of boundaries. A leap of this kind is sometimes called *transfer*.

One of the common ways in which transfer occurs is by the figurative use of a word, which, if it happens often enough, leads to a permanent new meaning. In eModE, the word *ceiling* could mean 'the lining of the roof of a room'. Relatively recent is the metaphorical extension of this to give the meaning 'upper limit', now quite normal. Such changes are going on all the time, and when we read eModE texts we have to remember, for example, that *budget* can mean 'a leather bag or wallet', but not 'financial proposals' or 'the money available for expenditure'; that *cell* can be used of a small room in a monastery, a prison, or a beehive, but not (before the 1670s) of the structural units of plants or animals; and that *headache* can mean 'pain in the head', but not 'problem, difficulty'.

It might be thought that the context would show clearly that the present-day meaning was inappropriate. This is not always the case, however. In *The Defence of Poesie*, Sidney speaks of:

> the high and excellent *Tragedie*, that openeth the greatest woundes, and sheweth forth the *Vlcers* that are couered with *Tissue*, that maketh Kings feare to be Tyrants.

It is tempting for the present-day reader to take *tissue* in its biological sense, but this cannot have been what Sidney meant. In the sixteenth century, *tissue* meant 'a rich kind of cloth (especially one that had gold and silver in it)', and more specifically 'a band or girdle of rich material'. In the second half of the sixteenth century it also came to be used of any woven fabric, whether rich or not. The figurative use, as when we speak of a tissue of lies, errors, absurdities,

251

and so on, is not recorded until the eighteenth century. The biological use (plant or animal tissue) is first recorded in the OED in 1831. Sidney is referring to rich material: the ulcer is concealed by magnificent clothes.

Sometimes the new figurative meaning develops in such a way that its connection with the original literal meaning is no longer obvious. The form is then apprehended as two different words, sometimes differentiated in spelling. The noun *mettle* was originally a figurative use of *metal*, meaning the 'stuff' a person or a horse is made of (perhaps with an implicit comparison with a sword-blade). Hence it came to mean 'quality, temperament', and especially 'ardent or spirited temperament'. The figurative use arose in the sixteenth century, and no distinction was made in spelling between this and other uses of *metal*. It was not until the eighteenth century that this distinction was established.

FORMAL INFLUENCE

Transfer can also arise by the influence of one word on another, because of a formal resemblance between them. The adjective *obnoxious*, first recorded in the late sixteenth century, originally meant 'exposed to injury or evil, liable to punishment or censure, subject to the power of another'. There is a well-known example near the beginning of Milton's *Samson Agonistes* (1671), where Samson complains that, because of his blindness, he is made more obnoxious to all the miseries of life. Joseph Glanvill is rather fond of the word, and always uses it with meanings of this kind, as when he remarks, in *The Vanity of Dogmatizing* (1661), that we human beings are:

> obnoxious to fallacy ['liable to be deceived or mistaken'] in our *apprehensions* and *judgments*, and so often imposed on by these deceptions.

The usual present-day meaning of *obnoxious*, 'offensive, objectionable', is due to the influence of the adjective *noxious*. This meaning is recorded as early as 1675, and the meaning 'injurious' (also due to the influence of *noxious*) as early as 1612. The earlier meanings are the normal ones in the seventeenth century, however, and continue to be found in the eighteenth century and even later, perhaps because educated people knew the meaning of the Latin word from which *obnoxious* had been derived.

Slightly different is the case of the verb *demean*. In eModE, *to demean oneself* usually meant 'to comport oneself' (cf. the noun *demeanour*). The now more usual meaning, 'to lower oneself', probably arose because speakers analysed the word as consisting of the prefix *de-* and the adjective *mean*, on the analogy of *debase*. The new meaning is found in the seventeenth century, but is rare before 1700.

EUPHEMISM

Another cause of transfer is euphemism. Under the influence of taboo or delicacy of feeling, a speaker replaces the normal word by some substitute. If this is done regularly, the substitute in time becomes the normal word, and in due course has to be replaced by another euphemism.

Today, a latrine is often called a *lavatory* or a *toilet*, but these are relatively recent words for the thing, having first been used as euphemisms. The eModE words are *privy*, *privy house*, *jakes*, and *draught* (which more often meant 'sewer'). There are also expressions with the word *easement*, like *place of easement*, and (in the later part of the period) with *ease*, like *closet of ease*.

Sir John Harington, a godchild of Queen Elizabeth I, invented a kind of water-closet, and in 1596 published a book about it, a mock-encomium called *The Metamorphosis of Aiax* (punning on *Ajax* and *a jakes*). In it he has an anecdote about a real-life contemporary, a certain Mr Jacques Wingfield:

> There was a very tall and seruiceable gentleman, somtime Lieutenant of the ordinance, called *M. Iaques Wingfield*; who coming one day, either of businesse, or of kindnesse, to visit a great Ladie in the Court; the Ladie bad her Gentlewoman aske, which of the *Wingfields* it was; he told her *Iaques Wingfield*: the modest gentlewoman, that was not so well seene in the French, as to know that *Iaques*, was but *Iames* in English, was so bashfoole, that to mend the matter (as she thought) she brought her Ladie word, not without blushing, that it was *M. Priuie Wingfield*; at which, I suppose, the Lady then, I am sure the Gentleman after, as long as he liued, was wont to make great sport.

The gentlewoman thought that *privy* was a politer word than *jakes*, and used it as a euphemism. In fact, *privy* appears to be the older word: the OED records it from the fourteenth century, whereas its first example of *jakes* is from the 1530s. It is probable, however, that *jakes* was a slangy and rather vulgar word, and it may well have existed in popular speech long before it appeared in writing.

The word *lavatory* existed all through the Early Modern period, but not in this sense. The earliest meaning was 'vessel for washing, bath'. It could also be used figuratively, and the word was so far from having unsavoury associations that it could be used in solemn religious contexts: the OED examples include *the lauatory of grace* (1526) and *The Lavatory of Baptisme* (1633). In the middle of the seventeenth century the word developed the meaning 'apartment for washing the hands and face', from which came the later euphemistic development to 'latrine' (probably in the nineteenth century).

The word *toilet* came later. It is first recorded in 1540, meaning 'a piece of stuff used as a wrapper for clothes'. In the second half of the seventeenth century it has a number of meanings connected with dressing – 'the articles used in dressing', 'a table for such articles, a toilet-table', 'a cloth cover for a toilet-table', 'the action or process of dressing'. Not until the nineteenth century did it take on the meaning 'a dressing-room', from which came the present euphemistic use.

Since in time euphemisms are likely to be supplanted by new ones, there are eModE expressions of this kind which have not survived, and whose meanings are not always self-evident. There are many in that area of strong taboo, sex. Here euphemism shades off into slang, and there are frequent examples in the drama, especially in plays which try to simulate everyday speech. There are numerous words for the penis, such as *bauble, carrot, date, lance, needle*, and *pike*. There are also many words for the female pudenda, such as *medlar, tail*, and *plum tree*. The last is illustrated in the following extract from Nash's *Haue with you to Saffron-walden* (1596):

> Yea, Madam *Gabriela*, are you such an old ierker? then Hey ding a ding, vp with your petticoate, haue at your plum-tree.

There are also many words for 'whore', 'prostitute', such as *callet, cockatrice, hackney, hobby-horse, (piece of) mutton, pagan, punk, stale*, and *wagtail*. Such euphemisms and slang words shade off into the arcane language of the underworld.

LOSS OF INTENSITY

One final kind of change which we can consider is loss of intensity. This arises from the common human habit of exaggerating for effect. The adjective *beastly* meant 'bestial, brutish', but exaggeration led speakers to use the word about people or actions that were not bestial but merely unpleasant or offensive. But the meaning of a word is determined by the ways in which speakers use it, and so *beastly* lost intensity, and came to mean merely 'offensive, unpleasant'; and today we can use it of the weather or of an inanimate object, with no animal suggestions at all. The first signs of this weakening can be seen in the Early Modern period, but on the whole *beastly* remains a strong word throughout the seventeenth century.

Another word which has undergone similar weakening is the adjective *naughty*. Today it suggests childish waywardness, but earlier it meant 'morally bad, wicked', as when Portia, in *The Merchant of Venice*, says:

> How farre that little candell throwes his beames,
> So shines a good deed in a naughty world.

Other examples of words which have lost intensity, together with typical eModE meanings, are *admire* 'to wonder, be astonished (at)', *amaze* 'to stun, bewilder, terrify', *astonish* 'to stun, paralyse, stupefy', *awful* 'awe-inspiring, terror-stricken', *baffle* 'to subject to public disgrace', *care* 'grief, sorrow', *confound* 'to destroy, overthrow, ruin', *dismal* 'unpropitious, malign, calamitous', *merely* 'absolutely, entirely', and *presently* 'at once, immediately'. This last word also had the meaning 'at present, now', which disappeared from the southern language in the seventeenth century, but which continued to occur in Scots, and is also normal in American English. The weakened meaning, 'after a short interval', which is usual in present-day British English, is first found round about 1600.

Some changes of meaning which have taken place since Early Modern times can easily be overlooked by the present-day reader. These are the ones that depend on a change in world view, in a whole set of attitudes: the word may look familiar, but the assumptions behind it may be quite different. Anybody reading the literature of the age needs to be familiar with the official world view that dominated intellectual life throughout the greater part of the period: the pervasive theological assumptions, which weight the meanings of words liked *grace* and *nature*, and which provide an overall view of the history of the universe (Creation, Fall, Redemption, Last Judgment); the belief in the Great Chain of Being, the hierarchy descending from God, through the nine orders of angels, to humankind, the animal kingdom, the vegetable kingdom, the minerals; the social hierarchy which forms part of this chain, and is therefore divinely sanctioned; the Ptolemaic cosmology, in which the central earth is surrounded by rotating spheres carrying the seven 'planets' and the fixed stars; the physics based on the four 'elements' of earth, water, fire, and air, themselves formed by combinations of the four 'qualities' hot, cold, wet, and dry; the corresponding theory of human physiology based on the four humours, melancholy, phlegm, blood, and choler, the combination of which determines a person's 'complexion' or temperament; and the complicated set of parallelisms which had been built up between these different areas of thought.

It does not follow that the whole of this complicated web of theory was accepted uncritically by everybody, even in the sixteenth century. It was, however, part of the intellectual equipment of every educated person, and is often assumed rather than stated: perhaps just one word in a sentence may give the clue, and the reader has to supply the rest. Consider, for example, the following stanza from Donne's poem 'A Valediction forbidding mourning':

> Dull sublunary lovers love
> (Whose soule is sense) cannot admit
> Absence, because it doth remove
> Those things which elemented it.

Why *sublunary*? Plainly it means 'beneath the moon', but what are the implications of this? In the traditional cosmology, the sphere carrying the moon was the one nearest to the earth: it marked the boundary between things earthly and things heavenly. Below the sphere of the moon was the world of the four ele-

255

ments, which underwent constant transformations. The heavens, on the other hand, were not composed of the four elements, but of a fifth element, the quintessence, which was perfect and immutable. Below the sphere of the moon, therefore, was the world of mutability and imperfection, while above it was the world of immutability and perfection. Donne is not merely implying that the inferior kind of love is ordinary, mundane: he is also implying that, by its very nature, it is subject to change. By contrast, the love between the poet and his mistress is perfect and immutable, like the universe above the sphere of the moon. These implications would have been plain to the original readers of the poem.

Again, consider a familiar couplet from Marvell's poem 'To his Coy Mistress':

> My Vegetable Love should grow
> Vaster then Empires, and more slow.

Why *vegetable*? In the Great Chain of Being, every grade had some particular quality at which it excelled. The excellence of humankind lay in their power of reason. The beasts excelled in their power of movement, and in the acuity of their senses, while minerals excelled in their hardness and durability. The quality at which plants excelled was growth. Marvell is drawing on a whole cosmological system to suggest the power of growth possessed by his love, which is like that of the vegetable kingdom. At this date, the associations of *vegetable* were not culinary (carrots and turnips in the kitchen): this use of the word did not arise until the second half of the eighteenth century. The suggestion is rather of the slow growth of something like an oak tree.

My third example is more problematical. It is a stanza from George Herbert's lovely poem 'Vertue':

> Sweet rose, whose hue angrie and brave
> Bids the rash gazer wipe his eye:
> Thy root is ever in its grave,
>   And thou must die.

Why *rash* gazer? There is nothing obviously rash in looking at a rose. F. E. Hutchinson, in his edition of Herbert, quotes a parallel from Spenser's *Faerie Queene*:

> So passing persant and so wondrous bright
> That quite bereau'd the rash beholders sight.

But this does not help much, for it obviously *is* rash to gaze at something which is so bright that it blinds you. My own view is that Herbert's *rash* has a precise implication: the gazer is not just any man, but one who resembles the rose in temperament. The colour red was associated with the humour called *choler* (hot and dry), an excess of which made a person violent and irascible (and therefore rash). The rose is *angrie and brave* in hue: its splendid red colour shows that it is choleric in temperament. The man who gazes at the rose has the same choleric temperament: he is *rash*; and, perceiving the resemblance between the rose and himself, weeps for its inevitable death (and his own).

During the seventeenth century, under the pressure of social and political change and of the new science, this traditional world view gave way to a different one. In astronomy, biology, chemistry, and physics, the old ideas were supplanted as serious scientific concepts by new ones. This indeed began to happen in the sixteenth century in advanced European thought, with the work of Paracelsus and Copernicus (though we have to remember that Copernicus retained the system of spheres). Early in the seventeenth century came the work of Kepler (the three laws of planetary motion) and of Harvey (circulation of the blood), while the great achievements of Galileo Galilei in physics and astronomy dominate the central part of the Early Modern period. But lay opinion, even educated lay opinion, lagged far behind, and it was only in the second half of the seventeenth century that the old concepts were supplanted. In *Paradise Lost* (1667), Milton still adheres to the old geocentric picture of the universe, spheres and all, even though he knew all about current heliocentric theories.

In the seventeenth century, the general effect of the new scientific ideas was to encourage a more mechanical view of the world. In the sixteenth century, on the other hand, the scientific development that probably had the greatest effect on English lay thought was that in anatomy. The great work of the Belgian anatomist Vesalius, *De humani corporis fabrica* (1543), with its wonderful plates, seems to have made a deep impression on the Elizabethan imagination. The word *anatomy* became commonly used in a figurative sense, meaning 'analysis' (but often with the implication that something was amiss, and surgery needed). The word occurs in the titles of many books in the middle of the Early Modern period, from Lyly's *Euphues: the Anatomy of Wit* (1579) to Burton's *Anatomy of Melancholy* (1621). But *anatomy* was also frequently used in its non-figurative senses, meaning 'the science of anatomy', 'a dissection', 'the object dissected'. There is an example in Jonson's *Volpone* (1607), when the jealous Corvino threatens his wife:

> Not looke toward the windore: if thou dost –
> (Nay stay, heare this) let me not prosper, Whore,
> But I will make thee an *Anatomy*,
> Dissect thee mine owne selfe, and read a *lecture*
> Vpon thee, to the citty, and in publique.

The reference is to the carrying out of public dissections by eminent

257

practitioners, who would simultaneously lecture. Corvino uses *anatomy* in the sense 'a subject for dissection, the object dissected'. The whole idea is typical of his obsessive imagination: he recurrently imagines his wife exposed to public view, while he himself commits physical violence on her.

Besides assimilating the earlier scientific ideas, we have to bear in mind the pervasiveness of religious ideas and of class concepts. Words with Christian connotations came so naturally that they are often used, apparently with no sense of incongruity, in non-Christian contexts, for example in plays set in pagan times, or in arguments with non-Christians. An example of the latter can be seen in *The Merchant of Venice*, when Portia exhorts the Jew, Shylock, to show mercy: she does so by referring to the Lord's Prayer, and by invoking Christian concepts such as salvation.

As for class connotations, we have already looked at a few words – *Mr*, *lady*, *gentleman*. The words *gentleman* and *gentlewoman* are probably the most important class-defining terms in use in the period, for they mark the divide between the privileged and the unprivileged. They could be used to denote all people of gentle rank, including esquires, knights, and peers, right up to the sovereign. In *Hamlet*, Laertes, who is a nobleman, is referred to as a gentleman ('pardon't as you are a Gentleman'). In *Henry V*, Ancient Pistol claims to be 'As good a Gentleman as the Emperor'. But the words could also be used to denote one particular rank in that gentle hierarchy, namely the lowest. In this sense, the word *gentleman* can be used as a term of contrast to *knight*, *lord*, *duke*, and so on. This is seen in the passage in *Henry V* in which the king is given a list of the French dead at Agincourt, categorised as princes, nobles, knights, esquires, and gallant gentlemen. This is also the meaning of the word when it is suffixed to a name, as when Nash's *Pierce Penniless* (1592) says on its title-page that it is 'Written by *Thomas Nash* Gentleman'. On the other hand the *Poems* (1645) of Waller, who was decidedly a cut above Nash socially, were 'Written by Mr. *Ed. Waller* of *Beckonsfield*, Esquire'.

On the other hand, many words with class connotations were ones referring to non-gentle rank. Some of these were purely neutral descriptive terms, such as *artificer*, *burgess*, *citizen*, *husbandman*, and *yeoman*, all of which occur in Smith's *De Republica Anglorum*. There were other words, however, which were often used pejoratively, at any rate when used by the gentry about the lower orders. Such are *base*, *cit* 'citizen', *mechanic(al)*, *peasant*, *popular*, and *vulgar*, which all had class implications. Sometimes these are obvious enough, as when Pistol says to the disguised Henry V:

> Discusse vnto me, art thou Officer, or art thou base, common, and popular?

Sometimes, however, the class implications are less obvious to the present-day reader. There is a well-known episode in *The Winter's Tale* in which

Polixenes argues with Perdita about the propriety of producing hybrid plants, of using art to interfere with nature. At one point he says

> you see (sweet Maid) we marry
> A gentler Sien, to the wildest Stocke,
> And make conceyue a barke of baser kinde
> By bud of nobler race.

He is talking about the horticultural techniques of grafting, but this is also a metaphor for human marriage: the key words can apply both to plants and to human families (*marry, scion, stock, conceive, race*). We then notice the class connotations of *gentler*, *baser*, and *nobler*: there is an implicit reference to marriages between the nobility and plebeians. One of the ironies here is that Perdita, the supposed peasant girl who is betrothed to a prince, is the one who opposes hybridisation. On the other hand, Polixenes, who defends it, is about to denounce this proposed marriage and forbid it.

FURTHER READING

On semantics in general, see Ullmann (1959), Lyons (1977), and Leech (1981). Stern (1964) deals with change of meaning in English. A shorter book, providing a good introduction, is Waldron (1979). Lewis (1967) examines the changes in meaning which have taken place in ten important English words; it is an entertaining book, and easy to read. Books on single words include Knox (1961) and Tucker (1972).

The essential dictionary is the OED, but there are a number of helpful shorter works, such as Onions (1919) and Onions (1966). Copley (1961) is a historical dictionary of about 250 words which are often misunderstood by present-day readers. Partridge (1968) contains much useful material on bawdy words, but perhaps does not distinguish clearly enough between regular and nonce usages.

A good introduction to the world view of the sixteenth century is provided by Tillyard (1943). The effect of Vesalius on the Elizabethan imagination has been discussed by Benton (1970).

Appendix

FURTHER PASSAGES
FOR STUDY

1.

On solely linguistic grounds, assign an approximate date to each of the following three passages of eModE prose. Obviously the range of possibilities is wide, especially as the passages are short, but try at any rate to suggest a period of (say) forty or fifty years within which each passage was written.

a.

Seyng there be so many poore vyllages in the countree abrode whiche can not fynde a shepeherde / there shold ye bestow your labours. there were conuenyent places for you to labour in / but now ye wyll be nowhere but in the houses of ryche men. ye face and crake vnder the name of popes / but your pryuyleges be not worth a strawe: but where as the bysshop, parsone, or vycare dooth not his duety. In my chyrche shall none of you preche so longe as I am the curate and haue my helthe. I am no bacheler, neyther saynt Martyn was ony bacheler, and yet he played the very bysshop. yf I lacke lernyng I wyll not aske it of you. Suppose ye that the worlde is yet so blynd and folysshe, that (whersoeuer they se saynt Domynyke or Fraunceys cote) they wyll thynke theyr sanctymony and holynes there to be? or is it to you ony mater at all what I do at my hous? what pageauntes ye play in your dennes, and what knauery ye vse with holy nonnes all the world knoweth ... To tell the what more was spoken I dare not. truly he handled those reuerend fathers with small reuerence. And none ende sholde haue ben, oneles Georgius had sygnyfied with waggyng of his hande, that he wolde say some thyng.

b.

Good things grow on verie hardlie at their first planting, bycause that profit, which theie promis at their entrie, hath not yet bene proued, and therefor wanteth the commendation of triall, which is the verie best mean to enforce persuasion: and their pretence to be profitable, vpon som probabilitie in sequele, is a great inducement in dede, but to those peple, which can forese ear theie fele, but of small importance to them, which cannot se till theie fele. Good things finde hard footing, when theie ar to be reformed after a corruption in vse, bycause of that enormitie which is in possession, and vsurpeth on their place, which hauing strengthened it self by all circumstances, that can dis-suade alteration, fighteth sore for it self, and hard against redresse, thorough the generall assistence of a preiudicate opinion in those mens heds, which might further the redresse ... To me it maie be replied, you medle in this matter alone, you do but truble your self: you can not turn the course, which is ordinarie and old, and therefore verie strong for you to striue against: this thing which you commend is not euerie mans ware: do you let it alone: if you will nedes write, turn your pen to other matters ... I know not anie book in this kinde so thoroughlie fitted for such a purpos, as I hope this shall proue. What there be in other kindes I will then shew mine opinion, when I com to their placing. I haue therefor fenced my hole choice in all these principles, with the best autoritie of most allowed writers, who commend the vse of them in one hole traine, which maie persuade vs thoroughlie to entertain them so, as their worthinesse deserues.

c.

Is that dissolution of body and soule, the last death that the body shall suffer (for of spirituall death wee speake not now)? It is not ... If we say, can this dust liue? perchance it cannot, it may be the meere dust of the earth, which neuer did liue, never shall. It may be the dust of that mans worme, which did liue, but shall no more. It may be the dust of another man, that concernes not him of whom it is askt ... I thanke him that prayes for me when the Bell tolles, but I thank him much more that Catechises mee, or preaches to mee, or instructs mee how to liue. *Fac hoc et viue*, there's my securitie, the mouth of the Lord hath sayd it, do this and thou shalt liue: But God neuer mentions, neuer seems to consider that death, the bodily, the naturall death. God doth not say, liue well and thou shalt dye well; But liue well here, and thou shalt liue well for euer. As the first part of a sentence peeces wel with the last, and neuer respects, neuer hearkens after the parenthesis that comes betweene, so doth a good life here flowe into an eternall life.

2.

The following is an extract from a work by the Scots poet William Dunbar, which was probably written in the early years of the sixteenth century. The punctuation has been modernised, as has the use of *u*, *v*, *ȝ* and *þ*. Study the passage, and point out the linguistic features which distinguish it from the standard southern language of the same period.

Apon the Midsummer evin, mirriest of nichtis,
I muvit furth allane neir ['almost'] as midnicht wes past,
Besyd ane gudlie grein garth, full of gay flouris,
Hegeit ['hedged, bordered'] of ane huge hicht ['height'] with hawthorne
   treis,
Quhairon ane bird on ane bransche so birst out hir notis
That never ane blythfullar bird was on the beuche ['bough'] harde
   ['heard'].
Quhat throw ['because of'] the sugarat sound of hir sang glaid ['glad'],
And throw the savour sanative ['healthful'] of the sueit flouris,
I drew in derne ['secrecy'] to the dyk ['wall'] to dirkin ['lurk'] efter
   mirthis.
The dew donkit ['wetted'] the daill, and dynnit ['made a noise'] the
   feulis.
I hard, under ane holyn ['holly'] hevinlie grein hewit ['hued'],
Ane hie speiche at my hand, with hautand ['proud'] wourdis;
With that in haist to the hege so hard I inthrang ['pushed in']
That I was heildit ['concealed'] with hawthorne and with heynd ['pleas-
   ant'] leveis:
Throw pykis ['sharp points'] of the plet ['intertwined'] thorne I presand-
   lie luikit
Gif ['if'] ony persoune wald approche within that pleasand garding.

3.

The following excerpts come from an early seventeenth-century play, and are put into the mouth of a Puritan from the citizen classes. Point to the features in the passage which, rightly or wrongly, were commonly believed at that time to characterise Puritan speech.

Verily, for the disease of longing, it is a disease, a carnall disease, or appetite incident to women: and as it is carnall, and incident, it is natu-rall, very naturall: Now Pigge, it is a meat, and a meat that is nourishing, and may be long'd for, and so consequently eaten: but in the Fayre, and as a Bartholmew pig, it cannot be eaten, for to eat it so, is a spice of Idolatry, and you make the Fayre, no better then one of the high places. This, I take it, is the state of the question. A high place ... Surely, it may be otherwise, but it hath a face of offence, with the weak, a great face, a foule face, but that face may haue a vaile put ouer it, and be shaddowed as it were, it may be eaten, and in the Fayre, I take it, in a Booth, the tents of the wicked: the place is not much, not very much, we may be religious in the midst of the prophane, so it be eaten with a reformed mouth, with sobriety: for, should she goe there, as taking pride in the place, or delight in the vncleane dressing, to feed the vanity of the eye, or the lust of the palat, it were not well, it were not fit, it were abominable, and not good ... In the way of comfort to the weak, I will goe, and eat. I will eate exceedingly, and prophesie; there may be good vse made of it, too, now I think on't: by the publike eating of Swines flesh, to professe our hate, and loathing of Iudaisme, whereof the brethren stand taxed. I will therefore eate, yea, I will eate exceedingly.

4.

The following is an extract from a comedy written in about 1605. Point to the features in the passage which help to give the illusion of informal everyday speech.

Lucre. Her name I prethee?

Host. It runnes there in the writings sir, among her Lands, widdow Medler.

Lucre. Meddler? Masse haue I neere heard of that widdow?

Host. Yes, I warrant you, haue you sir, not the riche widdowe in Staffordsheere?

Lucre. Cuds me, there tis indeede, thou hast put me into memorie, there's a widdow indeed, ah that I were a batchiler agen.

Host. No doubt your worship might do much then, but she's fayrely promist to a batchiler already.

Lucre. Ah what is he I prethee?

Host. A Country Gentleman too, one whome your worship knowes not Ime sure: has spent some fewe follies in his youth, but marriage by my fayth begins to call him home, my Mistris loues him sir, and loue couers faults you know, one maister Wit-good if euer you haue heard of the Gentleman.

Lucre. Ha? Wit-good sayst thou?

Host. Thats his name indeede sir; my Mistris is like to bring him to a goodly seate yonder, foure hundred a yeare by my faith.

Lucre. But I pray take me with you.

Host. I sir?

Lucre. What Countryman might this yong Wit-good be?

Host. A Lestershire gentleman sir.

Lucre. My Nephew, by the Masse my Nephew, Ile fetch out more of this yfaith, a simple Country fellow, Ile workte out of him [*Aside*], – and is that Gentleman sayst thou presently to marrie her?

Host. Fayth he brought her vp to towne sir, has the best card in all the bunch fort, her heart: and I know my Mistris will bee married, ere she goe downe, nay Ile sweare that, for she's none of those widdowes that will goe downe first, and bee married after, she hates that I can tell you sir.

Lucre. By my faith sir, shee is like to haue a proper Gentleman and a comelie, Ile giue her that gift.

Host. Why do's your worship know him sir?

Lucre. I know him! does not all the world knowe him, can a man of such exquisite qualities be hid vnder a bushell?

5.

The following are brief extracts from Thomas Wilson's *Arte of Rhetorique* (1553). Try to find answers to the questions that follow each extract.

a.

> Any one that will handle any matter, must fasten his mynde first of all, vppon these fiue especiall pointes that followe, and learne them euery one: (i) Inuention of matter. (ii) Disposition of the same. (iii) Elocution. (iv) Memorie. (v) Utteraunce.

In traditional rhetorical theory, what was the function of each of these five? What methods were recommended for the achieving of each of these functions?

b.

> There are seuen partes in euery Oration: (i) The Enterance or beginning. (ii) The Narration. (iii) The Proposition. (iv) The Deuision or seueral parting of things. (v) The confirmation. (vi) The confutation. (vii) The Conclusion.

What was the function of each of these seven parts? Did all the traditional rhetorics agree with this seven-part structure? Wilson says 'every oration'; for which of the three main types of oration was this structure originally developed?

c.

> There are three kindes of causes or Orations, which serue for euery matter.

What were the three types of oration, and in what circumstances was each to be used?

6.

In the following pieces of rhyming verse from the Early Modern period, the italicised words do not rhyme in PresE. Could any of them have been exact rhymes in eModE? If so, explain why they are no longer exact rhymes.

a. I am not he suche eloquence to boste
   To make the crow singing as the *swanne*,
   Nor call the lyon of cowarde bestes the moste,
   That cannot take a mows as the cat *can*.

b. Tis not enough that through the cloude thou *breake*,
   To dry the raine on my storme-beaten face,
   For no man well of such a salue can *speake*,
   That heales the wound, and cures not the disgrace.

c. But I protest I loue to heare him *lie*,
   And I will vse him for my *Minstrelsie*.

d. This is the flower that smiles on euerie *one*,
   To shew his teeth as white as Whales *bone*.

e. *King.* Norfolke, throw down we bidde; there is no *boote*.
   Mow. My selfe I throw (dread Soueraigne) at thye *foot*.

f. Nor Friends, nor Foes, to me welcome you *are*,
   Things past redresse, are now with me past *care*.

g. Against that time when thou shalt strangely *passe*,
   And scarcely greete me with that sunne, thine eye,
   When loue conuerted from the thing it *was*
   Shall reasons finde of setled grauitie

h.   those whom you curse
   Haue felt the worst of Deaths destroying *wound*,
   And lye full low, grau'd in the hollow *ground*.

7.

Ye old mule that thinck your self so fayre,
Leve of with craft your beautie to repaire,
    For it is true without any fable
    No man setteth more by riding in your saddell;
To muche travaill so do your train apaire,
        Ye old mule!
With fals savours though you deceve th'ayer,
Who so tast you shall well perceve your layer
    Savoureth som what of a Kappurs [colt's] stable,
        Ye old mule!
Ye must now serve to market and to faire,
All for the burden for pannyers a paire;

For syns gray heres ben powdered in your sable,
The thing ye seke for you must your self enable
To pourchase it by payement and by prayer,
Ye old mule!

(Sir Thomas Wyatt)

a. The poem is clearly addressed to a woman. What can we deduce about this woman from the opening word of the poem, *Ye*?

b. What kind of effect is achieved by the collocation *Ye old mule*? What characteristics have traditionally been attributed (rightly or wrongly) to mules? The mule is a hybrid between an ass and a mare: what characteristic of hybrids might be relevant to the poem?

c. With the aid of the OED, suggest appropriate meanings for the following expressions in the poem: (i) *craft*; (ii) *setteth ... by*; (iii) *travaill*; (iv) *train*; (v) *tast*; (vi) *layer*.

d. The poem is in a strict poetic form. Can you identify this form? In what kind of poetry would you expect to find it? What is the effect of Wyatt's use of it in this somewhat bawdy poem?

8.

Though no man lesser feares the Greeks then I,
As farre as touches my particular: yet dread Priam,
There is no Lady of more softer bowels,
More spungie, to sucke in the sense of Feare,
More ready to cry out, who knowes what followes   5
Then Hector is: the wound of peace is surety,
Surety secure: but modest Doubt is cal'd
The Beacon of the wise: the tent that searches
To'th bottome of the worst. Let Helen go,
Since the first sword was drawne about this question,   10
Euery tythe soule 'mongst many thousand dismes,
Hath bin as deere as Helen: I meane of ours:
If we haue lost so many tenths of ours
To guard a thing not ours, nor worth to vs
(Had it our name) the valew of one ten;   15
What merit's in that reason which denies
The yeelding of her vp?

This is a speech from a play first published in 1609. With the aid of the OED where necessary, explain the meaning (or meanings) of the following words and phrases in this context:

i. touches (2); ii. my particular (2); iii. softer bowels (3); iv. spungie (4);

266

v. the wound of peace (6); vi. surety (6); vii. secure (7); viii. modest Doubt (7); ix. tent (8); x. tythe (11); xi. dismes (11); xii. deere (12); xiii. I meane of ours (12); xiv. not ours (14); xv. Had it our name (15).

SELECT BIBLIOGRAPHY

The Bibliography is in two parts. Part I lists the primary texts quoted or referred to in the book. Part II gives a selection of secondary texts. For the primary texts, the place of publication is London unless otherwise stated.

PART I. PRIMARY TEXTS

A. B., *Merie Tales of the mad men of Gotam*, ed. S. J. Kahrl. Evanston, Illinois: Northwestern University Press (1965)

Anon, *The Trial and Execution of King Charles I. Facsimiles of the contemporary official accounts*, Leeds: Scolar Press (1966)

Ascham, Roger, *Toxophilus* (1545)

Ascham, Roger, *The Scholemaster* (1570)

Awdeley, John, *The Fraternitye of Vacabondes*, ed. E. Viles & F. J. Furnivall: EETS (1869)

Bacon, Francis, *Of the proficience and aduancement of Learning* (1605)

Bacon, Francis, *The Essayes or Counsells, Ciuill and Morall* (1625)

Bacon, Francis, *The Works*, ed. J. Spedding, R. L. Ellis, & D. D. Heath, 14 volumes (1857–74)

Barclay, Alexander, *The Egloges of Alexander Barclay, priest*, n.d. (?1548)

Barrett, Robert, *The Theorike and Praktike of Moderne Warres* (1598)

Beaumont, Francis, *The Knight of the Burning Pestle* (1613)

Bentley, Richard, *A Dissertation upon the Epistles of Phalaris. With an answer to the objections of the Honourable Charles Boyle* (1699)

Bible, The Holy, conteyning the Old Testament, and the New (1611) ('The King James Bible')

Blount, Thomas, *Glossographia* (1656)

The booke of the common praier and administracion of the Sacramentes (1549)

Boorde, Andrew, *The fyrst boke of the Introduction of knowledge*, n.d. (?1550)

Bullokar, John, *An English Expositor* (1616)

Bullokar, William, *Pamphlet for Grammar* (1586)

Bullokar, William, *A Short Introduction or Guiding 1580–81*, ed. B. Danielsson & R. C. Alston, Leeds Texts and Monographs N.S.I.: University of Leeds (1966)

SELECT BIBLIOGRAPHY

Bunyan, John, *The Pilgrim's Progress from this World to That which is to come* (1678)
Butler, Charles, *The English Grammar*. Oxford (1633)
Camden, William, R*emaines of a Greater Worke* (1605)
Cawdrey, Robert, *A Table Alphabeticall* (1604)
Caxton, William, *The Prologues and Epilogues*, ed. W. J. B. Crotch: EETS (1928)
Cheke, Sir John, *The Gospel according to Saint Matthew*, ed. J. Goodwin (1843)
Clarke, Sir William, *The Clarke Papers*, ed. C. H. Firth, Vol. 1: Camden Society N.S. 49 (1891)
Cockeram, Henry, *The English Dictionarie* (1623)
Coles, Elisha, *An English Dictionary* (1676)
Congreve, William, *The Old Batchelour, a Comedy* (1693)
Congreve, William, *Love for Love: A Comedy* (1695)
Congreve, William, *The Way of the World, A Comedy* (1700)
Cooper, Christopher, *Grammatica Linguae Anglicanae* (1685)
Crashaw, Richard, *Steps to the Temple* (1646)
Daines, Simon, *Orthoepia Anglicana* (1640)
Daniel, Samuel, *Delia* (1592)
Davenant, Sir William, *Gondibert: an Heroick Poem* (1651)
Dekker, Thomas, *The Shomakers Holiday* (1600)
Digges, Leonard, & Digges, Thomas, *An Arithmeticall Militare Treatise, named Stratioticos* (1579)
Donne, John, *Poems* (1633)
Donne, John, *LXXX Sermons* (1640)
Dowland, John, *Second Book of Airs 1600*, ed. E. H. Fellowes: Stainer & Bell (1922)
Drayton, Michael, *Poems* (1619)
Dryden, John, *Of Dramatick Poesie, an Essay* (1668)
Dryden, John, *Marriage A-la-Mode. A Comedy* (1673)
Dryden, John, *The Works of Virgil* (1697)
Dryden, John, *Fables Ancient and Modern* (1700)
Dunbar, William, *Poems*, ed. J. Kinsley. Oxford: Clarendon Press (1958)
Elyot, Sir Thomas, *The boke named the Gouernour* (1531)
Elyot, Sir Thomas, *Of the knowledg whiche maketh a wise man* (1533)
Elyot, Sir Thomas, *The Castell of Helth, corrected and in some places amended, by the first author therof* (1541)
Etherege, Sir George, *The Man of Mode, or Sir Fopling Flutter* (1676)
Fairfax, Nathaniel, *A Treatise of the Bulk and Selvedge of the World* (1674)
Fellowes, E. H. (ed.), *English Madrigal Verse 1588–1632*, third edition. Oxford: Clarendon Press (1967)
Fenner, Dudley, *The Artes of Logike and Rhetorike* (1584)
Fiennes, Celia, *The Journeys of Celia Fiennes*, ed. C. Morris, revised edition: Cresset Press (1949)
Ford, John, *'Tis Pitty Shee's a Whore* (1633)
Ford, Thomas, 'I know a Lady', in Fellowes (1967)
Fox, George, *The Journal of George Fox*, ed. N. Penney, two volumes. Cambridge: Cambridge University Press (1911)
Fox, George, Stubs, John, & Furly, Benjamin, *A Battle-Door for Teachers and Professors to Learn Singular and Plural* (1660)
Foxe, John, *Actes and monuments of these latter and perillous dayes* (1563)
Fraunce, Abraham, *The Arcadian Rhetorike*, n.d. (?1588)
Gascoigne, George, *Supposes*, in *A Hundreth sundrie Flowres* (1573)
Gil, Alexander, *Logonomia Anglica* (1619)
Glanvill, Joseph, *The Vanity of Dogmatizing* (1661)

269

SELECT BIBLIOGRAPHY

Grammaire générale et raisonnée, Paris (1660)

Greaves, Paul, *Grammatica Anglicana* (1594)

Greene, Robert, *The Scottish Historie of Iames the fourth* (1598)

Hakluyt, Richard, *The Principall Nauigations, Voiages, Traffiques and Discoueries of the English Nation*, three volumes (1598–1600)

Harington, Sir John, *A New Discourse of a Stale Subiect, called The Metamorphosis of Aiax*, ed. E. S. Donno: Routledge & Kegan Paul (1962)

Harman, Thomas, *A Caueat or Warening, for commen Cursetors* (1567)

Hart, John, *John Hart's Works on English Orthography and Pronunciation*, ed. B. Danielsson, two volumes. Stockholm: Almqvist & Wiksell (1955–63)

Harvey, Gabriel, *Foure Letters* (1592)

Harvey, Gabriel, *Pierces Supererogation* (1593)

Henslowe, Philip, *Henslowe's Diary*, ed. R. A. Foakes & R. T. Rickert. Cambridge: Cambridge University Press (1961)

Henryson, Robert, *The Poems*, ed. Denton Fox. Oxford: Clarendon Press (1981)

Herbert, George, *The Temple*, Cambridge (1633)

Heywood, Thomas, *A Woman kilde with Kindnesse* (1607)

Hobbes, Thomas, *Leviathen* (1651)

Hoby, Thomas, *The Courtyer of Count Baldessar Castilio* (1561)

Howard, Henry, *see* Surrey, Earl of

Hume, Alexander, *Of the Orthographie and Congruitie of the Britan Tongue*, ed. H. B. Wheatley: EETS (1865)

Jonson, Ben, *The comicall Satyre of Euery Man out of his humor* (1600)

Jonson, Ben, *Volpone or the Foxe* (1607)

Jonson, Ben, *Ben Ionson his Case is Alterd* (1609)

Jonson, Ben, *The Alchemist* (1612)

Jonson, Ben, *The Silent Woman* (1620)

Jonson, Ben, *Bartholomew Fayre* (1631)

Jonson, Ben, *The English Grammar*, in volume two of *The workes of Benjamin Jonson* (1640)

Latimer, Hugh, 'Sermon on the Ploughers', in *Specimens of English Literature 1394–1570*, ed. W. W. Skeat. Oxford: Clarendon Press (1871)

Lever, Ralph, *The Arte of Reason, rightly termed, Witcraft* (1573)

Lily, William, *A Shorte Introduction of Grammar* (1549)

Lisle, William, *A Saxon Treatise* (1623)

Locke, John, *An Essay concerning Humane Understanding* (1690)

Locke, John, *The Educational Writings*, ed. J. L. Axtell: Cambridge: Cambridge University Press (1968)

Lyly, John, *Euphues. The Anatomy of Wyt*. n.d. (?1579)

Marlowe, Christopher, *Tamburlaine the Great* (1590)

Marlowe, Christopher, *Hero and Leander* (1598)

Marprelate, Martin (pseud.), *The Marprelate Tracts (1588–89)*, Leeds: Scolar Press (1967)

Marvell, Andrew, *Miscellaneous Poems* (1681)

Middleton, Thomas, *The Reuengers Tragœdie* (1607)

Middleton, Thomas, *A Trick to catch the Old-one* (1608)

Middleton, Thomas, *A Chast Mayd in Cheape-side* (1630)

Milton, John, *Areopagitica* (1644)

Milton, John, *Paradise Lost. A Poem Written in Ten Books* (1667)

Milton, John, *Paradise Regain'd. A Poem in IV Books. To which is added Samson Agonistes* (1671)

More, Sir Thomas, *see* Robinson, Ralph

SELECT BIBLIOGRAPHY

Morley, Thomas, *Madrigalls to foure voyces* (1594)
Mulcaster, Richard, *The First Part of the Elementarie* (1582)
Nash, Thomas, *Pierce Penilesse his Supplication to the Diuell* (1592)
Nash, Thomas, *Strange Newes* (1592)
Nash, Thomas, *Haue with you to Saffron-walden* (1596)
Otway, Thomas, *Venice Preserv'd, or, the Plot discover'd* (1682)
Peacham, Henry, *The Garden of Eloquence* (1577)
Pettie, George, *The ciuile conuersation of M. Steeuen Guazzo* (1581)
Phillips, Edward, *The New World of English Words* (1658)
Port Royal Grammar, *see* Grammaire générale et raisonnée
Puttenham, George, *The Arte of English Poesie* (1589)
Ralegh, Sir Walter, *The discouerie of the large, rich, and bewtiful empyre of Guiana* (1596)
Ralegh, Sir Walter, *The Poems*, ed. A. Latham: Routledge & Kegan Paul (1951)
Ramus, Petrus, *The Logike of the Moste Excellent Philosopher P. Ramus Martyr* (1574)
Rich, Barnaby, *A Path-way to Military practise* (1587)
Robinson, Ralph, *A frutefull, pleasaunt, and wittie worke, of the beste state of a publique weale, and of the new yle, called Vtopia* (1556)
Rochester, John Wilmot, Earl of, *Poems on Several Occasions*, Antwerp, n.d.
Rosseter, Philip, *A Booke of Ayres* (1601)
Shakespeare, William, *The Tragedy of King Richard the third* (1597)
Shakespeare, William, *The History of Henrie the Fourth* (1598)
Shakespeare, William, *The Tragicall Historie of Hamlet, Prince of Denmarke* (1604)
Shakespeare, William, *M. William Shak-speare: His True Chronicle Historie of the life and death of King Lear and his three Daughters* (1608)
Shakespeare, William, *Sonnets* (1609)
Shakespeare, William, *Mr William Shakespeares Comedies, Histories, & Tragedies* ('The First Folio') (1623)
Sharpham, Edward, *Cupids Whirligig* (1607)
Sidney, Sir Philip, *The Defence of Poesie* (1595)
Skelton, John, *Pithy pleasaunt and profitable workes* (1568)
Smith, Sir Thomas, *De Republica Anglorum* (1583)
Spenser, Edmund, *The Shepheardes Calender* (1579)
Spenser, Edmund, *Amoretti and Epithalamion* (1595)
Spenser, Edmund, *Prothalamion* (1596)
Spenser, Edmund, *The Faerie Queene* (1596)
Sprat, Thomas, *The History of the Royal-Society of London* (1667)
Surrey, Henry Howard, Earl of, *Songes and Sonettes* ('Tottel's Miscellany') (1557)
Tyndale, William, *The obedience of a Christen man* (1528)
Tyndale, William, *The newe Testament, dylygently corrected and compared with the Greke*, Antwerp (1534)
Udall, Nicholas, *Roister Doister*, ed. G. Scheurweghs. Louvain: Librairie Universitaire (1939)
Vanbrugh, Sir John, *The Relapse: or, Virtue in Danger* (1697)
Verstegan, Richard, *A Restitution of Decayed Intelligence*, Antwerp (1605)
Waller, Edmund, *Poems* (1645)
Wallis, John, *Grammatica Linguae Anglicanae* (1653)
Wallis, John, *Grammar of the English Language, with translation and commentary by J. A. Kemp*, Longman (1972)
Walton, Izaak, *The Compleat Angler* (1653)
Webster, John, *The White Diuell* (1612)
Wharton, Jeremiah, *The English-Grammar* (1654)

SELECT BIBLIOGRAPHY

Wilbye, John, *The first set of English madrigals* (1598)
Wilkins, John, *An Essay Towards a Real Character, And a Philosophical Language* (1668) ·
Wilson, Sir Thomas, *The Arte of Rhetorique* (1553)
Wyatt, Sir Thomas, *Collected Poems*, ed. K. Muir. Routledge & Kegan Paul (1949)
Wyatt, Sir Thomas, *Collected Poems*, ed. K. Muir & P. Thomson. Liverpool: Liverpool University Press (1969)
Wycherley, William, *The Country-Wife, a Comedy* (1675)

PART II. SECONDARY TEXTS

Abbot, E. A. (1870) *A Shakesperian Grammar*, third edition, London: Macmillan
Adams, V. (1973) *An Introduction to Modern English Word-Formation*, London: Longman
Aitchison, J. (1981) *Language Change: Progress or Decay?*, London: Fontana Paperbacks
Alston, R. C. (1965–87) *A bibliography of the English language from the invention of printing to the year 1800*, twelve volumes, Leeds: printed for the author
Atkinson, M., Kilby, D., & Roca, I. (1988). *Foundations of General Linguistics*, second edition, London: Allen and Unwin
Baldwin, T. W. (1944) *William Shakspere's Small Latine & Lesse Greeke*, two volumes, Urbana: University of Illinois Press
Bambas, R. C. (1947) 'Verb Forms in *-s* and *eth* in Early Modern English Prose', *Journal of English and Germanic Philology* XLVI 183–7
Barber, C. (1964) *Linguistic Change in Present-Day English*, Edinburgh: Oliver & Boyd
Barber, C. (1981a) *York Notes on Shakespeare, Richard III*, Harlow: Longman
Barber, C. (1981b) *York Notes on Shakespeare, As You Like It*, Harlow: Longman
Barber, C. (1981c) '*You* and *thou* in Shakespeare's *Richard III*', *Leeds Studies in English* NS XII, 273–89. Reprinted in Salmon & Burness 1987
Barber, C. (1983) *Poetry in English: an Introduction*, London: Macmillan
Barber, C. (1987) *Macmillan Master Guides. Richard II by William Shakespeare*, Basingstoke: Macmillan
Barber, C. (1993) *The English Language: a Historical Introduction*, Cambridge: Cambridge University Press
Bately, J. M. (1964) 'Dryden's Revisions in the *Essay of Dramatic Poesy*: the Preposition at the End of the Sentence and the Expression of the Relative', *Review of English Studies* N.S. XV 268–82
Bauer, L. (1983) *English Word Formation*, Cambridge: Cambridge University Press
Baugh, A. C. (1993) *A History of the English Language*, fourth edition, London: Routledge & Kegan Paul
Bennett, H. S. (1973) *Chaucer and the Fifteenth Century*, second edition, Oxford: Clarendon Press
Benton, V. G. (1970) *The Prose Style of Thomas Nash*, unpublished doctoral dissertation: University of Leeds
Blake, N. F. (1969) *Caxton and his World*, London: Deutsch
Blake, N. F. (1983) *Shakespeare's Language: an Introduction*, London: Macmillan
Blake, N. F. (ed.) (1992) *The Cambridge History of the English Language: Vol. 2, 1066–1476*, Cambridge: Cambridge University Press
Bloomfield, L. (1935) *Language*, revised edition, London: Allen & Unwin
Bolton, W. F. & Crystal, D. (eds) (1966–9). *The English Language*, two volumes, Cambridge: Cambridge University Press

SELECT BIBLIOGRAPHY

Bolton, W. F. (1992) *Shakespeare's English: Language in the History Plays*, Oxford: Blackwell

Brinkley, R. F. (1967) *Arthurian Legend in the Seventeeth Century*, London: Frank Cass

Brook, G. L. (1965) *English Dialects*, second edition, London: Deutsch

Brook, G. L. (1976). *The Language of Shakespeare*, London: Deutsch

Brown, R. & Gilman, A. (1960) 'The pronouns of power and solidarity', in Sebeok, T. A. (ed.), *Style in Language*. Cambridge, Mass.: MIT

Brown, R., & Gilman, A. (1989) 'Politeness theory and Shakespeare's four major tragedies', *Language in Society* 18, 159–212

Bruce, F. F. (1961) *The English Bible. A History of Translations*, London: Lutterworth Press

Brunner, K. (1950–51) *Die englische Sprache. Ihre geschichliche Entwicklung*, two volumes, Halle (Saale): Max Niemeyer

Burton-Roberts, N. (1986) *Analysing Sentences*, London: Longman

Calvo, C. (1992) 'Pronouns of address and social negotiation in *As You Like It*', *Language and Literature* 1, 5–27

Carney, E. (1994) *A Survey of English Spelling*, London: Routledge

Cercignani, F. (1981) *Shakespeare's Works and Elizabethan Pronunciation*, Oxford: Clarendon Press

Chomsky, N. (1966) *Cartesian Linguistics*, London: Harper & Row

Conley, C. H. (1927) T*he First English Translators of the Classics*, New Haven: Yale University Press

Copley, J. (1961) *Shift of Meaning*, London: Oxford University Press

Craigie, Sir W. A. et al. (1931–88, ongoing). *A Dictionary of the Older Scottish Tongue*, Volumes 1–7, Chicago: Chicago University Press

Craigie, Sir W. A. (1946) *The Critique of Pure English from Caxton to Smollett*, S.P.E. Tract No. LXV, Oxford: Clarendon Press

Crystal, D. (1995) *The Cambridge Encyclopedia of the English Language*, Cambridge: Cambridge University Press

Crystal D. & Davy, D. (1969) *Investigating English Style*, London: Longman

Dahl, T. (1951) *An Inquiry into Aspects of the Language of Thomas Deloney*, Aarhus: Universitetsforlaget

Denison, D. (1993) *English Historical Syntax*, London: Longman

Devitt, A. J. (1989) *Standardizing Written English*, Cambridge: Cambridge University Press

Dobson, E. J. (1968) *English Pronunciation 1500–1700*, two volumes, second edition, Oxford: Clarendon Press

Douglas, D. C. (1939) *English Scholars*, London: Cape

Ekwall, E. (1975) *A History of Modern English Sounds and Morphology*, translated and edited by A. Ward, Oxford: Blackwell

Ellegård, A. (1953) *The Auxiliary Do. The Establishment and Regulation of its Use in English*, Stockholm: Almqvist & Wiksell

Emma, R. D. (1964) *Milton's Grammar*, The Hague: Mouton

Finkenstaedt, T. (1963) *You und Thou. Studien zur Anrede im englischen*, Berlin: Walter de Gruyter

Franz, W. (1939) *Die Sprache Shakespeares in Vers und Prosa*, Halle (Saale): Max Niemeyer

Fridén, G. (1948) *Studies on the Tenses of the English Verb from Chaucer to Shakespeare*, Upsala: Lundequist

Gimson, A. C. (1989) *An Introduction to the Pronunciation of English*, fourth edition, London: Edward Arnold

Görlach, M. (1991) *Introduction to Early Modern English*, Cambridge: Cambridge University Press

Halle, M. & Keyser, S. J. (1971) *English Stress*, London: Harper & Row

Haller, W. (1938) *The Rise of Puritanism*, New York: Columbia University Press

Halliday, M. A. K. (1961) 'Categories of the Theory of Grammar', *Word* 17, 241–92

Hill, C. (1958) *Puritanism and Revolution*, London: Secker & Warburg

Hogg, R. M. (ed.) (1992) *The Cambridge History of the English Language: Vol. 1. The Beginnings to 1066*, Cambridge: Cambridge University Press

Holmberg, B. (1964) *On the Concept of Standard English and the History of Modern English Pronunciation*, Lund: C. W. K. Gleerup

Hope, J. (1993) 'Second person singular pronouns in records of Early Modern spoken English', *Neuphilologische Mitteilungen* 1.XCIV, 83–100

Hope, J. (1994) *The Authorship of Shakespeare's Plays: a socio-historical linguistic study*, Cambridge: Cambridge University Press

Horn, W. (1954) *Laut und Leben. Englische Lautgeschichte der neueren Zeit (1400–1950)*, revised and edited by Martin Lehnert, two volumes, Berlin: Deutscher Verlag der Wissenschaften

Jacobsson, B. (1951) *Inversion in English with Special Reference to the Early Modern English Period*, Upsala: Almqvist & Wiksell

Jespersen, O. (1961) *A Modern English Grammar on Historical Principles*, new edition, seven volumes, London: Allen & Unwin

Jespersen, O. (1982) *Growth and Structure of the English Language*, tenth edition, Oxford: Blackwell

Jones, C. (1989) *A History of English Phonology*, Harlow: Longman

Jones, D. (1962) *The Phoneme: its Nature and Use*, second edition, Cambridge: Heffer

Jones, R. F. (1953) *The Triumph of the English Language*, Stanford California: Stanford University Press

Jordan, R. (1934) *Handbuch der mittelenglischen Grammatik*, Heidelberg: Carl Winter

Jordan, R. (1974) *Handbook of Middle English Grammar: Phonology*, translated and revised by E. J. Crook, The Hague: Mouton

Joseph, Sister Miriam (1947) *Shakespeare's Use of the Arts of Language*, New York: Columbia University Press

Kennedy, G. A. (1980) *Classical Rhetoric and its Christian and Secular Tradition from Ancient to Modern Times*, London: Croom Helm

King, A. H. (1941) *The Language of Satirized Characters in Poëtaster*, Lund: C. W. E. Gleerup

Knox, N. (1961) *The Word 'Irony' and its Context, 1500–1755*, Cambridge: Cambridge University Press

Kökeritz, H. (1953) *Shakespeare's Pronunciation*, New Haven: Yale University Press

Krapp, G. P. (1915) *The Rise of English Literary Prose*, New York: Frederick Ungar

Lake, D. J. (1975) *The Canon of Thomas Middleton's Plays*, Cambridge: Cambridge University Press

Lanham, R. A. (1968) *A Handlist of Rhetorical Terms*, Berkeley: University of California Press

Lass, R. (1969) *Approaches to English Historical Linguistics: an Anthology*, New York: Holt, Rinehart & Winston

Leech, G. (1981) *Semantics*, second edition, Harmondsworth: Penguin Books

Lehmberg, S. E. (1960) *Sir Thomas Elyot Tudor Humanist*, Austin: University of Texas Press

Leith, D. (1983) *A Social History of English*, London: Routledge & Kegan Paul

Lewis, C. S. (1967) *Studies in Words*, second edition, Cambridge: Cambridge University Press

SELECT BIBLIOGRAPHY

Luick, K. (1964) *Historische Grammatik der englischen Sprache*, two volumes, Oxford: Blackwell

Lyons, J. (1968) *Introduction to Theoretical Linguistics*, Cambridge: Cambridge University Press

Lyons, J. (1977) *Semantics*, two volumes, Cambridge: Cambridge University Press

McIntosh, A. (1963) '*As You Like It*: a grammatical clue to character', *Review of English Literature* IV.2, 68–81

McIntosh, A. & Williamson, C. F. (1963) '*King Lear*, Act I Scene 1. Two Stylistic Notes', *Review of English Studies* N.S. XIV, 54–6

McKerrow, R. B. (1927) *An Introduction to Bibliography for Literary Students*, Oxford: Oxford University Press

McKisack, M. (1971) *Medieval History in the Tudor Age*, Oxford: Clarendon Press

McKnight, G. H. (1968) *The Evolution of the English Language*, New York: Dover Publications

Marchand, H. (1969) *The Categories and Types of Present-day English Word-formation*, second edition, Munich: C. H. Beck

Matthiessen, F. O. (1965) *Translation: an Elizabethan Art*, New York: Octagon Books

Michael, I. (1970) *English Grammatical Categories and the Tradition to 1800*, Cambridge: Cambridge University Press

Moore, J. L. (1910) *Tudor-Stuart Views on the Growth Status and Destiny of the English Language*, Halle: Max Niemeyer

Muir K. (ed.) (1970). *Shakespeare Survey 23*, Cambridge: Cambridge University Press

Mulholland, J. (1967) 'Thou and You in Shakespeare: a study in the second person pronoun', *English Studies* 48, 34–43. Reprinted in Salmon & Burgess 1987

Murison, D. (1977) *The Guid Scots Tongue*, Edinburgh: Blackwood

O'Connor, J. D. & Arnold, G. F. (1973) *Intonation of Colloquial English*, second edition, London: Longman

Onions, C. T. (ed.) (1919) *A Shakespeare Glossary*, second edition, Oxford: Clarendon Press

Onions, C. T. (ed.) (1966) *The Oxford Dictionary of English Etymology*, Oxford: Clarendon Press

Orton, H. & Dieth, E. (1962–71) *Survey of English Dialects*, five volumes, Leeds: Edward Arnold

Oxford English Dictionary, The (1989). Second edition, twenty volumes, Oxford: Clarendon Press

Partridge, A. C. (1953a) *The Accidence of Ben Jonson's Plays Masques and Entertainments*, Cambridge: Bowes & Bowes

Partridge, A. C. (1953b) *Studies in the Syntax of Ben Jonson's Plays*, Cambridge: Bowes & Bowes

Partridge, A. C. (1964) *Orthography in Shakespeare and Elizabethan Drama*, London: Edward Arnold

Partridge, A. C. (1969) *Tudor to Augustan English*, London: Deutsch

Partridge, E. H. (1968) *Shakespeare's Bawdy*, revised edition, London: Routledge

Potter, S. (1975) *Changing English*, second edition, London: Deutsch

Quirk, R. (1957) 'Relative Clauses in Educated Spoken English', *English Studies* XXXVIII, 97–109

Quirk, R. (1962) *The Use of English*, London: Longman

Quirk, R. (1971) 'Shakespeare and the English Language', in *A New Companion to Shakespeare Studies*, ed. K. Muir & S. Schoenbaum, Cambridge: Cambridge University Press

Quirk, R. (1974) *The Linguist and the English Language*, London: Edward Arnold

Quirk, R., Greenbaum, S., Leech, G., & Svartvik, J. (1985). *A Comprehensive Gram-*

mar of the English Language, London: Longman

Roach, P. (1991) *English Phonetics and Phonology*, second edition, Cambridge: Cambridge University Press

Robertson, S. (1954) *The Development of Modern English*, second edition, revised by F. G. Cassidy, New York: Prentice-Hall

Robins, R. H. (1979) *A Short History of Linguistics*, second edition, London: Longman

Robins, R. H. (1980) *General Linguistics*, third edition, London: Longman

Romaine, S. (1982) *Socio-historical Linguistics*, Cambridge: Cambridge University Press

Rydén, M. (1966) *Relative Constructions in Early 16th Century English*, Upsala: Almqvist & Wiksell

Rydén, M. (1970) *Coordination of Relative Clauses in Sixteenth Century English*, Upsala: University of Upsala

Salmon, V. (1965) 'Sentence structures in colloquial Shakespearian English', *Transactions of the Philological Society*, 105–40. Reprinted in Salmon & Burgess 1987

Salmon, V. (1966) 'Language-Planning in Seventeenth-Century England: Its Context and Aims', in *In Memory of J. R. Firth*, ed. C. E. Bazell et al., London: Longman

Salmon, V. (1967) 'Elizabethan Colloquial English in the Falstaff Plays', *Leeds Studies in English* N.S. 1, 57–70

Salmon, V., & Burness, E. (1987) *Reader in the Language of Shakespearean Drama*, Amsterdam: Benjamins

Samuels, M. L. (1972) *Linguistic Evolution*, Cambridge: Cambridge University Press

Savory, T. H. (1967) *The Language of Science*, revised edition, London: Deutsch

Scragg, D. G. (1974) *A History of English Spelling*, Manchester: Manchester University Press

Serjeantson, M. S. (1935) *A History of Foreign Words in English*, London: Routledge & Kegan Paul

Sheard, J. A. (1954) *The Words We Use*, London: Deutsch

Skeat, W. W. (1911) *English Dialects from the Eighth Century to the Present Day*, Cambridge: Cambridge University Press

Sonnino, L. (1968) *A Handbook to sixteenth-century Rhetoric*, London: Routledge & Kegan Paul

Spevack, M. (1968–80) *A Complete and Systematic Concordance to the Works of Shakespeare*, nine volumes, Hildesheim: Olms

Spevack, M. (1973) *The Harvard Concordance to Shakespeare*, Cambridge, Mass.: Belknap Press

Starnes W. T. & Noyes G. E. (1946) *The English Dictionary from Cawdrey to Johnson*, Chapel Hill: University of North Carolina Press

Stern, G. (1964) *Meaning and Change of Meaning*, Bloomington: Indiana University Press

Strang, B. M. H. (1968) *Modern English Structure*, second edition, London: Edward Arnold

Strang, B. M. H. (1970) *A History of English*, London: Methuen

Sugden, H. W. (1936) *The Grammar of Spenser's Faerie Queene*, University of Pennsylvania, Philadelphia: Linguistic Society of America

Sweet, H. (1892–1903) *A New English Grammar, Logical and Historical*, two volumes, Oxford: Clarendon Press

Tillyard, E. M. W. (1943) *The Elizabethan World Picture*, London: Chatto & Windus

Traugott, E. C. (1972) *A History of English Syntax. A Transformational Approach to the History of English Sentence Structure*, New York: Holt, Rinehart & Winston

Trudgill, P. (1983) *Sociolinguistics: an Introduction to Language and Society*, revised edition, Harmondsworth: Penguin Books

SELECT BIBLIOGRAPHY

Tucker, S. I. (1961) *English Examined*, Cambridge: Cambridge University Press

Tucker, S. I. (1972) *Enthusiasm. A Study in Semantic Change*, Cambridge: Cambridge University Press

Twaddell, W. F. (1963) *The English Verb Auxiliaries*, second edition, Providence, Rhode Island: Brown University Press

Ullmann, S. (1959). *The Principles of Semantics*, revised edition, Glasgow: Jackson

Vallins, G. H. (1965) *Spelling*, revised by D. G. Scragg, London: Deutsch

van Beek, M. (1969) *An Enquiry into Puritan Vocabulary*, Groningen: Wolters-Noordhoff

Vickers, B. (1970) *Classical Rhetoric in English Poetry*, London: Macmillan

Visser, F. T. (1963–73) *An Historical Syntax of the English Language*, four volumes, Leiden: E. J. Brill

Wakelin, M. (1977) *English Dialects: an Introduction*, revised edition, London: Athlone Press

Waldron, R. A. (1979) *Sense and Sense Development*, second edition, London: Deutsch

Wales, K. (1983) 'Thou and You in early Modern English', *Studia Linguistica* 37.2, 107–25

Webb, H. J. (1965) *Elizabethan Military Science*, Madison: University of Wisconsin Press

Wells, J. C. (1982) *Accents of English*, three volumes, Cambridge: Cambridge University Press

Wright, L. (1995) 'Syntactic structure of witnesses' narratives from the sixteenth-century court minute books of the royal hospitals of Bridewell and Bedlam', *Neuphilologische Mitteilungen* 1.XCVI, 93–105

Wright, L. B. (1935) *Middle-Class Culture in Elizabethan England*, Chapel Hill, University of North Carolina Press

Wyld, H. C. (1923) *Studies in English Rhymes from Surrey to Pope*, London: John Murray

Wyld, H. C. (1936) *A History of Modern Colloquial English*, third edition, Oxford: Blackwell

Yamakawa, K. (1966) 'The Imperative accompanied by the Second Person Pronoun', *Hitotsubashi Journal of Arts and Sciences* (Tokyo) VII.1, 6–25

Yamakawa, K. (1982) 'The Adverbial Accusative of Duration and its Prepositional Equivalent Part II, Early Modern English', *Hitotsubashi Journal of Arts and Sciences* (Tokyo) 23.1, 1–52

Yamakawa, K. (1996) *Studies in Historical English Syntax*, Tokyo: Kenkyusha

Zachrisson, R. E. (1913) *Pronunciation of English Vowels 1400–1700*, Gothenburg: Wettergren & Kerber

INDEX

278

INDEX

INDEX